Competing Visions of World Order

PALGRAVE MACMILLAN TRANSNATIONAL HISTORY SERIES
Akira Iriye (Harvard University) and **Rana Mitter** (University of Oxford)
Series Editors

This distinguished series seeks to: develop scholarship on the transnational connections of societies and peoples in the nineteenth and twentieth centuries; provide a forum in which work on transnational history from different periods, subjects, and regions of the world can be brought together in fruitful connection; and explore the theoretical and methodological links between transnational and other related approaches such as comparative history and world history.

Editorial board:

Thomas Bender University Professor of the Humanities, Professor of History, and Director of the International Center for Advanced Studies, New York University

Jane Carruthers Professor of History, University of South Africa

Mariano Plotkin Professor, Universidad Nacional de Tres de Febrero, Buenos Aires, and member of the National Council of Scientific and Technological Research, Argentina

Pierre-Yves Saunier Researcher at the Centre National de la Recherche Scientifique, France and Visiting Professor at the University of Montreal

Ian Tyrrell Professor of History, University of New South Wales

Published by Palgrave Macmillan:

The Nation, Psychology and International Politics, 1870-1919
By Glenda Sluga

Competing Visions of World Order: Global Moments and Movements, 1880s-1930s
Edited by Sebastian Conrad and Dominic Sachsenmaier

European History in an Interconnected Word
By Matthias Middell, Michael Geyer, and Michel Espagne (forthcoming)

trade has experienced a massive loss of support. It has become evident that increasing entanglement does not automatically produce an open world society but, quite to the contrary, may generate antipathy and exclusionism. Consequently, globalization has come to stand not only for symphony and integration but also for cacophony and polarization. Indeed, recent developments seem to suggest growing political disintegration and a declining world order, at a time when economic globalization and rates of migration continue to accelerate. Signs of centrifugal global forces are manifold. The political culture of the United States has become increasingly parochial in recent years, and, at least for the time being, national self-interest has replaced global commitment as the lead paradigm of American foreign policy.[4] A strong resurgence of nationalism in East Asia, Latin America, and Eastern Europe has proven the earlier optimism about a flourishing international community to be rather short-lived.[5] In many parts of the world, organized religious movements fed by widespread fear of globalization and its discontents are gaining political influence. Most notably, this is the case with Islamic fundamentalism, a highly modern ideology that defines itself against internationalism and secularism—including the institution of the secular nation-state in the Islamic World.[6] Political aspirations coming out of right-wing religious movements can also be observed in India,[7] or in the case of the rising influence of certain evangelical movements in the United States.[8]

The growing trend toward national, respectively cultural essentialism is related to the sustained processes of economic globalization that continue to characterize our time. Despite the Asian economic miracles, the gap between the global rich and global poor continues to widen—increasingly also within single societies. A progressively mobile and flexible global economy is now in a position to relocate its production and transaction facilities to the cheapest environment. As a result of growing international corporate investment in low-wage countries, most notably China and India, the welfare systems of Western Europe, Japan, and North America are increasingly strained. Further, in other parts of the world a growing number of people are finding themselves losing to corporate globalization.

The sustained or even aggravated socioeconomic problems in many poor countries feed the mounting distrust of globalization. While modernization in principle continues to enjoy wide-ranging support in Asia, Africa, and Latin America, antipathy to the West, particularly the United States, is growing. In academic circles the reinvigorated search for cultural alternatives to Westernization programs has manifested itself in various schools of thought ranging from Orientalism to postcolonialism,[9] all of which problematize Western-centric discourses of civilization and their former role in colonial endeavors. Other related opinion camps suggest the possibility of culturally

CHAPTER 1

Introduction: Competing Visions of World Order: Global Moments and Movements, 1880s–1930s

Sebastian Conrad and Dominic Sachsenmaier

D uring the past two decades the discussions on world order have taken interesting turns. The collapse of the cold war constellation gave neoliberal visions of accelerating economic integration and global democratization a certain prominence within academic circles and a wider public sphere. For many observers the fall of the Berlin Wall and the removal of the iron curtain signified a future with the potential to grow into an era characterized by free trade, migration, and an ever-more tightly knit web of human interaction. Many deemed ideological fault lines and geopolitical rivalries to be outdated by the potentials that a new era of globalization brought to the international community. It was this optimistic branch of the late 1980s and early 1990s that brought widespread public attention to new programmatic terms ranging from "global village" to the "end of history" first and foremost in the United States but also in other parts of the world.[1] At that time a majority of Chinese intellectuals, for example, supported a new "Enlightenment" effort, widespread Westernization and internationalization programs for their society.[2] And in most countries of the former Warsaw Pact, liberal democratic parties won national elections—public endorsements to bring their societies closer to a more Western and more global world.[3]

This mood has changed. The confidence in the possibilities of a world order centered on the Washington consensus and the logics of international colonialism, and the history of science. His publications include a monograph on "Elective Affinities. Racial Discourse and Nationalism in the Late 19th Century" (in German, 2004).

Erez Manela is assistant professor of history at Harvard University. He is the author of several articles providing global perspectives on the Wilsonian Moment. He is the author of *The Wilsonian Moment: Self-Determination and the International Origins of Anticolonial Nationalism* (Oxford University Press, 2007).

Matthias Middell is the director of the Center for Advanced Study at Leipzig University and permanent visiting professor at the École des Hautes Études in Paris. He is the editor of the journal *Comparativ* as well as the founder and president of the European Network of Global History. Middell is widely published in various fields, particularly the history of historiography and historiographical theory.

Klaus Mühlhahn is professor for contemporary Chinese history at the University of Turku (Finland). His research interests include: Sino-Western relations, history of international law and human rights, modern Chinese social and cultural history. He just finished a book manuscript on "History of Criminal Justice and Legal Punishment in Twentieth Century China," which will be published by Harvard University Press.

Dominic Sachsenmaier is an assistant professor of transcultural and Chinese history at Duke University. He is widely published in fields such as Sino-Western relations, 20th century Chinese and transnational intellectual history as well as theory of history. He is currently working on a monograph entitled "Paths to Global History—Debates and Approaches in China, Germany and the United States." Together with Sebastian Conrad he directs a trans-Atlantic research network on "Conceptions of World Order. Global Historical Perspectives."

Notes on Contributors

Cemil Aydin is assistant professor of history at the University of North Carolina at Charlotte. In the past, Aydin held positions as an academy scholar at Harvard University and assistant professor of international history at Ohio State University. Aydin's main research focuses on civilizational identities in Japan and Turkey around the turn of the 20th century.

Sebastian Conrad is assistant professor of modern history at the Free University of Berlin (Germany). He is widely published in the fields of modern German and Japanese history, the history of historiography and the theory of postcolonialism. His publications include "The Quest for the Lost Nation. Writing History in Japan and West Germany, 1945–1960" (in German). Together with Dominic Sachsenmaier, he directs a trans-Atlantic research network on "Conceptions of World Order. Global Historical Perspectives."

Andreas Eckert is professor of African history at the University of Hamburg (Germany). He is widely published in the history of colonial and postcolonial Africa, social history of African elites, labor history, and colonialism. He is one of the editors of the "Journal of African History" and has published several monographs on the history of the Douala (Cameroon) and of the political elites in Tanzania (in German).

Harald Fischer-Tiné is professor of history at the International University Bremen (Germany). He has worked on the colonial history of India, theoretical problems of colonialism, and on low-class British subalterns in colonial India. His publications include *Colonialism as Civilising Mission. Cultural Ideology in British India*, coedited with Michael Mann, London (Anthem Press) 2004.

Christian Geulen is assistant professor of modern history at the University of Koblenz (Germany). His research interests include the history of nationalism,

The introduction to the volume by the two editors gives an excellent account of how the pieces are integrated, so we shall not run over that ground again here. Instead, we urge readers to digest the essays in this volume for reasons both historical and contemporary. In terms of historical interpretation, readers will find that the authors have put together a powerfully revisionist account of a period often considered one of Western hegemony (with Japan joining the imperial game late in the day). This reading of the period is one where colonized people around the world used the possibilities of technology and a new awareness of the global to create networks that transcended nation-state boundaries. At the same time, these essays also provide food for thought for those who wish to consider the complexities of contemporary globalization, which likewise is often regarded as a dominant machine incapable of being resisted or adapted. This is an exemplary set of historical essays with a strong significance for the present day.

Rana Mitter
Akira Iriye

Oxford, July 2006

Foreword

The present era has become obsessed by the idea of globalization. The idea that economies, societies, and cultures are becoming ever more deeply entwined has led to both utopian visions of a world without borders, and nightmare visions of multinational corporations and hegemonic states using technology and economic and military clout to seal their own dominance. What is lacking from a large part of the contemporary debate about globalization, its possibilities, and its discontents, is any real sense of historical perspective.

For this reason, we are delighted to publish this powerful new set of essays edited by Dominic Sachsenmeier and Sebastian Conrad. With patience and without hysteria, the essays in this volume analyze an earlier, almost forgotten period of global connections showing that transnational, globalized networks are neither new in our own era, nor are they necessarily driven by a purely Western agenda. Both the range of topics and the depth of scholarly endeavor in the pieces here are impressive. In their introduction, the editors promise to demonstrate a wide range of connections across national boundaries and that promise is amply fulfilled. Here we encounter important non-government organizations such as the Salvation Army; the impact of the Versailles Treaty, something usually associated with the European political world, on colonized peoples around the globe; and the doubts of Chinese intellectuals about the promise of Western modernity betrayed by the savagery of the Great War. Overall, the picture that emerges from the volume is an intriguing and liberatory one. Rather than a picture of a colonized world in thrall to the great Western empires, instead, the half-century from the 1880s to the 1930s was marked by an alternative discourse in which networks of the mind, of shared interests, and changing values, emerged among people who understood, but were not dominated by the Western version of global modernity.

Contents

First published in 2007 by
PALGRAVE MACMILLAN™
175 Fifth Avenue, New York, N.Y. 10010 and
Houndmills, Basingstoke, Hampshire, England RG21 6XS
Companies and representatives throughout the world.

PALGRAVE MACMILLAN is the global academic imprint of the Palgrave Macmillan division of St. Martin's Press, LLC and of Palgrave Macmillan Ltd. Macmillan® is a registered trademark in the United States, United Kingdom and other countries. Palgrave is a registered trademark in the European Union and other countries.

ISBN-13: 978–1–4039–7988–9
ISBN-10: 1–4039–7988–X

Library of Congress Cataloging-in-Publication Data

Competing visions of world order : global moments and movements, 1880s–1930s / edited by Sebastian Conrad and Dominic Sachsenmaier.
    p. cm.—(The Palgrave series in transnational history)
Includes bibliographical references and index.
ISBN 1–4039–7988–X (alk. paper)
    1. World politics—19th century. 2. World politics—1900–1945.
3. International cooperation—History—19th century. 4. International cooperation—History—20th century. I. Conrad, Sebastian.
II. Sachsenmaier, Dominic.

D395.C595 2007
327.09'034—dc22   2006051381

A catalogue record for this book is available from the British Library.

Design by Newgen Imaging Systems (P) Ltd., Chennai, India.

First edition: April 2007

10 9 8 7 6 5 4 3 2 1

Printed in the United States of America.

Competing Visions of World Order

Global Moments and Movements, 1880s–1930s

Edited by

Sebastian Conrad
and
Dominic Sachsenmaier

specific forms of modernity, that is, forms of democratic polity and market economy that lie outside the spectrum of Western experiences.[10] The criticism of Western imperialism and its intellectual underpinnings has also weakened support for global standards, values, and institutions.[11] For example, important assets such as international law and human rights increasingly come under attack and are held to be Western instruments of power and cultural imperialism.[12]

As a consequence, in recent years scenarios of conflict have become prominent on the intellectual agenda. In addition to the notorious "clash of civilizations," the term "empire" has aroused intensive discussions and polarized opinions. These range from the possibility of neoimperialist rivalries driven by the United States, China, and other powers,[13] to concerns about new deterritorialized forms of imperialism, centered around the global business world and the global financial markets.[14] In the eyes of many observers, the main actors of this arena may no longer be nation-states but transnational networks and alliances.[15] It remains rather doubtful whether other transnational networks such as non-governmental organizations that are often portrayed as the beginnings of a global civil society,[16] truly have the potential to reverse this trend.

The current situation makes transcultural and historical perspectives critical. If we look at parallels to the present challenges to a functional world order, the immediate predecessor of the current international system, the cold war constellation seems quite distant in terms of its international dynamics. The post-World War II period was largely typified by two ideologically charged superpower blocks with rather meager attempts of the third world and Europe to gain some degree of independent agency.[17] In many regards, more similar to the situation after the end of the cold war is the period between the early 1880s–1940s. Between the onset of high imperialism and the dusk of World War II, the world also experienced a confluence of globalization and polarization—with disastrous consequences that may contain some important historical lessons for today's world. Needless to say, history does not repeat itself, and the world of the early twentieth century was certainly structured in many ways structured in profoundly different ways. Yet, a new look at the possibilities and ultimate failures of this period that is often considered to have witnessed the first wave of globalization, may still provide some insights for the dynamics of our own time. This may prove quite significant for the current attempts to hold the balance of an arguably more modern but less Western, more interconnected, and yet more multipolar international system.

In many historical narratives the time span between the 1880–1930s is not depicted as a coherent period. For many historians the transformations around the end of World War I, most notably the decline of European supremacy, the rise of the United States as a global power, and the Russian

Revolution, marked a distinct historical watershed. For this very reason many accounts of the long nineteenth or the short twentieth century refer to the years 1914 or 1917, the year of the October revolution and the direct involvement of the United States in the Great War, as a major landmark in time.[18] The reasons for this kind of periodization are compelling, but they should not blind us to the great commonalities shared by the period from the beginning of the Scramble for Africa in the 1880s, to the end of the World War II. For example, Jürgen Habermas emphatically argues that the end of World War II must be seen as a clear break of a longer historical trajectory. After the 1945 fascist or proto-fascist ideologies of Social Darwinism, cultural or ethnic self-purification and international struggle had ceased playing a significant role in global politics.[19] Already in the immediate aftermath of World War II, Western and non-Western intellectuals such as Hannah Arendt and Aimé Césaire had established a connection between the imperialist mindset and the rise of fascist ideologies during the 1920s.[20]

The idea that fascism as well as Japanese expansionism radicalized the imperialist logic and—in the European case—transplanted colonial warfare onto new territories, is now shared by a growing number of historians.[21] The rise of national chauvinism, racism, Social Darwinism, and genocidal thinking was concomitant with the establishment of a world economy during the last decades of the nineteenth century. Whereas the global economy retained at least aspects of a polycentric character for almost a century after the Industrial Revolution, during the late-nineteenth century, Industrial Revolution, now regional markets had become integrated to such a degree as to cause key commodity prices to converge at a global level.[22] Furthermore, from the 1870s onward, one can observe global trade cycles and the onset of worldwide recessions and economic booms.[23]

However, it was also during the nineteenth century that the Enlightenment philosophers' ideal of cosmopolitanism started to give way to tropes of cultural belonging and national commitment. In his seminal work *The Great Transformation*, Karl Polanyi showed that during the late 1800s, international, largely European networks of capitalism and finance succumbed to national power politics. Contrary to many expectations of the time the international economy proved not to be the guarantor of peace that many had expected it to be.[24] According to Polanyi's interpretation, the imbalances created by a free-floating international economy were first countered by rising tides of nationalism, which then in some societies gave way to the pathological "solutions" that characterized fascist social economics.[25] The situation was certainly aggravated by the fact that colonial expansion had reached its natural limits around the turn of the twentieth century. The ensuing discourses of shortage of land and the predictions of future wars over space and raw materials for a mushrooming human population turned out to be self-fulfilling prophecies.[26]

World War I admittedly weakened the international global economy and put a dent on colonialism but in hindsight it did not mean a fundamental break from the patterns of imperialist competition. Also, with the only exception of Japan, the world economy of the late nineteenth and early twentieth centuries remained dominated by the North Atlantic World.[27] Today's world is characterized by the success of the East Asian tigers, the development of India and above all the rapid expansion of the Chinese economy that arguably constitutes the fastest and most profound economic upswing since the Industrial Revolution. Adding the fact that multinational corporations are now headquartered in non-Western societies[28] points to a more evenly distributed global economic output, which in the future may well lead to the center of the world economy shifting back to the Eastern and Southern fringes of the Eurasian landmass.[29] Parallel to this transition toward a more multipolar global economy, the "Hellenistic Period" of Western civilization may come to an end. Today, the global appeal of Eastern food and other aspects of daily life indicate that cultural flows no longer lead primarily from the West to the rest.

Furthermore, in contrast to today's world, where the nation-state model has at least formally been implemented, the first period of globalization was largely characterized by colonial rule. During that time almost only the Latin American elites had some degree of political autonomy and independence from direct interference by the established powers.[30] Also, countries such as China, Siam, or Ethiopia that had never been formally colonized, were de facto subject to direct and heavy Western interference. This situation did not change profoundly with the Great War, which left most colonial empires largely intact. The Wilsonian transformation toward independent states applied only to Eastern Europe and to the fragments of the former Ottoman Empire. The rest of the world, however, remained under the grip of colonial rule, and it did so until after World War II. Certainly, colonial rule was far more complex than mere exploitation and occupation. Some of the colonial powers undertook genuine, albeit half-hearted efforts to establish modern state apparatuses and institutions for controlled levels of self-administration.[31] Also, local elites regarded the transformation of their society according to Western standards as the only hope to survive in a Western-dominated world.

The sustained pattern of colonialism needs to be considered when analyzing the great efforts that international diplomacy undertook to achieve at least a balanceable world order. On many levels, Europe and increasingly the United States seemed to project themselves over the globe, even though both sides of the North Atlantic were equally transformed by the forces of globalization. The myriad intergovernmental organizations that began to transform and standardize different societies were dominated by Western representatives—diplomats from other world regions were often not more than onlookers. This had great consequences for the ways in which the world was ordered in technical and practical terms. For example, European metric systems quickly spread all over the globe, and the new world time was based on European traditions.[32] Furthermore, global events such as the world fairs or the Olympic Games did not even try to hide a sense of Western triumphalism. Even early forms of international nongovernmental activism such as the Red Cross could only spread from the West.[33]

Similarly the intergovernmental systems that were designed to prevent the world from slipping into conflict were almost exclusively centered on European powers. The Westphalian system of diplomatic regulations and international law between sovereign nation-state was only applied to a club of privileged countries. The beginnings of intergovernmental organizations that actively worked on a sustainable world order and international law eventually culminated in the Foundation of the League of Nations after World War I,[34] but it did not allow for full participation of the underdeveloped world. Often the colonial rhetoric of globalization was used to justify this condition—entire societies were denied the privilege of autonomy on the grounds of not being sufficiently civilized to determine their own fate within the international political arena. The standards of international law were only fully applied to those who met some ill-defined standards of civilization.[35] "Civilization" was commonly evoked to justify a world order divided into the privileged free and the unprivileged colonized.[36] In addition to hierarchies between cultures, the principle of racial and gender equality remained disputed in early intergovernmental organizations. Today, by contrast, cultural and biological inequality is no longer even an issue at the level of diplomatic consultation.

Needless to say, even during the age of high imperialism the term "Westernization," though highly suggestive, cannot adequately convey the complexity of mutual influence, hybridization, and cross-cultural entanglement. However, the idea that the non-Western world had to incorporate central aspects of European culture and political order remained basically shared by most influential circles outside Europe and the United States. During the mid-nineteenth century, the elites of much of Africa, China, Japan, and other world regions could at least try to uphold the myth of cultural and political autonomy. Not even half of a century later, Western dominance and the imperialist grip on the world had conjoined domestic and international politics all over the world. Visions of domestic order had become closely related to interpretations of the international system at large.

During the same period many concepts and institutions central to various interpretations of world order today had begun to spread globally during the decades around the turn of the twentieth century. For example, categories such as nation, class, and the rule of internationally anchored law started to become political realities in many parts of the world. Some intellectual and political concepts like modernity, tradition, and secularism have ever since been contested issues in such diverse regions as East Asia, the Middle East, and Latin America.[37] The Great War may have doomed European political supremacy but its immediate consequences did not profoundly challenge the position of the West as the global exporter of cultural and political models.

Still, seen from a global perspective, the catastrophes in Europe enhanced the diversification and confrontation of global ideologies. The 1920s witnessed the emergence of three rivaling ideological systems.[38] Each had a trans-cultural appeal, albeit with varying regional levels of influence. First there was the liberal vision, centered on ideals of development and free trade and mainly promoted by the United States and Western European powers, while in Latin America—a sort of liberal model continent in the mid-nineteenth century—most countries had largely moved away from liberal doctrines.[39] Second, with the founding of the Soviet Union, communism emerged as a real existing alternative to previously dominating visions of world order. Against discourses of civilization and liberalism, communism upheld the categories of class and hegemonic exploitation, and its opposition to imperialism and capitalism seemed to carry the promise of an egalitarian world.

The third main branch of ideologies that gained strength in the aftermath of World War I was the growing number of extreme rightist and fascist movements. Fascist ideologies did not contain elaborate conceptions of world order but were instead based on a critical attitude toward the existing international system. Social Darwinism and racial inequality were the key concepts shared by all fascist and proto-fascist ideologies.[40] As in the case of communism and liberalism, political support structures and financial networks facilitated the global appeal of fascism.[41] In other words, the rivaling ideologies of fascism, communism, and liberalism circulated in international networks, from where they were being applied to domestic arenas and intra-national power struggles. Quite contrary to the parameters of our time, local and trans-local religious groups, for instance, only rarely amounted to politically significant forces.

However, the great ideologies were by no means a mere projection of the critical issues inside Europe onto territories outside Europe. Rather, in each and every case ideological systems of European origin were being selectively applied, blended with local elements and often related to older, traditional conceptual frameworks. Chinese interpretations of communism, Japanese versions of imperialist rhetoric or the fascist-like Estado Novo of Getúlio Vargas in Brazil, for instance, differed from their Western counterparts, and they did so in profound and fundamental ways. The same is true for subordinate concepts that pertained to visions of world order such as nation, development, class, race, culture, or tradition. Almost all of these concepts played a role in the ideological systems as they emerged after World War I. For example, communism was almost exclusively successful in its Leninist version, from where it could be tied to discourses of national liberation. And most forms of fascism maintained some form of socialist rhetoric. However, the international prominence of sociopolitical concepts such as class or nation shows a trend of increasingly entangled political struggles around the globe. Whether in Western Europe or in colonized societies, whether in the United States, in Brazil or in crisis-ridden China, the domestic political debates started to refer to similar, if not entirely identical, political concepts. The prominence of categories such as class, modernity, and tradition means that the political struggles between different political groupings were increasingly being fought with concepts that carried explicit global connotations. Conversely, the notions of race or nation implied value judgments about global hierarchies and ideals of how the world should be structured and ordered.[42]

Conceptions of world order were part of an arsenal of political and cultural alternatives that rivaled one another on a global scale, even if the manifestations of the programs and agendas varied depending on the social and cultural context. For the most part, these alternative value systems such as cultural fundamentalisms have been studied in isolation. This perspective has generated questions concerning their internal origins and conditions. In particular, cultural fundamentalisms have been studied separately from each other,[43] mostly within a paradigm of uniqueness. This perspective precludes insights into the interactions that public spheres in East Asia, Southeast Asia, Latin America, and the Islamic world had with Europe and among each other. The national historiographies have impeded interpretations that see competing visions of order within an international context, for example as reactions to similar structural challenges.[44]

This book seeks to provide some trans-cultural lenses to visions of world order, their social carriers, cultural contexts, and political environments. Taken together and individually the chapters in this book aim to contribute to the growing fields of global and transcultural history. The term "global history" has quickly risen to prominence in recent years and is now used in many Western and non-Western languages. More and more historians around the world agree that so far their field has insufficiently explored the history of intercultural connections, worldwide exchanges, and global transformations. In many countries one can observe an emerging debate among historians about the possibilities of moving historiographic research beyond monocultural perspectives.[45] Since traditional world history tended to focus on the premodern period, the calls for global perspectives are particularly directed toward research on modern and contemporary history.

Most proponents of a new transnational and global history agree that steering historiography into the rather unknown ocean surrounding the isles of solidly explored nation-state does not aim at all-encompassing, universalizing visions reaching across time and space. The shift to multipolar and global approaches necessitates careful methodological reflections on how to balance the gains of a global perspective with the potential losses in local sensitivity. Any study with a global perspective will have to find ways to negotiate the attention to transnational processes with detailed archival source-work at various local levels. It may be the case that research teams will increasingly emerge as a solution pattern for bridging the gap between local expertise and transcultural perspectives.

Visions of world order since the late-nineteenth century were typically discussed and negotiated between networks extending beyond the boundaries of nation-states and cultural spheres. Some of the more influential projects and utopias were propagated by social and political movements seeking to garner support for their plans on a global scale. The emergence of a global consciousness linking hitherto unconnected public spheres facilitated the formation of these movements. For a better understanding of the transnational character of the debates about world order, it will be useful to look at both, the temporal and spatial dimension of this conjuncture: at global moments, that is, specific events such as World War I that had at least some degree of impact on most societies in the world, and the global movements connected to them. The following chapters' main emphasis lies in the time between the onset of high imperialism and the end of the interwar period. The Second World War itself caused such profound shifts in the previously existing visions of world orders—including the international connections between fascist programs, the anti-Western debates on "Overcoming Modernity" in Japan, and the anticolonial movements in Asia and Africa—that it is excluded from analysis here.

Global Movements

The phase of globalization between the 1880s–1930s was a period of global movements. This is true in a very literal sense: mobility of people was one of the hallmarks of the time and characteristic for the global integration before

World War II. In recent years, it has become increasingly obvious that mass long-distance migrations were not only a phenomenon of the Atlantic world, but rather of global extent. Close to 60 million people migrated from Europe to the Americas between 1846 and the 1930s, complemented, after the turn of the century, by large flows of Asian laborers to Brazil, Cuba, and California. At the same time, the frontiers of Manchuria and the rice fields and rubber plantations of Southeast Asia were the destinations for large migrations of Indians, Chinese, and Russians that added up to another roughly 100 million people. These flows into the Indian Ocean region and into Northeast Asia also challenge the received wisdom that mass migration largely came to an end in 1914. From a perspective of global history, mobility reached new peaks in the interwar period.[46]

Mobility was not just a sign of the times, but was also perceived as a major threat to the existing world order. Beginning in 1882, with the Chinese Exclusion Act in the United States, migration control emerged as one of the central devices with which the Western powers aimed to prevent the political status quo from dissolving. The anti-Chinese Policy in Australia, and the Alien Act in Great Britain in 1905, were important steps on a road, that, in the 1920s, led to immigration quotas in many countries, most notably the United States. The migration of large numbers of people around the globe was frequently met with xenophobic outbursts and violent pogroms. The limitation of mobility was an integral part of European colonial policy in Africa and Asia. Fingerprinting was used to check unwelcome immigrants in Argentina and India, and the passport developed into a universal tool for keeping the order of nations, culture, and race intact.[47] Mobility and the emergence of diaspora communities were seen, by the imperialist powers, as major forces undermining the political and legal order of the world.[48]

A more direct challenge was posed by the oppositional political movements that formed since the end of the nineteenth century. As "movements," many political groupings not only related themselves to the increasing social and international mobility of the time, they also were often entangled in transregional networks. While the integration of the world led to processes of homogenization and assimilation, at the same time it produced new borders and countermovements. This dialectic of "globalization and fragmentation" was characteristic for the way the global and the local were articulated under the auspices of intensified interaction.[49] These movements were a product of the emerging public spheres, and a response of local elites to the disenchantment of the modernizing promises of the imperial order. The intensified entanglement of communicative public spheres enabled the actors and agents of these movements to connect and their visions and agendas to influence each other, across national and cultural borders.

Four kinds of oppositional movements played a prominent role between the 1880s–1930s. *First*, a number of nongovernmental organizations were established to reform and revise the existing world order from within. Originating mostly (but not always) in the West, these movements formed what could be termed a "subversive internationalism" in the late-nineteenth century and in the interwar period. Philanthropic movements, the 1893 Chicago Parliament of World Religions, the international socialist and workers movement, the women's associations, and the 1927 Congress of the Suppressed Nations in Brussels (with participants like Jomo Kenyatta, Kwame Nkrumah, Ho Chi Minh, and Aimé Césaire) all were part of international endeavors to question and undermine certain forms of political, social, and cultural hegemony, while in principle operating within the existing order.[50]

Secondly, the various nationalist movements that mushroomed at the turn of the century posed a serious challenge to the international order based on large overseas empires and international law. The nationalization of the world had many facets. In many regions, like New Zealand, Australia, China, Persia, and Siam, nation-states were formed at the end of the nineteenth century. However, the rise of mass nationalism also affected Latin American states as well as European polities, like the Habsburg Empire, and challenged multiethnic political entities from within. Outside the West, nationalism emerged as the leading ideology and eroded more encompassing definitions of belonging in places as diverse as Egypt, the Balkans, and India. While the spread of nationalism and the nation-state may be seen as part and parcel of the Westernization of the world, at the same time it set fire to a balance of large colonial empires based on Western hegemony.

While nationalism tended to question multiethnic empires, the rise of regionalism can be seen as a concomitant—and *third*—movement aiming to revise the existing world order. The debate about the emergence of just a few "world empires"—the United States, Great Britain, Russia, and possibly Germany—caught the fancy of many politicians and commentators before World War I: "world empire or doom" was one of the slogans of the day.[51] Taking the Monroe doctrine as their model, visionaries like Friedrich Naumann in Germany aimed to construct larger geopolitical units like "Central Europe" (the title of Naumann's book in 1915) that enabled political and economic autarky. The Pan-movements advocated a different form of regionalism based on cultural and ethnic commonalities. In the political arena, these movements remained rather marginal since they were not able to establish a support base that was comparable to the nation-state. Their main challenge lay in the cultural claim they posed to the existing order, even though they were constructed around politicized concepts and geographical mappings that had originated in the West. Pan-Islamists and Pan-Asianists, in particular, expressed anti-Western resentments and pledged not to abandon their cultural traditions in the course of modernization. They were directed not only against imperialism as a form of political dominance, but also against colonialist ideologies and discrimination based on the discourses of "Orientalism" and race. However, this antipathy did not preclude the instrumentalization of "race" as the point of departure for a number of alternative, anti-imperialist visions of order that themselves frequently had imperialist overtones.[52]

A *fourth*, but closely related movement was the widespread turn toward traditionalism that frequently verged on cultural fundamentalism. Less an organized movement than a cultural and political trend and mentality, traditionalism in a broad (and not party-political) sense posed the antithesis of modern, European civilization allegedly devoid of true and inner meaning and a fuller, less alienated form of communal life to be found in the golden past, or outside the modern West. Thus, cultural values that traditionalists in Africa, China, India, and Japan presented as remedy were appropriated or actively supported by conservative thinkers in the West. These discursive coalitions attest to the fact that the ambivalent relationship to the modern West was not a monopoly of non-Western elites, but was shared by critical observers in the United States and Europe as well. A global turning point in the development of conservative ideologies was World War I, which had further eroded the trust in the benefits of Western civilization.[53]

In the late-nineteenth century, the political and cultural challenges had assumed global dimensions, and it is difficult to find social and intellectual actors operating autonomously and independent from each other.[54] Global structures of political domination and communication facilitated the flow of information between different regions. This led to the formation of movements and intellectual networks operating internationally and to a whole industry translating modernity into non-Western contexts.[55] Large universities, mainly in Western Europe, the United States, and Japan, developed into centers where competing global visions were negotiated.[56] Therefore, the parallels between different societies were not only the effect of similar structural conditions, but also due to the increase of contact and transfer between them.

Global Moments

As a point of departure, visions of world order frequently referred to events of a popular significance that appealed to people in discrete and distant locations. They were focal points for a whole set of different hopes and anxieties that coalesced around the notion of an interconnected future. These "global moments" were characteristic for the high time of globalization since the late nineteenth century. They allowed oppositional movements to connect with forces and political actors across a variety of social and cultural conditions.

While periodizations are the product of historians with the benefit of hindsight, global moments owed their existence to the attention and concerns of contemporaries. They referred to events that were conceived as epochal in their time, however ephemeral they may seem to the retrospective observer. Global moments were not necessarily the expression of deep structural changes, be it political or economical. Instead, they were charged with symbolic meaning that made them accessible to observers from a variety of diverse positions, as is obvious in the case of the Russo-Japanese war that was widely hailed as the end of the imperialist domination of the Western powers. In other words, their global reach was not always obvious, but rather the effect of a public discourse that turned particular constellations into moments of global import. But the focused attention with which they were endowed added to the significance of these events and produced real effects, both, locally and globally. While these moments were typically represented as global in reach, they were in fact appropriated very differently under diverse local conditions.

The precondition for the perception of global moments was the gradual emergence, in the last quarter of the nineteenth century, of a global consciousness throughout much of the world. The increased exchange across borders was accompanied by the recognition that the world had gradually become more integrated. Geographer David Harvey has written about a sense of "time-space compression" that accompanied the technological and informational changes at the end of the nineteenth century.[57] This did not go unnoticed by contemporaries. As the English historian James Bryce argued in 1901, it seemed as if "a new sort of unity is being created among mankind."[58] The intensification of global exchange was clearly accompanied by an awareness of transnational ties and processes.

This mental revolution, in turn, rested on a veritable revolution of information and communications technologies since the 1850s.[59] The steamship and the expansion of postal connections—especially overseas—the telephone, and the telegraph were among the elements of a technological transformation that produced a sense of a shrinking world.[60] Sandford Fleming declared at the International Meridian Conference in 1884, "The conditions under which we live are no longer the same. The application of science to the means of locomotion and to the instantaneous transmission of thought and speech have gradually contracted space and annihilated distance. The whole world is drawn into immediate neighborhood and near relationship."[61] It was the telegraph, in the first place, that contributed to the rapid distribution of news, information, and opinion. The spread of the telegraph system in the 1880s, was precipitated by the expansion of global capitalism and the integration of the world market. The borderless communication was further facilitated by the invention of wireless telegraphy.[62] After the first successful transatlantic message in 1901, the wireless enabled communications without cables and thus multiplied the nodal points of informational exchange.

These technological changes were an important factor in the development of public spheres in places as different as Japan, China, the Ottoman Empire, and Latin America. The emergence of a global consciousness—not only in Western Europe and the United States, but also around the world—was largely the work of the educated elites in the urban centers and port cities. Thus, it rested not only on technological developments, but also on the emergence of new metropolitan elites, closely tied to the integrated systems of education established mostly in the latter half of the nineteenth century. The circulation of newspapers, both on a local and national level, was crucial for the contact between discursive communities that soon coalesced into opinion camps on a national level.[63] The channels of information, the system of foreign correspondents and the large number of diaspora presses enabled a vivid exchange of ideas, even if the largely national public spheres did not add up to form an integrated world society. Nevertheless, even if the issues themselves were not necessarily global, crucial debates were now conducted increasingly under the influence of global constraints and pressures, of global expectations and fears.

This led to a number of standardizing measures that can be understood as reactions to the challenges of a unifying world. The adoption of standard world time, and of the Gregorian calendar in places that had not hitherto known it, attest to the widespread conviction of living on a shared globe that was also experienced by social strata outside and below the cosmopolitan circles. The sense of time and space, on a more general level, shifted markedly under the auspices of increased global exchange.[64] A global consciousness not only affected a general mentality, but also framed the context in which specific political measures were discussed. The gradual dissolution of the free-trade regime and the levying of high protective tariffs in places like Germany, France, and the United States since 1879, for example, show the close connections between debates that aroused national emotions but were clearly part of a global development and an effect of global pressures.[65] Likewise, the colonial world order was the frame of reference for the development of nationalist movements around the world, both in Euro-America and in the non-Western world. The fin-de-siècle turn toward a conception of "China" as a nation within "Asia," for example, cannot be severed from a growing awareness of the larger geopolitical landscape in an imperialist world.[66]

Against the backdrop of a developing global consciousness in diverse social contexts, global moments contributed to the integration and overlapping of distinct discursive communities. The global character of some of these moments, to be sure, varied. The world exhibitions, beginning with the Crystal Palace exhibition in 1851, and culminating in huge gatherings as in Paris in 1900 catered to a predominantly Western audience, even if an increasing number of non-Western countries participated.[67] The same can be said for the Vienna stock market crash in 1873, even though the ensuing recession was felt outside of Europe as well, in particular in Latin America with its heavy dependency upon European capital.[68] Other events were easier to appropriate without buying into a set of hegemonic political and cultural structures. The explosion of the volcano Krakatau in Indonesia in 1883, for example, has been called the first global media event, fascinating scientists and a large public locally and around the world.[69]

For the problematic at stake here, a few highly symbolic events allowed connecting visions of an alternative world order to changes in the global political landscape. The Russo-Japanese War in 1905 was registered and commented upon virtually everywhere, from the Unites States to Southeast Asia. In Great Britain, a debate on national efficiency ensued in which the Japanese example was presented as a model to follow in the face of an alleged British decline. In China and Southeast Asia, countless reform-minded students flocked to Tokyo to experience non-Western modernity first hand. In much of the Islamic world, as elsewhere, 1905 signaled the end of Western hegemony both militarily and politically. Japan's victory was interpreted as the refutation of assumptions that tied "civilization" to a certain race, culture, and religion. It also undermined the self-fashioning of the imperialist countries that had portrayed colonialism as a form of tutoring on the path to modernity. In terms of a larger history of decolonization, 1905 served as a point of departure for various anti-imperialist trajectories.[70]

Another set of global moments was connected to World War I and its immediate aftermath. The war itself may have had several regional focal points, but at the same time its global repercussions were felt and commented upon widely. Debates about the end of Western political and cultural hegemony, about the dissolution of the German colonial empire or about the use of colonial troops in combat and occupation, all testify to the sense of global entanglement that the war had reinforced. Outside of Europe and the United States, the war was taken to signal the failure of the Western "civilizing mission" and the concomitant beginning of a process of decolonization.[71] Politically and symbolically at least, as important as the war itself, were two events directly related to it—the Russian Revolution in 1917 and its world-political counterpoise, the declaration of Wilson's 14 points in January 1918. Both events were taken, by contemporaries and later commentators alike, as the symbolic beginning of a new world order.[72]

At the end of the period under discussion here, the World Economic Crisis of 1929 may also be considered a global moment. Although ostensibly not a political event, "Black Friday" nevertheless had a lasting impact on debates about the possible shape of a world beyond the League of Nations paradigm. As a response to economic plight, the quest for autonomy and autarky of larger geopolitical units took center stage in the Americas, Central Europe, and in East Asia. In the following years, Pan-movements and regionalisms lost much of their subaltern and subversive status and became a viable political alternative.[73]

These global moments were events with global repercussions. In many cases, they were not only perceived globally but also with the awareness of global connections. At the same time, they were appropriated locally and integrated into the dynamics of developments on local, national, and regional scales. Indeed, in national memories many of these global moments live on. The shock of 1929, for example, is still a constitutive element of public memory in many European countries and in the United States. Likewise, World War I is alive in public consciousness as a turning point in European history. The end of the war and the violent outbreaks in its wake are a central element in the narratives of national reassertion, like the March First Movement in Korea or the Fourth of May in China. Global moments, in other words, were charged with a multitude of complementary meanings through their incorporation into political and cultural movements that operated on a less-than-global scale.

Chapter Previews

Some of the conceptions of world order discussed in the following chapters aimed at spreading certain standards and rights beyond the circles of privileged nations. Others worked to unsettle the assumptions of the imperialist and internationalist order challenging the political and cultural hegemony of the "West." Part one of the book deals with perspectives on the world order before World War I largely from Western European and North American points of view. They attest to the high degree of global consciousness in the imperialist world, and at the same time to the currents that aimed at reforming and revising the existing order of which most commentators in principle approved.

This becomes particularly apparent in the case of nongovernmental organizations (NGOs), such as philanthropic societies. While in current political discourse, NGOs are hailed as the very antithesis of the "forces of empire" and instrumental in establishing a "global civil society," Harald Fischer-Tiné shows, in his contribution, how one of the early NGOs, the Salvation Army, closely interacted with the metropolis and British imperialism. Finally, the chapter argues that the activities of the Salvation Army were not confined to the colonial periphery, but rather tended to undermine the colonial dichotomy. The rhetoric and social practice of the Salvation Army's activities in India and England influenced and mutually informed each other. It becomes clear that the convenient division of colonizers and colonized that structures much scholarship of the nineteenth century, does not reflect the degree to which individuals and social movements had begun to act on a global scale.

In his contribution, Christian Geulen demonstrates that racial theories were among the first global categories used to give order to an increasingly entangled world. He shows that racial discourses survived the World War of 1914–1918 almost unharmed: until racial theories were officially banned from international political discourse after 1945, they were being equally applied to totalitarian programs as well as to more optimistic and peaceful visions of world order. Geulen's essay tries to uncover the historical origins, transcultural spread and complex semantics of racial thought in political discourse during the period from 1880–1940. Geulen particularly seeks to recover the specific function of popular racial theory as one of the transnational discourses of political belonging and self-reflection that flourished under the conditions of imperialism and internationalization. In this context he discusses the transnational reception of Darwinism and shows how racial thinking was diversified, multiplied and disseminated over the globe.

Among the facets of global consciousness in turn-of-the-century Europe, the United States, and in other parts of the world were the world histories written around the time of World War I. Matthias Middell looks at the subtext of these works to analyze the spatial frameworks with which the respective authors ordered the historical and contemporary world. Whereas some world histories used nations as the primary units of analysis, others referred to continents and civilizations. After a comparative account of a wide variety of ways to define such units, Middell goes on to focus on works that explicitly challenged the ontology of the nation. The article relates the transformations in world historical thinking to changing experience bases of historians during the decades around the turn of the twentieth century. In this manner Middell also analyzes the continuities and discontinuities in the field of world history during the aftermath of the Great War.

While a study of the Russo-Japanese war in 1905 as a global conjuncture is part of Cemil Aydin's project (see Part three), Part two of the book—focusing on global moments—is devoted to the study of the impact of World War I on debates about world order. Historians have long recognized the year 1919 as a pivotal moment in the international system, but its history has been written as a largely European affair. Erez Manela sets out to expand the historical lens through which we view the aftermath of the Great War, decentralizing Europe and focusing instead on the dynamics and implications of that moment for groups on the global periphery. From this perspective, he examines a number of the anticolonial and national uprisings that erupted almost simultaneously in the months after the armistice. These movements should be understood as part of a global shift in the international discourse of global legitimacy, epitomized at the time by U.S. President Woodrow Wilson's call for a "new world order" based on the principles of self-determination and national equality. These events can be conceptualized as a "Wilsonian moment" in the colonial world, a watershed in the modern transformation of the principles of world order from the imperial to the national, complemented by the emergence of non-European peoples as sovereign actors in an international arena.

The Great War was not only a global watershed in the eyes of nationalists but also other intellectual and political groupings. Dominic Sachsenmaier discusses a range of intellectual reactions patterns to the Great War in terms of their transnational connections. In the midst of the heated intellectual climate of the postwar years, World War I became a major trope in the politicized debates about the future trajectories of China. The chapter investigates how some of the rivalling sociopolitical milieus within China interpreted the global and local implications of the Great War. Sachsenmaier also investigates the connections between like-minded intellectuals and activists in China, Europe, and other parts of the world. During the early 1920s, distinct images and understandings of the Great War started to be circulated within international networks of likeminded scholars and activists.

Part three deals with movements that worked toward undermining the existing imperial world order. It starts out with an analysis of movements in a very literal sense. Sebastian Conrad and Klaus Mühlhahn argue that mass mobility produced reactions contributing to a reconceptualization of the nation on a global scale. Using the example of the migration of Chinese "coolies" and moving between global structures and local/national settings, they show that mobility influenced the trajectories of nationalism in locations as different as Germany, Australia, the United States, and China. In particular, the physical reinforcement of borders, the ethnicization of notions of belonging, and the increasing consciousness of a global-systemic context can be interpreted partly as a response to the transnational circulation of people in the decades before World War I. By complementing the long-standing national traditions with the synchronous entanglements across national borders, the authors aim to contribute to a spatial and global turn in studies of nationalism.

Cemil Aydin offers a comparative account on alternative visions of world order as well as anti-Western critiques in the Ottoman State and Meiji Japan. He analyzes how modern anti-Western discourses and alternative visions of world order emerged originally to criticize the imperialist "West" for violating its own proclaimed "standards of civilization." Aydin documents Ottoman and Japanese reflections on the global debate about ideas of race, empire, civilization, progress, and humanity from the 1880s–1910s. During that time, both Pan-Asianism and Pan-Islamism were utilized as what Aydin calls "alternative universalisms" by nationalist movements against the inherent contradictions of the civilizing mission ideology. In particular, the article focuses on the impact of the Russo-Japanese War as a global moment. The war deepened the legitimacy crisis of one single Eurocentric global polity, though it did not foster a rejection of Western modernity at large.

Following Paul Gilroy's groundbreaking study, Andreas Eckert attempts to investigate the social and intellectual history of African and African-American networks in the United States, Europe, and Africa as part of the "Black Atlantic" between the 1880s–1940s. His main focus is on networks that could be linked to Pan-Africanist ideas. Pan-Africanism was a very heterogeneous project initiated by African American intellectuals in the late-nineteenth century. The general vision of this project was to unify and integrate African societies (in Africa and elsewhere). Based upon the mobility of African and African American intellectuals and politicians, Pan-Africanism represented a very complex transnational network characterized by diverse origins, contexts, aims, ideologies, and forms of organization. Eckert specifically looks at the social actors and their visions of the world.

Notes

The nine authors of this book are the members of a trans-Atlantic research network, which was sponsored by the German National Research Foundation (DFG) from 2004 to 2007. The network sought to discover new research approaches and sets of questions by providing an exchange forum for scholars with different area expertise who worked on comparable and compatible topics. Over a period of three years, the group members worked on combining their disciplinary backgrounds into a coherent investigative framework. The members of this research network are grateful for the generous support by the German National Research Foundation and for the editorial work by Joshua Hoffman (UC Santa Barbara). For more information see www.global-history.de. Another segment of the network's work has been published in the issue "Beyond Hegemony?—'Europe' and the Politics of Non-Western Elites, 1900–1930," of *the Journal of Modern European History* 4–2 (2006).

1. See, for example, Thomas Friedman, *The Lexus and the Olive Tree: Understanding Globalization* (New York: Farrar, Straus & Giroux, 1999); Francis Fukuyama, *The End of History and the Last Man* (New York: Avon, 1993).

2. See, for example, Jing Wang, *High Culture Fever: Politics, Aesthetics, and Ideology in Deng's China* (Berkeley: University of California Press, 1996).

3. See, for example, Timothy Garton Ash, *The Magic Lantern: The Revolution of '89 Witnessed in Warsaw, Budapest, Berlin, and Prague* (New York: Random House, 1990).

4. See, for example, Richard A. Falk, *The Declining World Order: America's Imperial Geopolitics* (New York: Routledge, 2004).

5. For the rising tide of nationalism in Chinese intellectual discourse see Ben Xu, "From Modernity to Chineseness: The Nativist Cultural Discourse in Post-1989 China," *Positions* 6, no. 1 (1998): 203–37; for a Latin American case, see Stephen D. Morris, "Reforming the Nation: Mexican Nationalism in Context," *Journal of Latin American Studies* 31 (1999): 363–97.

6. About Islamic fundamentalism and its modern character see for example Olivier Roy, *Globalised Islam: Fundamentalism, De-territorialisation and the Search for a New Ummah* (London: Hurst, 2004).

7. See Thomas Blom Hansen, *The Saffron Wave: Democracy and Hindu Nationalism in Modern India* (Princeton: Princeton University Press, 1999).

8. See, for example, Michael Lienesch, *Redeeming America: Piety and Politics in the New Christian Right* (Chapel Hill: University of North Carolina Press, 1993).

9. See, for example, Dipesh Chakrabarty, *Provincializing Europe: Postcolonial Thought and Historical Difference* (Princeton: Princeton University Press, 2000). For the Orientalism debates consult Ulrike Freitag, "The Critique of Orientalism," in Michael Bentley, ed., *Companion to Historiography* (London: Routledge, 1997), pp. 620–38.

10. See Dominic Sachsenmaier, Jens Riedel, and Shmuel Eisenstadt, eds., *Reflections on Multiple Modernities: European, Chinese and Other Approaches* (Leiden: Brill, 2002).

11. Amartya Sen, *Rationality and Freedom* (Cambridge, Mass.: Belknap Press of Harvard University Press, 2002).

12. See, for example, Immanuel Wallerstein, "The End of What Modernity?" *Theory and Society* 24, no. 4 (1995): 471–88.

13. An example are the lively debates initiated by the rather apologetic account in Niall Ferguson, *Empire: The Rise and Demise of the British World Order and the Lessons for Global Power* (New York: Basic Books, 2003).

14. See, for example, Michael Hardt and Antonio Negri, *Empire* (Cambridge, Mass.: Harvard University Press, 2000). A slightly more optimistic account, which places some hope on the global elites' interest for international stability, is offered by Kees Van Der Pijl, *Transnational Classes and International Relations* (New York: Routledge, 1998).

15. An example for the widespread opinion that the leeway of the nation-state is withering away under the impact of economic globalization is Giovanni Arrighi,

The Long Twentieth Century: Money, Power, and the Origins of Our Times (New York: Verso, 1994).

16. See, for example, Akira Iriye, *Global Community: The Role of International Organizations in the Making of the Contemporary World* (Berkeley: University of California Press, 2002). For arguments for a stronger role of religious communities in a future global civil society, see Richard Falk, *Religion and Humane Global Governance* (New York: Palgrave, 2001).

17. See, for example, Robert Mortimer, *The Third World Coalition in International Politics*, 2nd, updated ed. (Boulder: Westview Press, 1984).

18. For example, Eric Hobsbawm, *The Age of Extremes: A History of the World, 1914–1991* (New York: Pantheon Books, 1994).

19. Jürgen Habermas, "Learning from Catastrophe? A Look Back at the Short Twentieth Century," in Jürgen Habermas, *The Postnational Constellation*, (Cambridge: MIT Press, 2001), pp. 38–57.

20. Most prominently by Hannah Arendt, *The Origins of Totalitarianism* (New York: Harcourt Brace, 1951); as well as Aimé Césaire, *Discourse on Colonialism*, trans. Joan Pinkham (New York: New York University Press, 2000).

21. Compare v. Theodor H. Laue, *The World Revolution of Westernization: The Twentieth Century in Global Perspective* (Oxford: Oxford University Press, 1987).

22. See Kevin O'Rourke and Jeffrey G. Williamson, "Once More: When did Globalization Begin?" *European Review of Economic History* 8 (2004): 109–17.

23. See W. Arthur Lewis, *Growth and Fluctuations, 1870–1913* (London: Allen & Unwin, 1978).

24. See Akira Iriye, *Cultural Internationalism and World Order* (Baltimore: Johns Hopkins University Press, 1997), pp. 25–27.

25. Karl Polanyi, *The Great Transformation: The Political and Economic Origins of Our Time* (New York: Rinehart & Co., Inc., 1944).

26. See Jürgen Osterhammel and Niels P. Petersson, *Globalization: A Short History* (Princeton: Princeton University Press, 2005), chapter 5.

27. See Michael D. Bordo, Alan M. Talor, and Jefferey G. Williamson, eds., *Globalization in Historical Perspective* (Chicago: University of Chicago Press, 2003).

28. See Alfred Chandler and Bruce Mazlish, "Introduction," in Alfred Chandler and Bruce Mazlish, eds., *Leviathans: Multinational Corporations and the New Global History* (Cambridge: Cambridge University Press), pp. 1–18.

29. An argument made by Andre Gunder Frank, *ReOrient: Global Economy in the Asian Age* (Berkeley: University of California Press, 1998).

30. See G. Pope Atkins, *Latin America in the International Political System*, 2nd ed. (Boulder: Westview Press, 1989).

31. For this reason the concept of colonial modernity has gained a certain prominence in recent years. See, for example, Tani E. Barlow, ed., *Formations of Colonial Modernity in East Asia* (Durham: Duke University Press, 1997).

32. See, for example, Stephen Kern, *The Culture of Time and Space, 1880–1918* (London: Weidenfeld and Nicholson 1983).

33. An overview is provided by Iriye, *Global Community*.
34. A good overview of early IGO activities is provided by Iriye, *Cultural Internationalism*.
35. Martti Koskenniemi, *The Gentle Civilizer of Nations: The Rise and Fall of International Law 1870–1960* (Cambridge: Cambridge University Press, 2001).
36. See Gerrit W. Gong, *The Standard of "Civilization" in International Society* (Oxford: Oxford University Press, 1984).
37. See, for example, Michael Featherstone, ed., *Global Culture: Nationalism, Globalization and Modernity* (London: Sage Publications, 1990).
38. See Hobsbawm, *The Age of Extremes*.
39. For the liberal tradition in Latin America, see for example Richard N. Sinkin, *The Mexican Reform, 1855–1876: A Study in Liberal Nation-Building* (Austin: University of Texas Press, 1979); Ralph L. Woodward, *Positivism in Latin America, 1850–1900: Are Order and Progress Reconcilable?* (Lexington: Heath, 1971).
40. For new accounts on fascism from an international perspective see, for example, Robert A. Paxton, *The Anatomy of Fascism* (New York: Knopf, 2004); and Stein Ugelvik Larsen, ed., *Fascism Outside Europe: The European Impulse against Domestic Conditions in the Diffusion of Global Fascism* (New York: Columbia University Press, 2001).
41. See Iriye, *Cultural Internationalism*, pp. 118–130.
42. For the global dimension of discourses on race, see Rebecca Karl, "Race, Ethnos, History in China at the Turn of the Twentieth Century," in Peter Osborne and Stella Sandford, eds., *Philosophy of Race and Ethnicity* (London: Continuum, 2002), pp. 97–113. For the Latin American case see Nancy S. Stepan, *The Hour of Eugenics: Race, Gender, and Nation in Latin America* (Ithaca: Cornell University Press, 1991).
43. An exception is Iriye, *Cultural Internationalism*. For East Asia, see James Mayall, "Nationalism and the International Order: The Asian Experience," in Michael Leifer, ed., *Asian Nationalism* (London: Routledge, 2000), pp. 187–96.
44. An attempt to transcend this kind of compartmentalization is, for instance, made by Iwo Amelung, Matthias Koch, and Joachim Kurtz, eds., *Selbstbehauptungsdiskurse in Asien: China-Japan-Korea* (Munich: Iudicium, 2003).
45. For the debates on global history see Michael Geyer and Charles Bright, "World History in a Global Age," *American Historical Review* 100, no. 4 (1995): 1034–60; Bruce Mazlish and Ralph Buultjens, eds., *Conceptualizing Global History* (Boulder: Westview Press, 1993); Anthony G. Hopkins, ed., *Globalization in World History* (London: Pimlico, 2002); Patrick Manning, *Navigating World History: Historians Create a Global Past* (New York: Palgrave Macmillan, 2003).
46. See Aaron Segal, *An Atlas of International Migration* (London: Hans Zell Publishers, 1993); Wang Gungwu, ed., *Global History and Migrations*, Global History Series, vol. 2 (Boulder: Westview Press, 1997); Adam McKeown, "Global Migration, 1846–1940," *Journal of World History* 15 (2004): 155–90.
47. Julia Rodriguez, "South Atlantic Crossings: Fingerprints, Science, and the State in Turn-of-the-Century Argentina," *American Historical Review* 109 (2004): 387–416; Carl Solberg, *Immigration and Nationalism: Argentina and Chile,*

1890–1914 (Austin: Texas University Press, 1970); John Torpey, *The Invention of the Passport: Surveillance, Citizenship and the State* (Cambridge: Cambridge University Press, 2000); Jane Caplan and John Torpey, eds., *Documenting Individual Identity: The Development of State Practices in the Modern World* (Princeton: Princeton University Press, 2001).

48. Dirk Hoerder, *Cultures in Contact: World Migrations in the Second Millennium* (Durham: Duke University Press, 2002); Aristide R. Zolberg, "Global Movements, Global Walls: Responses to Migration, 1885–1925," in Gungwu Wang, ed., *Global History and Migrations*, pp. 279–307. See also Joshua A. Sanborn, "Unsettling the Empire: Violent Migrations and Social Disaster in Russia during World War I," *Journal of Modern History* 77 (2005): 290–324.

49. Ian Clark, *Globalization and Fragmentation: International Relations in the Twentieth Century* (Oxford: Oxford University Press, 1997), p. 33f; Roland Robertson, *Globalization: Social Theory and Global Culture* (London: Sage Publications, 1992).

50. See Martin H. Geyer and Johannes Paulmann, eds., *The Mechanics of Internationalism: Culture, Society, and Politics from the 1840s to the First World War* (Oxford: Oxford University Press, 2001); Francis S. Lyons, *Internationalism in Europe, 1815–1914* (Leiden: A.W. Sythoff, 1963); Craig N. Murphy, *International Organization and Industrial Change: Global Governance since 1850* (New York: Oxford University Press, 1994); Micheline R. Ishay, *Internationalism and its Betrayal* (Minneapolis: University of Minnesota Press, 1995); Iriye, *Cultural Internationalism.*

51. See Sönke Neitzel, *Weltmacht oder Untergang: Die Weltreichslehre im Zeitalter des Imperialismus* (Paderborn: Schöningh, 2000).

52. See Louis L. Snyder, *Macro-Nationalisms: A History of the Pan-Movements* (Westport: Greenwood Press, 1984); Akira Iriye, *After Imperialism: The Search for a New Order in the Far East, 1921–1931* (Cambridge, Mass.: Harvard University Press, 1965); Prasenjit Duara, "The Discourse of Civilization and Pan-Asianism," *Journal of World History* 12 (2001): 99–130; Selcuk Esenbel, "Japan's Global Claim to Asia and the World of Islam: Transnational Nationalism and World Power, 1900–1945," *American Historical Review* 109 (2004): 1140–70; Hasan Kayali, *Arabs and Young Turks: Ottomanism, Arabism, and Islamism in the Ottoman Empire, 1908–1918* (Berkeley: University of California Press, 1997). For Pan-Africanism, see Immanuel Geiss, *The Pan-African Movement: A History of Pan-Africanism in America, Europe, and Africa* (London: Methuen & Co., 1974).

53. See, for example, Michael Adas, "The Great War and the Decline of the Civilizing Mission," in L.J. Sears, ed., *Autonomous Histories, Particular Truths* (Madison: University of Wisconsin Center for Southeast Asian Studies, 1993), pp. 101–21.

54. See Rebecca Karl, *Staging the World: Chinese Nationalism at the Turn of the Twentieth Century* (Durham: Duke University Press, 2002).

55. See Douglas Howland, *Translating the West: Language and Political Reason in 19th Century Japan* (Honolulu: University of Hawaii Press, 2002).

56. See Paula Harrell, *Sowing the Seeds of Change: Chinese Students, Japanese Teachers, 1895–1905* (Stanford: Stanford University Press, 1992).

24 • Sebastian Conrad and Dominic Sachsenmaier

57. David Harvey, *The Condition of Postmodernity: An Enquiry into the Origins of Cultural Change* (Oxford: Blackwell, 1989).
58. Quoted from T.N. Harper, "Diaspora and the Languages of Globalism, 1850–1914," in Hopkins, ed., *Globalization in World History.* pp. 141–166, Quote p. 143.
59. See Armand Mattelart, *Networking the World, 1794–2000,* trans. Liz Carey-Libbrecht and James A. Cohen (Minneapolis: University of Minnesota Press, 2000); Peter J. Hugill, *Global Communications since 1844: Geopolitics and Technology* (Baltimore: Johns Hopkins University Press, 1999); Daniel R. Headrick, *When Information Came of Age: Technologies of Knowledge in the Age of Reason and Revolution, 1700–1850* (New York: Oxford University Press, 2000).
60. See Robert S. Fortner, *International Communication: History, Conflict, and Control of the Global Metropolis* (Belmont: Wadsworth Publishing Co., 1993); Daniel R. Headrick, *The Tentacles of Progress: Technology Transfer in the Age of Imperialism, 1850–1940* (Oxford: Oxford University Press, 1988); Daniel R. Headrick, *The Invisible Weapon: Telecommunications and International Politics, 1851–1945* (Oxford: Oxford University Press, 1991).
61. Quoted from Matthias Dörries, "Krakatau 1883: Die Welt als Labor und Erfahrungsraum," in Iris Schröder and Sabine Hohler, eds., *Welt-Räume: Geschichte, Geographie und Globalisierung seit 1900* (Frankfurt: Campus, 2005), p. 68.
62. See G.E.C. Wedlake, *S.O.S.: The Story of Radio Communication* (New York: Crane, Russak & Co, 1973); Tom Standage, *The Victorian Internet: The Remarkable Story of the Telegraph and the Nineteenth-Century On-Line Pioneers* (New York: Walker and Co., 1998).
63. See, for example, Joan Judge, *Print and Politics: "Shibao" and the Culture of Reform in Late Qing China* (Stanford: Stanford University Press, 1996).
64. Kern, *The Culture of Time and Space.*
65. See Ivo Nikolai Lambi, *Free Trade and Protection in Germany 1868–1879* (Wiesbaden: F. Steiner, 1963); Rita Aldenhoff-Hübinger, *Agrarpolitik und Protektionismus, Deutschland und Frankreich im Vergleich, 1879–1914* (Göttingen: Vandenhoeck & Ruprecht, 2002).
66. Karl, *Staging the World.*
67. Paul Greenhalgh, *Ephemeral Vistas: The Expositions Universelles, Great Exhibitions and World's Fairs, 1851–1939* (Manchester: Manchester University Press, 1988).
68. See Carlos Marichal, *A Century of Debt Crises in Latin America* (Princeton: Princeton University Press, 1982), p. 107.
69. Simon Winchester, *Krakatoa: The Day the World Exploded, August 27, 1883* (New York: Harper Collins Publishers, 2003).
70. See Cemil Aydin, *Politics of Anti-Westernism in Asia. Visions of World Order in Pan-Islamic and Pan-Asian Thought (1882–1945)* (New York: Columbia University Press, 2007).
71. See Adas, "The Great War and the Decline of the Civilizing Mission."

72. Thomas J. Knock, *To End All Wars: Woodrow Wilson and the Quest for a New World Order* (New York: Oxford University Press, 1992).

73. See, from an economic point of view, Charles P. Kindleberger, *The World in Depression, 1929–1939* (Berkeley: University of California Press, 1973); Dietmar Rothermund, *The Global Impact of the Great Depression 1929–1939* (London: Routledge, 1996).

PART ONE

Conceptions of World Order and Global Consciousness in the Imperialist Age

CHAPTER 2

Global Civil Society and the Forces of Empire: The Salvation Army, British Imperialism, and the "Prehistory" of NGOs (ca. 1880–1920)

Harald Fischer-Tiné

"What, then, is my scheme? It is a very simple one, although in its ramifications and extensions it embraces the whole world"
—William Booth, *In Darkest England and the Way Out,* London, 1890

Nongovernmental organizations (NGOs)[1] play a pivotal role in the current debate on globalization. Particularly, critics of the asymmetrical economic and political relationships ensuing from the processes of intensified communication and exchange on a global scale warn of the new forces of Empire—that is, the hegemonic role of the United States and multinational trusts—in a new postcolonial and post-cold war world order.[2] The establishment of a global civil society, would provide the only effective means of resistance to these perilous developments.[3] The most recent world social fora held in Mumbai (formerly Bombay) in 2004 and in Porto Alegre in 2005 served as powerful demonstrations of the resolution of countless movements and organizations from all over the world—including many NGOs—to strengthen local interests and check the impact of the alleged neoimperial forces. Recent scholarship has rightly criticized the lack of interest in the historical dimension of globalization[4] that characterizes much of today's political discourse on the issue. While there is an abundance of historiographical writing on the prehistory of states and nations, we know comparatively little about the historical trajectory taken by what is today termed global civil society. Transnational interaction and communication on a global scale, however, is not as recent a phenomenon as is commonly understood. According to Jürgen Osterhammel, the intensity of globalizing processes had reached a first peak by the end of the nineteenth century.[5] This holds true not only for the economic, political, and cultural level, but also for the emerging religious and philanthropic organizations that could be seen as forerunners of today's NGOs.[6]

Building on Kathleen Wilson's important insight showing that the British Empire provides us with a particularly striking example of interdependent sites that "allow us to rethink the . . . historiographies of national belonging and exclusion,"[7] the present case study tries to illustrate these developments by analyzing the ideology as well as the practical endeavors of one of the most successful global philanthropic movements, in a transnational context: the Salvation Army. Founded as a modest lay-missionary organization in 1878 in England, the Salvation Army was represented in more than 30 states by 1910. It entertained a flourishing network of schools, hospitals, reformatories, factories, publishing houses, and other institutions almost all over the globe. Complementing and partly challenging previous work that tended to study the movement in isolation, either in Western—mostly British and American[8]—or non-Western contexts,[9] I want to stress the interrelation between the metropolitan and the imperial (or even global) dimension of the Salvation Army's work that mutually influenced and informed each other in significant ways.[10] Mainly focusing on the Army's activities in Britain and British India, I would like to make three basic arguments.

First, even when the Army's activities were largely confined to British or other European theaters, the epistemological base of Salvationist ideology was significantly shaped by what has been described as "imperial technologies of knowledge-gathering."[11] Britain's urban poor, the prime targets of the organization's reclamation activities, were constructed as "heathens" or "savages" in a rhetoric borrowing heavily from imperial travel writing. It is evident that extra-European points of reference had become commonplace in late Victorian public debates.

Second, apart from this ideological entanglement, the global outlook of Salvationism and the movement's imperial dimension became very concretely visible in its scheme to eradicate urban poverty in Britain. The Army's program of Social Salvation was conceived on a global scale, as one of its features was the emigration of unemployed plebeian elements of British society to overseas colonies. Thus, not only the epistemological tools of the empire but also its infrastructure and the practical possibilities it offered were very much present in public debates and shaped what can, from that point on, no longer merely be called a metropolitan discourse.

Third, in the beginning, the Salvation Army had to cope with official suspicion, in the United Kingdom as well as in the British colonies and various other countries. During the first two or three decades after its inception it acted not only without any support from the state but often suffered outright repression by the state authorities. However, an exploration of the Indian example shows that the state attitude changed as soon as it was realized that the Salvation Army could be used as a helpful tool to control and "reform" segments of the population that were deemed dangerous. Within a few decades, the role of the organization changed fundamentally. From being denounced as troublemakers raising the concern of the colonial administration, the Salvationists had been transformed into guardians of the empire by the second decade of the twentieth century. They supported the colonial state in various important projects concerned with inculcating the natives with civility, thereby spreading the British/European standard of civilization[12] into a corner of the world regarded as half civilized at best. Meanwhile, and arguably not entirely unconnected to its imperial usefulness—the organization had also won respectability at home after initially being attacked for decades from various sides including, as previously mentioned, government officials. One result of the eventual recognition by the establishment was that it could extend its services to other colonies and dominions of the British Empire and thus became a truly imperial force, active all over the globe.

Thus, the example of the Salvation Army can serve to demonstrate that the new internationalism carried by organizations and agents belonging to the realm of the civil society did not necessarily "challenge state power,"[13] nor did it unavoidably entail lofty aspirations "to a more peaceful and stable world order through transnational efforts"[14] because it was intrinsically linked to imperial ideologies and practices in manifold ways.

The Emergence of Salvationism in Mid-Victorian England

Changing Religious Landscapes

The Salvation Army was a typical product of the economic, social, and intellectual cataclysms that took place in mid- and late Victorian England. The processes of industrialization and urbanization, with their endemic features of hunger, housing problems, and unemployment had created two nations, not only in social and economic but also in religious terms.[15] They had alienated many members of the lower strata of British Society from the Church of England and even partly from the nonconformist sects, which had been very popular among the working classes in the eighteenth and early nineteenth centuries. The fact that the popularity of the conventional type of organized Christianity was "receding in unprecedented rapidity"[16] became evident in the nationwide religious census conducted in 1851 that unmistakably showed "how absolutely insignificant a proportion"[17] of the congregations was composed of members of the urban laboring classes. As a result, a whole wave of evangelist groups and individuals embarked on what became known as the Home Mission Movement from the late 1850s onward. It was their avowed aim to save Christianity—already under siege on a different level through the spread of scientific modes of explaining the world and man's place in it[18]—from further decline by reaching out for the working classes.

The Salvation Army has to be seen in the broader context of this religious revivalism that aimed to create a "middle of the road Christianity," whose middle-class values could be adapted lower on the social scale. Conversion thus had not only a religious significance, it could also be used to contain a laboring population that—in the eyes of many upper-class observers—had grown more and more "unruly," "degenerate" and "dangerous" by the 1880s.[19] That the process of downward diffusion of middle-class values through a large-scale re-Christianization was regarded as a viable method to counter such threats can be gathered from the report of a Salvationist officer dating from the 1890s. He observes with obvious relief that "[c]onversion has a wonderful effect on a man; he is very soon decently clothed; his home becomes better, and, although he remains a working man, outwardly he might pass with the clerks."[20] New techniques of organization, mobilization, and recruitment were used to convey this double message of spiritual and social upliftment, and traditional congregational religion was being increasingly supported (and sometimes replaced) by large-scale public organizations combining religious interests with an agenda of social reform.[21] The Salvation Army was perhaps the most successful and doubtlessly the most original of these newly emerging bodies.

William Booth and the Rise and Growth of
Aggressive Christianity

For what was to become a global movement, Salvationism had astonishingly narrow local origins. The movement's founder William Booth (1829–1912), originated from a humble working class family in Nottingham.[22] At the age of 15 he underwent a religious conversion experience and came under the influence of Methodism. He served for several years as a minister for a Methodist sect, before he declared his independence in the early 1860s. Nonetheless, Methodism seems to have influenced his religious teachings in at least two important ways. His rather simplistic belief that eternal damnation was the inescapable fate of the unconverted that went in tandem with a strong conviction that personal salvation was possible in this world only due to the grace of the holy spirit, certainly bore traits of Wesleyan teaching. Undoubtedly his strong social commitment and concern for the "poor and degraded" also has moorings in this tradition.[23] It was the combination of both factors that made him eventually settle down in the capital and found the East London Christian Mission in 1865.[24] After two years of preaching in tents or open air, a permanent headquarter of his mission was established in the Eastern Star, formerly a "low drinking saloon"[25] on Whitechapel road. This choice of place is significant, as the environs of Whitechapel were already infamous for being one of the most disreputable areas in the "heart of the empire" even before they acquired Jack-the-Ripper-fame.[26] The symbolic message was unambiguous: in England, as in India, later on the outcasts of society, were the main addressees of the Army's proselytizing.

From the very beginning William Booth and his wife Catherine, who played an important role in the movement and was later given the honorary title "Mother of the Salvation Army,"[27] made use of the print media to disseminate their message—a feature it shared with countless other modern religious movements and organizations all over the globe.[28] In addition to the impressive number of pamphlets that Booth had circulated from the inception of his career as a *homme public*, the *East London Evangelist* was published from 1868 as the first regular journal of his movement. Several other periodicals including the *Salvationist* (1878) and *The War Cry* (1879) that was to become its most important mouthpiece, followed later.

In spite of the extensive use of the mass-media available at the time,[29] the organization's rate of growth remained humble during the first decade of its existence. It was only during the years 1878–1880 that a major shift in matters of internal organization, strategy, and public appearance changed the course of its history: the "mission to the heathens of London"[30] became a quasi-military organization and was renamed Salvation Army. William Booth appointed himself as its General and introduced the complete range of military ranking for his fellow-Salvationists. The Army's brass bands parading through the streets of poorer urban quarters, together with the uniforms[31] and flags soon became one of the most powerful symbols of the restyled voluntary organization.

The adoption of military uniforms, terminology, music, and modes of organization reflected an important broader tendency in late Victorian intellectual and religious life: a growing militarization.[32] Interestingly, the ground for this change of attitudes had partly been prepared by geopolitical developments of the 1850s, when the British Empire was shaken by the almost simultaneous outbreaks of the Crimean War and the Indian "Mutiny."[33] The feelings of vulnerability and anxiety provoked by these conflicts that involved heavy losses of life on the side of the British, also led to a subtle change in religious sensibilities. Traditional concepts of peacefulness and piety slowly gave way to ideals of aggressive self-assertion of which the conspicuous popularity of military rhetoric and imagery in Christian circles is but one index. As Peter Van der Veer and others have argued, the new concept of "muscular Christianity," propagated by influential literary and public figures like Thomas Carlyle and Charles Kingsley, must also be seen in this wider imperial connection.[34]

One result of these masculinizing tendencies was a widespread enthusiasm for the figure of the soldier-saint, construed as a defender of the faith who was pious and yet strong, godly, and virile. By the middle of the 1860s, the phrase "Christian soldier" was becoming commonplace as warrior-like qualities seemed to be best fitted to spread Christianity in an age regarded as godless and impious. This was not only obvious in the case of missionary work in Britain's various colonies that was pursued with renewed zeal from mid-nineteenth century onward,[35] but also in the crusade to win over the "heathens" in the metropolis. In a seminal pamphlet, Catherine Booth justified the militarization of the former East London Christian Mission with the simple argument:

> [I]f you can't get them in by civil measures, use military measures. Go and COMPEL them to come in. It seems to me that we want more of this determined aggressive spirit. . . . Verily, we must make them look—tear the bandages off, open their eyes, make them bear it, and if they run away from you in one place, meet them in another, and let them have no peace until they submit to God and get their souls saved. This is what Christianity ought to be doing in this land.[36]

The advantages of an autocratic, army-like style of leadership for a religious outfit are outlined in even clearer terms by General Booth in a manual that was modeled after the British Army's "soldiers" pocket-book and handed out to every new "cadet." After denouncing the uselessness of any democratic system of church government[37] Booth pointed out that:

> Only with this absolute power over men can there be regularity. . . . [W]ith people who are always under the same control, it is possible, no matter who the officer may be, for the services to be continued day after day, and year after year, without a break or hitch. This is militarism—a settled, absolute, regular system of using men to accomplish a common settled purpose.[38]

It was precisely the high degree of organization and discipline achieved through this "militarism" that transformed the former "Christian mission" into an authoritarian "imperial structure"[39] able to "overcome, conquer, subdue [and] compel all nations . . . to become the disciples of the son of god"[40] that later on made it an attractive partner for the common settled purpose of "reforming" segments of the population viewed as degenerate and dangerous both in the metropolis and in the outposts of the empire.[41] Quite obviously, this scheme also fit in perfectly well with late Victorian society's more general obsession with regularity and national efficiency.[42] Whereas the attainment of a more effective style of leadership was thus the main goal of the organizational aspect of militarization[43] the expected results of its outward elements—the adoption of uniforms and other army paraphernalia—was threefold. First it was expected simply to "attract attention." Second, it was calculated to "excite respect in the rowdy population"[44] whose souls were the prime targets of the Army's religious zeal. Third, it was supposed to clearly demarcate the Salvationists from other Christian missionaries, making them distinguishable as a lay civil society organization that had nothing in common with the established churches. The latter point is significant insofar as it did indeed appeal to the members of the working classes, many of whom were, as we have already noticed, strongly prejudiced against the congregational versions of Christianity.

Whichever aspect may have been decisive, the restructuring along military lines doubtlessly was a tremendous success. From the 31 branches existing in 1878 the movement's strength grew to 519 branches (now called corps) all over the United Kingdom by 1883.[45] In the following decades the Army's rise across Britain steadily continued, though at a somewhat slower pace: there were 1507 corps by 1890 and 1557 by 1900.[46] These impressive figures could easily mislead one to believe that the Army's growth was a neat and uncomplicated success story. Quite the opposite: from the outset, the Salvationists' catchy methods of spreading their gospel provoked what one author has called "Salvophobism":[47] fierce opposition from various quarters.[48] Young workers formed so-called "Skeleton Armies" and disturbed the public sermons and procession of the Christian revivalists. The clergy of the Church of England and other established denominations were often hostile, and the local authorities not seldom regarded the zealous revivalists as troublemakers and had them arrested. It was only after the organization became significantly engaged in social service and philanthropic activities from the 1890s onward that things began to change slowly. By the turn of the century, the Army was increasingly recognized in official circles as an efficient agent of both social reform and social control.[49] George Bernard Shaw even saw it as a "sort of auxiliary police" as it was "taking off the insurrectionary edge of poverty"[50] thus "preserv[ing] the country from mob-violence and revolution."[51] The newly acquired official acclaim became most apparent in two symbolic acts. In 1904 General Booth was received by King Edward VII, and three years later he was even awarded an honorary doctorate from Oxford University.[52] Thus, by the end of the first decade of the twentieth century, there could no longer be a doubt about it: Salvationism had gone mainstream.

Long before such a recognition by the establishment was even imaginable, the international expansion of the movement had begun. As early as 1880 the first branches were opened in other countries, by 1910 the Salvationists had "seeded themselves"[53] in more than 30 countries (including British colonial territories)[54] and by the 1930s the movement had become an almost universal force, entertaining branches in 41 countries and territories spanning 5 continents.[55] Before we look more closely at the Army's actual activities overseas, it is worth exploring the ideological base of its social and philanthropic work in the metropolis, which eventually made the organization respectable in official circles. An analysis of this discursive dimension also demonstrates the importance of global (mostly colonial or exotic) metaphors and points of reference. On the basis of the conspicuous omnipresence of imperial rhetoric in the core texts produced by leading figures of the Salvation movement, I would suggest reading the Army as a colonizing agency within the boundaries of the United Kingdom.

The Imperial Mission Within

"Darkest England" and the Tools of Empire

In the first decade after the foundation of the Salvation Army, the organization's religious objective—"saving" as many souls as possible—seems to have clearly outweighed its ambitions for social reform.[56] Soon it became evident that the targeted *Lumpen* elements of urban society would be hard to convince in terms of focusing their attention on their spiritual "sanctification"[57] whilst they had to struggle with their utter material distress. Social reform thus appeared to be the first necessary step to realize the more ambitious goal of the "the devil's children's"[58] spiritual regeneration.

The publication of William Booth's[59] controversial book *From Darkest England and the Way Out* in 1890 reflects this reorientation toward the material needs of the "submerged tenth" of England's population.[60] *In Darkest England* is today rightly regarded as a classic of Victorian reform literature. Apart from being a tremendous commercial success (more than 300,000 copies were sold within one and a half years after its release),[61] the book provoked a vibrant public debate about poverty, philanthropy, and the responsibilities of civil society, involving such prominent intellectuals as T.H. Huxley and George Bernard Shaw.[62] In spite of the fact that Booth focuses on England—almost all the examples he gives are taken from the London poor—the arguments brought forward in the book and in the ensuing debate reveal not only the omnipresence of imperial points of reference, they also show the extent to which Victorians were used to thinking in a global framework. The catchy title itself is a perfect illustration for this point. It capitalizes on the popularity of a book written by one of Britain's imperial heroes, brought out shortly before Booth's manifesto appeared: Henry Morton Stanley's *In Darkest Africa*.[63] Whereas Stanley describes his expedition through Central Africa as a voyage into the heart of a hostile, repulsive, and dangerous wilderness, inhabited by uncivilized and degraded specimens of the human race "nearly approaching the baboon,"[64] Booth takes his readers to the poorer parts of London, the "urban jungle" whose "denizens" he describes in astonishingly similar terms:

> Darkest England like Darkest Africa reeks with malaria. The foul and fetid breath of our slums is almost as poisonous as that of the African Swamp. . . . Just as in Darkest Africa . . . much of the misery of those whose lot we are considering arises from their own habits. Drunkenness and all manner of uncleanness, moral and physical abound. . . . A population sodden with drink, steeped in vice eaten up by every social and physical malady, these are the denizens of Darkest England among whom my life has been spent and to whose rescue I would now summon all that is best in the manhood and womanhood of our land.[65]

A painstakingly detailed description of the slum areas in the heart of the empire and a meticulous categorization of its populace (the homeless, the out-of-work, the vicious, the criminals, etc.) follows.[66] The sociologist Mariana Valverde has persuasively argued that Booth's description of Darkest England and her "degenerate" inhabitants is a typical example for the impact of imperial technologies of knowledge production on the emerging metropolitan discipline of urban social studies.[67] Cartographical mapping of "spaces of disease and disorder" as well as taxonomic projects like the classification of human types (later on called ethnology or race science) had first been developed in an imperial context by explorers, surveyors, and "scholar administrators."[68] In a process Valverde describes as "the dialectic of the familiar and the unfamiliar" hegemonial knowledge, based on metropolitan premises but produced in the colonial "contact zone"[69] was re-imported into the metropolis to provide the attempts at categorization and hierarchization in the more familiar arena "with scientific authorisation."[70] Booth's tropical-ization of London's East End—some of his contemporaries were indeed engaged in the drawing of an ethnographic map of the capital—shows that these imperial technologies of exploration, far from being objective scientific methods, were shot through with pre-assumptions and laden with value judgements.[71] One certainly has to admit that General Booth had a genuine interest in the poor, and helped considerably in improving their material lot. Yet at the same time his "benevolent despotism,"[72] characterized by the constant use of the "language of empire,"[73] resulted in a widening of the gap between middle-class "explorers" and the slum dwellers in England's industrial cities whose life-world was put under scrutiny.[74] Ultimately, the "Sunken Millions"[75] of the urban poor were put on par with the savage "natives," "pygmies," and "baboons" out there in the colonies. Such rhetoric compellingly demonstrates the impact of the powerful late Victorian trope of race and more specifically the fear of "racial degeneration."[76]

Booth was perfectly aware of the fact that the prevalence of excessive poverty and low life in London and other English cities severely threatened the credibility of an imperial nation that boasted of spreading "moral and material progress" over the globe and held it to be "a satire . . . upon our Christianity and our civilisation that these colonies of heathens and savages in the heart of our capital should attract so little attention!"[77] He was convinced, however, that "for Darkest England as for Darkest Africa, there [wa]s a light beyond"[78] in the form of responsible representatives of superior "races" or individuals embarking on a civilizing mission "to snatch from the abyss those who, if left to themselves, w[ould] perish."[79]

Global Solutions for Domestic Problems

Booth's diagnosis of poverty in Britain was gloomy. According to his calculations no less than three million, 10 percent of the country's population, were living beneath the poverty line, but there were substantial differences between them, even if the boundaries between the groups were fuzzy. According to Booth, Darkest England could be imagined as a territory demarcated by three concentric circles.[80] The outer was inhabited by the homeless and unemployed but honest poor. Next came the vicious, and the innermost was the domain of the criminals. All of them were threatened by the constant temptation of the brothels and gin shops in their vicinity. Echoing a current stereotype,[81] Booth believed that moral weakness and particularly the affinity to drink was almost a natural character trait of the urban "residuum."[82] His program of "social salvation" hence had two basic goals that could be aptly described in the imperial rhetoric of the time as "material and moral improvement."[83] Both were centered on the notion of work as a panacea for various kinds of evils and the ultimate key to salvation.[84] Work not only as a key to self-help, that is, economic self-sufficiency, but also as a moralizing force,[85] inculcating virtues like regularity and self-discipline, encompassed in the Victorian omnibus term "character."[86] The actual instrument of upliftment was to be a threefold scheme of self-sustaining communities, significantly termed "colonies." This scheme, Booth argued, should be entirely financed by donations and public subscriptions, thus setting an example for the self-healing capabilities of civil society. The "city colonies" were supposed to be "harbours of refuge" in the "centre of the ocean of misery" and had the task of saving the "poor destitute creatures"[87] from the most immediate forms of distress by providing shelter, food, and temporary employment in factories and industrial workshops.

Those who had passed a test "as to their sincerity, industry and honesty"[88] could then proceed to the farm colony, situated a safe distance from the temptations of the city and the unhealthy and corrupting influences of urban life. Booth made it unmistakably clear that every person admitted into the settlement would not only be "instructed in the needful arts of husbandry, or some other method of earning his bread" but also "taught the elementary lesson of obedience."[89] Drunkenness, falsehood, and even the use of "profane language" would be severely punished.[90] The rule that repeat offenders were to be expelled from the rural colony was designed to ensure that the "scum of Cockneydom"[91] was sorted out and only the "deserving," the refined products of this process of internal colonization, should reach the third and final stage in the Salvationists' regenerative scheme. For our present purpose the proposed establishment of New Britain or the colony over-sea is certainly the most interesting aspect of Booth's ambitious plan. The General's awareness of the significance of recent improvements in transport and communication and the resulting intensity of ongoing processes of globalization was at the bottom of the whole project. His description of an Anglophone global village must strike today's readers.

The world has grown much smaller since the electric telegraph was discovered and side by side with the shrinkage of this planet under the influence of steam and electricity there has come a sense of brotherhood and a consciousness of community of interest and nationality on the part of the English-speaking peoples throughout the world. The change from Devon to Australia is not such a change in many respects as merely to cross over from Devon to Normandy.[92]

Given his awareness of the global character of his age and the resulting possibilities, it seems to be logical for the founder of the Salvation Army to solve Britain's domestic problems of recurrent economic crises and unemployment by exporting surplus labor to other parts of the world. That this new type of expansion of England was only conceivable thanks to Britain's imperial expertise becomes evident when Booth assured that he would revise the details of his scheme according to the "best wisdom and matured experience of the practical men of every colony in the empire."[93] The importance of the existing imperial infrastructure comes out even more sharply when one considers the places Booth suggests for his proposed New Britain Colony: South Africa was his first choice but Australia and Canada were also considered suitable to establish similar settlements in the future. Borrowing again heavily from the imperial rhetoric of his times, the general made it a point that emigration did not mean a clean break with the motherland. Quite the reverse: the family ties would become even stronger through the diaspora situation:

It will resemble nothing so much as the unmooring of a little piece of England, and towing it across the sea to find a safe anchorage in a sunnier clime. The ship which takes out emigrants will bring back the produce of the farms, and constant travelling to and fro will lead more than ever to the feeling that we and our ocean-sundered brethren are members of one family.[94]

The Salvationists' gravest concern seems to have been the right selection and adequate preparation of the would-be colonists for their new lives overseas. Booth was fully aware of the fact that the sending of colonists, "whose first enquiry on reaching a foreign land was for a Whisky shop,"[95] could endanger the whole scheme. He therefore wanted to make sure, through a rigid training program, that only the most "trustworthy characters" were eventually sent out. At the same time, he pointed to the necessity for the establishment of a "strong and efficient government" in the colony and constant control and surveillance of the immigrants, as "nothing less than the irresistible pressure of a friendly and stronger purpose" would constrain them to give up their old degraded ways.[96]

Another obstacle to overcome was the problem of transport.[97] Here again, Booth was most anxious about the moral state of the passengers. Being onboard the ship for several weeks without an occupation could easily lead to

Figure 2.1 The colored centerfold from *In Darkest England* powerfully illustrates the global dimension of William Booth's threefold scheme of social salvation

Source: William Booth, *In Darkest England and the Way Out*, London: International Headquarters of the Salvation Army 1890.

the "downfall" of female passengers and to the men "contracting habits of idleness." He therefore opted for the Army acquiring a ship of its own, wherein the female colonists would be compelled to engage in "knitting, sewing, tailoring, and other kindred occupations" and the men could perform manual work on the ship. To ensure that unskilled men would be sufficiently occupied and the "Salvation Ship" could indeed become both a "floating temple" and a "hive of industry," Booth recommended buying a sailing vessel rather than a steamer.

Anybody with only cursory knowledge of the rhetoric of the British colonial civilizing mission[98] will see how closely the twin enterprises of imperial philanthropy and the rescuing of the lower classes in the metropolis were intertwined both on a discursive and practical level: England's regenerated jungle population would eventually contribute to the providential task of spreading the English version of civilization in the dark corners of the world. It should not come as a surprise, therefore, that the plan was received very warmly by the usual advocates of British imperialism, such as Rudyard Kipling, Henry Rider Haggard,[99] Cecil Rhodes, and Winston Churchill[100] as a useful strategy to foster imperial unity.[101] However, whereas Booth's appeal to pledge funds in order to finance the Darkest England Scheme was by and large a success, and both city and farm colonies soon became a reality, the proposed overseas colonies were "destined to be still-born."[102] Therefore, we have so far mainly been concerned with analogies, influences, and mutual borrowings between Christian revivalism and the forces of empire. In the concluding part of this chapter we see how the Army ultimately became an active *agent* of British imperialism. This can best be demonstrated by analyzing the Salvationist engagement in Britain's oldest and most important colony: India.

The Imperial Mission Without

A Difficult Passage to India

In-house histories of the Salvation Army mention that the movement "recognized its obligation to assume an international character"[103] immediately after it had been refashioned into a quasi-military body. The international expansion began in 1880 with the founding of a branch in the United States. Australia and several European countries (including France and Switzerland) followed almost immediately. India was thus only the sixth country to be "invaded,"[104] as the Salvationist rhetoric had it. Nevertheless, it is also emphasized that India was the army's first "Missionary field in the East," and was hence regarded as a country of "vast opportunities"[105] and a convenient bridgehead for the conquest of Asia's "teeming millions."[106]

It would be no exaggeration to say that the Indian campaign was in its initial phase a one-man enterprise, driven almost entirely by the missionary zeal of Frederick St. George De Lautour Tucker (1854–1928), who had the vision "to see the whole of India kneeling at the feet of Jesus."[107] For a Salvationist—most officers came from the lower middle or "respectable" working classes—De Lautour Tucker had a rather untypical "gentlemanly" background.[108] A graduate of Cheltenham College and fluent in several Indian languages, he had served as magistrate in the Indian Civil Service, a highly paid and very prestigious post in British India. The legend has it that, after reading the Christmas 1880 issue of *The War Cry* while posted in the Punjab, he was so impressed that he took home leave to hear William Booth's sermons in London and immediately afterward offered his services to the general.[109] He resigned from his lucrative post, joined the Salvation Army, and became not only Booth's most loyal lieutenant but also his son-in-law a few years later.[110] In September 1882, De Lautour-Tucker returned to India as the head of a small invading force consisting of merely four officers. In spite of the numerical insignificance of the expedition corps, both colonial officials and the Anglo-Indian public seem to have been extremely alarmed when it arrived in Bombay. Ironically, one British magistrate suggested dealing with them under the European Vagrancy Act, a law that allowed for the deportation of unemployed and distressed Europeans back to the country of their origin.[111] Nobody would have imagined at the time that three decades later, the Salvation Army would become a state-financed agency to reclaim European vagrants. The reasons for this official distrust are obvious. First, the traumatic experience of the Indian "Mutiny" had made the colonial government extremely sensitive toward a possible provocation of native religious sensibilities. The Queen's proclamation of 1858 had therefore stressed the absolute neutrality of the government of India in matters of religion.[112] In addition, it was well known that the Army's aggressive style of conveying its religious propaganda to the public had provoked controversies and outright disturbances even in England and some other European countries—much worse things could happen, it was feared, in the delicate religious landscape of India.[113]

Second, what was regarded by the Salvationists as the quintessential strategy for the successful evangelization of non-European races was considered a taboo in the extremely race- and class-conscious social environment of British India:[114] "going native." As with what happened later on in other Asian and African countries,[115] the complete assimilation of indigenous modes of dressing, eating, and living and even the adoption of local names was attempted in India from the outset. De Lautour-Tucker (who changed his name to Booth-Tucker in 1888) thus became Fakir Singh. General Booth himself had instructed him before leaving Britain that "to the Indians you must be Indian . . . in order that you may win them to your Master."[116] This transgression of the unwritten imperial law of keeping social distance toward the natives at any cost must have been even more disturbing because of Fakir Singh's biography. To see a former representative of "the conquering race, the white aristocracy, the civilising power"[117] traveling in third class railway compartments or walking around barefooted, begging for funds, wearing turbans and a long Indian *kurta* (shirt) could not cause but the gravest concern of the British-Indian authorities.[118] Whether such a tactic of "go[ing] down low enough to meet the lowest India on its own level"[119] indeed signified the denial of a fundamental racial or civilizational difference, as Jeffrey Cox has recently argued,[120] remains doubtful if one takes into account the heavily racialized language of contemporary Salvationist publications on India, not even to speak of the organization's later activities. It is beyond doubt, however, that most colonial officials tended to read it that way. Fully aware of the provocative effect, Fakir Singh paraded his exotic dress through the streets of London a few years later when he led members of the Army's Indian division through the imperial metropolis on the occasion of the first International Salvation Congress in 1886.[121]

From Conflict to Cooperation

Accordingly, the newly arrived invasion force was closely observed by the Bombay police. When Major De Lautour Tucker (*alias* Fakir-Singh) and his four subalterns tried to organize a musical procession, parading on "war chariots" (converted bullock-carts) through the Bazaars of Bombay,[122] they were immediately arrested on the ground that their activities "would be the cause of disorder and serious breaches of peace."[123] Once again, it became obvious that the Army possessed a remarkable flair for publicity: Booth-Tucker's first arrest (several others followed) was stylized as "martyrdom"[124] and brought the Army unprecedented sympathy from Europeans and declarations of solidarity from Indian elites. The Hindu reformer Keshav Chandra Sen, for instance, sent a memorial to the viceroy complaining that "the action of the government of Bombay against the Salvationists . . . has been most unjust, arbitrary, and improper and contrary to the enlightened policy of the Government."[125]

Despite the growing popularity of Salvationism, the Bombay Presidency continued its hostile politics toward the religious body. Thus, Frederick De

Lautour-Tucker was denied the right to solemnize marriages as a minister of religion in 1884. The central government—anxious to avoid another storm of protest—somewhat uneasily asked the Bombay authorities to reconsider their decision, reminding them that the Salvationists were "as much a Christian sect as the Jumpers of Wales or a dozen of odd bodies that could be named."[126] Nonetheless, the relationship between the Salvationists and colonial authorities remained a strained one in other provinces as well. In Punjab, for instance, W.M. Drysdale, an English police officer who had been converted to Salvationism during his home leave and started preaching to the natives and selling *The War Cry* in public places, was reported to his superiors as "being both mad and a fool" by the district magistrate. Having refused to "give up all interference with the religion of the Natives" he was eventually dismissed from service in 1891 for disobedience.[127]

Regardless of the continuing distrust of many colonial administrators, the Army managed to quickly extend its network from Bombay to other provincial cities and from there make inroads into the rural areas, getting increasingly engaged in what they termed "village warfare."[128] The pioneers were reinforced by scores of new officers from England, Sweden, Switzerland, Australia, the United States, Canada, and other countries.[129] By 1889, Fakir Singh could boast of his "devoted band of 170 officers gathered from all around the world" supported by "more than 100 Indian officers . . . who have caught from them the real Army spirit."[130] *The War Cry* started an Indian edition that was soon translated into several vernaculars.[131] Other periodicals and pamphlets followed. Salvationist popularity also benefited considerably from two visits by William Booth in the early 1890s. The General's rhetorical skills were proverbial and his brief Indian tours seem to have resulted in thousands of conversions, although most of them were from Christian communities.[132] In order to further widen its basis among the native population—the main attention was focused once again on the outcast[e]s of Indian society[133]—the organization's commitment to social service was also intensified. Educational institutions were established and many of the Salvationist Corps regularly engaged in philanthropic activities during famines and natural catastrophes.[134] In the early 1890s, rescue homes for "fallen women" were opened in the red-light districts of Colombo, Calcutta, Bombay, and Madras.[135] The year 1895 witnessed the inauguration of a medical institution in Travancore, South India and several other dispensaries and hospitals followed in other parts of the country[136] although the professional qualification of the Salvationists running these institutions was sometimes rather doubtful.[137]

Acting as a fully self-financed nongovernmental organization *stricto sensu*, the Army had made considerable progress. However, it had also become evident that a truly large-scale expansion would remain impossible without the approval and financial aid of the colonial state. This is probably the reason why the Army gave up its policy of strict autonomy and the first attempts to curry the favor of the colonial authorities began. In early 1907, "Commissioner" Booth-Tucker asked the government of India for financial support to extend the Army's activities to the medical field.[138] The proposal was declined as the majority of the colonial officials were still of the opinion that hospitals run by the Army would "tend to become . . . instruments of religious propaganda."[139] Some of the reports on which the government's refusal was based betray the continuing distrust toward an organization that was at times denigrated as a "safe haven for the mentally disturbed,"[140] even by fellow missionaries of other denominations. The assessment of one of the Salvationists' medical institutions in the Bombay Presidency by the responsible district collector is quite typical for the position of the colonial authorities. He states:

> I have the honour to report that the Salvation Army Hospital at Anand is a superfluous institution, founded for the purpose of competing for patients and possible converts with other Missions previously planted at the place. . . . Had they been guided by unmixed motives, whether philanthropic or even Christian, they could not have selected Anand for their centre . . . I . . . express my strong opinion against Government mixing itself up with any form of Missionary activity, and least of all with anything undertaken by the Salvation Army.[141]

The interests of the British-Indian Empire thus still seemed to be clearly at odds with the interests of the "Kingdom of Christ" after more than two decades of the Salvationists' presence in India. Despite such discouraging reactions, Booth-Tucker and his fellow officers did not give up, and eventually the considerable ideological overlap in the common project of "civilising the native population" began slowly to be acknowledged by representatives of the colonial state. Education was one field where the Salvationists sought the recognition and financial support of the colonial government by bringing attention to the imperial value of the Army's work. By 1908 they had managed to establish more than 200 day-schools all over the subcontinent, daily attended by about 10,000 pupils without receiving any grants-in-aid.[142] In his effort to convince the highest representatives of the state[143] the Commissioner not only mentions that "physical drills ha[d] been introduced" in these primary schools "with great success"[144]; he also tries bringing to bear the organization's worldwide experience. In connection with the appropriate language and script to be taught to transform the Indian populace into loyal citizens of the empire, he draws on his experience in the United States, where he had been working in the Army's headquarters from 1896–1903:[145]

> It seems to us further that an improvement might be made in these schools by an adoption throughout India of the Roman character. This would greatly simplify the teaching of the various languages, and would tend toward the unification of the country. A similar result would . . . be obtained by extending largely the study of the English language. . . . Having spent so many years in the United States, I should like to have an opportunity of explaining something of the general policy of that country with regard to that question. For instance the despatch of one thousand "school marms" [sic!] to teach the Philippinos English probably did more for the pacification of those turbulent and many-languaged Islanders than could have been accomplished by fifty times that number of soldiers.[146]

With the government of India's eventual approval to integrate the primary day-schools run by the Salvationists into their grants-in-aid scheme, the "imperial romance" of the organization had begun. It was going to last until the end of the British rule in India.

Reclaiming "Savages," Brown and White

We have already discussed at length the homologies occurring in the Salvationists' (as in other Victorian reformers') discourse on the British working classes on the one hand and the "heathens" or "savages" on the other. The formula "Soup, Soap and Salvation" coined by William Booth to describe the pillars of the Army's reclamation work[147] was believed to be applicable to savages worldwide—regardless of their color. As early as 1890, Commissioner Booth-Tucker had written a book entitled *Darkest India*, echoing General Booth's *In Darkest England*, in which he claimed that "the gospel of social salvation, which has so electrified all classes in England can be adopted on this country almost as it stands."[148] From about 1908 onward, more and more imperial administrators recognized that this potential as a civilizing agency made the Salvationists an ideal partner of the colonizing state. One could assume that the sudden change of attitude by representatives of the colonial state was facilitated by the growing influence of Indian philanthropic organizations that often combined their social agenda with nascent forms of nation-building and hence posed a serious threat to the legitimacy of colonial rule.[149] A joint venture with the Salvation Army promised to regain some of the lost ground in this particular situation.[150] It seems also likely that the general fear of losing grip over the Indian population has played a certain role—a fear that was prevalent among the British in the wake of the Swadeshi Campaign 1905–1907 and the first wave of "terrorist" activities that accompanied it. Whatever may have been the exact reason for the government's conciliatory position, there is no doubt that the most spectacular cooperation between the Salvation Army and the British-Indian state was largely based on the official acknowledgment of the former's ability to teach "the elementary lesson of obedience": the "reclamation" of criminals and particularly of entire communities that were regarded as "criminals by birth."[151]

The so-called Criminal Tribes were itinerant groups of the rural Indian population whose uncontrolled mobility and "predatory propensities" were seen as a threat to British authority and that were hence discriminated against as "hereditary criminals."[152] Two Criminal Tribes Acts were passed in 1871 and 1911 to provide for their confinement in segregated settlements and their gradual education to a sedentary lifestyle. Initially, the settlements had been run directly by the state. However, they soon turned out to be extremely costly and inefficient. The Salvation Army became the chief agency in this program, as it was believed that it could do a better and, more importantly, a cheaper job. Already in 1908 prominent government officials approached the Army offering them a grant to open a weaving school and industrial homes for the Doms, a low-caste community classed as "criminal,"[153] with a view of "bringing them into discipline and subjection."[154] A few years later the Indian edition of *The War Cry* would celebrate the way in which "these poor despised off-scourings of the U.P.[155] were adopted, civilised and evangelised by . . . saintly Salvation Army Officers."[156]

Soon afterward the Lieutenant Governor of the Punjab entrusted the reeducation of ex-convicts from Lahore prison in state-financed reformatories to the Salvationists, and was obviously pleased with the results of the Army's work as "prison sub-contractors,"[157] described by one of his highest officers as "unqualified success."[158] In an effort to capitalize on the positive reaction of colonial officials, General Booth addressed the British Secretary of State for India, in person, to make a more far-reaching offer of cooperation. He suggested the introduction of a "system of reformation and employment" for all the "tribes to whom, by force of circumstance, criminality has become a hereditary occupation."[159] That the program was apparently based on the Army's Social Salvation scheme developed for the "savages" at home becomes clear when he explains the details of the proposed "treatment":

To carry out this scheme two kinds of treatment are essential: (*a*) Reformatory and kindly influences must be brought to bear on them which will appeal to their better instincts and . . . (*b*) they must not be allowed to wander about disposing of the products of their labour, as this will probably result in their relapsing into crime. Markets must be found and their produce must be sold for them. To the attainment of both these objects, our numerous agencies and extensive ramifications are favourable.[160]

To further strengthen his argument, Booth pointed to the success of the industrial homes and agricultural settlements already existing in the Punjab and the United Provinces. He apparently managed to overcome the initial skepticism of the colonial government, and the cooperation between the colonial state and what had been a nongovernmental social service organization was extended to an unprecedented scale. By 1919, the Army entertained 28 settlements (varying in size from 100 to 1,800)[161] for altogether 6,812 "Crims"[162] and had become a sort of a huge service business in social control. There can be no doubt that it played a crucial role in sustaining colonial rule. The work of Rachel Tolen and Meena Radhakrishna has shown that the transformation of "very unpromising material"[163] into "decent, law-abiding citizens"[164] of the empire, living up to civilized standards of cleanliness and self-discipline and productivity, was at the core of the Army's reclamation work.[165] The results of the reeducation processes were shown in quasi-imperial exhibitions, organized in Simla, British India's summer capital in the Himalayas, and displaying various agricultural and industrial goods produced by the "reformed tribesmen."[166] These products were also available in special shops run by the Army that provided a handsome extra income in addition to the government grants.

During World War I women of the Haburah tribe, "whose entire character had . . . undergone a radical change" under the firm tutelage of the Salvationists, were employed to make uniforms for the military department, and actively supported the imperial war effort.[167] An even bigger contribution to Britain's warfare was the role the Salvation Army played in the recruitment of a Porter's coolie corps from among their "depressed" clientele for service in Mesopotamia.[168] The successful conversion of some of the "reclaimed" was, of course, another welcome side-effect.[169]

The cooperation with the colonial state was extended to several related fields, one of which, perhaps, deserves special mention. The so-called "European loafers" (mostly unemployed railway men or sailors and ex-soldiers), roaming all over the subcontinent, often behaving in a way that was hardly suited to enhance the prestige of the ruling race, had become a major problem by the late 1860s.[170] As already conveyed, a special European Vagrancy Act was promulgated in 1869 to deal with the problem. But similar to the "Crim" settlements run by the government, the workhouses opened in its wake proved to be expensive rather than effective institutions. Here opened another opportunity for the Salvationists who possessed matchless experience in "reclaiming" members of the lowest classes at home. Frederick Booth-Tucker approached the government of Bombay with a scheme for running an industrial home for European vagrants in 1910. Pointing to the expertise tried and tested in similar fields in England as well as in India, the Commissioner promised to run the institution with the utmost efficiency:

> But the reformatory influence thus exercised is not limited to the "deserving" men, who come within our reach. The undeserving and most degraded are frequently reformed. Cut off from their old associates, protected from those who often prey upon their weaknesses, surrounded with good and kindly influences, fed well, clothed well and found work of a not too repulsive and severe character, supplied with good wholesome literature, looked after during their leisure moments as well as when employed, with a firm, yet fatherly counsellor always at their side, thousands of them respond to the new atmosphere of hope and help.[171]

Booth-Tucker was allowed to proceed with his project and an industrial home for the deserving cases was opened with grand *éclat* by the Governor of Bombay in December 1910[172] in addition to the already existing government workhouse. The colonial authorities were so satisfied with the working of the King Edward Home[173] that the Salvation Army was soon asked to take over the government institution as well, which it subsequently did.[174] Such was the official acclaim of the Army's achievement, that the government sponsored the establishment of two more industrial homes for stranded Europeans: a house called The Bridge was opened in Calcutta in November 1914, and in March 1915 the Chief Commissioner of Delhi inaugurated a branch of the Institution in the new capital of British India,[175] justifying his approval by stating that

> the institution . . . is desirable in order to obviate the difficulties arising from the fact that Europeans and Eurasians of this class at present resort in some numbers to Delhi, and that their numbers are likely to increase rather than diminish in the future. [T]he Salvation Army offers an excellent agency for dealing with this class and the proposed terms appear to me very economical.[176]

The financial support of the government for the various Salvation Army projects was continually extended until the 1920s,[177] and the organization continued to blossom under the protection of the colonial state. By 1922, the Salvationists' British Indian detachment counted 3,700 officers and cadets as well as 100,000 soldiers in the rank and file. The Army had established more than 4,500 centers in India and developed into a "well-organized fighting force, ready and eager to be led on to the attack on the millions of non-Christians who surround each Corps and institution."[178]

Most Salvationists seem to have been proud of their newly acquired respectability within the empire framework. In an article in *The War Cry* one writer celebrates the Army as a "regenerative force" of imperialism and asks the rhetorical question "In what do the imperial services of the Army consist?" The answer he subsequently provides himself is revealing:

> In its endeavours to soften and remove the effect of extreme poverty, to raise the fallen to succour to the needy and assist the distressed, the products of a civilisation which turns out an appalling proportion of waste products—paupers, prostitutes, criminals and lunatics in every class of society, and by this means to soften the conflict between the "haves" and the "have-nots" which constitute a fertile soil for the seeds of the rebellion that threatens the mother country.[179]

By the same time, Booth-Tucker, who had been arrested several times in the 1880s, came to be held in the highest esteem by the colonial authorities. He was regarded as *the* expert on the reclamation of criminal and dangerous segments both in the Indian as well in the white colonial society. In 1913, the prestigious *Kaiser-i-Hind* medal was conferred upon him for "public services in India"[180] and few years later he was asked to lecture on "Criminocurology"—the Army's scientific method of classification and treatment of people infected with the "disease" of criminality—before an audience of high government officials including the Lieutenant-Governor of the Punjab.[181] He also published a book with the same title,[182] explaining in detail how to transform "criminals" into "productive and subjected bodies."[183] With *Criminocurology* the imperial taxonomic techniques that had shaped the understanding of the London poor, had finally come back to the environment from where they had originated: the colonial outposts of the British Empire.

Concluding Remarks

Our probes into the history of the Salvation Army from a transnational perspective have thus produced some significant, if preliminary, results. First and foremost, the close entanglement of Europe with the wider non-European world not only in economic, social, and political, but also in epistemological terms has been made clear. In the case of Britain, as with many other colonizing European countries, this global framework was predetermined to a large extent by the infrastructure of the empire. Even organizations and historical actors like the Salvationists who, at the outset, viewed themselves as distinctly apolitical and sometimes even antigovernment, were marked by the imperial rhetoric and modes of knowledge production that were regarded as authoritative at the time: the imperial social formation heavily influenced the ways to look at and make sense of the world. The Salvationists' venture to map the "swamps" and "jungles" of Darkest England and "rescue" their denizens by civilizing them through a paternal but rigorous course of training, have vividly illustrated this point. The fact that General Booth's plan to deport the Sunken Millions to overseas colonies was seriously discussed (and partly realized through the practice of assisted emigration) shows the extent to which global thinking prevailed at the time under survey.

Most intriguing, perhaps, was the analysis of the Salvation Army's transformation from a Home Mission movement, based on traditions of lower middle and upper working-class religiosity and often viewed as disturbing by the authorities, into a worldwide service business for social control. As we have seen, this transformation happened almost simultaneously in India and Great Britain and the developments on both sides mutually influenced each other. As a recent study on the role of the Salvationists in East Asia suggests, similar developments seem to have taken place in Meiji Japan, where Charles Booth was granted an audience with the emperor in 1907 and his organization accepted as a "useful handmaiden of the state."[184]

The Army's metamorphosis in India was particularly spectacular. From a small band of idealists "gone native" and placed under the constant surveillance of a colonial government anxious to avoid blurring the colonial boundaries, it developed into a powerful force whose high degree of organization, rigid discipline, experience in projects of disciplining and reforming "unruly" segments of society, and, last but not least, entrepreneurial skills, turned it into an attractive partner in empire-building. The knowledge gathered about "criminals by birth" and other marginalized groups in British India then circulated back to England and onward to other parts of the world, including the United States, Scandinavia, Canada, Japan, and Africa—together with the officers, who usually served only a limited time in one foreign field—and arguably played a role in further shaping the view on the "waste products" of their respective home societies. Although the present discussion has focused on these two sites for analytical purposes, the worldwide ramifications underscore once more that the phenomenon under study cannot be reduced to a simple Britain-India relationship. As the Salvation Army was already a universal organization by the

1910s, its impact went much further once the imperial connection had been established. Thus the Salvationists also acted as prison-subcontractors in Canada, and were engaged in the reeducation of ex-convicts in Japan, Australia, South Africa, and French Guyana, to give just a few examples.[185]

On a more general level, the Army's undeniable contribution to the softening of the effects of extreme poverty helped sustain the existing asymmetrical power relations both at home and in the various colonies and dominions. The social activities of the movement were therefore ultimately welcomed by the establishment: the harbingers of global civil society had been hijacked, as it were, by the empire. Being aware of this ambiguous relationship between British imperialism and a predecessor of today's NGOs, one would probably have to be cautious *vis-à-vis* the fashionable uncritical view that postulates an "epic struggle" between global civil society and the "forces of empire," extending back "to the earliest human experience."[186] At least the example of the Salvation Army should help to stir up our interest in gaining a better historical understanding of institutions that characterize globalizing processes in today's world.

Appendix

Statistics on the Salvation Army's social, industrial, agricultural, educational, and training work in British India in 1918.

28	Settlements for criminal tribes with population of	6,812
3	Homes for released prisoners and beggars	106
8	Industrial boarding schools for Crim children, inmates	246
4	Non-Crim colonies and farms	1,314
5	Women's industrial homes accommodating	110
2	Weaving and silk schools	100
5	Centers for nonresident workers, employing	960
2	Industrial homes for Europeans and Anglo-Indians accommodating	45
1	Military hospital for wounded soldiers, beds	100
10	Dispensaries, beds	45
3	General hospitals, beds	90
3	Naval and military Furlo homes accommodating	115
4	Hut and refreshment bars for troops	6
6	Depots for sale of institutions	
17	No-criminal hostels for boys and girls, inmates	775
14	Training garrisons for cadets	181
118	Institutions providing food, shelter, and employment for	11,059
550	Day schools for education for children	16,664
668	**Institutions caring for**	**27,723**

Source: *The War Cry*, 24, no. 10 (October 1918): 6.

Notes

The archival research for this chapter has been conducted at the Staatsbibliothek, Berlin, the National Archives of India, New Delhi, the Maharashtra State Archives in Mumbai, the Oriental and India Office collection of the British Library, and the Salvation Army Heritage Centre in London. I wish to express my gratitude to Francis Meynell, Vanessa Ogle, Margrit Pernau, Carey Watt, Clare Anderson, and the members of the "global history group" for reading earlier drafts of this chapter and making valuable suggestions for its improvement.

1. According to a recent study "the term nongovernmental organization . . . represents any organisation of a voluntary nature engaged in either welfare or developmental activities." R. Sooryamoorthy and K.D. Gangrade, *NGOs in India: A Cross-Sectional Study* (Westport, Conn: Greenwood Press, 2001), p. 15. On the basis of this working definition, I think it is safe to treat the Salvation Army as an NGO.
2. For one of the most influential treatments of these forces see Michael Hardt and Antonio Negri, *Empire* (Cambridge, Mass.: Harvard University Press, 2000).
3. For a typical, though not very sophisticated, articulation of this position see, for instance, David C. Korten, Nicanor Perlas, and Vandana Shiva, "Global Civil Society: The Path Ahead," available online at http: //www.pcdf.org /civilsociety/ path.htm. This discussion paper was put on the Internet in November 2002.
4. See, for instance, Arif Dirlik, "Is there History after Eurocentrism? Globalism, Postcolonialism and the Disavowal of History," in Arif Dirlik, Vinay Bahl, and Peter Gran, eds., *History after the Three Worlds: Post-Eurocentric Historiographies* (Lanham: Rowman and Littlefield, 2000), pp. 25–47; Prasenjit Duara, "Transnationalism and the Challenge to National Histories," in Thomas Bender, ed., *Rethinking American History in a Global Age* (Berkeley: University of California Press, 2002), pp. 25–46. See also Akira Iriye, "The Internationalisation of History," *American Historical Review* 94 (1989): 1–10, especially 3–7 for an early statement to that effect.
5. Jürgen Osterhammel and Niels Petersson, *Geschichte der Globalisierung. Dimensionen, Prozesse, Epochen* (München: Beck, 2003), pp. 60–70.
6. This point has been most recently made in Frank L. Lechner and John Boli, *World Culture: Origins and Consequences* (Malden: Blackwell, 2005), especially pp. 119–34. See also Carey A. Watt, *Serving the Nation: Cultures of Service, Association and Citizenship* (New Delhi: Oxford University Press, 2005), pp. 30–33. See also John Boli and George M. Thomas, eds., *Constructing World Culture: International Nongovernmental Organizations since 1875* (Stanford: Stanford University Press, 1999).
7. Kathleen Wilson, "Introduction: Histories, Empires, Modernities," in Kathleen Wilson, ed., *A New Imperial History: Culture, Identity and Modernity in Britain and the Empire 1660–1840* (Cambridge: Cambridge University Press, 2004), pp. 1–26. See also Catherine Hall, *Civilising Subjects: Metropole and Colony in the English Imagination* (Chicago: University of Chicago Press, 2002), pp. 10–19. Both authors, in turn, are drawing on the well-known models of the "common

analytical field" and the "imperial social formation" as introduced by Cooper and Stoler, and Mrinalini Sinha respectively.

8. The most valuable newer research includes Pamela J. Walker, *Pulling the Devil's Kingdom Down: The Salvation Army in Victorian Britain* (Berkeley: University of California Press, 2001); Roy Hattersley, *Blood & Fire: William and Catherine Booth and their Salvation Army* (London: Little, Brown, 1999); Norman H. Murdoch, *Origins of the Salvation Army* (Knoxville: University of Tennessee Press, 1994); Lillian Taiz, *Hallelujah Lads & Lasses: Remaking the Salvation Army in America, 1880–1930* (Chapel Hill: University of North Carolina Press, 2001).

9. The only comprehensive work to date of the movement in a non-Western context is on Japan: R. David Rightmire, *Salvationist Samurai: Gunpei Yamamuro and the Rise of the Salvation Army in Japan*, Pietist and Wesleyan Studies, vol. 8 (Lanham: Scarecrow Press, 1997). In her masterly study on the emergence of the Salvation Army in Britain, Pamela Walker deplores that the imperial significance of the movement has only met with scant scholarly attention. Walker, *Pulling the devil's Kingdom Down*, p. 245, endnote 2. The only attempt so far to understand the Salvation Army in a transnational perspective has recently been undertaken by Peter Van der Veer. However, the army does not feature very prominently in his book on *Imperial Encounters*, as he devotes only four pages to the topic. See Peter Van Der Veer, *Imperial Encounters: Religion and Modernity in India and Britain* (Princeton: Princeton University Press, 2001), pp. 151, 153–55. Nevertheless, his stimulating but somewhat superficial exercise in "interactional history" was the main inspiration to pursue this project.

10. A somewhat similar argument has been persuasively made by Laura Thorn with regard to earlier forms of missionary activity in Britain and its colonies. See Laura Thorn, "Missionary Imperialism and the Language of Class," in F. Cooper, and A.L. Stoler, eds., *Tensions of Empire: Colonial Cultures in a Bourgeois World* (Berkeley: University of California Press, 1997), pp. 238–62.

11. Mariana Valverde, "The Dialectic of the Familiar and the Unfamiliar: 'The Jungle' in Early Slum Travel Writing," *Sociology* 30, no. 3 (1996): 493–509. See also John Marriott, *The Other Empire: Metropolis, India, and Progress in the Colonial Imagination* (Manchester: Manchester University Press, 2003), pp. 130–59.

12. See also Roland Robertson's interesting discussion of the political implications of Norbert Elias' concept of the "civilizing process" in a global framework: Roland Robertson, *Globalization: Social Theory and Global Culture* (London: Sage, 1992), pp. 115–28.

13. Michael Walzer, "The Concept of Civil Society," in Michael Walzer, ed., *Toward a Global Civil Society* (New York: Berghahn, 1995), pp. 7–27, 23–24. For a similar optimistic view see Tony Spybey, *Globalization and World Society* (Cambridge: Polity Press, 1996), chapter 7.

14. Akira Iriye, *Cultural Internationalism and World Order* (Baltimore & London: Johns Hopkins University Press, 1997), p. 3.

15. The metaphor was famously introduced by Benjamin Disraeli in the 1840s to describe the growing gap between the rich and the poor. See Deborah E. Nord, "The Social Explorer as Anthropologist: Victorian Travellers among the Urban Poor," in

W. Sharp and L. Wallock, eds., *Visions of the Modern City: Essays in History Art and Literature* (Baltimore: Johns Hopkins University Press, 1987), pp. 122–34, 123. For an exhaustive discussion of Victorian readings of poverty see also the two monumental volumes by Gertrude Himmelfarb, *The Idea of Poverty: England in the Early Industrial Age* (New York: Knopf, 1984), especially pp. 489–503; and Gertrude Himmelfarb, *Poverty and Compassion: The Moral Imagination of the Late Victorians* (New York: Knopf, 1991). A more concise account can be found in Gertrude Himmelfarb, "The Colour of poverty," in H.J. Dyos and M. Wolff, eds., *The Victorian City: Images and Realities*, vol. 2 (London and Boston: Routledge & Keegan, Paul, 1973), pp. 707–38. For the late Victorian development of the "two-nation theorie" see David Cannadine, *Class in Britain* (New Haven: Yale University Press, 1999), p. 112–13.

16. Eric Hobsbawm, *The Age of Empire, 1875–1914* (London: Weidenfeld and Nicolson, 2000), p. 265. See also Himmelfarb, *Poverty and Compassion*, pp. 150–52.
17. Quoted in K.T. Hoppen, *The Mid-Victorian Generation, 1846–1886* (Oxford and New York: Clarendon Press, 1998), p. 453.
18. Gareth Stedman Jones, *Outcast London: A Study in the Relationship between Classes in Victorian Society* (Harmondsworth: Penguin, 1976), p. 5.
19. Ibid., pp. 286–300; Marriott, *The Other Empire*, pp. 171–81.
20. Quoted in Victor Bailey, "In Darkest England and the Way Out: The Salvation Army, Social Reform and the Labour Movement, 1885–1910," *International Review of Social History* 29 (1984): 133–71.
21. Jose Harris, *Private Lives, Public Spirit: Britain 1870–1914* (London: Penguin Books, 1994), p. 163. As studies of continental countries indicate, this seems to have been a broader European trend. See, for instance, the essays in Collette Bec, Catherine Duprat, Jean-Noël Luc, and Jacques-Guy Petit, eds., *Philanthropies et Politiques Sociales en Europe (XVIIIe-XXe Siècles)* (Paris: Anthropos, 1994).
22. For biographical details on Booth see Walker, *Pulling the Devil's Kingdom Down*, pp. 13–22; The general of the Salvation Army, ed., *The Salvation Army. Its Origin and Development* (London: Salvation Army, 1938), pp. 1–15. The most comprehensive, though uncritical, treatment remains in Harold Begbie, *Life of William Booth, Founder of the Salvation Army*, 2 vols. (New York: The Macmillan Company, 1920).
23. See also Murdoch, *Origins of the Salvation Army*, pp. 21–39.
24. A more comprehensive account on the background and early years of the Salvationist movement can be found in Glenn K. Horridge, *The Salvation Army: Origins and Early Days*, 1865–1900 (Godalming: Ammonite Books, 1993).
25. Salvation Army, ed., *The Salvation Army. Its Origin and Development*, p. 20. This choice is typical for the Army's strategy of consciously "capturing" places associated with leisure activities of the working classes that were regarded as corrupting, like pubs, music-halls, theaters, etc. Walker, *Pulling the Devil's Kingdom Down*, p. 188. See also Robert Sandall, *The History of the Salvation Army*, vol. 1 *(1865–1878)* (London: Nelson, 1947), pp. 150–51, 220.

26. See Peter Keating, "Fact and Fiction in the East End," in H.J. Dyos and M. Wolff, eds., *The Victorian City*, p. 589–93. See also Judith R. Walkowitz, *City of Dreadful Delight: Narratives of Sexual Danger in Late Victorian London* (Chicago: University of Chicago Press, 1992), p. 30.

27. Salvation Army, ed., *The Salvation Army Year Book. 1939, Thirty Fourth Year of Issue* (London: Salvation Army, 1938), p. 39.

28. C.A. Bayly, *The Birth of the Modern World 1780–1914: Global Connections and Comparisons* (Malden: Blackwell, 2004), pp. 357–59.

29. In the early twentieth century, the organization also played a pioneering role in using film and radio as media for religious propaganda. See Jeffrey Cox, *Imperial Fault Lines: Christianity and Colonial Power in India, 1818–1940* (Stanford: Stanford University Press, 2002), p. 238; and Salvation Army, *The Salvation Army Year Book. 1939*, pp. 7–10.

30. Christian Mission Report 1867, quoted in Horridge, *The Salvation Army*, p. 17. See also the programmatical statements in William Booth, *Heathen England: Being a Description of the Utterly Godless Condition of the Vast Majority of the English Nation, and of the Establishment, Growth, System and Success of an Army for Its Salvation Consisting of Working People etc.*, 3rd ed. (London: 1879), passim.

31. The uniforms made out of plain simple dark blue cloth, trimmed with red braid, and marked with the letter "S" on the collar, were worn by both male and female members of the organization, which was regarded as repulsive by quite a few contemporaries.

32. The following is based on Olive Anderson, "The Growth of Christian Militarism in mid-Victorian Britain," *The English Historical Review* 86, no. 338 (1971): 46–71. See also Walker, *Pulling the Devil's Kingdom Down*, pp. 60–63.

33. Anderson, "The Growth of Christian Militarism," pp. 46–52; Brian Stanley, "Christian Responses to the Indian Mutiny," in W.J. Shiels, *The Church and War*, Studies in Church History, vol. 20 (Oxford: Blackwell, 1983), pp. 277–99. See also Victor Bailey, "Salvation Army Riots: The 'Skeleton Army' and Legal Authority in a Provincial Town," in A.P. Donajgrodzkij, ed., *Social Control in Nineteenth Century Britain* (Totowa, N.J.: Rowman and Littlefield, 1977), pp. 231–53, 236–37.

34. Van Der Veer, *Imperial Encounters*, pp. 83–94. See also H.J. Field, *Toward a Programme for Imperial Life: The British Empire at the Turn of the Century* (Westport, Conn.: Greenwood Press, 1982). For a thorough discussion of "Muscular Christianity" see also Norman Vance, *Sinews of the Spirit: The Ideal of Christian Manliness in Victorian Literature and Religion* (Cambridge: Cambridge University Press, 1985); Donald Hall, ed., *Muscular Christianity: Embodying the Victorian Age* (Cambridge: Cambridge University Press, 1994).

35. Hoppen, *The Mid-Victorian Generation 1846–1886*, p. 454.

36. Mrs. [i.e., Catherine] Booth, "Aggressive Christianity," in Catherine Booth, *Papers on Aggressive Christianity* (London: 1891), pp. 1–19, p. 13. (Emphasis in the original text.) See also The Salvation Army, ed., *All about the Salvation Army* (London: 1882), pp. 4–5.

37. "Now surely the least-witted person can see that it cannot be possible to do a great spiritual work for the deliverance of people from what is wrong about them by a system under their own direction!" William Booth, *Orders and Regulations for the Salvation Army*, Pt. I. (London: ca. 1880), p. 3.

38. Ibid., p. 5. See also Horridge, *The Salvation Army*, pp. 52–59.

39. Murdoch, *Origins of the Salvation Army*, p. xi.

40. William Booth, "The Salvation Army," in William Booth, *Salvation Soldiery. A Series of Addresses on the Requirements of Jesus Christ's Service* (London: S.W. Partridge & Co., 1882), pp. 27–33.

41. A Salvationist pamphlet published in 1882 states that "We have 300 officers and thousands of the rank and file, who are so far disciplined as to regularly discharge their duty, or who are willing to go to any part of the world simply at the word of command." The Salvation Army, ed., *All about the Salvation Army*, p. 23.

42. See Geoffrey R. Searle, *The Quest for National Efficiency: A Study of British Politics and Political Thought, 1899–1914* (Berkeley and Los Angeles: University of California Press, 1971).

43. When the adoption of a military strategy was discussed in autumn 1877, the General's entourage was convinced that "if we can only drill and mobilize fast enough, we can overrun the country before Christmas." Letter of G.S. Railton to W. Booth, October 11, 1877, cited in Sandall, *History of the Savation Army*, vol. 1, p. 225.

44. Booth, *Orders and Regulations for the Salvation Army*, pp. 11–12.

45. Horridge, *The Salvation Army*, p. 38.

46. Peter Adolf Clasen, *Der Salutismus: eine sozialwissenschaftliche Monographie über General Booth und seine Heilsarmee*, Schriften zur Soziologie der Kultur, vol. 2 (Jena: E. Diederichs, 1913), p. 322.

47. F. Booth-Tucker, *The Short Life of Catherine Booth the Mother of the Salvation Army*, 2nd ed. (London: The Salvation Army, 1895), pp. 332–41.

48. For the following see Walker, *Pulling the Devil's Kingdom Down*, pp. 206–34; Bailey, "Salvation Army Riots," pp. 241–49; and Horridge, *The Salvation Army*, pp. 101–13.

49. The "social control" argument has been brought forward most clearly in Bailey, "Salvation Army Riots." Bailey, however, later revised his thesis somewhat by pointing to the similarities between the socialist workers' movement and the army's work. For a critical general discussion of the concept of social control see also Karel Williams, *From Pauperism to Poverty* (London: Routledge & Keegan, Paul, 1981), pp. 136–39.

50. Cited in Meena Radhakrishna, *Dishonoured by History: "Criminal Tribes" and British Colonial Policy* (New Delhi: Orient Longman, 2001), p. 78.

51. Cited in Bailey, "Salvation Army Riots," p. 236.

52. Walker, *Pulling the Devil's Kingdom Down*, p. 242.

53. Salvation Army, *The Salvation Army Year Book.1939*, p. 28.

54. Clasen, *Der Salutismus*, p. 322.

55. Salvation Army, *The Salvation Army. Its Origin and Development*, pp. 29, 41–50.

56. Bailey, "In Darkest England and the Way Out," p. 136.

57. William Booth, *Holy Living: Or What the Salvation Army Teaches about Sanctification* (London: ca. 1880), passim.
58. William Booth, *Sociales Elend und Abhülfe. Vortrag gehalten in der Schweiz etc.* (Bern: Buchdruckerei K.J. Wyß, 1896), p. 21.
59. For the sake of convenience, I refer to William Booth as the author. It is almost certain, however, that the book was not the product of Booth's limited literary talent, but at least partly ghost-written by the investigative journalist and social reformer W.T. Stead of the *Pall Mall Gazette*. See Joseph McLaughlin, *Writing the Urban Jungle: Reading Empire in London from Doyle to Eliot* (Charlottesville: University Press of Virginia, 2000), p. 209, endnote 6.
60. After being largely neglected for a long time, *In Darkest England* has only in recent decades received some critical scholarly attention. The most insightful treatments are: Bailey, "In Darkest England and the Way Out"; McLaughlin, *Writing the Urban Jungle*, pp. 79–103; and Valverde, "The Dialectic of the Familiar and the Unfamiliar," passim.
61. McLaughlin, *Writing the Urban Jungle*, p. 94.
62. For a detailed account of the debate between "Boothites" and "anti-Boothites" see Herman Ausubel, "General Booth's Scheme of Social Salvation," in *American Historical Review* 56, no. 3 (1953): 519–25.
63. Henry Morton Stanley, *In Darkest Africa, or the Quest, Rescue and Retreat of Emin, Governor of Equatoria* (London: S. Low, Marston, Searle, and Rivington, 1890).
64. Cited in Booth, *In Darkest England and the Way Out*, p. 11.
65. Ibid., pp. 14–15. For a similar powerful example of Booth's rhetoric see William Booth, "Getting Rid of the Filth," in William Booth, *Salvation Soldiery*, pp. 34–40.
66. Booth, *In Darkest England and the Way Out*, pp. 24–66.
67. Valverde, "The Dialectic of the Familiar and the Unfamiliar," pp. 495–500.
68. Sudipta Sen, *Distant Sovereignty: National Imperialism and the Origins of British India* (New York and London: Routledge, 2002), pp. 57–84; Bernard S. Cohn, *Colonialism and Its Forms of Knowledge: The British in India* (Princeton: Princeton University Press, 1996), pp. 3–5; and Marriott, *The Other Empire*, pp. 130–59. See also Melitta Waligora, "What Is Your Caste?" in H. Fischer-Tiné and M. Mann, eds., *Colonialism as Civilizing Mission: Cultural Ideology in British India* (London: Anthem Press, 2004), pp. 141–62 for categorization of human "tribes" and Ian J. Barrow, *Making History, Drawing Territory: British Mapping in India, c. 1756–1905* (New Delhi: Oxford University Press, 2003), as well as Matthew H. Edney, *Mapping and Empire: The Geographical Construction of British India, 1765–1843* (Chicago: University of Chicago Press, 1997) for the imperial relevance of topographical mapping. For a concise general discussion of colonial knowledge production, see Trutz Von Trotha, "Was war Kolonialismus? Einige zusammen-fassende Befunde zur Soziologie und Geschichte des Kolonialismus und der Kolonialherrschaft," *Saeculum* 55, no. 1 (2004): 49–95, 81–86.
69. Mariel Louise Pratt, *Imperial Eyes: Travel Writing and Transculturation* (London and New York: Routledge, 1992).
70. Valverde, "The Dialectic of the Familiar and the Unfamiliar," p. 494.

71. For an analysis of the symbolical meanings of such value judgements see also Peter Stallybrass and Allon White, *The Politics and Poetics of Transgression* (London: Methuen, 1986), pp. 125–48.
72. The term, perhaps most frequently used by contemporaries to describe the nature of British rule in India during the later nineteenth century, is employed by Anthony Wohl to describe the social philosophy coupling material improvement with moral reformation that was underlying much of the philanthropic efforts in Victorian England. See Anthony S. Wohl, *The Eternal Slum: Housing and Social Policy in Victorian London* (New Brunswick: Transaction Publishers, 2002), pp. 179–99.
73. Walkowitz, *City of Dreadful Delight*, p. 28. See also McLaughlin, *Writing the Urban Jungle*, p. 80.
74. For the diverse motives and contradictory effects of Victorian urban philanthropy see also Seth Koven, *Slumming: Sexual and Social Politics in Victorian London* (Princeton: Princeton University Press, 2004), particularly pp. 3–14, and Anne McClintock, *Imperial Leather: Race, Gender and Sexuality in the Colonial Contest* (New York and London: Routledge, 1995), pp. 75–100.
75. Booth, *In Darkest England and the Way Out*, p. 40.
76. For a further exploration of this impact see Sally Ledger, "In Darkest England: The Terror of Degeneration in *fin de siécle*-Britain," *Literature and History* 4, no. 2 (1995): 71–86; Kenan Malik, *The Meaning of Race: Race, History and Culture in Western Society* (Basingstoke: Macmillan, 1996), pp. 91–100; Daniel Pick, *Faces of Degeneration: a European Disorder ca. 1848–1918* (Cambridge: Cambridge University Press, 1989), pp. 189–203; and Tim Barringer, "Images of Otherness and the Visual Production of Difference: Race and Labour in Illustrated Texts, 1850–1865," in Shearer West, ed., *The Victorians and Race* (Aldershot: Scholar Press, 1996), pp. 34–52.
77. Booth, *In Darkest England and the Way Out*, p. 16.
78. Ibid., p. 15.
79. Ibid., p. 43.
80. See also the analysis of Booth's scheme in Clasen, *Der Salutismus*, pp. 237–39.
81. See for instance John Briggs et al., *Crime and Punishment in England: An Introductory History* (London: UCL Press, 1996), p. 194.
82. Interestingly, the term "residuum," frequently used by Booth, was soon employed by the advocates of eugenics. See Pauline M.H. Mazumdar, "The Eugenicists and the Residuum: The Problem of the Urban Poor," *Bulletin of the History of Medicine* 54, no. 2 (1980): 204–15.
83. For a discussion of the Salvation Army's program of "religious colonisation" of the working classes see Himmelfarb, *Poverty and Compassion*, pp. 228–30. For the twin aim of moral and material improvement in a colonial setting see also Michael Mann: "Torchbearers upon the Path of Progress," in Fischer-Tiné and Mann, eds., *Colonialism as Civilizing Mission*, pp. 1–26.
84. Booth, *Sociales Elend und Abhülfe*, p. 18.
85. That similar discourses existed in continental Europe is evident from recent work on the policies of "education to work" in late-nineteenth-century Germany and the German colonies in Africa. See Sebastian Conrad, "Eingeborenenpolitik

in Kolonie und Metropole. 'Erziehung zur Arbeit' in Ostafrika und Ost-Westfalen," in Sebastian Conrad and Jürgen Osterhammel, eds., *Das Kaiserreich transnational. Deutschland in der Welt 1871–1914* (Göttingen: Vandenhoeck & Ruprecht, 2004), pp. 107–28.

86. Stefan Collini, *Public Moralists: Political Thought and Intellectual Life in Britain, 1850–1930* (New York: Oxford University Press, 1991), pp. 92–118, and Richard Bellamy, *Liberalism and Modern Society: A Historical Argument* (Cambridge: Polity Press, 1992), pp. 9–14.

87. Booth, *In Darkest England and the Way Out*, p. 92.

88. Ibid.

89. Ibid., p. 134.

90. Ibid., pp. 137–38.

91. Ibid., p. 129. In spite of quoting this phrase, Booth places emphasis on the fact that most of the urban poor were not "real" Cockneys but country dwellers who had moved to the capital only recently, and hence it could be expected that they proved useful in the farm colony. He thus implies that "the real Cockney" was a lesser species, unfit for rural life.

92. Ibid., p. 143.

93. Ibid., p. 149.

94. Ibid., p. 152. This idea of a global "Greater Britain" had earlier been formulated in Charles Wentworth Dilke, *Greater Britain: A Record of Travel in English-Speaking Countries During 1866 and 1867*, 2 Vols. (London: 1869).

95. Booth, *In Darkest England and the Way Out*, p. 145.

96. Ibid., pp. 146 and 157. See also F. Booth-Tucker, *The Short Life of Catherine Booth*, p. 515.

97. For the following see Booth, *In Darkest England and the Way Out*, pp. 152–55.

98. For a general discussion and case studies of the concept's application see Boris Barth and Jürgen Osterhammel, eds., *Zivilisierungsmissionen. Imperiale Weltverbesserung seit dem 18. Jahrhundert* (Konstanz: UVK Verlag, 2005), passim.

99. Agricultural reformer Sir Henry Rider Haggard, better known for his adventure novels like *King Solomon's Mines* or *She*, was appointed as the head of an inspection committee by the Colonial Secretary to evaluate the Army's farm colonies in Britain and the United States. He recommended them as an appropriate means to stop the "racial degeneration" supposedly resulting from urbanization. See H. Rider Haggard, *The Poor and the Land: Being a Report on the Salvation Army Colonies in the United States and at Hadleigh, England* (London: Longmans, Green & Co., 1905). See also Jose Harris, *Unemployment and Politics: A Study in English Social Policy, 1886–1914* (Oxford: Clarendon Press, 1972), p. 130.

100. Clasen, *Der Salutismus*, p. 273, and Murdoch, *Origins of the Salvation Army*, pp. 163, 213, end note 34.

101. See McLaughlin, *Writing the Urban Jungle*, p. 211, fn. 37.

102. Hattersley, *Blood & Fire*, p. 370. The Salvation Army did, however, support schemes of aided emigration, especially to Canada, see Clasen, *Der Salutismus*, pp. 272–73; Marjory Harper, "British Migration and the Peopling of the Empire," in Andrew Porter, ed., *The Nineteenth Century: The Oxford History of*

the British Empire, vol. 3 (Oxford: Oxford University Press, 1999), pp. 75–87, p. 82; Harris, *Unemployment and Politics*, pp. 131–32; and Desmond Glynn, " 'Exporting Outcast London': Assisted Emigration to Canada, 1886–1914," in *Social History* 15, no. 29 (1982): 209–38.

103. Salvation Army, *The Salvation Army. Its Origin and Development*, p. 41

104. Booth-Tucker, *The Short Life of Catherine Booth*, p. 374.

105. Clasen, *Der Salutismus*, p. 89. See also Salvation Army, *The Salvation Army. Its Origin and Development*, pp. 41, 45.

106. *India's Cry: A Monthly Record of the Spiritual and Social Operations of The Salvation Army in India and Ceylon*, 1 (2) (May 1896), p. 1.

107. Solveig Smith, *By Love Compelled: The Salvation Army's One Hundred Years in India and Adjacent Lands* (London: Salvationist Pub. & Supplies, 1981), p. 9.

108. See Harry Williams, *Booth-Tucker: William Booth's First Gentleman* (London: Hodder & Stoughton Ltd., 1980). Other biographical monographs include Madge Unsworth, *Bridging the Gap: Frederick Booth-Tucker of India*, Eagle Books no. 52 (London & Edinburgh, 1944); and F.A., Mackenzie, *Booth-Tucker: Sadhu and Saint* (London: Hodder & Stoughton Ltd., 1930).

109. Hattersley, *Blood & Fire*, pp. 289–90; and Clasen, *Der Salutismus*, pp. 85–86.

110. Hattersley, *Blood & Fire*, Ibid., p. 300.

111. For details see David Arnold, "European Orphans and Vagrants in India in the Nineteenth Century," *Journal of Imperial and Commonwealth History* 7, no. 2 (1979): 104–27, especially pp. 119–21, and Aravind Ganachari, "White Man's Embarassment: European Vagrancy in 19th Century Bombay," *Economic and Political Weekly* 37, no. 2 (2002): 2477–85, especially pp. 2481–84.

112. Reprinted in A.B. Keith, ed., *Speeches and Documents on Indian Policy, 1750–1921*, vol. 1 (London: H. Milford, Oxford University Press, 1922), pp. 370–86.

113. Williams, *Booth-Tucker*, p. 71.

114. See, for instance, Kenneth Ballhatchet, *Race, Sex and Class under the Raj: Imperial Attitudes and Policies and Their Critics, 1793–1905* (London: Weidenfeld & Nicolson, 1980), passim. See also E.M. Collingham, *Imperial Bodies: The Physical Experience of the Raj, ca. 1800–1947* (Cambridge: Polity Press, 2001), particularly chapter 4. For an interesting compilation of insiders' accounts see Charles Allen, *Plain Tales from the Raj: Images of British India in the Twentieth-Century* (London: Futura Publications, 1999).

115. The "native policy" proved to be counterproductive in Japan, where people "roared with laughter" at the sight of the Salvationists wearing night kimonos they had erroneously bought in Hong Kong as typical "native dress." Rightmire, *Salvationist Samurai*, pp. 16–17.

116. Quoted in Smith, *By Love Compelled*, p. 3.

117. According to a typical British self-representation in a contemporary weekly journal for Europeans: *The Friend of India* 24, no. 5 (1866): 607.

118. On a completely different level, the Salvationists also transgressed cultural and "civilizational" boundaries by arranging their pious songs in the style of traditional

Indian music and playing them with Indian instruments. See e.g. Salvation Army (India), *Salvation Army Songs*, rev. and enl. ed. (in Kannarese), (Bapatla: The Salvation Army, 1918).

119. Anonymous, *Catherine Bannister: Given for India* (London: The Salvation Army's Miniature Biographies no. 10, 1930), p. 10.

120. Cox, *Imperial Fault Lines*, pp. 236–37.

121. *The War Cry*, 25 no. 10 (1919): 5, and Williams, *Booth-Tucker*, p. 220.

122. F. Booth-Tucker, *Muktifauj, or, Forty Years with the Salvation Army in India and Ceylon* (London: Salvationist Publishing & Supplies, 1923), p. 14.

123. National Archives of India (hereafter quoted as NAI), GoI, Home Dept. Progs., Public A—201–202, October 1882, Viceroy Lord Ripon to members of the Viceregal Council, October 25, 1882.

124. Booth-Tucker, *Muktifauj*, pp. 15–35; Mackenzie, *Booth-Tucker: Sadhu and Saint*, pp. 65–81; and Smith, *By Love Compelled*, pp. 6–9, 13–15.

125. NAI, GoI, Home Dept. Progs., Public A—202, Oct. 1882, "Petition of the inhabitants of Calcutta protesting against the treatment of some members of the Salvation Army."

126. NAI, Home Dept. Progs., Ecclesiastical, A—19–30, September 1884, Letter No. 158, dated Simla, September 15, 1884, A Mackenzie, Secretary to the Government of India to the Government of Bombay.

127. Oriental and India Office Collection, India Office Records [hereafter OIOC, IOR] L/PJ/6/411, File No. 2249, "Letter of W. McG. Drysdale to William Booth."

128. *India's Cry (Special Self-Denial Number)* 11, no. 11 (November 1906): 5.

129. Smith, *By Love Compelled*, pp. 34–35, 39.

130. Quoted ibid., p. 43.

131. Ibid., p. 44 and Salvation Army, *The Salvation Army Year Book. 1939*, p. 92. The journal was renamed *India's Cry* between 1896 and 1908.

132. Murdoch, *Origins of the Salvation Army*, p. 138. See also Booth-Tucker, *The Short Life of Catherine Booth*, p. 376. For a more detailed account of Booth's visits see Booth-Tucker, *Muktifauj*, pp. 140–48.

133. Williams, *Booth-Tucker*, pp. 100–08. The pragmatic reasons for this were made plain by Fakir Singh in 1891: "Religious by instinct, obedient to discipline, . . . inured to hardship, and accustomed to support life on the scantiest conceivable pittance we cannot imagine a more fitting object for our pity, nor a more encouraging one for our effort, than the members of India's submerged tenth." F. Booth-Tucker, "Preface," in F. Booth-Tucker, *Darkest India: A Supplement to General Booth's In Darkest England and the Way Out* (Bombay: Bombay Gazette Steam Printing Works, 1891), pp. 5–6. See also *The War Cry*, 14, no. 3 (March 1910): 6.

134. See for instance *India's Cry* 1, no. 6 (September 1896): 4; 1, no. 9 (December 1896): 1–2; 2, no. 1 (April 1897): 1–6; 2, no. 3 (June 1897): 3–6, 11–13; 5, no. 7 (July 1900): 1–2. See also Smith, *By Love Compelled*, pp. 71–72.

135. *India's Cry* 1, no. 6 (September 1896): 5; 1, no. 7 (October 1896): 1; 2, no. 4 (July 1897): 1–2; 2, no. 3 (September 1897): 3. See also Salvation Army, *A Year's Advance: Being the Eleventh Annual Report of the Salvation Army in India*

and Ceylon 1892–93 (Bombay: 1893), pp. 47–48; *The Bombay Guardian*, March 8, 1890, p. 10, Matilda Hatcher, *The Undauntables: Being Thrilling Stories of the Salvation Army's Pioneering Days in India* (London: Hodder & Stoughton, 1933), pp. 133–34; and *The Sentinel. Organ of Movements for Social Purity and National Righteousness* 17, no. 10 (October 1895): 145. See also F. Booth-Tucker, *Darkest India*, p. 94.

136. Salvation Army, *The Salvation Army Year Book. 1939*, p. 91. See also Smith, *By Love Compelled*, pp. 77–79.

137. OIOC. IOR: L/PJ/6/544 File No. 1291. "Salvation Army Headquarter's Enquiries Regarding the Practice of Medicine in India by Persons Not Having the Legal Medical Qualifications Required in Great Britain."

138. NAI, Home Dept. Progs., Medical, A—19–21, July 1907.

139. NAI, Home Dept. Progs., Medical, A—14–19, June 1908, "Offer Made by the Salvation Army to Cooperate with the Government in Supplying Medical Assistance to the People of India."

140. Cox, *Imperial Fault Lines*, p. 228.

141. NAI, Home Dept. Progs., Medical, A—15, June 1908, Letter No. 4424, Arthur Wood, ICS, Collector of Kaira to the Commissioner, Northern Division, dated Kaira, September 25, 1907.

142. NAI, Home Dept. Progs., Educational, A—48, July 1908, Letter No. 596, dated June 18, 1907, E.D. Maclagan, Chief Secretary to the Govt. Of Punjab to the Director of Public Instruction, Punjab, "Forwarding extracts of a letter dated 19-2-1907 from Mr. F de L. Booth Tucker, Commissioner, Salvation Army." Three years later the figures in *The War Cry*, 17, no. 11 (November 1911): 6, mention even 400 day schools.

143. Booth-Tucker was granted interviews by Lord Minto, Viceroy of British India and Herbert Hope Risley, one of the most influential members of his Council on February 5, 1905. He was also in contact with John Morley, the Secretary of State for India in Whitehall.

144. NAI, Home Dept. Progs., Educational, A—48, July 1908, Letter No. 596, "Forwarding extracts of a letter dated 19-2-1907 from Mr. F. de L. Booth Tucker, Commissioner, Salvation Army." To impart "English Drill" was indeed one of the most prominent features of the Salvationists schools. See *India's Cry*, 1, no. 11 (February 1897): 3.

145. Walker, *Pulling the Devil's Kingdom Down*, p. 236. Interestingly, Booth-Tucker had been engaged in the United States amongst other places in the founding of "farm colonies," an experience that would prove valuable for his later work in India. For an account of his American career see Taiz *Hallelujah Lads & Lasses*, pp. 108–30.

146. NAI, Home Dept. Progs., Educational, A—48, July 1908, Letter No. 596, "Forwarding extracts of a letter dated 19-2-1907 from Mr. F de L. Booth Tucker, Commissioner, Salvation Army."

147. See *The War Cry*, 22, no. 5 (May 1916): 6.

148. Booth-Tucker, "Preface," in Booth-Tucker, *Darkest India*, p. 3.

149. See Watt, *Serving the Nation*, pp. 2–13. passim. I am grateful to Carey Watt for guiding my attention to this likely interconnection. Before drawing final conclusions, however, further research on this point is required.

150. For the context of the Swadeshi movement and Indian "terrorism" see Sumit Sarkar, *Modern India, 1885–1947* (Madras, New Delhi: Macmillan India, 1983), pp. 111–47 and Rajat Kanta Ray, *Social Conflict and Political Unrest in Bengal, 1875–1927* (Delhi: Oxford University Press, 1984), pp. 160–206.

151. As this particular aspect has received some scholarly attention recently I will confine myself largely to a brief summary. For a more exhaustive treatment of the Salvation Army's work with the "Criminal Tribes" see also Radhakrishna, *Dishonoured by History*, and the same author's "Surveillance and Settlements under the Criminal Tribes Act in Madras," *Indian Economic and Social History Review* 29, no. 2 (1992): 171–98, as well as Rachel Tolen, "Colonizing and Transforming the Criminal Tribesman: The Salvation Army in British India," in Jennifer Terry and Jacqueline Urla, eds., *Deviant Bodies: Critical Perspectives on Difference in Science and Popular Culture* (Bloomington: Indiana University Press, 1995), pp. 78–108.

152. There is a vast body of literature on "hereditary criminality" in colonial India. For some recent general accounts see, for instance, Marie Fourcade, "The So-Called Criminal Tribes of India: Colonial Violence and Traditional Violence," in D. Vidal, G. Tarabout, and E. Meyer, eds., *Violence/Non-Violence. Some Hindu Perspectives* (New Delhi: Manohar, 2004), pp. 143–73;. Mark Brown, "Race, Science and the Construction of Native Criminality in Colonial India," *Theoretical Criminology* 5, no. 3 (2001): 345–68. Mark Brown, "Ethnology and Colonial Administration in Nineteenth-Century British India: The Question of Native Crime and Criminality," *British Journal of the History of Science* 36, no. 2 (2003): 201–19; A. Major, "State and Criminal Tribes in Colonial Punjab: Surveillance, Control, and Reclamation of the 'Dangerous Classes,' " *Modern Asian Studies* 33, no. 3 (1999): 657–88; Sandria B. Freitag, "Crime in the Social Order of Colonial North India," *Modern Asian Studies* 25, no. 2 (1991): 227–61; Jacques Pouchepadass, "Criminal Tribes of British India: A Repressive Concept in Theory and Practice," *International Journal of Asian Studies* 2, no. 1 (1982): 41–59.

153. Booth-Tucker, *Muktifauj*, p. 164; Smith, *By Love Compelled*, pp. 103–104; Cox, *Imperial Fault Lines*, p. 240; and Radhakrishna, "Surveillance and Settlements," p. 179.

154. *The War Cry*, 16, no. 4 (April 1910): 13.

155. United Provinces: One of the British Presidencies in Northern India.

156. *The War Cry*, 25, no. 11 (November 1919): 6. See also Charles, R. Henderson, "Control of Crime in India," *Journal of the American Institute of Criminal Law and Criminology* 4, no. 3 (1913): 378–401.

157. Tolen, "Colonizing and Transforming the Criminal Tribesman," p. 94. See also NAI, Home Dept. Progs., Jails, A—35–36, April 1914, "Report on the Experimental Salvation Army Settlement, Lahore for the Reclamation of Juvenile Criminals."

158. The OIOC, IOR: P/9453, GoI, Home Dept., Jail Progs., 1914, Letter No. 364 G.I., Lieut.-Col. G.F.W. Braide, IMS, Inspector-General of Prisons, Punjab to the Revenue Secretary to the Government of Punjab, January 30, 1914.

159. NAI, Home Dept. Progs., Police, A—102–03, November 1910, "Letter from General Booth of the Salvation Army Making Certain Proposals in Connection with the Reclamation of Criminal Tribes."

160. Ibid.

161. Commissioner Booth-Tucker, *India's Millions: Being a Summary of a Lecture on the Work of the Salvation Army in India* (London-Edinburgh s.a. 1923), p. 13.

162. *The War Cry*, 25, no. 11 (November 1919): 6.

163. Booth-Tucker, *Muktifauj*, p. 208.

164. Smith, *By Love Compelled*, p. 103.

165. See Radhakrishna, *Dishonoured by History*, chapter 3; and Tolen, "Colonizing and Transforming the Criminal Tribesman," pp. 94–99.

166. *The War Cry*, 17, no. 7 (July 1911): 1; 21, no. 7 (July 1915): 1–4; Cox, *Imperial Fault Lines*, p. 241; and Booth-Tucker, *Muktifauj*, pp. 163–64. See also *The War Cry*, 22, no. 1 (January 1916): 5–7 for a similar exhibition in Bombay, inaugurated by the governor of that presidency.

167. "Address Presented to his Excellency the Viceroy by Commissioner Fakir Singh. At the Industrial Exhibition and Sale of Work at Simla," *The War Cry*, 21, no. 7 (July 1915): 2; and Booth-Tucker, *Muktifauj*, pp. 212–13.

168. In 1916, two corps consisting of 800 "coolies" each were sent to the Persian Gulf under the command of European Salvation Army officers; they served in loading and unloading ships in Basra. *The War Cry*, 22, no. 10 (October 1916): 11 and *The War Cry*, 24, no. 8 (August 1918): 1.

169. Salvation Army, *The Salvation Army. Its origin and development*, pp. 61–62. Quite astonishingly, a critical evaluation of the army's role in the reeducation of the so-called Crims seems not to have taken place, as the reclamation work it is still described as "one of the greatest and most successful enterprises in the history of the Salvation Army in India" in semiofficial accounts published in the 1980s. See Smith, *By Love Compelled*, p. 103, and Williams, *Booth-Tucker*, p. 178.

170. For the following see also Harald Fischer-Tiné, "Britain's Other Civilising Mission: Class Prejudice, European Loaferism and the Workhouse-System in Colonial India," *Indian Economic and Social History Review* 42, no. 3 (2005): 295–338, 323–26.

171. Maharashtra State Archives, Government of Bombay, Judicial Dept. Progs., Vol. 134, 1910, "The Loafer Problem in Bombay," Memorandum by F. Booth-Tucker, Salvation Army.

172. *The War Cry*, 17, no. 1 (January 1911): 6, 9; OIOC, IOR: P/8599, Government of Bombay Judicial Progs., September–December 1910 A—30 November 1910, "Opening of the Industrial Home for Europeans Vagrants in the City of Bombay."

173. OIOC, IOR: P/9851, Government of Bombay, Judicial Progs., 1915, Letter No. 13538-6, December 10, 1914. S.M. Edwardes, Commissioner of Police,

Bombay, to Under Secretary, Judicial Dept., Bombay A-24, January 1915, "Report on the Working of the European Vagrants Labour Home, Managed by the Salvation Army," and NAI, GoI, Home Dept. Progs., Police, A—141–52, April 1915, "Despatch from the Secretary of State for India (Public) No. 56 to the Governor General of India in Council," March 12, 1915.

174. OIOC, IOR: P/10054 Government of Bombay, Judicial Progs., No. A-5, March 1916, Letter No. 1476, March 6, 1915. Secy. to Government of Bombay to Commissioner Booth-Tucker of the Salvation Army, "Proposal to Transfer to the Salvation Army the Management of the Government Workhouses in Bombay and the Erection and Provision of New Buildings for the Male and Female Workhouses." See also "The Salvation Army (Western India Territory)," *Reclamation. A Review of the Salvation Army's Social and Medical Activities*, (Bombay n.d. [ca. 1927]), p. 14.

175. *The War Cry*, 21, no. 4 (April 1915): 18; 21, no. 7 (July 1915): 8. See also NAI, Home Dept. Progs., Judl., A—28–29, February 1915, "Establishment by the Salvation Army of a Labour Home for Indigent Europeans and Eurasians at Delhi."

176. Ibid., Prog. 28, Letter No. 8854, W. M. Hailey, Chief Commissioner of Delhi, to GoI, Home Dept., December 14, 1915.

177. See for instance NAI, Home Dept. Progs., Judicial, A—61–62, July 1912, "Further Continuance of the Scheme Relating to the Establishment of a Labour Home for European Vagrants, by the Salvation Army, Bombay," NAI, Home Dept. Progs., Police, A—36–50, November 1912, "Reclamation Of Criminal Tribes Through the Salvation Army and Grant to the Salvation Army of a Plot of Land in Madras Presidency"; NAI, Home Dept. Progs., Jail, A—62–63, March 1918 "Proposal to Increase Grants to the SA in Madras for Reclamation Work."

178. Commissioner Booth-Tucker, *India's Millions*, p. 9.

179. *The War Cry*, 17, no. 1 (January 1911): 14.

180. At least four other Salvation Army officers (Col. E. Sheard, Brig. S. Smith and W. Francis and Maj. L. Gale) engaged in the reclamation of "Crims" later received the same award. See also Smith, *By Love Compelled*, p. 110.

181. Cox, *Imperial fault lines*, p. 240.

182. F. Booth-Tucker, *Criminocurology or the Indian Criminal and what to do with him: being a review of the work of the Salvation army among the prisoners, habituals and criminal tribes of India*, 4th ed. (Simla: Liddell's Printing Works, 1916).

183. Tolen, "Colonizing and Transforming the Criminal Tribesman," p. 98.

184. Cited in Rightmire, *Salvationist Samurai*, p. 111.

185. See Clasen, *Der Salutismus*, pp. 84–85, 103–04; Rightmire, *Salvationist Samurai*, p. 90 and Salvation Army, *The Salvation Army Year Book 1939*, pp. 61, 63–64.

186. Korten, Perlas and Shiva, "Global Civil Society: The Path Ahead." http://www.pcdf.org/civilsociety/path.htm, accessed February 1, 2005.

CHAPTER 3

The Common Grounds of Conflict: Racial Visions of World Order 1880–1940

Christian Geulen

The era of high imperialism can be regarded as the first period in which a global order was seriously imagined as at least a possibility for the near future. Imperialism had not only made the globality of the world perceivable as an empirical reality, but also produced a whole range of theories and ideologies supposedly proving the irreversibility and quasi-natural character of imperial expansion. Some of those ideologies had only a short life and quickly disappeared when, after 1918, the nationalist movements in the non-Western world became more powerful and the process of decolonization began to take shape. Among those imperialist ideologies that survived the World War of 1914–1918 almost unharmed and served as an important mediator between the national and the global was most significantly the imperialist attempt to envision a new world order by the means of science and racial theory. What today is implied by catchphrases such as clash of civilizations, cultural conflict, or intercultural relations was—in the era between the late nineteenth century and World War II—primarily articulated in terms of race. Until it became officially banned from the international political discourse after 1945, the concept of race was the most common and central idea around which the global relation between peoples, nations, classes, groups, and even individuals was reflected upon in scientific and popular-scientific terms. From evolutionism to eugenics and from nationalism and fascism to imperialism and even socialism, the discourse of race served as a recurring field of controversy, debate, and struggle over different visions of the global "order of things."[1]

In order to gain a full picture of this multifunctional role of racial discourse between the late nineteenth century and World War II, we have to abandon the traditional idea that the term race always signifies a strict biological determinism, and to acknowledge how complex the actual semantics of the term have always been. For, one of the aspects that turned racism into such a successful ideology was its ability to completely confuse binary notions such as nature versus culture by pretending to refer only to strict biological matters while in fact talking about everything from medicine to art. Thus, the concrete historical origins of the popularity of racial thought need to be uncovered, instead of presupposing that race and biological thinking were convincing notions as such. The point to be made here is that the racial discourse for many decades functioned as one of the first and most important media through which the globality of the imperial age could be envisioned, communicated, and reflected upon. Race was one of the first global terms used to give order to an increasingly entangled and postnational world. It lifted the common longing for a determined political identity and sense of belonging onto a global scale.

The main reason for this ability of the racial discourse to provide notions of identity and belonging fitting the conditions of an age of globalization was the increasingly popularized idea that the scientific knowledge about races and racial development provided the means to improve and strengthen the racial basis of a political or cultural community and thus to adapt it to changing conditions. Here the evolutionary paradigm, especially in its Darwinian form, was the major link between the idea of race and racially determined forms of belonging on the one hand, and the transnational and transcultural challenges of the imperial age on the other. Primarily through evolutionism the idea of race, although still conceived of as a biological category, became an idée fixe for imperialists and nationalists as well as for universalists and members of the early peace movement, and for the colonizers as well as for many of the educated colonized. Thus, there was never such a thing as "the" racial vision of world order. Instead, the evolutionary racial discourse—itself transnational—produced various alternative visions of how to instrumentalize the scientific knowledge about the biological mechanisms of racial development for political purposes—ranging from regional communities to global humanity.

To sketch this story of the relationship between racial theory and visions of world order in the period between 1880–1940 is the aim of this chapter.[2] It does not intend to overvalue the historical significance of racial thinking or the influence of racism in this period. Rather, the intention is to recover the specific function of popular racial theory as one of the "postnational" discourses of political belonging and self-reflection flourishing under the conditions of an empirical globality of which many among the educated classes all over the world became increasingly aware. After a short introduction to the modern history of the race concept until the middle of the nineteenth century, this chapter briefly sketches the transnational reception of Darwinism in order to show how racial thinking diversified, multiplied, and disseminated over the globe as soon as the evolutionary paradigm had introduced the idea of flexible races, developing and changing over time. How that notion was transformed into visions of a global world order is then exemplified by the First Universal Races Congress held in London in 1911. Whereas here, shortly before World War I, a harmonistic and optimistic version of a global racial order was imagined, the transnational development of eugenics after the war is examined as a case in which the idea of racial manipulation and creating new races tended to turn this vision of globality into totalitarian programs. However, the major aim of these surveys is to show that the development of racial thinking and racial ideologies in the period between 1880–1940 was at least partly a reaction to the globalizing forces of the imperial age and can be interpreted as a global intellectual movement trying to envision and create, by the means of science, new forms of collective belonging fitting the conditions of a globalized world.

Race and Evolutionism in the Nineteenth Century

Just as imperialism has long been regarded by historians primarily as a system of suppression and competition, the concept of race has usually been associated with phenomena of difference, conflict, and subordination. Neither of these perspectives is, of course, wrong. But they do tend to ignore the more projective and utopian promises that were connected with imperialist expansionism as well as with racialist worldviews. Especially in respect to racial discourse we hesitate to perceive it as anything but an ideology of suppressing others, designed to scientifically legitimate this suppression. However, the important question of why this ideology was so successful and so popular over such a long period of time has not very often been a subject of detailed analysis and reflection.

The universalist dimension of the race concept is one aspect of international racial thinking in the nineteenth and twentieth centuries that has long been neglected in favor of a classic critique of ideology. Even though the term race in most contexts implied a strong notion of particularism and inequality between human collectives, precisely its biological and anthropological semantics also implied a moment of universal integration: in the racial worldview nobody was really excluded from the universe of races—just as nobody could escape it. For, at its core, race was not a political, asymmetrical concept of particularity, but a symmetrical and generic concept of universality. Even the most radically excluded or suppressed racial enemy, in this perspective, never ceased to be an integral part of the imagined global constellation and struggle of races, which is precisely the reason why other races could be described as a constant threat and fundamental danger to one's own culture and way of life, no matter if they were actually near and present or far away and excluded. Thus, the racial discourse always functioned as a particularistic ideology, but it did so in a very special way, insofar it was based upon a concept that, whenever used to point out difference and inequality, inevitably invoked the vision of a universal compatibility. In this sense, universalism and racism were, as the French philosopher Étienne Balibar puts it, "determined opposites"—they related to each other "from within."[3] In other words, racial thinking was not only a particularistic way of claiming the superiority of one's own community or population over others, but it was always also a form of interpreting the entire world. It is this aspect of racial thinking, often overlooked today, that will be at the center of the following analysis.

Historically, race manifested itself especially in two periods: during the very emergence and origin of the modern race concept in the context of the eighteenth-century Enlightenment and in the period of its substantial reformulation and reinterpretation in the context of the global success of evolutionism since the 1870s. In the categorical systems of Natural History as developed by eighteenth-century naturalists such as Carl von Linné, Johann Friedrich Blumenbach, Georges Buffon, or Christoph Meiners, race was primarily a classifying concept. It was a central notion of imagining an encyclopaedic order of a world that, in the universalist view of the Enlightenment thinkers, had become at least potentially global. Even though large parts of this world were neither discovered nor explored at the time, Enlightenment theorists envisioned its rational order based upon the conviction that absolutely nothing was out of the potential reach of scientific reasoning. Thus, the categories of eighteenth-century European science constantly transformed the "unknown" into the merely "not yet known."[4]

Alongside other classic Enlightenment concepts such as reason, mind, humanity, nature, and climate, the concept of race also provided such a category of a projective, prefigured, and in this sense a priori world order. The concept of race achieved something in this context, that has been lost in our understanding of the term: a categorical and universalist description of the variety of the human world, a description that, of course, started with and indeed was triggered by the narrations of travellers and explorers, but that was principally independent from such empirical data.[5] Once the notion of race as a category of natural history was established, there was no form of human life, however strange or far away, that could not be described and understood in racial terms. This view became further supported by the Enlightenment's theory of progress that declared the non-European races to represent archetypes of the natural history of humanity.[6] Here, the integral universalism of the notion of race started to take on an authoritarian form: as "early stages" of one's own natural development, the non-European "others" became integrated (and hierarchically placed in the imagined world order) even before they actually appeared as concrete "others." The ontological notion of a global "human kind" or "human race" preceded and predetermined the universal and political notion of humanity.[7]

When the naturalist models of the Enlightenment started to be replaced around 1800 by a new modern biology that turned away from classifying systems and started searching for the underlying laws of the natural world, the concept of race played a much less prominent role among natural scientists for a certain time period. Instead, and precisely because of its classifying function, it now became quite prominent among historians. From Augustine Thierry and Johann Gottfried Herder to Arthur Gobineau, the term was now used to explore—against the universalist view of the Enlightenment—the empirical diversity and heterogeneity of the world, its division into various and completely different cultures, nations and ways of life. Only in this historiographical context was the notion of race given its status and meaning as a radically particularistic concept that still predominates in our own understanding.[8]

The second major turn in the history of the racial discourse took place when modern evolutionism, as founded by Herbert Spencer and Charles Darwin, managed to re-fuse the two semantic traditions of the race concept: its historical-particularist and its biological-universalist meaning. The Darwinian evolution theory made the modern idea of a continuously changing natural world plausible by uncovering the universal forces and mechanisms that produce those changes and lie behind the development of species. It was not the species and races themselves that were now perceived as being universal and stable, but the forces supposed to shape and transform them on a daily basis such as, the principle of natural selection. The core element of evolutionism was the idea that races that are best adapted to their environment have the best chance to exist for a longer period of time. Paradoxically, what evolutionism thereby introduced into the racial discourse precisely by pointing to the daily evolutionary forces of selection, adaptation, and survival, was the idea of biological self-responsibility. In the long run, every race was itself responsible for its development, insofar as it had to prove itself fit enough for survival. For, from the perspective of Darwin's theory, species do not survive because they adapt, but they turn out to be well adapted, insofar as they survive.[9]

More than any other scientific theory, Darwinian evolutionism combined the promise of scientifically discernable (and technically applicable) natural forces and racial principles with the discovery of the eternal instability and daily transformation of races that were now themselves responsible for their own "natural" development. Therefore, most evolutionists and disciples of Darwinism explained in their writings not only the theory itself and its possible implications, but also came up with various suggestions of how to intervene and bring the evolutionary process under some kind of rational control. They often supplemented Darwin's ideas with additional principles in order to let evolution appear more calculable or to guarantee possible ways of manipulation. For instance, Herbert Spencer, whose early writings had been an important source for Darwin himself and who soon became the world's most influential popularizer of Darwinism, was a strong advocate of such an additional principle that Darwin too, had once considered but then discarded.[10]

Since Spencer did not want to believe that merely the selection of accidental mutations would drive evolution forward, he forcefully reintroduced the idea (formulated already around 1800 by the French biologist Jean Baptiste Lamarck) that the physical characteristics that an individual acquired during lifetime could be transmitted to the next generation. In the late 1880s, when the German biologist August Weismann experimentally proved that neither physical nor mental characteristics, biographically acquired, had any hereditary influence on the offspring, Spencer devoted much of his writing to the attempt of proving the opposite.[11] He even quoted racist myths as scientific evidence such as the idea of "telegony" that had been particularly prominent among slave owners of the old American South. The core idea of telegony was that sexual intercourse could leave hereditary marks even though it did not lead to pregnancy. American slave owners had turned this idea into the racist myth that a white woman who had sex with a black man might reveal her "sin" even years later by conceiving (from a white father) children with racially black characteristics. Spencer quoted this myth as clear evidence and proof for the influence of environmental and behavioural factors on the hereditary and thus evolutionary process.[12]

However, even though founded on clearly false ideas, Neo-Lamarckianism and telegony were, in fact, nothing but radicalized versions of the core notion of evolutionism: whatever people (or peoples) do, they shape the evolutionary process. Their daily behavior determines how the human races (and the human race as a whole) will "naturally" develop. For, selection, adaptation, and survival were everyday principles, effective at any given moment. In this sense, evolutionism can be interpreted as a broad and very popular attempt to cast history and historical contingency into the form of a natural principle. This explains why a mere translation of Darwin's writings was never enough to spread the idea of evolution. In most cases it needed commentators and popularizers to translate and present the theory in accordance with the respective cultural traditions, intellectual climates, and political contexts.

The Global Dissemination of Darwinian Concepts of Race

A short transnational sketch of the reception of Darwinism shows that in many cases the social scientific applications of Darwinism often became popular long before Darwin's own writings were received or even translated.[13] For instance, in Spain the popularization of Herbert Spencer's ideas and even the reception of the German sociobiologist Ernst Haeckel preceded the first Spanish translations of Charles Darwin's works. Haeckel's amazing success, not only in Spain, but also in South America and elsewhere around the globe, is a good illustration of the widespread international and transnational desire to receive evolutionism as something much bigger and more important than a mere biological theory about the origins of species. From the very beginning it was perceived as a universal theory reaching far beyond the differences between nature and culture, biology and history, as well as across national boundaries.

In his *Natural Creation*, Haeckel had gone even further in this direction by presenting Darwinism not only as a science of nature *and* society, but as a new kind of secular religion. What he coined as "monism" was nothing less than a Darwinian evolutionism turned into a religious worldview apparently explaining and making sense of virtually every aspect of life, from racial issues to politics and economics, to history, art, and faith.[14] The Spanish physician Peregrin Casanova Ciurana, who was politically engaged in the revolution of 1868, later became the most influential translator, popularizer, and also a true disciple of Haeckel, with whom he was in personal contact. This primary influence of Haeckel in Spain and thereby also in the Spanish speaking countries of Latin America, was one of the reasons why the debate over evolutionism became soon mixed up with broader cultural and nationalist issues. On the one side, conservative Catholics opposed evolutionism not only for its anticreationist view on the origin of humanity but also as an unpatriotic import of a German (!) ideology. On the other side, liberal scientists defended the new theory in the name of modern rationality, but also argued that the German monist versions of evolutionism would suit the Spanish mind and culture much better than the purely materialist and crude forms of Anglo-American social Darwinism as represented by Herbert Spencer or William G. Sumner.[15]

A similar pattern can be found in all predominantly Catholic countries such as France, Italy, or Mexico. Here, a social Darwinism in the strict sense, understood as the biologically legitimated doctrine of laissez faire, was much less (or became only later) prominent. Instead, evolutionism's more general theses on human nature and the question of the origin of mankind were far more important issues. Thus, in the beginning, only those evolutionary positions were received and discussed that offered a harmonic, universalist, and peaceful worldview that could make up, at least partly, for the major scandal that Darwin's "ape-theory" presented to the Catholic system of belief. Although the term itself did not exist at the time, the idea of an "intelligent design" was clearly articulated in these early debates: the idea that evolution might function according to the purely natural principles Darwin had discovered, but that the process as a whole followed a creational plan. Among those harmonistic models of evolution that could at least be read as fitting these claims, Haeckel's monism was the most prominent one. Although presenting, especially in Haeckel's own view, quite a competition to the Catholic system of faith, it was still widely received by Catholics around the world precisely for its integration of nature and culture by means of a specific religious rhetoric.[16]

A different but equivalent form of reception can be found in the Islamic regions of the world, especially in Egypt and Arabia, where an increasing interest in the scientific theories of the West emerged at the end of the nineteenth century. Interestingly enough, it was again a German Darwinist, Ludwig Büchner, whose ideas helped to integrate evolutionism into the Islamic worldview. in the 1850s, Büchner had published popular scientific writings in which he tried to transform the various discoveries and theories of the modern sciences into an integrated cosmic ideology and worldview. After the publication of Darwin's works, Büchner quickly picked up the evolutionary concepts as a general paradigm that supported his own cosmological theses. Until the later works of Haeckel, Büchner's books were the bestselling works of German popular materialism. The major difference between Haeckel and Büchner was that Büchner avoided any religious rhetoric in his writings, instead he presented his ideas either as scientific commentaries or as visions of a near future and rationalistic, materialist blueprints of the coming forms of world order.[17]

When the Egyptian physician Shibli Shumayyil—who had studied in Beirut and Paris, where he became familiar with evolutionism—introduced the new theory in a series of publications to his mostly Muslim audience, he repeatedly pointed out that the actual implications of evolutionism were of a social and philosophical nature rather than of a merely biological kind. The major source for such an interpretation of Darwinism was Ludwig Büchner, whom Shumayyil quite appropriately called a "Darwinian Philosopher." However, as elsewhere, a fundamental critique of the new theory did not take long to be voiced. But in its sharpest form it came neither from the Christian nor from the Muslim clergy, but was raised by Jamal al-Din al-Afghani, a well-known political thinker of late nineteenth century Islam. Al-Afghani was a critical modernist who attempted to rationalize Muslim faith and Islamic culture on the basis of a pan-Islamic ideal of uniting the Islamic countries against Western and especially British colonial domination.[18] From this perspective, he perceived the reception of evolutionism and German materialism as an uncritical and dangerous import of Western ideologies. Even though in many of his later writings al-Afghani himself argued in evolutionary terms, proposing, for instance, a "natural selection of thoughts and ideas," he always warned of the fatal consequences an uncritical reception of Western scientific ideas could have for the Islamic culture. However, he could not change the fact that between the 1880s and the 1930s evolutionism, mostly in its already ideologically transformed versions of Büchner, Haeckel, Spencer, or E.B. Tylor, was widely received among the educated classes of the Islamic world.[19]

In other parts of the world too, the seemingly more harmonic and philosophical German versions of evolutionism such as those of Haeckel or Büchner sometimes played the role of an alternative to the strictly Darwinian discourse.[20] However, the social Darwinist principles of survival of the fittest and natural selection as well as the idea of a universal racial struggle for existence most prominently formulated in the writings of Herbert Spencer, remained the dominant form of evolutionary thinking. Only in Russia did scholars develop a very specific form of evolutionism that promised, mostly from a socialist perspective, to deduce from the laws of the biological world principles of a social evolution that would be based upon justice and equality. For instance, the anarchist Petr Kropotkin combined Darwin's evolution theory with Proudhon's concept of "mutualité," in order to sketch out a possible social development, in the course of which the selective pressure of a brutal nature would lead to a just and peaceful social order among human beings. In the United States, Benjmain Kidd popularized similar ideas, although his focus was less on a coming world peace, and more on the global superiority and final success of the Anglo-Saxon race.[21]

However, even the classic and apparently strictly deterministic models of social Darwinism should not be misunderstood as the simple idea that society and politics could do nothing but fulfill nature's supposed demands. As became already clear in Herbert Spencer's stubborn defense of the Lamarckian idea of the inheritance of acquired characters, the evolutionary principles, laws, and mechanisms were first and foremost regarded as means to bring the evolutionary process under human control, both on a physical and on a cultural or political level. For Spencer, humanity as a whole, just as well as every individual race or nation, was (by the law of nature itself) supposed and indeed committed to make use of the finally uncovered biological principles in order to improve its own physical and cultural development through conscious selection, education, and intervention. Only through consciously applying nature's forces would an individual or race prove itself fit and worthwhile to survive the global struggle for existence.

Thus, it is no surprise that Spencer, even though he was a philosopher rather than a biologist, also became the most prominent reference for the new biological science of eugenics, founded by Francis Galton in the 1880s, that was entirely devoted to the question of how to instrumentalize the biological knowledge for the physical improvement of individuals and races.[22] One of the first international debates initiated by this new scientific discipline was the long controversy about the biological effects of war, an issue discussed by scientists, politicians, and the educated public around the world. The main question was, whether warfare, biologically understood as a gigantic mechanism of selection, had only positive and cleansing effects upon the physical development of races and nations or whether it tended to destroy the racial substance of given populations.[23] From the 1880s all the way into the 1940s, this question was a constantly recurring subject of public debates, political considerations, scientific research, and military strategic discussions.

However, in the eugenic worldview it was not just actual war in which the principle of natural selection became manifest. In much the same way, but on a more general level, the eugenicists also regarded the everyday competition between individuals, races, and populations as an ongoing struggle, as a sort of slow, daily warfare following the same principles and posing the same problems. From social class-structures to the economy, to racial enmity, colonial competition, migration, and cultural discord—any kind of conflict constellation was perceived under the aspect of its eugenic effects of selection and with a view of finding ways to instrumentalize these mechanisms for racial self-improvement.[24]

The eugenic paradigm opened the way for another type of non-European reception of evolutionism and racial theory, a reception in which the Western ideas of racial struggle and competition were turned into a scientific legitimization of cultural self-consciousness and anticolonial resistance. In many Asian regions, eugenic evolutionism (in the wide sense of an evolutionism focusing on racial self-improvement) was received by liberation or self-strengthening movements. These movements were searching for a theoretical foundation for their emancipatory goals by reinventing the racial value of their own culture. Just as in today's multicultural societies, ethnic minorities forcefully underline their cultural particularities, classic imperialism also triggered new forms of self-evaluation that at the time were expressed in some cases, in the terms of racial theory. Japan was the forerunner and also a role model to some, in this respect, wherein the reception and nationalist interpretation of Spencer's and Darwin's writings began early and could be instrumentalized after the Japanese-Russian war in much the same way as in the Western imperial states. Also among Hindu nationalists in India as well as in other regions of Asia, evolutionism played a significant role as a medium for the articulation of "self-civilizational" and anticolonial claims among the educated and politically engaged classes. Here again, it was primarily Herbert Spencer's writings that initiated the developments of non-European versions of evolutionism.[25]

The reason for Spencer's global popularity was not only the fact that he was the most prominent philosopher of the British Empire. It was also his oft repeated insistence that, despite all the "iron lawfulness" of evolution, its political control, instrumentalization, and indeed manipulation was possible—providing his readers with the hopes of rationally controlling the evolution of their own race. It was this eugenic control-fantasy that continued to be the dominant and most prominent form of evolutionary and racial thought until the middle of the twentieth century. Although modern genetics uncovered ever more details of what used to be called "germ plasm" and although the geneticists from the 1920s onward started to conceive of heredity much more in terms of information, codes, and molecular patterns than in racial concepts, the eugenic paradigm preserved its dominance, especially in the popular scientific realm,[26] because it promised to direct the evolutionary process not by manipulating some biochemical substances only specialists would know of, but through the means of social medicine: the regulation of populations and the control of behavior. The foundation of this general paradigm had been formulated by Herbert Spencer already in the 1860s, when he envisioned possible methods of a "physiological education" as a means to improve the racial stock.[27] The idea of influencing human nature through human will and the conscious application of scientific knowledge were perhaps the most important reasons for the immense transnational and indeed global impact of his writings.

However, the eugenic paradigm proved to be not only transnationally and transculturally compatible, but it is also important to note that politically it was anything but one-sided. The fatal role that eugenic thinking played in the fascist regimes and especially in the Third Reich is well known. But in the Soviet Union too, eugenic concepts and ideas were an important part of Stalin's brutal population policy responsible for millions of victims. How much even here a Spencerian version of evolutionism was employed is illustrated by the fact that Russian scientists until the late 1950s desperately tried to proof the validity of that old Lamarckian principle of the inheritance of acquired characters that Spencer himself had defended so forcefully. Such a direct effect of the environment upon the genetic heredity would have suited the Stalinist concepts of progress and development much better than Darwin's irrational system of chance and selection.[28] In Germany as well as in Britain and France, eugenic organizations did not consist only of right wing conservatives; just as many socialists, social democrats, and liberals can be found on their membership lists.[29] And even such an explicitly anti-biologist thinker as Sigmund Freud considered for a while the idea that individual experiences might manifest themselves on a genetic hereditarian level—a possibility that would have provided the Freudian concept of trauma with a whole new, physiological dimension.[30]

In the United States too, the liberal German-American anthropologist Franz Boas, in arguing against an immigration restriction in 1910, went even so far as to claim that the American environment physically transformed the immigrants and especially their head-form (from a "southern European" to a "Caucasian-American" type) and that this transformation would be transmitted to the next generations. In the name of a liberal, antiracist immigration policy, Boas declared Americanization to be a biological fact. Once convinced of this Lamarckian effect of the environment upon physiology and heredity, Boas even reflected upon a possible long term solution for the racial problems in the United States as well as on a global scale. In letters to colleagues, he envisioned the complete erasure of racial differences brought about by a careful combination of controlled racial mixture and systematic transport of populations to suitable, that is effective, environments. Thus Boas represented a form of scientific liberalism that seriously considered the disappearance of races as one possible solution to the problem of racial conflict.[31]

In the general features of the transnational discourse of race and evolution—sketched only roughly here—some structural aspects need to be pointed out in order to understand its function as a medium of articulating and reflecting the globality of the imperial age and the challenges it posed. The racial discourse of the late nineteenth and early twentieth centuries was not only an international phenomenon, but a transnational one as well, insofar as it was produced and reproduced beyond and across national boundaries and independently from the national origins of the specific concepts and ideas. Only Friedrich Nietzsche insisted, rather hatefully, on the "specifically English character of Darwinism," but to the broad majority of his contemporaries it was a universal theory—concerning everyone and therefore adaptable by everyone. Understood in most parts of the world as a new philosophy of and for the modern word rather than as scientific study on the origins of biological life, evolutionism could be transformed and reinterpreted in various ways according to different contexts and circumstances. Moreover, the rhetoric of selection, adaptation, and survival itself invited such a manipulative reading once the realm of culture was seen as but a part of the global evolutionary system. Thus Darwin's evolution theory and evolutionary racial thinking provided both a direct access to the most advanced knowledge of modernity and a way to articulate alternative visions of what was called and generally admired as evolutionary progress. For at its core, evolutionism articulated a world order of difference.

Thus, the global attraction of evolutionary racial theory was based upon the specific structure of its basic assumptions: it combined the universality of the modern concepts of nature and humanity with the empirical factuality of differences and particularities. This combination made the shaping and arrangements of particular racial characteristics and differences appear as the most direct way to shape and arrange the human nature as such, no matter whether such intervention was thought of as direct individual manipulation or as a strategy in the global struggle of races. Because of this causal nexus between the universal and the particular, every racial or even racialist attitude, as long as it placed itself within the framework of the transnational discourse of evolutionary racial theory (and only few did not), had a utopian side to it, an embedded vision of a racial world order. In this sense and once the concept of race was predominantly linked to modern science and the universal mechanisms of evolution, racial thinking was, by definition, global. This is not to say that the racial discourse ceased to be a subordination. However, evolutionary racism derived this legitimating element no longer from nature as such, but from a utopian knowledge of how to manipulate it. Thus, racial thinking at the beginning of the twentieth century was less an ideology of crude natural determinism and much more a widely shared fantasy of the great faith in power.

The transnational reception of Darwinism makes clear the fact that the many different forms in which the original scientific ideas were translated, rearranged, and even manipulated, were precisely the ways in which the evolutionary racial discourse gained its function as a global discourse on the very problem of globality. Because of their global dissemination and inherent scientific universality, race and evolution gained the status of categories through which the global racial conflicts could be interpreted as mere variations of the same general phenomenon. At the same time, the biological dimension of the concepts still guaranteed the validity of differences and hierarchies. In a racial world order, globality is being scientifically categorized and controlled. This became especially manifest during an event that can be regarded as a paradigmatic example for the visionary dimension of the race concept: the First Universal Races Congress, held in London in the summer of 1911.

Visions of Racial Harmony in 1911

The First Universal Races Congress was an international meeting of racial theorists and evolutionists as well as of sociologists, economists, historians, and political intellectuals from Europe, America, and especially from Africa, Australia, India, Japan, China, Southeast Asia, Russia, and Latin America. Organized by prominent members of international peace and ethical culture movements, the prime intention of the Congress was to "discuss, in the light of science and modern conscience, the general relations subsisting between the peoples of the West and those of the East, between so-called white and so-called coloured peoples, with a view to encouraging between them a fuller understanding, the most friendly feelings, and a heartier co-operation."[32]

With over one thousand participants and an extensive accompanying program including an ethnographic exhibition, the Congress was probably the largest event devoted to international cooperation before World War I. Originally designed to concentrate on the relationship between the Orient and the Occident and in this way reacting to what was called the "Awakening of Asia," the leader of the African-American delegation, W.E.B. du Bois, successfully demanded, during the preparation of the Congress, that it should also discuss African issues and the situation of blacks around the world. Even though this decision further increased the heterogeneity of the event, a fact that was critically pointed out in many of the public commentaries, it also helped to truly globalize the Congress and to create the impression that here indeed the entire world was gathered to discuss its major problems.

The proud claim of the organizers to initiate the beginning of a whole new era of peaceful global communication, development, and interracial conduct at the eve of World War I, retrospectively seems quite naive. On the other hand, the Congress indeed raised issues and discussed ideas that later would become central topics during the foundation of the League of Nations (and later of the UN) as well as in the developmental politics of the second half of the twentieth century: The right to national self-determination, the notion of a politics of cultural recognition, the idea of modernization as a globally effective historical tendency, and the concepts of "cultural conflict" and "cultural contact" were explicitly introduced and openly discussed in the London Congress of 1911. Moreover, the event was an impressive illustration of how conscious the educated classes were in 1911 of the globality of their own era. Although the term globalization itself was not used (instead the most often mentioned name for the period was "era of internationalism"), most speakers referred explicitly to phenomena that we, today, clearly associate with the first wave of globalization: the shrinking of the world through new communication and transport technologies, the ever closer entanglement of the earth's most distant regions through economic networks and imperial expansion, the final end of the period of discovery, and the necessity to develop new forms of international cooperation in a world that no longer offered undiscovered spaces but had to be shared. Finally, even though the organizers strictly tried to keep the Congress clean from directly political issues and to prohibit any form of political commentary, even some anti-imperial and anticolonial views were articulated by at least a few of the many speakers.

However, criticizing imperialism was not part of the program nor intended to be so by the organizers. Instead, the Congress stressed the educational responsibility of the imperial powers to gradually "lift up" the colonized races for the sake of general progress of humanity. The practices of imperial politics as such were never questioned. In addition, the group of participants and speakers was also too heterogeneous to form a common anticolonial critique. For instance, among the German delegation, were not only such intellectuals as Georg Simmel, Friedrich Meinecke, and Ferdinand Tönnies, but also strictly racialist thinkers and eugenicists such as Ernst Haeckel, Ludwig Schemann, Wilhelm Ostwald, and Felix von Luschan. If these two groups already did not have much in common, the heterogeneity was multiplied when they met formerly probably unknown scientists and thinkers from India, Persia, Africa, and South America. Thus, Felix von Luschan, in some of his later commentaries, described his trip to London rather as visiting an ethnographic revue than as participating in a scientific Congress.[33] Nevertheless, no serious conflict or heated debates occurred during the event and von Luschan as well as others of the many rather critical observers had to admit that the Congress indeed managed to raise some globally important issue, to articulate insights into an important signature of the era, and to create a surprising spirit of unity despite its own racial and cultural diversity.

As to the question of what exactly provided and supported this harmony, two aspects appear most significant: the generally shared faith in the power of modern science and an equally shared concept of race. Already in the general invitation to the Congress, the organizers declared that the scientific discovery most important for the global situation of 1911 was the new insight that races were not fixed, stable, and given entities but changeable, flexible, and capable for development. This understanding of race as a fluid and flexible phenomenon was the basic evolutionary consensus that held the various theoretical positions, articulated in London, together. Within this consensus the difference between a physical understanding of "racial change," as stated by

Franz Boas (who presented his work on immigrants) and a more general understanding of racial change as, for instance, the potential for social and cultural development among the non-European races, became almost irrelevant. Instead the Congress celebrated—in one way or the other—the flexibility and possible change of races as such and envisioned a future world order in which the unity of mankind was represented precisely in its newly fashioned racial diversity. This became especially clear in the opening lecture on the concepts of race, tribe, and nation, held by the Indian scientist Brajendranath Seal:

> If modern civilisation is distinguished from all other civilisations by its scientific basis, the problems that this civilisation presents must be solved by the methods of Science. . . . Modern Science, first directed to the conquest of Nature, must now be increasingly applied to the organisation of society. . . . A synthetic view of Race is possible, only when we consider it not as a statical, but as a dynamic entity, plastic, fluent, growing, with energies not exhaust, but superimposing layer upon layer like the earth, its scene, still subject to the primal forces that have built up the bed-rocks in their order of sequence and distribution. This is the point of view of genetic Anthropology. It will study Race and Racial types as developing entities, tracing the formation of physical stocks or types as radicles, their growth and transmutation into ethnic cultural units (clans, tribes, peoples), and finally, the course of their evolution into historical nationalities. A study of genetic conditions and causes, of the biological, psychological, sociological forces at work, which have shaped and governed the rise, growth, and decadence of Races of Man, can alone enable us to guide and control the future evolution of Humanity by conscious selection in intelligent adaptation to the system and procedure of Nature.

And at the end of his talk, Seal came to the issue of a possible future world order:

> . . . Nationalism, Imperialism and Federationism are world-building forces, working often unconsciously, and in apparent strife, towards the one far-off divine event, a realised Universal Humanity with an organic and organised constitution, superintending as a *primum mobile* the movements of subordinate members of the Worldsystem, each within its own sphere and orbit. Respecting each National Personality, and each scheme of National values and ideals, Universal Humanity will regulate the conflict of Nations and National Ideals and Values on the immutable foundation of Justice, which is but the conscious formulation of the fundamental

bio-sociological law. . . . A realised Universal Humanity on this immutable basis is the goal of a Universal Races Congress like this. . . . Our motto is harmony.[34]

Here, it is hard to decide where the biological meaning of the term "race" ends and where its purely metaphorical function takes over. However, Seal—and with him the organizers as well as most of the other speakers of the Congress—declared racial change and development to be the keystone of a coming world order. At its core, this idea went perfectly hand in hand with the basic assumptions of Darwinian evolutionism as well as of the eugenic paradigm. Thus the main message voiced by the London Congress was that the development of races could be guided and that such guidance and controlled intervention now, in the context of a world that finally had become empirically global, was absolutely necessary for the sake of world peace. What the notion of race signified in this context was, therefore, not a given determining natural order, but the forces and principles through which such a natural order could be created. To understand and rationally apply those forces and principles in order to develop and shape the world's racial constellation for the sake of human progress—that was the indeed pacifist, but in its inner logic also racialist and eugenic ideal to which the majority of the participants and speakers of the London Congress felt committed.

Eugenics and the Invention of a New Racial World Order

Only one year later, the very same city of London hosted another world congress, this time the First World Congress of Eugenics. In almost every respect this event was much less universal than the Races Congress of 1911. The number of non-Western participants was reduced to only a few scientists from Latin America, Japan, and India and the great majority of racial theorists came from Germany, Britain, France, Italy, and the United States. Moreover, the entire tone of this Congress was much less optimistic. Although the eugenicists principally shared the same evolutionary assumptions and discussed quite similar problems, they constructed a much more pessimistic vision of the coming world order. There were basically two reasons for this pessimism: First of all, most of the eugenicists finally had started to dismiss the idea that the environment had any direct effects upon the heredity. Empirical research had made clear that heredity was an accidental molecular process, largely independent from the environment. But instead of questioning, on this very basis, the significance of heredity and evolution for the social and political realms of life, the eugenicists stressed all the more the dominant importance of racial issues and the necessity to carefully guide and control racial development. As a result of this, the eugenicists reduced all the hopes that had been invested so far into a possible scientific control of evolution—hopes that the Races Congress had expressed in many varieties—to but one central problem of a eugenic population policy: Who was to be encouraged to reproduce (positive eugenics) and who should be excluded from reproduction (negative eugenics).[35]

Along with this reduction of the entire problem to the alternatives of positive and negative eugenics, a second issue became relevant that further increased the new pessimism: the empirical observation that within the Western societies it seemed to be lower classes and on a global level it seemed to be the non-European races that apparently reproduced themselves to a much higher degree than the eugenicists' favoured racial group of the educated, white or Caucasian higher classes of Europe and North America. On the basis of this observation, the vision of a global degeneration was developed and extensively discussed first on the London Congress of 1912, and even more so on the follow-up event in New York in 1921. Although such a notion of degeneration seems to imply a static concept of race and the idea that lower and higher races will always be what they are, a closer look at the eugenic discourse of the time reveals that this was actually not the case.

The eugenic understanding of degeneration, especially when referring to the global situation, did not have much in common with the traditional concept of degeneration as the physical weakening of a given population. Instead, with the phantasmagorical idea of a global degeneration, the eugenicists articulated their fear that the white, "Arian" or Caucasian race, so far still dominating the world, in the long run, might prove itself unfit for the future. Thus the issue was not degeneration as such, but the question of success or failure in the global racial struggle. This idea of a global struggle of races that had been very popular already in the early twentieth century, was strongly revitalized by the eugenic discourse of the 1920s. Precisely because the hopes for directly influencing and controlling heredity had been disappointed, the notion of a global racial struggle as being the main engine of the evolutionary process, suddenly appeared plausible.[36]

Furthermore, the idea of a global racial struggle, the outcome of which was not predetermined, but open, fitted neatly into the more general intellectual *zeitgeist* of the time. The World War I and the attempts to establish systems of global conflict regulation that followed it, challenged the global consciousness of the period that until then had celebrated itself mainly in the terms of imperialism. Now, and not only in the eyes of those who lost the war, the possibility became conceivable that in the future, even more drastic changes in the global constellations of power might occur. What Oswald Spengler immediately after the War coined as the *The Decline of the West* and what he extensively described in a book that was almost as globally successful as Darwin's, Spencer's, or Haeckel's works had been before the war, was part of a widespread cultural pessimism among the intellectuals and educated classes all over Europe. In the English-speaking world, it was Madison Grant's *Passing of the Great Race* that played a similar role. Never before had the possibility of the downfall of Western culture and civilization been as intensively discussed and imagined as in the years after 1918.[37]

A central part of that pessimism was the fear and worry that the eugenicists articulated in ever more popular versions. Already in the context of the colonial debates over racial mixture, acclimatization, and racial education, the idea had been developed that the colonized races somehow might pose a threat to the purity and greatness of the white European races—an idea that somehow did not fit the self-confidence of a colonizing imperial "Master Race."[38] After World War I, the eugenicists turned this idea into the key concept of their new racial vision of world order that lived on and continued to be the internationally predominant form of racial thought until the World War II.

Within this new paradigm, the notion of a global struggle had, to a certain degree, replaced the idea of manipulation and self-improvement. The evolutionary struggle itself seemed to be the only principle and mechanism left to be applied for the betterment of races. In a way, the eugenic racial visions of the 1920s and 1930s came full circle and reintroduced what Darwin had proposed in the first place for the natural world: The so called "survival of the fittest" actually meant nothing but the survival of those who survive, the survival of the victors in the ongoing struggle for existence. Only insofar as a race turns out to have survived (for the time being), could it claim for itself an evolutionary fitness. In a Darwinian perspective, it is the racial struggle that precedes and in fact determines fitness, not the other way around. Thus, what the new eugenic discourse increasingly pointed out and tried to popularize was the idea that any attempt to guide and improve the development of races, either in relation to one specific race or on a global scale, was bound to take the most basic evolutionary principle into account: no improvement (no fitness) without struggle, competition, conflict, and war.

Moreover, in this new eugenic version, racial theory was truly globalized. Models of racial self-improvement as Herbert Spencer and other evolutionists of the late nineteenth century had developed, based upon the idea that every race can improve itself through the careful application of biological principles, were no longer conceivable. If a race was to improve itself it had to enter and then survive the conflict with other races. Practical racial politics was by definition global politics. Accordingly, it was no longer possible that the eugenic paradigm would receive as many different and diverse readings and reinterpretations in the various regions of the world as the classic evolutionism of the nineteenth century had, which is one of the reasons why the eugenics movement institutionalized itself much faster and had established a huge and strictly ordered international organization by the end of the 1920s.[39]

Also by definition, natural fitness was finally and completely identical with political power, since the lawfulness of the evolutionary process was reduced to the game of struggle and survival, manifesting itself in the human world predominantly as a fight for political power. One could expect that under the condition of such presupposed assumptions, the initial pessimism among the eugenicists continued or even increased. But that was not the case. Instead they managed to celebrate their idea that nothing but struggle, conflict, and war could elevate the human races and improve their physical fitness as the final breakthrough in the search for principles of a biologically guided world politics.

At the beginning of the 1920s, almost every Western country had its own national eugenic society, and the 1921 Congress in New York helped to establish regular contact and exchange between them. Moreover, this second International Congress of Eugenics—in contrast to the first one in London in 1912—was joined by scientists from all over the world, including Latin America, Asia, India, and some of the Arabic countries. Just as evolutionary thought, especially in its German versions, had been received in parts of the non-Western world in various ways before World War I, a straighter, less ambivalent and less harmonistic version of eugenic thinking spread around the globe after 1918, and was widely received for a variety of reasons. By and large, the success of eugenics in the non-Western world, despite its pessimism and its reductionist way of conceiving racial development, had origins similar to the success of the older evolutionary discourse. Especially in non-Western countries such as Japan that had managed to avoid colonial rule, or most of Latin America that had already achieved their independence, or India and parts of the Islamic world that were on the brink of achieving that goal, eugenics provided a way of adopting a Western modernist ideology of progress and social control that, at the same time, could at least potentially be used to demand independence from Western domination.[40]

Since the eugenic paradigm transformed the concept of race from an abstract notion, signifying biological destinies and hierarchies, into a much more practical agenda, calling for a form of racial politics that had to begin with a given population in order to racially transform and design it by controlling its future reproduction, the idea of a naturally and eternally given structure of racial dominance was banned from the centre of the international racial discourse. It was still a prominent part of the political self-image of the imperial powers as well as of the new radical nationalisms and pan-movements of the interwar period. However, even in these contexts it had virtually no reassuring effects any more, and functioned increasingly as a mere ideal image of a racial purity, the revitalization of which (by all means) became the new central trope of the biopolitical discourse of the time. By the same token, in the non-Western world, at least to the educated upper classes, the eugenic idea of healing societies from the degenerative forces of a false population politics provided not only modern scientific methods of social control to be easily applied, but also good arguments for an application of such methods, independent from foreign control and domination.[41]

This is why we see in the midst of the 1920s and 1930s, otherwise dominated by emerging fascism, radically nationalist pan-movements and anti-colonial resistance all over the world, a far-reaching global entanglement and cooperation between the various eugenic societies and scientific institutions. Congresses and conferences devoted to eugenics, genetics, and population politics were the most "international" meetings and cooperation efforts of modern science during the interwar era. By the late 1930s, the basic rules and assumptions of eugenic thinking had entered schoolbooks around the world and eugenic sterilization laws had been passed in parts of Latin America, the United States, Germany, Italy, and Scandinavia. The 1932 International Congress of Eugenics in New York established an especially close link between German and American scientists that was further strengthened by the institutional networks of the closely related discipline of genetics.[42]

Only as late as 1939, in the Seventh International Congress of Genetics in Edinburgh, did new biochemical ways of conceiving the phenomenon of heredity start to replace the classic biopolitical notions of eugenics.[43] However, at that point, the core idea of the eugenic paradigm—that racial superiority was not given, but depended upon a healthy reproduction of the population and on its success in the global struggle of races—had already become a central part of totalitarian politics, certainly in Nazi-Germany, but also in other fascist regimes as well as in Stalin's attempts to erase "classes" and class-conflicts by means of population politics. Moreover, the notion of a racial war, conceived as a war that was to be won for the sake of the very survival of one's own population and by the corresponding means of destroying other populations, determined much of the violence, mass-destruction, and mass-migration that accompanied and followed the World War II.

Race as a Global Concept

Eugenics and the racial discourse were neither the primary origin of the various forms of mass violence during World War II, nor necessarily a primary motivation for the actors and perpetrators. But they provided powerful forms of self-explanation by declaring acts of suppression, dispelling, and destruction as nothing but the manifestation of a natural and universal lawfulness of history and social development. Racial thinking, over the course of the preceding decades, had increasingly accepted the Darwinian notion that the laws and principles of evolution were everyday world-building forces, active at any given moment and thus—in the human realm—principally identical with the behaviour, movement, and struggle of individuals and collectives as such. Thus, under the conditions of totalitarian regimes or total warfare, when this natural lawfulness increasingly tended to replace the given legal systems of positive law, acts of violence no longer had to be justified, for they *were* nothing but the laws of nature in action.[44]

However, racial thinking, the laws of evolution, and the logic of eugenics were certainly not invented by the totalitarian regimes. Instead, the evolutionary and eugenic racial discourse had been out there in various forms and variations for decades. But is it appropriate and satisfying in this context to regard racial thinking as a popular ideology simply picked up by totalitarian regimes at the right time? Was the global spread of racial and eugenic ideas merely a matter of popularity and its central role in totalitarianism simply a matter of politically instrumentalizing this popularity? Or is there something that the various forms of receiving and making use of the racial principles from early Darwinism to the totalitarian mass destruction of the 1930s and 1940s have in common, something that connects them and turns the story that has been roughly outlined here into something that can be called a "global movement"?

One of the most important elements in this respect seems to be the development of the term race itself, from a universal category invented to make sense of the diversity of human cultures into a global concept increasingly employed to shape and design particularity and difference. In the era of high imperialism, bringing the cultures and nations of the world in ever closer contact and diversifying global power relationships, it was evolutionism that provided an understanding of races as being self-responsible for their own biological survival and development in relation to others. From then on, racial thought, however diverse and politically multifaceted, was primarily a discourse of scientific self-improvement. As such it was quickly and widely received around the globe as promising to legitimate and practically increase the specific character, particularity, independence and superiority of nations. But even in this nationalist context the global validity and effectiveness of the principles of racial development were acknowledged and celebrated as globally uniting forces that suited the claims of superiority and domination among the imperialist powers or the new pan-movements. The eugenic paradigm, then, in radicalizing the notion of racial self-improvement through its identification with the strictly Darwinian mechanisms of selection, struggle, and survival, represented a re-fusion of the universalist and the particularist dimensions of the race concept.

Racial self-improvement was now no longer conceived as something that each nation could achieve by itself through simply applying, according to its own needs, the universal laws of nature that science had discovered. Instead, if a nation was to be regulated by scientific principles and the laws of nature, it had to take its relation to the rest of the world into account, for only its success and survival in the life-and-death struggle between races was to prove, and in fact, to bring about its own racial fitness. Within this eugenic form of racial thinking, the nation itself lost its character as a fixed entity, for the racial struggle was conceived as a social process of constant purification and improvement just as well as an ongoing global conflict to be survived. Thus, the racial discourse introduced a transnational dimension into the political self-understanding of modern societies by popularizing the idea that collective belonging, distinctness, and power was to be gained and stabilized only in relation to the rest of the world. In this sense, the concept of race was one of the first—if fatal—attempts to think particularity under the conditions of globality.

Notes

1. One of the first scholars who pointed to this aspect of globality and its importance for both imperialism and its racialist ideologies in order to understand the era of high imperialism was Hannah Arendt in her classic *The Origins of Totalitarianism* (New York: Harcourt, Brace, 1951). See also Michael Geyer and Charles Bright, "World History in a Global Age," *American Historical Review* 100 (1995): 1034–60. For the German see Sebastian Conrad and Jürgen Osterhammel, eds., *Das Kaiserreich transnational: Deutschland in der Welt 1871–1914* (Göttingen: Vandenhoeck & Ruprecht, 2004). From a philosophical perspective, the importance of globality not just as a result or effect, but as a condition of modernity and modern history has also been outlined by Peter Sloterdijk, *Im Weltinnenraum des Kapitals: Für eine philosophische Theorie der Globalisierung* (Frankfurt am Main: Suhrkamp, 2005). Arendt's interpretation of the racial discourse relied heavily on a study, less prominent today, by Eric Voegelin, *Rasse und Staat* (Tübingen: Mohr, 1933). See also George M. Frederickson, *Racism: A Short History* (Princeton: Princeton University Press, 2002); Christian Geulen, *Wahlverwandte: Rassendiskurs und Nationalismus im späten 19. Jahrhundert* (Hamburg: Hamburger Edition, 2004). See also Hugh Tinker, *Race, Conflict, and the International Order: From Empire to United Nations* (New York: St. Martin's Press, 1977). In the more general fields of postcolonialism and cultural studies, strong and provocative arguments for acknowledging and analyzing the concept of race and its history not just as an antimodern ideology, but as an attempt of modern thought to conceptualize and control the problem of intercultural relations in a global world, have been

made by Walter Benn Michaels, *Our America: Nativism, Modernism and Pluralism* (Durham: Duke University Press, 1995); Robert J.C. Young, *Colonial Desire: Hybridity in Theory, Culture and Race* (London: Routledge, 1995); and—from a Foucauldian perspective—Ann L. Stoler, *Race and the Education of Desire: Foucault's History of Sexuality and the Colonial Order of Things* (Durham: Duke University Press, 1997).

2. A second essay will focus on the colonial popular culture of the 1920s and 1930s, reconstructing the ways in which colonialist visions of world order were propagated through the heroicization of certain colonial adventurers of the late nineteenth century.

3. See Étienne Balibar, "Der Rassismus: Auch noch ein Universalismus," in Ulrich Bielefeld, ed., *Das Eigene und das Fremde: Neuer Rassismus in der alten Welt?* (Hamburg: Hamburger Edition, 1998), pp. 175–88, here p. 182. See also Voegelin, *Rasse*.

4. See Frederickson, *Racism*; Werner Conze, "Rasse," in Werner Conze, von Otto Brunner, and Reinhart Koselleck, eds., *Geschichtliche Grundbegriffe*, historisches Lexikon zur politisch-sozialen Sprache in Deutschland, vol. 5 (Stuttgart: Klett, 1984), pp. 135–78; see also Foucault's lectures on the subject of racism as collected in Michel Foucault, *Society Must Be Defended* (New York: Picador, 2003).

5. See Urs Bitterli, *Die Wilden und die Zivilisierten: Grundzüge einer Geistes- und Kulturgeschichte der europäisch-überseeischen Begegnung* (München: Beck, 1976) Karl-Heinz Kohl, *Entzauberter Blick. Das Bild vom Guten Wilden* (Frankfurt am Main: Suhrkamp, 1986); on the historical development from Enlightenment anthropological thinking to modern anthropology see George W. Stocking, *Race, Culture, and Evolution: Essays in the History of Anthropology* (New York: Free Press, 1968).

6. A typical representative of this kind of reasoning was, for instance, A.R. Jacques Turgot. See Kohl, *Entzauberter Blick*.

7. See Arendt's chapters on the concept humanity and human rights in her *Origins*. See also Reinhart Koselleck, *Critique and Crisis: Enlightenment and the Pathogenesis of Modern Society* (Cambridge, Mass.: MIT Press, 1988).

8. Voegelin, *Rasse*; Foucault, *Society*. See also the classic studies by Thomas F. Gossett, *Race: The History of an Idea in America* (New York: Schocken Books, 1963); Leon Poliakov, *Aryan Myth: A History of Racist and Nationalist Ideas in Europe* (New York: Basic Books, 1974); George L. Mosse, *Toward the Final Solution: A History of European Racism* (New York: Fertig, 1978).

9. One of the first to fully grasp this core idea of the Darwinian model was John Dewey, "The Influence of Darwinism on Philosophy" [1909], in J.A. Boydston, ed., *The Collected Works of John Dewey*, vol. 4 (Carbondale: Southern Illinois University Press, 1977), pp. 3–14. See also Stephen J. Gould, *The Structure of Evolutionary Theory* (Cambridge, Mass.: Belknap Press of Harvard University Press, 2002).

10. Herbert Spencer, *Principles of Biology* (London: William and Norgate, 1863); Herbert Spencer, *The Study of Sociology* (New York: D. Appleton, 1874); Herbert Spencer, *The Factors of Organic Evolution* (London: Williams and Norgate, 1887).

See also Carl N. Degler, *In Search of Human Nature: The Decline and Revival of Darwinism in American Social Thought* (Oxford: Oxford University Press, 1991); Greta Jones, *Social Darwinism and English Thought: The Interaction between Biological and Social Theory* (Brighton: Harvester Press, 1980); Rolf-Peter Sieferle, *Die Krise der menschlichen Natur: Zur Geschichte eines Konzepts* (Frankfurt am Main: Suhrkamp, 1989); on Spencer himself see T.S. Gray, *The Political Philosophy of Herbert Spencer: Individualism and Organicism* (Aldershot: Avebury, 1996).

11. Frederick B. Churchill, "The Weismann-Spencer-Controversy," in E.G. Forbes, ed., *Human Implications of Scientific Advance* (Edinburgh: Edinburgh University Press, 1978), pp. 451–68; Peter J. Bowler, *Evolution: The History of an Idea* (Berkeley: University of California Press, 1984); Peter J. Bowler, *The Invention of Progress: Victorians and the Past* (Oxford and New York: B. Blackwell, 1989).

12. Hamilton Cravens, *The Triumph of Evolution: The Heredity-Environment Controversy 1900–1941* (Philadelphia: University of Pennsylvania Press, 1978); Richard W. Burckhardt, "Closing the Doors on Lord Morton's Mare: The Rise and Fall of Telegony," in W. Coleman and C. Limoges, eds., *Studies in the History of Biology* (Baltimore: John Hopkins University Press, 1979), pp. 1–21.

13. Along the works on the history of evolutionary thinking already mentioned see especially the comparative volumes by Thomas F. Glick, ed., *The Comparative Reception of Darwinism* (Austin: University of Texas Press, 1974); David Kohn, ed., *The Darwinian Heritage* (Princeton: Princeton University Press, 1985); Ronald L. Numbers and John Stenhouse, eds., *Disseminating Darwinism: The Role of Place, Race, Religion, and Gender* (Cambridge: Cambridge University Press, 1999).

14. Ernst Haeckel, *Natürliche Schöpfungsgeschichte* (Berlin: G. Reimer, 1868). See also Ernst Haeckel, *Die Welträtsel: Gemeinverständliche Studien über Monistische Philosophie* (Leipzig: A. Kröner, 1908); in English: Ernst Haeckel, *Riddle of the Universe*, trans. Joseph McCabe (New York: Prometheus Books, 1992).

15. See Thomas F. Glick, "Spain," in Thomas F. Glick, ed., *Comparative Reception*, pp. 307–45; M. Hawkins, *Social Darwinism in European and American Thought, 1860–1945: Nature as Model and Nature as Threat* (Cambridge and New York: Cambridge University Press, 1997); Numbers and Stenhouse, *Disseminating Darwinism*.

16. Robert E. Stebbins, "France," in Glick, ed., *Comparative Reception*, pp. 117–63; Linda L. Clark, *Social Darwinism in France* (Auburn: University of Alabama Press, 1984); Robert Moreno, "Mexico," in Glick, ed., *Comparative Reception*, pp. 346–73; Pietro Corsi and Paul J. Weindling, "Darwinism in Germany, France and Italy," in Kohn, *Heritage*, pp. 683–730.

17. Ludwig Büchner, *Kraft und Stoff* (Frankfurt: Meidinger, 1855); Ludwig Büchner, *Das künftige Leben und die moderne Wissenschaft* (Leipzig: Thomas, 1889). On the development and popularization of Haeckel, Büchner and others see Geulen, *Wahlverwandte*; Christoph Daum, *Wissenschaftspopularisierung im 19. Jahrhundert* (München: R. Oldenbourg, 1998).

18. On the ambiguous forms and functions of Pan-Islamism in this era see also Cemil Aydin, *The Politics of Anti-Westernism in Asia: Visions of World Order in Pan-Islamic and Pan-Asian Thought, 1882–1945* (New York: Columbia University Press, forthcoming in 2007), and his contribution to this volume.

19. Naijm A. Bezirgan, "The Islamic World," in Glick, ed., *Comparative Reception*, pp. 375–87; Adel A. Ziadat, *Western Science in the Arab World: The Impact of Darwinism 1860–1930* (Basingstoke: Macmillan, 1986); Albert Hourani, *Arabic Thought in the Liberal Age, 1789–1939* (New York and Oxford: Oxford University Press, 1967); Charles Kurzman, ed., *Modernist Islam, 1840–1940* (New York/ Oxford: Oxford University Press, 2002).

20. See also Peter J. Bowler, *The Eclipse of Darwinism: Anti-Darwinian Evolution Theories in the Decades around 1900* (Baltimore: Johns Hopkins University Press, 1983).

21. See Petr Kropotkin, *Mutual Aid: A Factor in Evolution* (London: William Heinemann, 1902); Benjamin Kidd, *Social Evolution* (New York: Macmillan, 1895).

22. See David J. Keyles, *In the Name of Eugenics: Genetics and the Uses of Heredity* (New York: Random House, 1995).

23. See David P. Crook, *Darwinism, War and History: The Debate over the Biology of War from the "Origin of Species" to the First World War* (Cambridge: Cambridge University Press, 1994).

24. On the international history of eugenics see Diane B. Paul, *The Politics of Heredity: Essays on Eugenics, Biomedicine and the Nature-Nurture Debate* (Albany: State University of New York Press, 1998); Nancy L. Stepan, *The Hour of Eugenics: Race, Gender and Nation in Latin America* (Ithaca: Cornell University Press, 1991); Marc B. Adams, ed., *The Wellborn Science: Eugenics in Germany, France, Brazil, and Russia* (Oxford and New York: Oxford University Press, 1990); Stephan Kühl, *The Nazi-Connection: Eugenics, American Racism, and German National Socialism* (Oxford and New York: Oxford University Press, 1994); Gunnar Broberg, ed., *Eugenics and the Welfare State: Sterilization Policy in Denmark, Sweden, Norway, and Finland* (East Lansing: Michigan State University Press, 1996).

25. See Harald Fischer-Tiné and Michael Mann, eds., *Colonialism as Civilizing Mission: Cultural Ideology in British India* (London: Anthem Press, 2004); Shingo Shimada, *Die Erfindung Japans: Kulturelle Wechselwirkung und nationale Identitätskonstruktion* (Frankfurt: Campus, 2000); Prasenjit Duara, "The Discourse of Civilization and Pan-Asianism," *Journal of World History* 12, no. 1 (2001): 99–130.

26. See Lily Kay, *Who Wrote the Book of Life? A History of the Genetic Code* (Stanford: Stanford University Press, 2000); Karl Heinz Roth, "Schöner Neuer Mensch: Der Paradimenwechsel der klassischen Genetik und seine Auswirkungen auf die Bevölkerungsbiologie des Dritten Reichs," in Heidrun Kaupen-Haas and Christian Saller, eds., *Wissenschaftlicher Rassismus: Analysen einer Kontinuität in den Human- und Naturwissenschaften* (Frankfurt: Campus, 1999), pp. 346–424.

27. Herbert Spencer, *Principles of Psychology* (London: Longman, Brown, Green, and Longmans, 1855).

28. The most prominent figure of this Russian revival of biological concepts dismissed by most of the scientific community at the time was Trofim D. Lysenko who promised to scientifically solve Russia's agricultural problems by an applied Lamarckianism. The Soviet political leaders strongly supported him despite the lack of scientific evidence until the late 1950s. See David Joravsky, *The Lysenko Affair* (Chicago: University of Chicago Press, 1970).

29. See Michael Schwartz, *Sozialistische Eugenik: Eugenische Sozialtechnologien in Debatten und Politik der deutschen Sozialdemokratie 1890–1933* (Bonn: J.H.W. Dietz, 1995); Donald K. Pickens, *Eugenics and the Progressives* (Nashville: Vanderbilt University Press, 1968); Michael Freeden, "Eugenics and Progressive Thought: A Study in Political Affinity," *Historical Journal* 22 (1979): 645–71; Kühl, *The Nazi-Connection*.

30. See Roland Burkholz, *Reflexe der Darwinismus-Debatte in der Theorie Freuds* (Stuttgart: Frommann-Holzboog, 1995).

31. Franz Boas, *Changes in Bodily Form of Descendants of Immigrants* (New York: Columbia University Press, 1912); George W. Stocking, ed., *The Shaping of American Anthropology, 1883–1911: A Franz Boas Reader* (New York: Basic Books, 1974), p. 213; see also Christian Geulen, "Blonde bevorzugt: Virchow und Boas—eine Fallstudie über 'Rasse' und 'Kultur' im ideologischen Feld der Ethnizität um 1900," *Archiv für Sozialgeschichte* 40 (2000): 147–70.

32. Gustav Spiller, *Inter-Racial Problems. Papers from the First Universal Races Congress Held in London 1911* (Boston: World's Peace Foundation, 1911), repr. (New York: Citadel Press, 1970); Gabriele Schirbel, *Strukturen des Internationalismus. The First Universal Races Congress London 1911: Der Weg zur Gemeinschaft der Völker* (Münster: Lit, 1991); see also Akira Iriye, *Cultural Internationalism and World Order* (Baltimore: Johns Hopkins University Press, 1997).

33. See Schirbel, *Strukturen*, pp. 954–63.

34. Spiller, *Inter-Racial Problems*, pp. 1–12.

35. See especially Kühl, *The Nazi-Connection*; Roth, "Schöner Neuer Mensch."

36. On the early uses of the term racial struggle to describe what today would be labeled social conflicts see Ludwig Gumplowicz, *Der Rassenkampf: Soziologische Untersuchungen* [1883] (Ausgewählte Werke vol. 3) (Innsbruck: Wagner. University, Buchhandlung, 1909). This is the first German book that had the term "sociology" in its title. Most widely used was the concept of racial struggle or racial war in the colonial context. See, for example, Jürgen Zimmerer and Joachim Zeller, eds., *Völkermord in Deutsch-Südwestafrika: Der Kolonialkrieg in Namibia und seine Folgen* (Berlin: Links, 2003).

37. Oswald Spengler, *Der Untergang des Abendlandes* (München: Beck, 1922–1923). In English: Oswald Spengler, *The Decline of the West*, trans. Charles Francis Atkinson (New York: A.A. Knopf, 1926); Madison Grant, *The Passing of the Great Race* (New York: C. Scribner's Sons, 1916).

38. See, for example, Pascal Grosse, *Kolonialismus, Eugenik und bürgerliche Gesellschaft in Deutschland 1850–1918* (Frankfurt: Campus Verlag, 2000).

39. See especially Kühl, *Nazi-Connection*; Adams, ed., *Wellborn Science*; Peter Weingart, Jürgen Kroll, and Kurt Bayertz, eds., *Rasse, Blut und Gene: Geschichte*

der Eugenik und Rassenhygiene in Deutschland (Frankfurt am Main: Suhrkamp, 1988).

40. The fact that eugenics was never conceived just as a scientific discipline, but was always connected with much broader hopes for social control and a global politics of racial improvement is especially worked out in Paul, *Politics of Heredity*.
41. See Glick, ed., *Comparative Reception*.
42. See Kaupen-Haas, *Wissenschaftlicher Rassismus*.
43. Roth, "Schöner Neuer Mensch."
44. In referring to Arendt as well as Foucault, this dissolution of the difference between positive law and natural lawfulness as an element not just of totalitarian regimes but of the modern notion of sovereignty in general has forcefully been pointed out by Giorgio Agamben, *Homo Sacer: Sovereign Power and Bare Life* (Stanford: Stanford University Press, 1998).

CHAPTER 4

World Orders in World Histories before and after World War I

Matthias Middell

The Internationalization of Historiography Around the Time of the Great War

Historical arguments have always played an important role in debates on world order. In this context the question of continuities and discontinuities has often been a contested issue, and so has the necessity to choose between threatening and promising historical trajectories as well as between obsolete and promising elements of the past. Since interpretations of the past figured so prominently in debates about world order, theoretical and methodological debates on history were often related to the political discourses on possible world orders. Especially transitory situations in world politics inspired historians to try to answer the challenge of new perspectives on the future by reconsidering their conceptions of the past. Particularly global moments, when decisions about new world orders are on stage, are also moments of increasing theoretical activity for historians to look for new approaches and to find new ways to rewrite the history of what they think the world is. The ongoing ideological contestations over new world orders typically resorted to narratives of the past in order to legitimatize their proposals for the future. In many cases historians were invited to produce or mobilize existing narratives for these purposes.

It has been argued that the Great War of 1914–1918 was a sort of watershed in debates on world orders, and some observers have emphasized a specific "Wilsonian moment" as a clear caesura that was echoed by intellectuals in Europe as well as in the South who interpreted the message of the American president as a promise that the principle of national self-determination would also be applied to their countries.[1] Akira Iriye, when discussing the reasons for the rejection of the Parisian treaties by the U.S. Senate, underlines the importance of Wilson's program that for the first time outlined a new principle for the international system:

> One should realize that it was not so much idealism as internationalism that informed Wilsonian thought, an internationalism solidly grounded on shared interests of nations and on aspirations of men and women everywhere transcending national boundaries. These are fundamentally cultural forces, so that in a way Wilsonianism was an agenda for putting culture at the centre of international relations. Although naked power was to be a crucial determinant of international affairs in the decade after Wilson, who at the end of the twentieth century can deny that culture has reasserted itself time and again?

Iriye links this new element of the world order to the "emergence of the United States as an international player" at the beginning of the twentieth century and sees Wilsonianism as "a potent definer of contemporary history."[2]

A second element that marks the end of the war as a global moment is of course the Russian Revolution. Lenin expressed the same interest in peace, disarmament, and putting an end to secret diplomacy as the basis for a new order of the international arena when he addressed his first message to the global community as the successful leader of the Bolshevik uprising in St. Petersburg. However, at the same time, he was convinced that only a worldwide revolution could bring success to the first attempt of forming a society that would no longer be dominated by private property, and would instead be based upon the more direct-democratic organized Soviets. The failure of left wing groups to establish similar regimes during the postwar revolutionary crisis in Central and West Europe, and the civil war supported by foreign intervention resulted in a regime of "war communism" and the concept of the "establishment of socialism in one country alone." Both developments strengthened the state against the Soviets and other concepts of societal self-administration. For the future world order it became important that the Communist International, as a disciplined world communist party, shift its emphasis further away from proletarian internationalism.[3] It increasingly concentrated on gaining support from Asian and Latin American countries by referring to discourses of decolonization.

Another element that characterized the new world order was the increasing participation of intellectuals from India, China, Vietnam, and Central Africa in the international debates during the postwar crisis.[4] All of them were quickly confronted with disillusionment about the hopes expressed in 1917 and 1918 in the League of Nations when it became clear that the American Senate would not ratify the covenant of the new organization, while revolutionary Russia, temporarily became a sort of pariah or reluctant player in the international diplomatic activities during the 1920s. Its decision to establish a state monopoly for transborder trade amounted to a withdrawal from one arena of the globalized economy, which after World War II fed into the establishment of a second arena with countries coming under Soviet control and the founding of the People's Republic of China. American isolationism in some political fields during the 1920s was accompanied by a different form of withdrawal from transcontinental trade: during the war the United States and some parts of South America had become largely independent from the importation of manufactured European goods. The resulting economic boom across large parts of the American continent thus resulted in a decline of trade with the Old World, while at the same time country quotas for immigration were introduced that rapidly stemmed the migration flows from Europe to North America and which shrunk from 11.6 million people in 1901–1910 to 1.9 million in the 1930s.[5]

However, some historians emphasize those patterns of longue durée in the "mechanics of internationalism" that survived the cataclysm of 1914.[6] From the perspective of economic history, authors like Niels Petersson have argued that international economic affairs did not decline after the war, but rather the character of globalization had been changing since the 1880s, when the British paradigm based on free trade (mainly within its huge empire) was increasingly challenged by the German model that was more characterized by great companies and state intervention.[7] Thus, globalization and nationalization were not in complete contradiction but became more and more intertwined. From this point of view the developments of the 1920s look more like continuations of trends that had emerged before the war.

Similar arguments can be found in recent literature about academic internationalism. The first boom of academic exchanges such as visiting scholar or student programs, or the rise of international conferences occurred during the last quarter of the nineteenth century. This tendency was not only inspired by cosmopolitan ideas,[8] but also by a sense of competition among the nations to "conquer empty academic territories" overseas by presenting leading scholars to the international community. What changed after 1914 was firstly, the exclusion of German scholars and their institutions as a consequence of their ardent propaganda for the war goals of the German Empire. Second, there was a higher participation of Japanese people and representatives from Latin America in international circles, most notably in the negotiations on cultural and academic affairs in the various commissions of the League of Nations.[9] Also the contacts with Russian scholars changed: while some of them were emigrating from the revolutionary state, others remained citizens of the Soviet Union when lecturing in the West.[10] Yet the number of overseas Russian students, extremely high before 1914 due to enrolment restrictions at Russian universities, remained high due to the political situation in Russia.[11]

When professional historiography developed and experienced its institutionalization as an academic discipline, it was shaped by the nation-state, which had a profound impact on the spatial dimensions of historical thinking.[12] Yet, at the same time one should not overlook the fact that the older traditions of universal history provided the frameworks in which the new national histories were being situated. It is by no means accidental that serious doubts about world history as a genre first arose in Germany, where the new field experienced a boom of diverse approaches and a rising tide of methodological debates.[13] The professionalization of historiography had occurred in the German-language territories a few years earlier than in France,[14] the United States,[15] England,[16] and Eastern Central Europe,[17] that made German methodologies highly influential in other countries.[18] As a role model for historians outside of Germany, different facets of German universal histories deemed useful were merged with other traditions,[19] but this process resulted in the recognition and simultaneous questioning[20] of German hegemony in international historiography.[21] Even though their leading status was declining before 1914, German historians were arguing about the methodological controversies of their historiography as if they were doing so in the name of international historiography.

In any case, influential academics such as Karl Lamprecht, who became rector of Leipzig University in 1910–1911, built international contacts for political and intellectual purposes.[22] Germany became one of the motors in an internationalizing academic environment in which scholars increasingly used foreign contacts as support in methodological quarrels. In some cases scholars even formed international quotation cartels in order to enhance their own prominence.[23] Apart from academic motivations the geopolitical context also played a decisive role in the changing international roles and concepts prevailing among German historians. Germany's economic boom after 1875, as well as sustained levels of demographic growth, nourished the idea that there was a legitimate claim to a "place in the sun" among the established colonial powers. This ambition inspired a debate among German scholars about the appropriate ways to stake colonial claims,[24] in which the more belligerent groups called for increasing armaments while others advocated the primacy of cultural diplomacy.[25]

The whole program of academic exchange that had been started by the Prussian administration of research and university matters was subordinated to the concept of "Weltpolitik." Friedrich Althoff, the head of this administration, regarded the exchange of scholars and students as "a first step towards the coming rapprochement of people. . . . All together with trade and diplomacy the intellectual exchange between peoples and nations should pave the way for a world culture."[26] While mobilizing private sponsorship and money from the German Empire's budget, he started to develop a truly international system of interlibrary loans. Furthermore, he attempted to build an International Association of Academies of Sciences that was supposed to operate in different countries and world regions. A bimonthly journal commenting on this process of internationalization received funding from a foundation created by Althoff. The foundation also provided other players with a nationwide forum to discuss matters concerning academic exchange. Statistics proved that Germany and France were the countries hosting the most international students, followed by the United States,[27] and leading German universities for the first time created offices in order to meet the foreign students' specific needs.[28] After Althoff's retirement in 1907, the Prussian ministry was less active in this field[29] and the initiative shifted more to single regional centres, where entrepreneurial professors like Wilhelm Ostwald[30] and Karl Lamprecht in Leipzig or Wilhelm Harms in Kiel[31] developed new strategies to strengthen exchange activities. The latter was criticized by some colleagues from Berlin who argued that such academic exchanges would be far more advantageous to the less prestigious American institutions than to the internationally renowned German universities.[32]

World Histories and World Orders

World histories can be used as indicators for changing ideas about world order. In the following, I will mainly concentrate on the short period from the 1890s to the 1920s and predominantly refer to German examples that were widely recognized in the international community during this time period. Of course, world history was not invented at the end of the nineteenth century, but drew on earlier antecedents and conceptual debates. For example, during the Enlightenment period historians started to think about aspects of interculturality in a world that—in European eyes—began to be split among the imaginary civilized/uncivilized divide. Abbé Raynal's *Histoire des Deux Indes* stands out among these attempts because it applies the same categories to Europe and the non-Western world.[33] In the late eighteenth century, the *Amis des Noirs* called for equality as demanded in the French Revolution for the slaves in the colonies. This implied taking Africa with an eye on abolishing slavery. This also opened to take Africa, the continent where plantation workers originated, seriously as a historical realm.[34]

By contrast, advocates of folkloristic national memories such as Johann Gottfried Herder pleaded more for notions of historical difference.[35] Hegel, who in his treatise on universal history, showed that he was not impressed by this concept of different historical realms, declared large parts of the world to be the home of people without histories. For Hegel, European expansion had given the impulse for development to the extra-European world that had either come to a standstill before or had not even been initiated in other parts of the world. Hegel's enthusiasm for the historical power of the Revolution and his teleological concept of historical progress blinded him to information that was available at his own time and contradicted a Europe-centered understanding of history. For example, neither the revolution in Haiti nor the Latin American independence movements figure prominently in his writings about world history.[36]

The narratives of universal history that dominated the period from the Enlightenment to the resurgence of world historical writings during the last quarter of the nineteenth century focused exclusively on the power of European expansion that was partly admired because of its spatial efficiency and partly criticized because of its victims. Christian missionary zeal, arguing for the necessity of colonial expansion and capitalist euphoria about the extension of markets and sources of raw material, both fell into the same categories. These Euro-centric types of universal history shared the notion that development was tantamount to the diffusion of modern technologies from the North Western European center to the peripheral zones of the world system.[37] Those who chose to participate in the "progress" characteristic of so-called modernity were to side with inevitable Westernization or were doomed to perish. Modernity in this context necessitates the removal of the traditional, seen as the locally or regionally rooted obstacle of the swift and uniform expansion of "Western" practices,[38] and gave Europeans the idea to fulfill a "civilizing mission."[39]

Euro-centrism remained and was, paradoxically, even strengthened by the critiques of capitalism formulated by Karl Marx and others around the middle of the nineteenth century.[40] From the perspective of the alleged metropolitan center, all that could be discerned was the unbelievable growth in the power of the British Empire and its French junior partner. Both powers not only appeared to draw considerable resources from their overseas possessions but also seemed to be technologically capable of shaping the entire world according to their own ideas and needs. Traveling times were shortened proportionally to the importance of the region to the center, and informational development of the world by telegraph and sea cable followed the logic of the leading colonial powers. The English pound was the undisputed leading currency of international exchange processes.[41]

During the internationalization of the academic world, around the turn of the nineteenth century, new conceptions of world history were increasingly being debated. For example, during a lecture delivered at Columbia University in 1904, Karl Lamprecht argued that a new period in world history was only just beginning—a period which would give much more importance to international exchange than to warfare. Lamprecht concluded that in the future a nation's capacity to learn from other cultures, to incorporate foreign knowledge, would be far more important than military might. This new constellation, Lamprecht predicted, would not necessarily be to the advantage of the most advanced societies.[42] In fact, Lamprecht was referring to a world that was beginning to change at breakneck speed: in 1898, Germany was participating in the so-called "opening of China,"[43] which was followed by the Russo-Japanese war of 1904–1905.[44] Due to these events and the continued colonial expansion, the conception of space and the notion of the interdependence of a European and an extra-European world changed: "For the first time, the feeling of closure and unity of the planetary context emerged."[45] For those who were ready to face the challenge of a world historiography under such circumstances it was necessary to confront extremely local research interests with the conviction that "generality/universality is the work field of the educated."[46]

An important landmark in the publication of world histories in Germany was Hans E. Helmolt's nine-volume *World History* that appeared starting from 1899. In this work Helmolt argued that the tendencies of internationalization would give new impetus for the return of historiography to the history of mankind. For example, in his introduction he stated that "under this aspect the Universal Postal Union, the Bern Agreement on the Protection of Intellectual Property, the Geneva

Convention and the international measurement of the globe deserve special attention. The world is small."[47] In his review of the *World History* Walter Bruchmüller saw a new era dawning and argued that new forms of historiographical thinking would need to be developed: "There has not been any world history so far. And this new world history is indeed not *a new one* but *the very first* world history!" With translations into English (London, 1901 ff) and into Russian (St. Petersburg, 1902 ff), the reach of this entirely new approach was not restricted to the German language.[48]

Born in Dresden in 1865, Hans Ferdinand Helmolt had maintained close contact with Lamprecht. From 1894–1919, he edited the *Quarterly for World History*[49] that helped him in the preparation of the ambitious *World History* commissioned by Meyer's Encyclopedic Empire. Helmolt admitted in his introduction that he took ethnological research as the starting point for his *World History* since it seemed to him the only possible approach for a comprehensive inclusion of all peoples and regions of the earth. The introduction states that "by consciously deviating from all previous works of this kind hitherto written, a 'History of All Mankind on Earth' was to appear, for which the only choice was the classification according to ethno-geographical criteria."[50]

Any Euro-centrism was to be avoided in this way: "The error is widespread to deem the part of the world one covers by one's own horizon to be the whole (world). Good old Cato saw the fulfillment of history in being Roman, and the Chinese call their Empire the Empire of the Middle. The German chronicler of the thirteenth century did not report anything about the Turks, and even as late as the seventeenth century, hardly any educated Western European would recognize Russia as an equal member." For this reason, Helmolt continues, all previous universal histories related "to real world history like the biography of a man to the history of his time."[51] According to him, excluding any peoples from this history of mankind was out of the question, "for there were neither peoples without a history of their own, nor any others that would not have had any influence on others, and even for Africa, which was generally described as having very little influence on others, no evidence exists of such isolation."[52] The program of this ecumenical world history referred—contrary to Hegel—to the tradition of the Enlightenment of the eighteenth century: "[T]he idea that some human tribes were more suited for full development than others would have gone against an Alexander von Humboldt's feelings."[53]

Helmolt was well aware of the fact that this meant a breach with previously held opinions: "The cultured European indulges in talking about the Negroes as bastards of humankind." And he admitted that the existing asymmetries of power served to promote such hubris: "Yet, it has something intoxicating to it that at present almost the whole earth is being controlled by the smallest continent and that . . . the smallest island empire is holding the most extensive share of power." In a similar way, the superiority of the Teutons, the French and the Prussians as well as of Slavism had been described by various authors as the culmination of cultural development. Against such notions Helmolt warned that "world historiography should not be based on the error of taking the momentary for the perpetual and the particular for the general."[54] But Helmolt was equally critical of the countertype, namely unifying world histories that were typically being preached by committed internationalists who themselves could not reach agreement over whether Russian or English should become the new common language. Helmolt did not see any empirical evidence for the notion of a homogenizing world and opined that if "any contrasts disappeared, everything would have to wither away. At the moment, reality mocked the attempt to favour all peoples with a universal equilibration."[55] Thus for Helmolt, neither a Western-centered world history nor the "return to primeval unity" could really be the frameworks for adequately presenting the world's increasing entanglements. Only the awareness of diversity, mutual influences, and interactions between the cultures, based on the most comprehensive depiction of the "Werdegang aller Völker," (development of all peoples) seemed possible.[56]

In his work Helmolt referred to the Enlightened tradition of the Humboldt brothers to support his view that historiography was, in the face of the contingency of historical events, an empirical science and could not to be mistaken for philosophy: "It is not the business of a historian to give a philosophy of history for, as Thomas Hobbes had found out, rationally concluding philosophy has nothing to do with history, which is based on experience."[57] Therefore the road from world history did not lead from the elaboration/conception of a philosophy of history,[58] but only from the collection of the knowledge available and its presentation as free as possible from prejudice. However, Helmolt also wanted to counter the danger of an empiricism based solely on the collection of facts. He polemicized against the pseudo-objectivism of the Historicist school, which in his eyes produced myths of origin. Helmolt did not only fling down the gauntlet to traditional historiography in the introductory passages but the very composition of his work was meant to challenge other schools of thought. The decision to begin the presentation with the early history of America made the intended breach with Hegel's teleological approach of an extension of European culture all over the world, quite obvious. He emphasized that "applying one standard of value to all cultural development should be rejected as arbitrary and . . . methodologically questionable." And he concluded that "not an uncertain theory of the origin of humankind, but practice is our guideline."[59]

This unusual starting point departed from any idea of a regular course of world history: "If we start with America and end up with Europe, we do not wish to say that the original source of all historical development will have to be sought in America and to be followed up from there towards the West (previously the 'East')."[60] Neither an assumption about the oldest culture nor a prophecy of a rising world power had been responsible for this choice but only "practical aspects," that Helmolt saw in the early interaction across oceans, which he chose as the central motives of history in his presentation. In his work the description of the historical course of events on individual continents is regularly superseded by the description of the oceans as the elements linking the continents through trade, travel, and migration.

Not unlike some current works on global history, Helmolt chose a decidedly presentist approach that took descriptions of the actual effects of globalization as points of departure. A century ago, Helmolt's endeavor was criticized as an aberration from the well-known tracks of historiography, because the arrangement of the historical material was cribbed from another science, as a critic disapprovingly remarked in the *Historische Zeitschrift* of 1911.[61] Thus, Helmolt's *World History* was not representative of the academic guild of historians. It was not so much the fruit of a development within the discipline, but rather an attempt initiated by the commercial interest of a far-sighted publisher to explain the complexities of globalization in new ways. From this perspective the discovery of the global context of history appeared to be more important than the normative ideas of historicism. The exceptional attention given to intercultural phenomena, especially encounters between the European and the non-European worlds, was seen from the tradition of the late Enlightenment. Helmolt skillfully integrated the then most advanced trends within geography, ethnography, and the nascent-area studies. Even though Helmolt's terminology was influenced by Darwinian and progressivist notions, he succeeded in devising a *bona fide* comprehensive history of humankind that no longer resorted to the discourse of peoples without history.[62]

However, the implementation of Helmolt's program confronted numerous difficulties. At first it was an insurmountable impasse that, contrary to the wishes of the editor, the *World History* turned out to be just a sequence of monographs on various peoples ("Völkerkreise"). The theoretically envisaged interactions between the "Völkerkreise," which according to Helmolt's idea could have provided the only legitimate context of a scientifically founded world history had, by then, been only poorly researched. For this reason, Helmolt defensively pointed to a geographically-conditioned unity resulting from maritime streams of traffic. Helmolt's *World History* was by no means an isolated example, but with its understanding that the extra-European world needed to be allotted a new role and with its orientation toward a history of relationships, mutual influences, and inspirations, it became part of a broader movement.[63] One of the first historians to take up that principle was the universal historian Kurt Breysig,[64] who extended it to the problem of migration. Breysig argued that the great cultural achievements in world history should be attributed to migrating rather than to autochthonous peoples and concluded that world historical narratives needed to be organized around the diversity of influences. Such an argument went squarely against the assumption that the history of a people was tied to its home soil and thus had to be treated independently in narratives of the past.[65]

An important step toward new understandings of world history was eventually taken by Karl Lamprecht. During a lecture series at Columbia University he summed up his *Deutsche Geschichte* (*German History*) and pointed out that this 12-volume work was just dealing with a special national case that could be integrated into the intended synopsis of universal history. He argued that world historical analysis should not be structured around isolated national developments but what mattered was the observation of increasing contacts, of interactions among the individual societies.[66] In his New York lecture, Lamprecht stayed within the limits of theory. He knew that, on the one hand, classical national history could basically be overcome by means of his formulated approach,[67] but on the other hand, he was well aware of the enormous problems that had to be tackled empirically, so that he spoke of a field into which the historian went "only timidly." He saw a promising development in this approach that tried to overcome isolated national history by providing comparative perspectives: "how openly the gold bars of grandiose scientific discovery are lying in the street for him who wants to find them!"[68]

Lamprecht's historical analysis was tightly interwoven with a diagnosis of the present that can be seen, for example, in his contribution to the publisher Ullstein's *World History* about the colonial expansion of Europe. Lamprecht concluded his section with the prediction that the non-European world would very soon take up the European lead. He saw collective learning processes in the United States, Japan, China, and other countries proceeding much faster since people in these societies did not concentrate on the preservation of military power.[69] Based on this hypothesis he advised the German government to pursue foreign cultural policy rather than naval armament.[70]

The Great War and its Impact on
World Historical Writings in Germany

After World War I, German scholars and their academic institutions were largely excluded from international academic cooperation due to their involvement in the German war propaganda.[71] It would be tempting to conclude that the war separated an international community that before the war had nourished world histories based on transfer processes. There is some evidence for such a conclusion that would underline the character of the Great War as a caesura in international conceptions of world orders. In the immediate aftermath of the war a flood of publications dealt with the question of responsibility for the atrocities between 1914–1918. German intellectuals tended to refuse the Versailles definition, and many historians portrayed their French colleagues as much more nationalist than they had been during the war. Even liberal historians like Walter Goetz, the successor to Lamprecht's chair in 1915, published ardent condemnations of French academics.[72]

But astonishingly enough, only after a very short period, during which nationalist discourses superseded transregional approaches, debates on world history regained international attention. After the Great War, doubts about the European civilizing mission became more pronounced, and the cultural pessimism that permeated Oswald Spengler's *Decline of the Occident* could now also be frequently found in other world histories. But at the same time, H.G. Wells published his essay on world history that was meant as an alternative view, and was echoed in the middle of the 1920s, by Kurt Breysig,[73] who tried to discern patterns in world history from a socialist perspective of humankind. Herbert Schönebaum, a much less well-known German scholar, opened up a new wave of discussions on world history as early as 1922 with an article published in the *Archiv für Kulturgeschichte* (Archive of Cultural History). The piece is remarkable since Schönebaum invoked the cooperation between geographers and historians, which he deemed fruitful for the conceptualization of spatial organization of world histories. He emphasized that all empires were forced to adopt a strategy of copying cultural patterns from the dominated people in order to integrate them into a coherent system of rule, whereas smaller societies were able to produce original features of social organization and culture that were able to overcome dominance by apparently much stronger empires.[74]

Not all of these authors were newcomers to the field. Breysig, for example, had been in correspondence with Lamprecht since the beginning of the century,[75] and most of the French historians who were supportive of comparative social and cultural historiography had been disciples of Henri Berr or linked to his Center of Universal History before 1914.[76] Henri Pirenne embodied the arguably most well-known link between the period before the war and the aftermath of 1918.[77] While being involved in Lamprecht's attempt to compose a comparative history of modern states, Pirenne was then in full disagreement with him concerning his political attitude during the first months of the war. Pirenne's basic approach for the development of a research-based study of world history was a comparative one. The main contributions by himself in 1922, and by Marc Bloch in 1928, emphasized the enormous potential of historical comparisons for a better, that is, scientifically valid understanding of history and society. But what linked this kind of comparison to the debates before World War I was the recognition that different elements of comparison were connected with each other.[78] The notion that the future world would be mainly characterized by connections and cultural transfers was not anathema to postwar comparative historiographies. People like Bloch were very well aware of the insights that had been formulated by Lamprecht, 20 years before:

> The recently established principle of cosmopolitism is to some extent quite the opposite of the old liberal cosmopolitism, which was totally ideal, abstract and far from reality like the famous text by Schiller "Seid umschlungen Millionen.". . . Essential to this cosmopolitism were only nations, and therefore the period of this liberalism was to a large extent the age of movements of national unification. He was national to the degree that national egoism has gone over all. Just to the contrary, the new democratic cosmopolitism is practical and will solve a couple of problems raised by the European expansion.[79]

In Lamprecht's mind, the liberal principle of competition and concurrence represented an attractive model for non-Western societies due to its alleged combination with the democratic principle of worldwide solidarity and cultural exchange. Since he believed in the spread of liberalism and democracy, he argued that world historical writing could not be limited to the nation as the only unit of analysis. One can hear an echo of this statement in Marc Bloch's reflections upon the necessity of bringing mutual influences into the framework of comparison. This sensibility to transnational factors that characterized parts of historiography during the first half of the twentieth century was mainly rooted in the experience of the first wave of globalization and the practice of internationalism in academic affairs before and after the World War I.

After the war, many German world historians were convinced that the only underlying principle of modern history was an inevitable march toward democracy. This notion was combined with favourable views of revolution and emancipation from colonial rule in the case of North America. But this creed in democracy also paved the way toward a more nation-state oriented interpretation of modern history, and it contributed to the decline of world histories based on alternative spatial concepts such as oceans, nomadic territories, or immigration regions.[80] Furthermore, the aftermath of the war witnessed the formation of new methodological and ideological frontlines in the writing of world histories. Liberal perspectives underlining the importance of democratic institutions in modern world history were confronted with socialist approaches that tended to see world history as evidence of an uncertain future. This boom only regained its dynamic in the period after World War II. In any case, the center of conceptual innovation went from Germany to France and Belgium, where well-known authors of manifestos on comparative history such as Pirenne and Bloch created the Annales d'histoire économique et sociale.

The whole period between 1890 and 1930, during which decisive steps toward the professionalization of historiographies were taken, was also a period of internationalization and national competition. [81] One may conclude that the trajectories of world historical conceptions were partly determined by inner-academic transformations and partly by the changing problems in the development of globalization. This dual context placed world histories in the middle of changing visions of world order within academia and popular discourses. If we look back to problems raised and discussed by the authors mentioned in this chapter, it seems that their concern with interconnectedness and comparison, and with the historically changing patterns of spatial organization of societies, came from an experience not just with ongoing economic and cultural globalization, but also with the first boom of international academic organizations.

Notes

1. See the contribution by Erez Manela in this volume.
2. Akira Iriye, *The Globalizing of America: United States Foreign Relations, 1913–1945* (Cambridge: Cambridge University Press, 1993), p. 72. The link goes not only from the "Wilsonian Moment" forward to the present but also back to some "Jeffersonian origins" of Wilson's concept. See also Akira Iriye, *Cultural Internationalism and World Order* (Baltimore: Johns Hopkins University Press, 1997).
3. For tendencies within the international workers movement before World War I see Moira Donald, "Workers of the World Unite? Exploring the Enigma of the Second International," in Martin Geyer and Johannes Paulmann, eds., *The Mechanics of Internationalism: Culture, Society, and Politics from the 1840s to the First World War* (Oxford: Oxford University Press, 2001), pp. 177–204.

4. See for China, Africa, Turkey, Egypt, and Japan the contributions by Dominic Sachsenmaier, Andreas Eckert, Cemil Aydin, and Erez Manela to this volume.

5. James Foreman-Peck, *A History of the World Economy: International Economic Relations since 1850* (Brighton: Wheatsheaf, 1983), p. 194. See also Adam McKeown, "Global Migration, 1846–1940," *Journal of World History* 15, no. 2 (2004): 155–89.

6. Geyer and Paulmann, "Introduction," in Geyer and Paulmann, eds., *Mechanics*, pp. 1–26; F.S. Lyons, *Internationalism in Europe, 1815–1914* (Leiden: A.W. Sythoff, 1963).

7. Niels Petersson, "Das Kaiserreich in Prozessen ökonomischer Globalisierung," in Sebastian Conrad and Jürgen Osterhammel, eds., *Das Kaiserreich transnational. Deutschland in der Welt 1871–1914* (Göttingen: Vandenhoek & Ruprecht, 2004), pp. 49–67.

8. Christophe Charle, *La république des universitaires 1870–1940* (Paris: Seuil, 1994); Eckhardt Fuchs, "Nationale Wissenschaft und internationale scientific community," *Berliner Debatte Initial* 3 (1996): 66–70; Ralph Jessen and Jakob Vogel, eds., *Wissenschaft und Nation in der europäischen Geschichte* (Frankfurt and New York: Campus, 2002)

9. Akira Iriye, *Global Community. The Role of International Organizations in the Making of the Contemporary World* (Berkeley: University of California Press, 2002), chapter 3. On the creation of an international school of archaeology (Escuela Internacional de Arqueología y Etnografía Americanas) in Mexico just before the outbreak of the Mexican Revolution in 1911, as an example for the cultural transfers between Europe, the United States, and Latin America see Eckhardt Fuchs, "Institutionalisierung zwischen Politik und Wissenschaft: Die Internationale Schule für Amerikanische Archäologie und Ethnologie in Mexiko," in Matthias Middell, Gabrielle Lingelbach, and Frank Hadler, eds., *Historische Institute im internationalen Vergleich* (Leipzig: Akademische Verlagsanstalt, 2001), pp. 395–428. About the role of international circles of anthropologists in this event see R. Godoy, "Franz Boas and His Plans for an International School of American Archaeology and Ethnology in Mexico," *Journal of the History of the Behavorial Sciences* 13 (1977): 228–42.

10. To quote an example I would like to mention Friedrich Braun, a former professor of Petersburg's university, who became the chair for East European history at the University of Leipzig while also working for the Russian embassy in Berlin and holding contact with academic institutions in the Soviet Union for getting original literature even after 1933. See the chapter on East European history as part of world history approaches in Matthias Middell, *Weltgeschichtsschreibung im Zeitalter der Verfachlichung und Professionalisierung. Das Leipziger Institut für Kultur- und Universalgeschichte 1890–1990*, vol. 2 (Leipzig: Akademische Verlagsanstalt, 2005), pp. 576–601.

11. Karl Schlögel, *Die Mitte liegt ostwärts. Europa im Übergang* (München and Wien: Hanser, 2002); Karl Schlögel, ed., *Russische Emigration in Deutschland 1918 bis 1941: Leben im europäischen Bürgerkrieg* (Berlin: Akademie-Verlag, 1995).

12. Jerry H. Bentley, "From National History toward World History," in Matthias Middell, ed., *Vom Brasilienvertrag zur Globalgeschichte* (Leipzig: Leipziger Universitätsverlag, 2002), pp. 169–82.

13. Hartmut Bergenthum, "Weltgeschichten im Wilhelminischen Deutschland: Innovative Ansätze in der populären Geschichtsschreibung," *Comparativ* 12 (2002): 16–56.

14. Pim den Boer, *History as a Profession: The Study of History in France, 1818–1914* (Princeton: Princeton University Press, 1998).

15. Gabriele Lingelbach, *Klio macht Karriere. Die Institutionalisierung der Geschichtswissenschaft in Frankreich und den USA in der zweiten Hälfte des 19. Jahrhunderts* (Göttingen: Vandenhoeck & Ruprecht, 2003).

16. Marc Schalenberg, "Oxford und die deutsche Wissenschaft: Eine Wahlfremdheit des 19. Jahrhunderts," in Marc Schalenberg, ed., *Kulturtransfer im 19. Jahrhundert* (Berlin: Centre Marc Bloch, 1998), pp. 109–122; and Marc Schalenberg, *Humboldt auf Reisen? Die Rezeption des "deutschen Universitätsmodells" in den französischen und britischen Reformdiskursen (1810–1870)* (Basel: Schwabe & Co. AG Verlag, 2002).

17. See the contributions of Bianca Valota, "Institutionalisierungsverläufe der rumänischen Geschichtswissenschaft bis zum Zweiten Weltkrieg," pp. 149–72; Jan Havranek, "Institutionen der tschechischen Geschichtswissenschaft bis zum Zweiten Weltkrieg," pp. 173–84; Tibor Frank, "Ideologie und Strukturwandel. Aufgaben und Organisation der ungarischen Geschichtswissenschaft in der ersten Hälfte des 20. Jahrhunderts," pp. 185–98; Markus Krszoska, "Die institutionelle und personelle Verankerung der polnischen Deutschlandforschung der Zwischenkriegszeit und der unmittelbaren Nachkriegszeit," pp. 269–84; Frank Hadler, "Geschichtsinstitute an ostmitteleuropäischen Wissenschaftsakademien. Budapes, Prag und Warschau im Vergleich," pp. 285–310 in Middell, Lingelbach, and Hadler, eds. *Historische Institute.*

18. Georg G. Iggers, "The 'Methodenstreit' in International Perspective: The Reorientation of Historical Studies at the Turn from the Nineteenth to the Twentieth Century," *Storia della Storiografia* 6 (1984): 21–32; Lutz Raphael, "Historikerkontroversen im Spannungsfeld zwischen Berufshabitus, Fächerkonkurrenz und sozialen Deutungsmustern: Lamprecht-Streit und französischer Methodenstreit der Jahrhundertwende in vergleichender Perspektive," *Historische Zeitschrift* 251 (1990): 325–63

19. See Christophe Charle, "L'élite universitaire française et le système universitaire allemand," in Michel Espagne and Michael Werner, eds., *Transferts. Les relations interculturelles dans l'espace franco-allemand (XVIIIe-XIXe siècle)* (Paris: Éditions Recherche sur les Civilisations, 1988), pp. 327–58; Michel Espagne, *Le paradigme de l'étranger. Les chaires de littérature étrangère au XIXe siècle* (Paris: Editions du Cerf, 1993).

20. Charle, *La république des universitaires, 1870–1940.*

21. Carlos Aguirre Rojas, *Los Annales y la historiografía francesa: tradiciones críticas de Marc Bloch a Michel Foucault / Carlos Antonio Aguirre Rojas* (Mexico, D.F.: Ediciones Quinto Sol, 1996). See also Patrick Manning, *Navigating World*

History: Historians Create a Global Past (New York: Palgrave Macmillan, 2003). Paul Costello, *World Historians and their Goals: Twentieth-Century Answers to Modernism* (DeKalb: Northern Illinois University Press, 1993) remains at the level of the history of ideas and neglects the institutionalistic explanation.

22. For a detailed description of Lamprecht's program of inviting visiting scholars from France, Belgium, Japan, and China see Katharina Middell, "Das Institut für Kultur- und Universalgeschichte bei der Universität Leipzig und seine Beziehungen zu Frankreich bis zum Ausbruch des Ersten Weltkrieges," in Michel Espagne and Matthias Middell, eds., *Von der Elbe bis an die Seine, Kulturtransfer zwischen Sachsen und Frankreich im 18. und 19. Jahrhundert* (Leipzig: Leipziger Universitätsverlag, 1993), pp. 379–408; Roger Chickering, *Karl Lamprecht: A German Academic Life, 1856–1915* (New Jersey: Humanities Press, 1993), chapter 11.

23. Eckhardt Fuchs and Henry Thomas Buckle, Geschichtsschreibung und Positivismus in England und Deutschland (Leipzig: Leipziger Universitatsverlag, 1994); Luise Schorn-Schütte, "Karl Lamprecht und die internationale Geschichtsschreibung," *Archiv für Kulturgeschichte* 67 (1985): 417–64; Bryce Lyon and Henri Pirenne, *A Biographical and Intellectual Study* (Ghent: E. Story-Scientia, 1974).

24. Rüdiger vom Bruch, *Wissenschaft, Politik und öffentliche Meinung. Gelehrtenpolitik im Wilhelminischen Deutschland (1890–1914)* (Husum: Matthiesen, 1980).

25. Roger Chickering, *Imperial Germany and a World without War: The Peace Movement and German Society, 1892–1914* (Princeton: Princeton University Press, 1975); Jürgen Kloosterhuis, *"Friedliche Imperialisten." Deutsche Auslandsvereine und auswärtige Kulturpolitik 1906–1918* (Frankfurt am Main: Lang, 1994)

26. Marie Althoff, ed., *Aus Friedrich Althoffs Berliner Zeit. Erinnerungen für seine Freunde* (Jena: Diederichs, 1918), p. 52.

27. The figures were the following for Germany: 840 students coming from Russia, 338 from North and South-America, 184 from Asia, and another 78 from Turkey. See G.W. Namsyth, "Auswärtige Kulturpolitik und die deutschen Universitäten," *Akademische Rundschau* 1, no. 11 (1913): 660–69, for the numbers listed for all German universities in the winter term of 1912–1913.

28. Arthur Köhler, "Über akademische Auskunftsstellen," *Akademische Rundschau* 1, no. 7 (1913): 411–19.

29. For the new experience of German professors with internationalization, see Bernhard vom Brocke, "Der deutsch-amerikanische Professorenaustausch. Preußische Wissenschaftspolitik, internationale Wissenschaftsbeziehungen und die Anfänge einer deutschen auswärtigen Kulturpolitik vor dem Ersten Weltkrieg," *Zeitschrift für Kulturaustausch* 31 (1981): 128–82.

30. On his experience as a visiting professor see Wilhelm Ostwald, *Lebenslinien. Eine Selbstbiographie* (Berlin: Klasing & Co., g.m.b.h., 1927), p. 262.

31. On Harms, the founder of the Kiel-based Institute for World Economics see especially J. Jessen, "Das Lebenswerk von Bernhard Harms," *Schmollers Jahrbuch für Gesetzgebung, Verwaltung und Volkswirtschaft im Deutschen Reich* 64 (1940), pp. 1–12; A. Predöl, "Bernhard Harms," *Weltwirtschaftliches Archiv* 50, no. 2 (1939): 489–91; A. Predöl, "Harms, Bernhard," in E. von Beckerath, Carl Brinkmann, Erich Gutenberg, Gottfried Harberler, Horst Jecht, Walter Adolf Jöhr, eds., *Handwörterbuch der Staatswissenschaften* (Stuttgart: G. Fischer, 1956), pp. 63–64; A. Rottmann, "Die Entwicklung des Instituts für Weltwirtschaft von der Gründung bis zur Gegenwart," in Anton Zottmann, ed., *Institut für Weltwirtschaft an der Universität Kiel 1914–1964* (Kiel: Institut für Weltwirtschaft, 1964).

32. Eduard Meyer, *Vereinigte Staaten von Amerika. Ihre Geschichte, Kultur, Verfassung, Politik* (Frankfurt am Main: H. Keller, 1920), pp. 180–81. The judgment of the famous historian of ancient times, himself spending the academic year 1909–1910 at Harvard University, was also partly due to the disappointment about the American positions toward Germany during the war. On this see Wilhelm P. Adams, "Geschichte Nordamerikas in Berlin," in Reimar Hansen and Wolfgang Ribbe, eds., *Geschichtswissenschaft in Berlin im 19. und 20. Jahrhundert. Persönlichkeiten und Institutionen* (Berlin: De Gruyter, 1992), p. 615.

33. Bernd Lenz and Hans-Jürgen Lusebrink, eds., *Fremdheitserfahrung und Fremdheitsdarstellung in okzidentalen Kulturen. Theorieansätze, Medien/Textsorten, Diskursformen* (Passau: R. Rothe, 1999).

34. Hans-Jürgen Lusebrink, " 'Les chaines de l'esclavage'—Perceptions et formes de conceptualisation de l'esclavage des noirs, des Lumières à la Revolution Française," in Wolfgang Binder, ed., *Slavery in the Americas* (Würzburg: Königshausen & Neumann, 1992), pp. 205–23.

35. On Herder and his romantic concept of history see János Rathmann, *Historizität in der deutschen Aufklärung* (Frankfurt am Main: Peter Lang, 1993).

36. This interpretation is developed in Charles Bright and Michael Geyer, "Globalgeschichte und die Einheit der Welt im 20. Jahrhundert," *Comparativ* 4 (1994): 13–45; Charles Bright and Michael Geyer, "World History in a Global Age," *American Historical Review* 100 (October 1995): 1034–1060.

37. The World System approach developed by Immanuel Wallerstein and his colleagues has focused on this core-periphery scenario, challenged now by Andre Gunder Frank's attempt to reorient the World System research and by the Californian School in World History (Kenneth Pomeranz, R. Bin Wong and others) that gives much more attention to Asia.

38. Sebastian Conrad and Shalini Randeria, "Einleitung," in Sebastian Conrad and Shalini Randeria, eds., *Jenseits des Eurozentrismus. Postkoloniale Perspektiven in den Geschichts- und Kulturwissenschaften* (Frankfurt am Main and New York: Campus, 2002), pp. 9–49.

39. An important attempt to put the various forms of this figure of thought and practice under the comparative microscope is now Boris Barth and Jürgen

Osterhammel, eds., *Zivilisierungsmissionen. Imperiale Weltverbesserung seit dem 18. Jahrhundert* (Konstanz: UVK, 2005).

40. Karl Marx, *Das Kapital*, vols. 1–3 (Berlin: Dietz, 1961).

41. Niall Ferguson, *Empire: The Rise and Demise of the British World Order and the Lessons for Global Power* (New York: Basic Books, 2004); but for the problem of establishing such a currency see Martin H. Geyer, "One Language for the World," in Geyer and Paulmann, eds., *Mechanics*, pp. 55–92.

42. See especially the last part of Karl Lamprecht, *What Is History? Five lectures in the Modern Science of History*, trans. E.A. Andrews (New York: Macmillan Company, 1905).

43. Heinz Gollwitzer, *Geschichte des weltpolitischen Denkens, Bd. 2: Zeitalter des Imperialismus und der Weltkriege* (Göttingen: Vandenhoeck & Ruprecht, 1982); Michael Frohlich, *Imperialismus. Deutsche Kolonial- und Weltpolitik 1880–1914* (Munchen: Deutscher Taschenbuch Verlag, 1994). The consequences for German world history writing are discussed in Andreas Pigulla, *China in der deutschen Weltgeschichtsschreibung vom 18. bis zum 20. Jahrhundert* (Wiesbaden: Harrassowitz, 1996).

44. W.G. Beasly, *Japanese Imperialism, 1894–1945* (Oxford: Clarendon Press, 1987). On the effects of the war of 1905, see the contribution by Cemil Aydin to this volume.

45. Jürgen Osterhammel, "Raumerfassung und Universalgeschichte im 20. Jahrhundert," in Jürgen Osterhammel, Gangolf Hübinger, and Erich Pelzer, eds., *Universalgeschichte und Nationalgeschichten. Ernst Schulin zum 65. Geburtstag* (Freiburg: Rombach, 1994), pp. 51–72.

46. Hans F. Helmolt, "Gegenstand und Ziel einer Weltgeschichte," in Hans F. Helmolt, ed., *Weltgeschichte*, vol. 1 (Leipzig: Bibliographisches Institut, 1899), p. 4.

47. Ibid.

48. Walter Bruchmuller, "Eine neue Weltgeschichte," *Nord und Süd* 23 (1899): 277–85.

49. Armin Tille, "Vorwort zur zweiten Auflage," in Helmolt, ed., *Weltgeschichte*.

50. Herbert Helbig, "Helmolt, Hans Ferdinand," in *Neue Deutsche Biographie*, vol. 8 (Berlin: Duncker & Humblot, 1969), pp. 502–03.

51. Helmolt, p. V.

52. Ibid., p. 3.

53. Ibid.

54. Ibid., p. 5.

55. Ibid..

56. Ibid., p. 6.

57. Ibid., pp. 6–7.

58. Ibid., p. 7.

59. Ibid., p. 17.

60. Ibid., p. 6.

61. Karl Uhlirz, "Rezension zu Helmolts Weltgeschichte," vols. 6 and 9, *Historische Zeitschrift* 106 (1911): 610–17.

62. Christoph Marx, "Die 'Geschichtslosigkeit Afrikas' und die Geschichte der deutschen Afrikaforschung im späten 19. Jahrhundert," in Wolfgang Küttler,

Jörn Rüsen, and Ernst Schulin, eds., *Geschichtsdiskurs, Bd. 3: Die Epoche der Historisierung* (Frankfurt am Main, 1997), pp. 272–81.

63. The argument that today's trends in world history go more in the direction of a history of interconnectedness more so then in the old fashioned way of comparison, where mainly isolated cases were contrasted with one another and that this development goes back to the early twentieth century is developed in more length in Middell, *Weltgeschichtsschreibung im Zeitalter der Verfachlichung und Professionalisierung*, chapters 19, 23, and 28.

64. Hartmut Böhme, " 'Der Dämon des Zwiewegs.' Kurt Breysigs Kampf um die Universalhistorie," in Kurt Breysig, *Die Geschichte der Menschheit* (New York: originally published in 1955), pp. 5–41.

65. Kurt Breysig, "Formen der Weltgeschichtsschreibung," *Die Zukunft* 7 (1903): 399–409.

66. Karl Lamprecht, *Moderne Geschichtswissenschaft. Fünf Vorträge* (Freiburg and Breisgau: Heyfelder, 1905), p. 108.

67. Ibid., p. 114.

68. Ibid., p. 112; Matthias Middell, "Méthodes de l'historiographie culturelle: Karl Lamprecht," *Revue Germanique Internationale* 10 (1998): 93–116.

69. Karl Lamprecht, "Europäische Expansion in Vergangenheit und Gegenwart," in J. von Pflugk-Harttung, ed., *Ullsteins Weltgeschichte* vol. 6 (Berlin: Ullstein, 1908), pp. 598–625.

70. Kurt Duwell, *Deutschlands auswärtige Kulturpolitik 1918–1932. Grundlinien und Dokumente* (Cologne: Böhlau, 1976), pp. 255–57; Jürgen Kloosterhuis, *Friedliche Imperialisten*; Chickering, *Imperial Germany and a World without War*.

71. K. Böhme, ed., *Aufrufe und Reden deutscher Professoren im Ersten Weltkrieg* (Stuttgart: Reclam, 1975).

72. Walter Goetz, ed., *Deutschland und der Friede. Notwendigkeiten und Möglichkeiten deutscher Zukunft* (Leipzig and Berlin: Teubner, 1918); Walter Goetz, *Das Wesen der deutschen Kultur* (Darmstadt: O. Reichl, 1919); Walter Goetz, *Die deutsche Geschichtsschreibung des letzten Jahrhunderts und die Nation* (Dresden, 1919).

73. On Breysig see Böhme, "Der Dämon des Zwiewegs," pp. 5–41.

74. Herbert Schönebaum, "Skizze zur Weltgeschichte," *Archiv für Kulturgeschichte* 15 (1922): 1–20.

75. Kurt Breysig, "Formen der Weltgeschichtsschreibung," pp. 399–409.

76. Agnes Biard, Dominique Bourel, Eric Brian, eds., *Henri Berr et la culture du XXe siècle* (Paris: Albin Michel/Centre international de synthèse, 1997).

77. Peter Schöttler, "Henri Pirenne, l'Allemagne et la (re)naissance du comparatisme," manuscript presented at the Conference of the European Science Foundation Program "Writing National Histories in Europe," Cardiff, November 2003.

78. See my more detailed analysis of Marc Bloch's text on comparative historiography. Matthias Middell, "Kulturtransfer und Historische Komparatistik—Thesen zu ihrem Verhältnis," *Comparativ* 10, no. 1 (2000): 7–41

79. Karl Lamprecht, "Europäische Expansion," in Julius v. Pflugk-Harttung, ed., *Ullsteins Weltgeschichte*, p. 621.

80. Partly, Hans Freyer later on in the 1940s came back to these issues in his *Weltgeschichte Europas*, published only in 1948. See on that Jerry Z. Muller, *The Other God that Failed: Hans Freyer and the Deradicalization of German Conservatism* (Princeton: Princeton University Press, 1987), and my interpretation of Freyer's work in Middell, *Weltgeschichtsschreibung*, chapter 23.

81. Petersson, "Das Kaiserreich in Prozessen ökonomischer Globalisierung," in Conrad and Osterhammel, eds., *Das Kaiserreich transnational*, pp. 49–67.

PART TWO

World War I as a Global Moment: Implications for Conceptions of World Order

CHAPTER 5

Dawn of a New Era: The "Wilsonian Moment" in Colonial Contexts and the Transformation of World Order, 1917–1920

Erez Manela

Introduction

When Woodrow Wilson, the president of the United States, steamed into the harbor of Brest on the French Atlantic coast on Friday, December 13, 1918, the mayor of Brest, who met the president at the dock, hailed him as an apostle of liberty, come to relieve the peoples of Europe from their suffering.[1] The next morning, driving along the streets of Paris, Wilson was cheered by crowds of ecstatic Parisians: "Vive Wilson! Vive l'Amérique, vive la liberté!" The press in France and elsewhere sang his praises, and labor leaders hailed him as "the incarnation of the hope of the future."[2] Similar receptions met Wilson when he traveled to London and Rome in the next several weeks.[3] The French pacifist author and Nobel laureate, Romain Rolland, seemed to express these widespread sentiments when he hailed Wilson as a figure poised to lead humanity toward a better, more just world, and called on him "to establish the new Charter of enfranchisement and of union" that would bring together all peoples.[4]

Great wars are transformative events; they destroy not only lives and property, but also established world orders—norms, institutions, ideas, perceptions—in short, the old ways of thought and practice. The Great War of 1914–1918 was an event unprecedented in the sheer scale of its destruction. It extinguished millions of lives and caused untold devastation; it also threatened the collapse of all order and stability in international relations. In the wake of the war many around the world hoped, and expected, the postwar world to be entirely different from that which came before it. The aftermath of World War I was unusual in the intensity of such feelings, of such expectations, even compared to other cataclysmic conflicts. In 1919, anticipation for a new and better world ran much higher and wider than, say, in the period following the Napoleonic wars some hundred years earlier, or World War II a quarter century later. There were no messiahs on the horizon in the aftermaths of those wars, only hard-headed men of affairs working to fashion a semblance of order out of the chaos of war. In 1919 there was such a millennial figure, a prophet of a new world order; a man who, for a fleeting, illusory moment, came to symbolize to millions worldwide their own hopes and aspirations.

Moreover, Wilsonian rhetoric captured imaginations not only in America and Europe, but also of many in Asia and Africa. In the immediate wake of the war, it captivated both elites and the "masses," though to varying extents and with varying meanings. One such story was that of Nguyen Tat Thanh, a 28-year-old kitchen assistant from the French colony of Indochina, who in June 1919 set out to present a petition to the world leaders then assembled in Paris for the Peace Conference. The document, entitled "The Claims of the People of Annam," echoed the liberal internationalist rhetoric of the American president. The young man from Indochina, who signed the petition as Nguyen Ai Quoc, or Nguyen the Patriot, sought a personal audience with the American president to plead his people's case before him. According to some accounts, he even rented a formal morning suit in preparation for the occasion. The meeting, however, never materialized; Wilson most likely never even saw Nguyen's petition, and he certainly did not respond to it. Within less than a year this man, who would later become known to the world as Ho Chi Minh, adopted Bolshevism as his new creed, and the Bolshevik leader V.I. Lenin replaced Wilson as his inspiration on the road to self-determination for his people.[5]

Ho's experience in Paris was far from unique. As the peace conference convened in early 1919, representatives from around the world—Chinese and Koreans, Arabs and Jews, Armenians and Kurds, and many others—scrambled to stake their claims in the new world order. To these representatives of emerging national aspirations, Woodrow Wilson was a symbol and a savior, a towering figure in the world arena committed, as he had declared, to the principle of self-determination for all peoples, the weak as well as the strong. They adopted Wilsonian rhetoric to formulate and justify their demands and aspirations, and often expected to have the president's support in attaining them. Most, however, were soon met with bitter disappointment. By the spring of 1919 it was becoming clear that in the emerging settlement the principle of self-determination would not be immediately applied anywhere outside Europe. This realization brought widespread disillusionment with the Wilsonian promise and fueled a series of nationalist upheavals across the colonized world, upheavals that marked a watershed in the rise of anticolonial nationalism as an international phenomenon. This "Wilsonian moment" constituted an important stage in the evolution of international society from an imperial world order to a postcolonial one, as colonized and marginalized peoples began to demand, and eventually attain recognition as sovereign actors in international society.

Although prodigious and outstanding scholarship has been produced on the genesis and impact of Wilsonian ideals and on the role of the United States and its president at the Paris Peace Conference, such studies have most often focused on the American perspective, the Western Powers, and the European settlement.[6] To the extent that non-Western regions and peoples figure in narratives of 1919 at all, it is mostly as inert masses of territory and humanity ruled or partitioned by the powers in a process usually understood as an unprecedented expansion of European imperialism. Although it is sometimes mentioned in passing that the new discourse of international power and legitimacy resonated widely across large sections of the colonized world, this phenomenon has received little sustained attention from scholars of this period in international history.[7] A recent survey of the current state of the scholarship on Woodrow Wilson and his influence in the international arena concluded that understanding how "the call for self-determination fired the imaginations of countless nationalists in the colonial world . . . is the most fertile ground for further writing about Wilsonianism."[8] But it is more than that: it is also essential to understanding the rise, since 1919, of anticolonial nationalism as a global trend, and the emergence of the self-determining nation-state as the sole legitimate unit of international society.

Method and Arguments

This chapter sets out to uncover the nature and significance of the responses of colonized peoples to that Wilsonian moment, and in the process reintegrate the voices of non-Western peoples back into the narrative of this pivotal era in international history. It endeavors to do this by analyzing the impact of the Wilsonian imagery and rhetoric, and of the opportunities that appeared to open with Wilson's arrival in Europe, on the perceptions, presentations, expectations, and actions in the international arena of four groups—Chinese,

Koreans, Indians, and Egyptians. In 1919, each of these groups was a nation, and nation-state, in the making; for each of them the spring of that year was a watershed in the development of nationalist sentiments and movements, heralding the emergence of nationalism as the central imperative of political life. This moment, under different names, is now etched into the national historiography of each of these nations—the May Fourth movement in China; the launching of Gandhi's passive resistance in India, which culminated in the infamous massacre at Amritsar; the 1919 Revolution in Egypt, and the March First Movement in Korea.

In none of these cases, of course, were the international developments that unfolded at the Wilsonian moment the only factor that precipitated the watershed events of 1919. In each case there were myriad domestic forces—political, economic, social, and cultural—that converged at that moment of crisis and transformation. The impacts of wartime hardships were also important contributing factors in a number of the cases, but their influence was uneven: wartime economic dislocations, for example, were a significant factor in India and Egypt, but not in Korea. Despite these and other differences, however, it is surely notable that in all four cases discussed here, with their disparate domestic circumstances and wartime experiences, the upheavals erupted almost simultaneously in the spring of 1919, and were precipitated by crises intimately tied to expectations and disappointments related to the new world order that was expected to emerge after the armistice. Indeed, one of the central features of the Wilsonian moment was its simultaneity across space—people all over the world experienced it at the same time, if not in the same manner, with an intensity that was unprecedented in modern international history. Rather than treating each movement separately, this chapter seeks to illustrate the simultaneity of the widespread significance of the Wilsonian moment by integrating the stories of these four disparate groups—Chinese, Indians, Egyptians, and Koreans—into a single narrative within a relatively narrow timeframe.

The period in international history described here as the Wilsonian moment stretches roughly from the promulgation of the Fourteen Points in January 1918 to the conclusion of the Versailles Peace Treaty in June 1919. Why, and in what ways, was the moment Wilsonian? Certainly not because Woodrow Wilson single-handedly created, intended, or even imagined it, either in the arena of world politics or in the realm of ideas. Politically, the unprecedented turmoil of the Great War itself, the carnage it spread, and the challenge it presented to established notions of European imperial supremacy was indispensable in creating the requisite context for the events that surrounded the convening of the peace conference in Paris. And in terms of ideals, the U.S. president was hardly the first world leader to articulate the vision of an international order based on self-determination. The notion itself had a long history in the liberal tradition from which Wilson came, going back at least as far as the late eighteenth century, when Immanuel Kant published his celebrated essay, *Perpetual Peace.*[9] Even among the wartime leaders, Wilson was not the first to propose a peace based on self-determination; he was preceded, most prominently, by the leaders of the Russian Bolsheviks, including Lenin and Leo Trotsky, as well as by the British Prime Minister David Lloyd George.[10] But, this chapter shows, as the American president entered the fray with increasing gusto in the concluding phases of the war, he soon eclipsed all others in the imaginations of peoples across the world, not the least in the colonial world, as a quasi-Messianic figure who symbolized the promise of the coming postwar era.

The fact that the rise of Lenin and the Bolsheviks to power in Russia paralleled the emergence of Wilson and the United States into international preeminence has long tempted historians to conceptualize the moment of 1919 as a clash between these two antagonistic global forces. Perhaps One of the most influential and oft-cited expositions of this view was first presented in the early years of the cold war by Arno J. Mayer. But Mayer's original focus was on the specific struggle within the European Left between the Wilsonian and Leninist options, and even there he concluded that Wilson had won, as evidenced in the general failure of the revolution to spread beyond the borders of Russia. Mayer's work says nothing of the colonial world. Indeed, trying to expand the Wilson vs. Lenin interpretive framework to include the events there during this period risks anachronism, since it predates the importance of Communism to anticolonial and anti-imperial movements. As this chapter argues, from the perspective of colonial nationalists at the time, there could be no equivalence between Wilson and Lenin, at least until the spring of 1919. Wilson received far more prominent and favorable press coverage across these regions, and was depicted and imagined as the preeminent and most powerful world leader at the time, arriving in Europe as a savior. Concurrently, Lenin and the Bolsheviks were far less prominent and were often reviled in press coverage, and were commonly believed, at least until their consolidation of power at the very end of 1919, to be on the verge of annihilation. Only after it became clear that colonial peoples would be largely excluded from the application of Wilsonian principles did Lenin and the Russian Bolsheviks begin to emerge, as they did for Ho Chi Minh, as alternative sources of guidance and support in their struggle for self-determination.

Three related arguments are woven into the unearthing of this hitherto submerged aspect of the global aftermath of World War I. First, that the combination of rhetorical iconoclasm and political opportunity that characterized the Wilsonian moment played an important—though by no means exclusive—role in galvanizing major movements of anticolonial nationalist resistance in Asia and the Middle East in 1919. Second, that viewed from this perspective, the Paris Peace Conference, often interpreted as heralding an unprecedented expansion of European imperialism, in fact marked the beginning of the end of the European imperial project by fatally undermining its legitimacy at home and abroad—not least among the colonized peoples themselves, whose general acquiescence was a *sine qua non* for the stability of colonial regimes. Third, that the evolution of anticolonial nationalist sentiments among elites in the colonies was inseparable from the new world order that they perceived emerging around them in the immediate wake of the war; one that encouraged, indeed required, that groups who wished to rule themselves appeal to the doctrine of national self-determination and re-imagine themselves as nascent nation-states as keys to claiming legitimate places within the expanding and reconfiguring space of international society.

The Emergence of Self-Determination

The notion of a right to national self-determination was first introduced into the international debate over war aims by Russian revolutionaries in mid-1917. The term had long been present in internal debates among socialists, though it was controversial: Marx himself had shown only intermittent support for nationalist movements in Europe during his lifetime, depending on their perceived relationship to the interests of the proletariat. During the Great War, the Bolsheviks remained divided on the issue, with one camp viewing nationalism as a dangerous, irrational force in conflict with the goal of international proletarian solidarity. Lenin, however, felt that Bolshevik support for national self-determination, defined as a right of secession from imperial rule, was crucial in undermining the imperial regime in Russia and gaining the support of subject peoples for the revolution.[11] In March 1917, Lenin declared that when the Bolsheviks came to power in Russia their peace plan would include "the liberation of all colonies; the liberation of all dependent, oppressed, and non-sovereign peoples."[12] That spring the Provisional Government in Russia, under pressure from the Bolshevik-controlled Petrograd Soviet, became the first among the belligerent governments to officially call for a peace settlement based on a right of "self-determination of peoples."[13]

Soon after the Bolsheviks took control of the revolution in October, Trotsky, as the newly appointed commissar of foreign affairs, announced a peace plan that denounced as hypocritical the Allied claims that they were fighting to guarantee the freedom of small nations, such as Belgium and Serbia. He called on the imperial powers to face the full implications of their claim to be fighting for the rights of small nations in Europe, while at the same time oppressing other national groups within their own empires:

> Are they willing on their part to give the right of self-determination to the peoples of Ireland, Egypt, India, Madagascar, Indochina, et cetera . . . ? For it is clear that to demand self determination for the peoples that are comprised within the borders of enemy states and to refuse self determination to the peoples of their own state or of their own colonies would mean the defense of the most naked, the most cynical imperialism.

Such cynicism was nothing more than what Trotsky expected from the capitalist governments of the Allies, since their "class character," he thought, precluded them from working for a truly democratic peace. Their real attitude toward the principle of national self-determination could be "not less suspicious and hostile" than that of the Central Powers.[14]

The Bolsheviks' calls for a settlement based on national self-determination were aimed not so much at the subject peoples of Asia themselves as at the anti-imperialist left in Europe, especially in Britain, France, and Germany.[15] It was in this context—the battle for European opinion—that the British Prime Minister David Lloyd George, first incorporated the term into the war-aims rhetoric of the Western allies. President Wilson had already spoken repeatedly of the need for a postwar settlement based on "the consent of the governed"—a favorite phrase that he had borrowed from a tradition of American political discourses going back to the Declaration of Independence. Lloyd George, increasingly worried about the enthusiasm for the rhetoric of both Wilson and Lenin on the domestic left in Britain and other Allied countries, moved quickly to redefine British war aims in line with it.[16] Coming before the British Trades Union League on January 5, 1918, Lloyd George managed a rhetorical coup, merging the statements of Wilson and Lenin into one: the peace, he said, must be based "on the right of self-determination or the consent of the governed."[17] By assimilating the Bolshevik call for self-determination to Wilson's notion of the "consent of the governed," the Welsh wizard managed to obfuscate the wide gap between the radical anti-imperialist agenda of the former and the gradualist liberal reformism implied in the latter.

Wilson and Lenin, who came from very different political backgrounds and experiences, had in mind two significantly different things when they spoke of self-determination: Wilson, thinking mainly of the need to stabilize postwar Europe, envisioned a peace based on the republican principles of government by consent, while Lenin, whose most immediate concern was toppling the Russian imperial state and gaining the support of its subject peoples, explicitly defined national self-determination as a right of secession. Even the term used was not identical. The Bolsheviks invariably spoke of the right to "national" self-determination, a qualification reflecting the term's origin in Marxist theory as distinct from other forms of self-determination—individual, or proletarian. In its broader sense within the Bolshevik revolutionary strategy, it was a call for the overthrow of imperialist rule through an appeal to nationalism among subject peoples, though the final goal remained the institution of a global communist world order in which national distinctions would be subsumed. Wilson, on the other hand, seldom described the right to self-determination as specifically national. Instead, he equated it with the traditional Enlightenment-derived notions of popular sovereignty, of government by consent, and though in his speeches he did not explicitly limit its application to Europe, it is clear that he saw it as immediately relevant only to the territories of the defeated empires—German, Austrian-Hungarian, and Ottoman. Eventually, he imagined, it might apply in other colonial situations, but if so it would be through gradual processes of tutelage and reform such as he himself initiated in the U.S. colonial administration of the Philippines, and not through the revolutionary overthrow of colonial rule.[18]

Nonetheless, Wilson himself completed this conflation/assimilation in the following months, adopting the term self-determination as his own with growing fervor and emphasis. Despite popular conceptions to the contrary, the term itself was nowhere to be found in the Fourteen Points, though several of the points—the resurrection of Poland, the evacuation of Belgium, and the call for the "autonomous development" of the peoples of the Ottoman and Habsburg empires—implied at least a partial application of this principle.[19] Wilson first spoke explicitly of the right of self-determination the following month, when he came before Congress again to outline the U.S. peace plan. In the coming settlement, he said, "national aspirations must be respected; people may now be dominated and governed only by their own consent. 'Self-determination' is not a mere phrase. It is an imperative principle of action, which statesmen will henceforth ignore at their peril."[20] In his draft of the address—he typically composed his speeches himself—Wilson had placed the term self-determination within quotation marks, indicating that he realized that he was incorporating a novel term into his lexicon. Calls for a peace based on self-determination would thereafter recur regularly, alongside references to the "consent of the governed," in Wilson's wartime rhetorical arsenal. This incorporation was designed to co-opt Bolshevik rhetoric and thus neutralize its influence within the European left. It did not change the essence of Wilson's vision in his own mind, but it lent his pronouncements a more radical tone, amplifying their impact on the imaginations of colonial peoples worldwide.[21]

As noted above, neither Wilson and Lloyd George nor Lenin and Trotsky saw the subject peoples of Asia as the main audience for their declarations in support of self-determination, which were part of the wartime struggle for the hearts and minds of the peoples of Europe. Nevertheless, this rhetoric echoed widely far beyond the European audiences for which it was primarily intended.[22] By the time of the armistice, nationalists all across Asia had adopted the language of self-determination, adapted it to their own specific situations, and launched concerted campaigns to bring their claims for this novel right to the peace conference and the assembled world leaders, Wilson foremost among them. By late 1918, the notion that the postwar settlement would be based on "President Wilson's principle of self-determination" was a central tenet of political discourse across the colonial world. A contemporary Indian intellectual, noting the rapturous reception Wilson encountered in London in December 1918, wrote: "Imagination fails to picture the wild delirium of joy with which he would have been welcomed in Asiatic capitals. It would have been as though one of the great teachers of humanity, Christ or Buddha, had come back to his home."[23]

Dissemination and Perceptions

What explains the widespread dissemination of Wilsonian iconography by 1918? One factor is undoubtedly the relatively recent rapid expansion in the technologies of the telegraph and of mass print media in many sections of Asia and the Middle East. As early as 1905, India, for example, already had more than 1,300 newspapers in English and Indian languages, which were estimated to have reached two million subscribers, and in China, the political press first appeared in coastal cities in the 1890s, and burgeoned in the first decades of the twentieth century with the expansion of literacy.[24] The press in Egypt, too, had developed considerably by the time of the World War I, and though censorship did exist, it was largely directed against critiques of the government. In China, India, and Egypt vernacular dailies published news about international affairs, and elites also had access to periodicals published in European languages by foreign residents. Moreover, copies of European papers were often widely available to educated native readers.[25] Audiences in these regions were still a small minority of literate elites, but they were far wider than in the past and by 1918 they constituted a nationally aware, articulate public opinion interested in and informed about international developments.[26]

In some cases, these new venues were also the targets of direct American propaganda efforts aimed at spreading the Wilsonian message. These efforts, which reflected Wilson's strong belief in the importance of influencing "world opinion," were carried out by branches of George Creel's Committee for Public Information (CPI). Creel was fiercely loyal to the president and his ideals and saw the CPI as an opportunity to spread the Wilsonian gospel of progressivism and democracy on an unprecedented scale, both domestically and abroad. The goal of the CPI propaganda efforts abroad, Creel believed, was "to drive home the absolute justice of America's cause, the absolute self-lessness of America's aims."[27] He made ingenious use of recent advances in communication and media technologies, such as the wireless and the moving picture, in the efforts to advertise America's war aims and peace plans at home and abroad: "The printed word, the spoken word, the motion picture, the poster, the signboard—all these were used in our campaign," Creel boasted.[28] The CPI produced and distributed movies about the successes of the American war effort, as well as about the ideals and advantages of American society that were then carried "to every corner of the world."[29]

It is significant in examining the creation and the global scope of the Wilsonian moment that Wilson's public addresses and declarations—the Fourteen Points, the Four Points, the Fourth of July Address, among others—soon became the lynchpins of CPI propaganda, especially in its for-eign operations. Wilson's messages were disseminated by wireless and cable worldwide in order to "tell all the people on earth what President Wilson was saying about the war and what the aroused American people were doing to win it."[30] As Creel testified:

> Early in its history the committee recognized the importance of distribution throughout the world of the speeches and messages to Congress of President Wilson. The President of the United States was looked upon as the spokesman for the Allies. It was he who sounded the keynote of America's policy in the war. . . . [The CPI] therefore undertook the work of distributing these keynote speeches textually, at first to England, France, Italy, and Russia, then, in response to a demand, to the four quarters of the civilized globe.[31]

In China, as Hans Schmidt has shown, CPI agents distributed news summaries, posters and newsreels, both independently and through local press organizations, with Wilson's wartime speeches at the center of American propaganda. Already in mid-1917, more than a year before formal CPI oper-ations in China had begun, missionary volunteers translated Wilson's speeches into Chinese and distributed them free of charge to the vernacular press or published in pamphlet form. In the fall of 1918, at about the time of the armistice, the full texts of Wilson's wartime speeches were published in Chinese translation and the volume quickly became a bestseller and went through several printings.[32] Carl Crow, the CPI head in China, later wrote that he received thousands of letters from Chinese expressing "an air of confidence in the future, a faith in the idea that President Wilson's words would prevail and that China, as well as all other oppressed nations, would be liberated."[33] A bilingual edition of Wilson's speeches, with the original English text side-by-side with the Chinese translation, was also published. It was circulated for use in Chinese schools as a textbook for English instruction, and soon some Chinese students could recite the Fourteen Points by heart.[34] Crow also ordered 20,000 large photographs of Wilson to be distributed among students at missionary schools, as well as buttons and engravings carrying his image.[35]

It is hard to measure with accuracy the impact of CPI propaganda in China. It is clear, however, that at the time of the armistice in November, enthusiasm for the promise of a new world order, and for Wilson himself, ran high among Chinese officials and intellectuals. Many leading intellectuals of the time, who perceived China's relations with the outside world in the preceding decades as a series of humiliations, eagerly awaited the implementation of the Wilsonian vision for the postwar order based on respect for the equality and self-determination of nations. One leading scholar, convinced that Wilson stood poised to transform the nature of international affairs, welcomed the end of the age of inequality and the coming of a new era of openness,[36] and a second described the American president as the "number one good man in the world."[37] China should consider itself fortunate to participate in the peace conference, wrote longtime reform advocate Kang Youwei, where it would have the opportunity "of one thousand years" to "recover its lost sovereignty and enjoy equality and freedom."[38] Animated by the widespread faith that a "new era" was ready to dawn in international affairs and, no less importantly, by indications of concrete American support for their cause, the Chinese delegates to the peace conference, as well as politically aware Chinese at home and abroad, prepared to stake their claim for equality among nations.[39]

However, we should not overestimate the role of direct American propaganda in disseminating the Wilsonian message beyond Europe, as indicated by the fact that Wilson's fame also spread in regions where no such efforts were made. In Egypt, under effective British control since 1882, direct American propaganda efforts were negligible but the Wilsonian message nevertheless echoed widely, causing a stir "even in the remotest villages."[40] The recent spread of telegraph technology and the ubiquity of news services, led by Reuters, which were sympathetic to the Allied cause, meant that the CPI's efforts elsewhere in the world and especially its propaganda in Great Britain were widely reflected in the Egyptian press. The texts of Wilson's wartime speeches, including his Fourteen Points, were widely available to educated Egyptians.[41] By mid-1918, many Egyptian nationalists had come to expect that the emerging postwar order would reflect Wilson's wartime rhetoric. "The principles that were announced by Dr. Wilson," one Egyptian historian has written, "exerted a great influence on everyone without exception," and another explained that Wilson's principles had such "a quick and decisive influence on Egyptian public opinion" because they reflected "the feelings that filled the hearts of the educated class in Egypt."[42]

In Korea, which had been annexed into the Japanese Empire in 1910, interest in the doctrine of self-determination became rather common among the younger generation despite Japanese attempts at censorship—for example, banning the showing of a foreign film on the ground that included some pictures of President Wilson. News of the Fourteen Points and Wilson's subsequent declarations seeped in through contacts with exiled nationalists and with Westerners living in Korea, and interest in the doctrine of self-determination and its potential applicability to Korea became increasingly widespread.[43] The American consul-general in Seoul reported on this rise of interest in the novel Wilsonian discourse, especially as it pertained to colonized peoples: "There can be no doubt that the present general movement throughout the world looking towards the self-determination of peoples, and particularly of the subject races, has produced its effect on the thought of the people in this country."[44] In the summer of 1918, prompted by Wilson's July 4 address, two Korean nationalists then studying in Japan traveled to Shanghai to found the New Korea Youth Association and began to make their postwar plans.[45] If Wilson's principle of self-determination was to be the basis for the peace conference—and the Koreans had every reason to think that would be the case—then the Korean claim that the Japanese rule over their homeland was illegitimate would have a firm leg to stand on.[46]

Even India, deeply embedded within the British Empire, was not left untouched as the vernacular press reported extensively on Wilson's statements and his vision for a new era in world affairs.[47] In a wartime episode that raised howls of condemnation in parliament in London, a retired Indian judge and prominent campaigner for Indian home-rule wrote Wilson after his war speech to the Senate in April 1917 to express his hope that the president would "completely convert England to your ideals of world liberation." The people of India, he added, had faith in Wilson and saw him "an instrument of God in the reconstruction of the world."[48] The Indian nationalist leader Lala Lajpat Rai, in exile in the United States, wrote the president several months later to thank him for his Fourteen Points, which, he said, were bound to "thrill the millions of the world's 'subject races.' " Wilson, he wrote, had introduced "a new charter of world's freedom."[49] Others among the Indian nationalist elite shared the sense that the world was on the cusp of a new era.[50] If Wilson's principles are to be the basis for the conference, opined one editorial, then "England has no other go but to frame her policy of governing India in accordance with them."[51] Another exclaimed that the end of the war was "in one word, nothing but the freedom of nations, their right of self-determination."[52] A window of opportunity, it seemed, was opening, and India, like other emerging nations, had to stake its claim. "We should put forward our demands" declared another writer. "It will be a sin if India does not lay her ailments before Dr. Wilson."[53]

Even at the height of the "Wilsonian moment," there were dissenting voices among colonial intellectuals, who did not believe that Wilson and the United States would be of much help to colonial peoples in their struggle for self-determination. One was the Indian revolutionary M.N. Roy, who would later become a leading figure in the Comintern and a founder of Indian communism, and who spent much of the war in Mexico. Influenced by the hostility of Mexican revolutionaries to the United States, Roy doubted the sincerity of the president's commitment to his declared ideals, though he still published an open letter calling on Wilson to implement them.[54] In China, the Beijing University librarian and future cofounder of the Chinese Communist Party, Li Dazhao, had praised Wilson early on for his "deep love of world peace," but by the time of the armistice clearly discerned and criticized the gap between the radical social revolution advocated by the Bolsheviks and Wilson's rather vague notions of political—not social—revolution.[55] Still, in the early days of victory, even those few in the colonial world who thought Wilson's ideals insufficient or doubted his true commitment to them adopted his rhetoric as their most effective tool for bringing their claims before the Peace Conference. With the Russian Bolsheviks excluded from Paris and mired in civil war and the other major powers—Britain, France, Japan—clamoring for the retrenchment and even expansion of the imperial order, Wilson remained, until the spring of 1919, the only influential world figure who seemed committed to a settlement that would reject the extension of empire and promote self-determination as a principle of international order.

Mobilization

In December 1918, as the Peace Conference loomed ahead, the Indian National Congress convened in Delhi for its annual session. Among the most important resolutions adopted was one that called for the "application of the Principle of Self-Determination to India." The Congress demanded that, "[i]n view of the pronouncement of President Wilson, Mr. Lloyd George, and other British statesmen, that to ensure the future peace of the world, the principle of Self-Determination should be applied to all progressive nations," and that India be recognized by the powers as "one of the progressive nations to whom, the principle of self-determination should be applied." The Delhi Congress further urged that India be represented at the peace table by elected delegates, and nominated three men for the position: veteran nationalist leader B.G. Tilak, Mohandas Gandhi, recently returned from South Africa, and the Muslim leader Syed Hasan Imam.[56] Dozens of local "self-rule leagues" throughout India authored petitions to the Peace Conference asking that India be granted self-determination in accordance with Wilsonian principles.[57]

Gandhi would remain in India throughout the conference, but Tilak, the fiery Marathi journalist and scholar who was the leading figure in the Indian national movement at the time, had already arrived in London in October to launch his campaign for Indian home-rule in conjunction with the Peace Conference. Tilak's letters to his followers back in India suggest that the goal of internationalizing India's demand for self-determination as a means to force the hand of the British government was a central one throughout Tilak's stay in England. Although the Peace Conference in Paris would deal directly with the Indian question, he reasoned, more importantly it would lay down the principles for a new order, and therefore must be informed of India's demand for self-determination.[58] Throughout the month of January 1919 Tilak remained optimistic about the opportunities afforded to them by the world gathering in Paris: "I am sure the question of India will not go unnoticed in the present sitting of the Conference. It is for us to see that the decision is in our favour. Government may not like the idea of our appealing to the Peace Conference. But that is no reason why we should not do so."[59] As part of his campaign, he wrote to President Wilson that "the world's hope for peace and justice is centered in you as the author of the great principle of self-determination" and asked that this principle be applied to India.[60]

China's position, of course, was markedly different, since it was formally recognized as a sovereign state, even if in practice its sovereignty was thoroughly penetrated and circumscribed by a legacy of "unequal treaties" with the great powers. By declaring war on the Central Powers the Beijing regime managed to get a seat at the peace table, and, inspired by notions of a "new era" in international affairs, politically aware Chinese at home and abroad felt that the time was ripe to demand real equality for China in the international arena. This meant the abrogation of the "unequal treaties" with the powers and the restoration of full Chinese sovereignty over its territory, especially the German concession in Shandong Province, which Japan had captured during the war and was now claiming her right to keep. Chinese elites, including intellectuals, students, merchants, and other groups both in China and abroad, produced a stream of petitions and pamphlets calling for "the establishment of a new international order" based on "the exalted ideas inspiring the immortal message of President Wilson" and demanding the application of his principles of self-determination and of the equality of nations to China.[61] The construction of Woodrow Wilson not as a mere flesh-and-blood politician, but rather as an icon of the coming new era in international relations was common to many of the texts produced by Chinese nationalists at the time, and served as a recurring reference point in the effort to define China's rightful place in the international arena.[62]

The leaders of the Chinese delegation in Paris—and it was largely they, rather than the weak regime in Beijing, who spoke for China—were young and American-educated, and believed that with the United States on its side China would win her case at the conference.[63] The two most prominent Chinese peace delegates were V.K. Wellington Koo, who had a PhD from Columbia University, and Chengting Thomas Wang, a graduate of Yale College. Both were ardent Chinese nationalists who wanted to see China emerge from its state of weakness, disunity, and humiliation to take its place among the nations of the world. At the same time, they were internationalist and cosmopolitan, acculturated and accomplished in both the Chinese and the Western worlds, and they hoped that Wilson's new order would allow China to be accepted as a full member of international society. In a pamphlet they coauthored to lay out their views, they drew a parallel between Confucius and Wilson as sages of international thought: "Confucius saw, just as the illustrious author of the present League of Nations has seen, the danger to civilization and humanity involved in the continued existence of such a sad plight [of constant war], and therefore spared no effort in emphasizing the need of creating and preserving a new order of things which would ensure universal peace."[64] Wilson's project of fashioning a more harmonious international order, they suggested, was the culmination of thousands of years of Confucian teachings, and the establishment of a League of Nations would be the fulfillment of Confucian ideals. The Chinese, therefore, could hardly fail to support it, and the world could not afford to exclude them.

Egyptians, too, were moving to seize the opportunity of the moment. Since 1882 Egypt had been, in essence if not in name, a British protectorate. Now, a delegation of prominent Egyptian leaders, galvanized by the sense of opportunity and urgency created by Wilson's pronouncements and the coming of the Peace Conference, prepared to head for Europe to stake their claim for Egyptian self-determination. The British authorities, however, would not allow the Egyptian delegation to travel. In response, its leadership, headed by veteran politician Sa'd Zaghlul—later celebrated by Egyptians as the Father of the Nation—mobilized popular protests against the British and launched an international campaign to press them to change their decision. By December, the American delegation in Cairo received petitions daily, protesting the refusal of the British authorities to allow the Egyptian delegation to travel to Paris and asking the United States to support Egyptian self-determination.[65] One telegram, from Zaghlul to Wilson himself, assured the president that "no people more than the Egyptian people has felt strongly the joyous emotion of the birth of a new era which, thanks to your virile action, is soon going to impose itself upon the universe," and asked "the eminent philosopher and statesman" to help release Egypt from foreign domination.[66] Other petitions were signed by a cross-section of the Egyptian upper and middle classes: legislators, government officials, local politicians, merchants, lawyers, doctors, and army officers.[67] Egyptians believed that the support of the American president and his principles would enable them to make a successful bid for self-rule. They were basing their claims to independence, the U.S. consul on Cairo reported, on the president's advocacy of the self-determination clause, and would "endeavor to obtain an expression of opinion from him during his visit in Europe".[68]

Like Egyptians, Koreans also strove to get a hearing at the Peace Conference. Korean nationalists in China, Japan, and the United States organized patriotic associations and produced numerous petitions and pamphlets that laid out the Korean case and appealed to Wilsonian principles to argue for self-determination for Korea.[69] In Shanghai, Korean nationalist activists prepared a petition for Korean independence, describing the plight of Koreans under Japanese rule and calling on the United States to "uphold the grand principles of President Wilson that a nation should be ruled in accordance with the consent of the governed."[70] In addition, Kim Kyu-sik, a young Korean Christian who had graduated from Roanoke College in Virginia and from Princeton, was selected to travel to Paris to represent Korea officially at the Peace Conference.[71] Korean students in Japan were also energized by the sense of opportunity that seemed to permeate the international atmosphere. Spurred to action by news of the activities of their compatriots in the United States and elsewhere, on February 8, 1919, a group of Korean students in Tokyo issued a declaration of independence "before those nations of the world which have secured victory for Freedom and Justice."[72] In the meantime, a young Korean exile in the United States, Syngman Rhee, declared himself president of the independent Republic of Korea and prepared to travel to Paris to speak for his people. As a doctoral student at Princeton from 1908 to 1910, Rhee had met Wilson when the latter served as president of that university. When Rhee graduated in 1910 it was Wilson who handed him his diploma.[73] Such connections, however, now helped Rhee little. The State Department, wary of inciting Japanese ire, refused to grant him a visa to travel to France, and Rhee, as he wrote to Wilson himself, was left with "a mingling of determination and despair."[74]

Upheaval

The flurry of activity in expatriate communities spurred similar expectations within Korea itself. The death of a former emperor in late February 1919 afforded a convenient opportunity for activists to mobilize the public around the call for self-determination.[75] On March 1, a group of eminent religious leaders released a declaration that proclaimed the independence of Korea. Drawing on Wilsonian imagery, the signers associated themselves "with the worldwide movement for reform," which was "the central force of our age and a just movement for the right of all peoples to determine their own existence." A new dawn, they asserted, was upon the world:

> A new era unfolds before our eyes. The old age of force is gone and an age of justice is here. A humane spirit, nurtured through all the centuries of human experience, has begun to cast the brilliant light of a new civilized morality upon human history. . . . We have a great opportunity to recover our country and we move with a new current of world thought. . . . We are now on the move. The conscience of mankind is with us and we march forward with right on our side.[76]

Over the following months more than a million people participated in demonstrations, as they spread all over the peninsula.[77] The wave of protests was also fueled by the spread of rumors that the United States and President Wilson were supporting Korean claims—made all the more effective since, due to Japanese censorship, few sources of reliable information were available. The rumors suggested, among other things, that "President Wilson was to come to Korea by airplane to assist Korean independence; that scores of United States battleships had been dispatched for Korea; that American troops had already landed at Inchon; that the peace conference had recognized the independence of Korea."[78] With the protests spreading, the colonial authorities launched a brutal campaign of suppression that left thousands of casualties in its wake.[79]

By early March the tense situation in Egypt also came to a head, and the British authorities, increasingly anxious over nationalist "agitation," decided to move forcefully against its leadership. Zaghlul and three of his colleagues were arrested by British troops, and the following morning, March 9, they were deported to be interned on the Mediterranean island of Malta.[80] According to at least one biographer, the one item found on Zaghlul's person when he was arrested and searched was a clipping from the *Daily Express* listing Wilson's Fourteen Points.[81] The arrest was a fateful move. It sparked a massive wave of strikes and demonstrations across Egypt and precipitated a period of violent clashes known in Egyptian history as the "1919 Revolution." Egyptians from all walks of life took part in the upheaval: students, urban workers, professionals, and peasants.[82] Members of religious and ethnic minorities also expressed their solidarity with the movement, and even women took to the streets—an unprecedented development in Egyptian society. As violent clashes with British troops proliferated and railway and telegraph lines were sabotaged, the British countered with a strict enforcement of martial law. Over the next several months some 800 Egyptians were killed in clashes and many more wounded, while 60 British soldiers and civilians also died.[83] The 1919 Revolution was a major watershed in the development of the Egyptian national struggle, which, according to a prominent Egyptian historian, "forms the basis for all the developments that followed" in the modern history of Egypt.[84] The violence unleashed during this period and the harshness of the British response sharply escalated Anglo-Egyptian tensions, heightening mutual fear and mistrust, hardening attitudes and positions on both sides, and casting a long shadow over all subsequent attempts at negotiation.

As the Wilsonian promise appeared to collapse in Egypt, Indian hopes to gain a hearing in Paris for their demands of self-determination were also being dashed. Though Tilak continued his campaign in London throughout the spring, by March it was becoming clear that the British government was determined to block the discussion of the Indian question in Paris.[85] When Tilak, citing his appointment by the Delhi Congress as its delegate to the Peace Conference, applied for a passport to go to Paris, his application was summarily denied: "The idea of our going to the Peace Conference is not relishable to them," he wrote, "and any deputation coming here after the Peace Conference is over will be . . . not of much use."[86] On the subcontinent itself, the anticipation of far-reaching change in the colonial relationship that had built up among Indians during the latter war years was replaced by bitter disillusionment as the government tried to stem the tide of "sedition" by introducing the oppressive Rowlatt Bills that extended its wartime powers of internment without trial. Indian nationalists, who had expected the war to be followed by an immediate push toward self-government, were incensed. Gandhi, who had been cutting his teeth in Indian politics through involvement in local issues since his return from South Africa in 1914, now emerged as a figure of national stature, leading the movement to oppose these "Black Acts." A staunch supporter of the Empire throughout the war, Gandhi now found that his hopes of achieving equality for Indians within the Empire had been in vain and called for civil disobedience and a nationwide strike in protest.[87] The British response was violent, most infamously with the killing, on April 13, 1919, of nearly 400 unarmed persons gathered in Jallianwala Bagh, in the Punjab city of Amritsar. The massacre at Amritsar dealt the final blow to Indians' faith in British intentions to move India expeditiously toward self-determination, and sealed Indian disillusionment with the promise of the Wilsonian moment. This bloody episode quickly became a symbol of colonialism, a defining event that epitomized in Indian eyes, the oppressive nature of British rule and marked a new stage in the evolution of Indian anticolonialism.

Three weeks later, when, in order to placate the Japanese, Wilson agreed to award them the former German concessions in the Shandong Peninsula, the Chinese leaders and public, who had placed great faith in Wilson, were shocked. On May 4, when students in Beijing learned of the Shandong decision, they took to the streets in violent protest. The students, who not long before filled the streets to chant "long live Wilson" now saw the American president as a liar, his promise of a new world exposed as a mere illusion. Street protests and strikes continued to spread throughout the country over the next several weeks. A contemporary pamphlet summed up the prevailing sentiments: "Throughout the world like the voice of a prophet has gone the word of Woodrow Wilson strengthening the weak and giving courage to the struggling. And the Chinese people . . . looked for the dawn of this new Messiah; but no sun rose for China." As one student recalled, they "at once awoke to the fact that foreign nations . . . were all great liars. . . . [We] could no longer depend upon the principle of any so-called great leader like Woodrow Wilson . . . we couldn't help feel that we must struggle!" The May Fourth incident served to galvanize hitherto inchoate strands of political, social, and cultural discontent, marking a defining moment in the evolution of Chinese nationalism.[88]

Conclusion

In November 1918, on the deck of the George Washington en route to France, Woodrow Wilson had ruminated about the task ahead of him and the unsettled state of much of the world. George Creel recalled one conversation with the president:

> One evening, as we walked the deck, I spoke to the President of the tremendous help that his addresses had been to us in our work—of the wholehearted response of the people of the earth, their gladness in his words, the joyful liberation of their thought . . .
>
> The President stood silent for quite a while, and when he turned to me at last his face was as bleak as the gray stretch of sunless water.
>
> It is a great thing that you have done, he said, but I am wondering if you have not unconsciously spun a net for me from which there is no escape. It is to America that the whole world turns to-day, not only with its wrongs, but with its hopes and grievances. The hungry expect us to feed them, the roofless look to us for shelter, the sick of heart and body depend on us for cure. All of these expectations have in them the quality of terrible urgency. There must be no delay. It has been so always. People will endure their tyrants for years, but they will tear their deliverers to pieces if a millennium is not created immediately. Yet you know, and I know, that these ancient wrongs, these present unhappinesses, are not to be remedied in a day or with a wave of the hand. What I seem to see—with all my heart I hope that I am wrong—is a tragedy of disappointment.
>
> —George Creel, *The War, the World and Wilson*
> (New York: Harper, 1920), pp. 161–62

The events that unfolded in the next several months validated Wilson's apprehensions. Indians, Chinese, Koreans, and Egyptians had envisioned the coming of a new era in which the newly articulated right to self-determination would be implemented for all peoples—expectations in which Woodrow Wilson was given a central role both as a symbol and a facilitator. Now, as it became clear that the American president had no intention of applying his avowed principles to their own cases, their faith in Wilson, and in the birth of a new international order in which they would have a place as equals, began to crumble.

However, even as the Wilsonian moment in the colonial world faded away, it had left its mark. During its brief but intense unfolding, Indians, Chinese, Koreans, and Egyptians staked their claims for full and immediate self-determination, and public mobilization behind this goal, often leading to violent clashes with the authorities, galvanized even further the commitment to an uncompromising nationalist agenda.[89] This dynamic was well captured by the apostle of Chinese nationalism, Sun Yat-sen, who observed: "Wilson's proposals, once set forth, could not be recalled; each one of the weaker, smaller nations . . . stirred with a great, new consciousness;

they saw how completely they had been deceived by the Great Powers' advocacy of self-determination and began independently and separately to carry out the principle of the 'self-determination of peoples.' "[90]

Recognizing a relationship between the Wilsonian moment and the rise of anticolonial nationalism does not discount other explanations commonly given for the upsurge of anticolonial sentiments in 1919, whether related to domestic factors, the depravations of war, or the blow it dealt to the imperial powers. It does, however, bring out a pattern that seems intriguingly similar across a number of diverse cases, one that illuminates the international context in which modern national identities and movements in the colonial world were shaped. Both Wilson and Lenin articulated a vision for international order that offered a voice in the international arena to groups that had not had one before, and suggested that such a voice could be claimed by asserting a right to "national self-determination." It conjured an international society in which the claim to nationhood would be the ticket to membership; in which nationhood, in effect, would be the currency of identity, of personhood. The importance of the Wilsonian moment in the colonial world does not reside solely, or even centrally, in the novelty of the rhetoric of self-determination. Rather, it lies in the specific efforts by Chinese and Indians, Egyptians and Koreans, as well as many others across the colonial world, to adopt, adapt, and deploy effectively these discursive strategies to make use of the international political space created by wartime pronouncements in order to transcend the imperial enclosures that had hitherto bound their struggles, and carry their struggle for identity, sovereignty, and equality, and shift them directly into the international arena.

A sort of "domino effect" developed in the international arena at the time. As the claims for self-determination put before the Peace Conference multiplied, some even being recognized, a window of opportunity seemed to open, requiring immediate and determined action to stake one's own claims. In practice, of course, some claims for self-determination were recognized while others were not. However, once a commitment, both ideological and political, was made to staking these claims; once expectations were dramatically raised, publics were mobilized to demand self-determination, and, often, blood was shed in its name; once all that had occurred, as it did at the Wilsonian moment in the four cases examined above, there was no turning back, and the relationships of colonized peoples with the colonizing powers, and with international society more generally, were irrevocably transformed. If, as I have argued here, the Wilsonian moment played an important role in galvanizing major nationalist movements in Asia and the Middle East, this suggests the need to view the evolution of such movements within the broader context of international history, rather than framing them exclusively within narratives of "national" history.

The perspective presented here also suggests a need to reevaluate the common view of the Versailles Peace as auguring an unprecedented expansion of European imperialism. On one level, this interpretation is undoubtedly true. However, as James Mayall has noted, "The European imperial powers . . . may have attempted to outwit the American president whenever they thought it necessary to protect their state patrimony . . . but in the end they had nothing to put in the place of national self-determination as an ordering principle for international society."[91] The Wilsonian moment firmly planted the newly articulated right to self-determination in the international discourse of legitimacy, gravely undermining what A.P. Thornton has called the "imperial idea" not only among the colonizers, but also, and more significantly, among the colonized themselves.[92] From this perspective, the Versailles Peace can be seen as the swan song, rather than the apex, of the European imperial order, as the new discourse of self-determination, relentlessly wielded by colonized groups, proceeded to undermine its legitimacy.

It is typical historical irony that Woodrow Wilson's rhetoric inspired aspirations and actions that he neither anticipated nor approved. On May 9, 1919, as the anticolonial upheavals I described above were raging, Wilson expressed his grave concerns. He was "disturbed," he told a gathering of dignitaries in Paris, by "the unqualified hope that men have entertained everywhere of immediate emancipation from the things that have hampered them and oppressed them. You cannot in human experience rush into the light," he added. "You have to go through the twilight into the broadening day before the noon comes and the full sun is upon the landscape."[93] Such a gradualist view was not usually shared by colonized peoples seeking self-determination; even if, with the benefit of retrospect, we know that the road from the imperial to the postcolonial order in international society has been tortuous. Understanding the role of the Wilsonian moment in the rise of anticolonial nationalism is a step toward unraveling that complexity, illuminating a crucial stage in the emergence of non-Western peoples as independent actors in international society and the construction of the postcolonial world order.

Notes

This essay is based on my forthcoming book, *The Wilsonian Moment: Self-Determination and the International Origins of Anticolonial Nationalism* (Oxford University Press, 2007). I would like to thank the editors of this volume and the other members of the Global History Network for their comments on previous versions of this essay.

1. Charles T. Thompson, *The Peace Conference Day by Day: A Presidential Pilgrimage Leading to the Discovery of Europe* (New York: Brentano's, 1920), p. 6.
2. "Two Million Cheer Wilson," *New York Times*, December 15, 1918, p. 1.

3. Thompson, *The Peace Conference Day by Day*, pp. 55–56, 67–68. See also Arthur Walworth, *Woodrow Wilson*, 3rd ed. (New York: W.W. Norton, 1978), 2: 221–34.

4. Stephen Bonsal, *Suitors and Supplicants: The Little Nations at Versailles* (New York: Prentice-Hall, 1946), p. 262.

5. Ho's original petition, dated June 18, 1919, is in United States National Archives, College Park, Maryland [USNA], Record Group [RG] 256, 851G.00/1. On Ho's petition and its consequences see also Loren Baritz, *Backfire: A History of How American Culture Led Us into Vietnam and Made Us Fight the Way We Did* (New York: William Morrow, 1985), p. 36; Mark Philip Bradley, *Imagining Vietnam and America: The Making of Postcolonial Vietnam, 1919–1950* (Chapel Hill: University of North Carolina Press, 2000), pp. 10–11; Hue-Tam Ho Tai, *Radicalism and the Origins of the Vietnamese Revolution* (Cambridge, Mass.: Harvard University Press, 1992), pp. 68–69.

6. For a survey of recent scholarship, see David Steigerwald, "The Reclamation of Woodrow Wilson?" *Diplomatic History* 23 (1999): 79–99.

7. See, for example, Henri Grimal, *Decolonization: The British, French, Dutch, and Belgian Empires, 1919–1963* (Boulder: Westview Press, 1978), pp. 17–18.

8. Steigerwald, "The Reclamation of Woodrow Wilson?" pp. 97–98.

9. Immanuel Kant, *Perpetual Peace: A Philosophical Sketch*, in Ted Humphrey, trans., *Immanuel Kant, Perpetual Peace and Other Essays* (Indianapolis: Hackett, 1983).

10. See Max Beloff, *Imperial Sunset, Vol. 1: Britain's Liberal Empire, 1897–1921* (New York: Knopf, 1970), pp. 265–66; Arno J. Mayer, *Wilson vs. Lenin: Political Origins of the New Diplomacy, 1917–1918* (New York: Meridian, 1967), pp. 245–66.

11. Lenin's ideas on self-determination crystallized in 1915–1916. See V.I. Lenin, "The Socialist Revolution and the Right of Nations to Self-Determination," in his *Collected Works*, 45 vols. (Moscow: Progress Publishers, 1960–1970), 22: 143–56 (first published in October 1916). For detailed analysis of the Marxist debate on nationalism see Jeremy Smith, *The Bolsheviks and the National Question, 1917–1923* (London: Macmillan, 1999), pp. 8–20.

12. Mayer, *Political Origins*, pp. 248, 298–303.

13. Ibid., pp. 74–76.

14. Address from the Bolsheviks "To Peoples and Governments of Allied Countries," December 31, 1917, included in David Rowland Francis to Robert Lansing, in Arthur S. Link, ed., *The Papers of Woodrow Wilson* [*PWW*], 69 vols. (Princeton: Princeton University Press, 1966–1994), 45: 412–13. For more on the Bolshevik impact on the postwar settlement, see John M. Thompson, *Russia, Bolshevism, and the Versailles Peace* (Princeton: Princeton University Press, 1966).

15. Mayer, *Political Origins*, pp. 385–87.

16. Seth P. Tillman, *Anglo-American Relations at the Paris Peace Conference of 1919* (Princeton: Princeton University Press, 1961), p. 26; George W. Egerton, *Great Britain and the Creation of the League of Nations: Strategy, Politics, and*

International Organization, 1914–1919 (Chapel Hill: University of North Carolina Press, 1978), pp. 57–59.

17. Thomas J. Knock, *To End All Wars: Woodrow Wilson and the Quest for a New World Order* (New York: Oxford University Press, 1992), p. 143. This address has been published as David Lloyd George, *British War Aims: Statement by the Prime Minister, the Right Honourable David Lloyd George, on January 5, 1918* (London: Hazell, Watson & Viney, 1918).

18. Lloyd E. Ambrosius, "Dilemmas of National Self-Determination: Woodrow Wilson's Legacy," in idem., *Wilsonianism: Woodrow Wilson and His Legacy in American Foreign Relations* (New York: Palgrave Macmillan, 2002), pp. 125–43; William R. Keylor, "Versailles and International Diplomacy," in Manfred F. Boemeke, Gerald D. Feldman, and Elisabeth Glaser, eds., *The Treaty of Versailles: A Reassessment after 75 Years* (Cambridge: Cambridge University Press, 1998), pp. 469–507, especially p. 475 and note 12; N. Gordon Levin, *Woodrow Wilson and World Politics: America's Response to War and Revolution* (New York: Oxford University Press, 1968), pp. 247–51. The literature on Wilson's policy in the Philippines is surprisingly sparse, but see William Christopher Hamel, "Race and Responsible Government: Woodrow Wilson and the Philippines" (Ph.D. diss., Michigan State University, 2002), especially chapter 6.

19. Address to a joint session of Congress, January 8, 1918, *PWW*, 45: 534–39.

20. Address to Congress, February 11, 1918, *PWW*, 46: 321.

21. For a comprehensive analysis of the origins and meanings of Wilson's notion of self-determination see Michla Pomerance, "The United States and Self-Determination: Perspectives on the Wilsonian Conception," *American Journal of International Law* 70 (1976): 1–27.

22. For a general treatment of this phenomenon see Daniel R. Headrick, *The Invisible Weapon: Telecommunications and International Politics, 1851–1945* (New York: Oxford University Press, 1991).

23. V.S. Srinivasa Sastri, Foreword, in *Woodrow Wilson's Message for Eastern Nations, Selected by Himself from His Public Addresses* (Calcutta: Association Press, 1925), pp. iv–v.

24. For detailed analysis of the emergence of a popular press and a mass audience in China, see Leo Lee and Andrew J. Nathan, "The Beginnings of Mass Culture," in David Johnson, Andrew J. Nathan, and Evelyn S. Rawski, eds., *Popular Culture in Late Imperial China* (Berkeley: University of California Press, 1985), pp. 368–78; and Joan Judge, *Print and Politics: "Shibao" and the Culture of Reform in Late Qing China* (Stanford: Stanford University Press, 1996).

25. P.J. Vatikiotis, *The History of Modern Egypt* (London: Weidenfeld and Nicholson, 1980), pp. 179–88.

26. This group constituted what Ernest May has dubbed a "foreign policy public." See Ernest May, *American Imperialism: A Speculative Essay* (New York: Antheneum, 1968). The role of "print capitalism" in the formation of national identity was, of course, a major theme in Benedict Anderson's influential text, *Imagined Communities: Reflections on the Origin and Spread of Nationalism*, rev. ed. (London: Verso, 1991).

27. George Creel (U.S. Committee on Public Information), *Complete Report of the Chairman of the Committee on Public Information* (Washington, D.C.: Government Printing Office, 1920), p. 1.

28. Ibid., p. 2.

29. Ibid., p. 4.

30. James R. Mock and Cedric Larson, *Words That Won the War: The Story on the Committee on Public Information* (Princeton: Princeton University Press, 1939), pp. 240–41.

31. Creel, *Complete Report*, p. 112.

32. George Creel, *How We Advertised America: The First Telling of the Amazing Story of the Committee on Public Information that Carried the Gospel of Americanism to Every Corner of the Globe* (New York: Harper & Brothers, 1920), p. 362; Hans Schmidt, "Democracy for China: American Propaganda and the May Fourth Movement," *Diplomatic History* 22, no. 1 (1998): 1–28, p. 3.

33. See Carl Crow, *China Takes Her Place* (New York: Harper & Brothers, 1944), pp. 113–15; also Carl Crow, *I Speak for the Chinese* (New York: Harper & Brothers, 1937), pp. 27–29. On Feng see James E. Sheridan, *Chinese Warlord: The Career of Feng Yü-hsiang* (Stanford: Stanford University Press, 1966).

34. Creel, *How We Advertised America*, p. 362; Kazuyuki Matsuo, "American Propaganda in China: The U.S. Committee on Public Information, 1918–1919," *Journal of American and Canadian Studies* 14, no. 2 (1996): 19–42, 29; Xu Guoqi, "The Age of Innocence: The First World War and China's Quest for National Identity" (Ph.D. diss., Harvard University, 1999), p. 328.

35. Schmidt, "Democracy for China," pp. 11–12.

36. See, for example, Tang Zhenchang, *Cai Yuanpei Zhuan* [The Biography of Cai Yuanpei] (Shanghai: Shanghai Renmin Chubanshe, 1985), p. 159. Cai was a leading intellectual in China at the time. On him see William J. Duiker, *T'ai Yuan-pei: Educator of Modern China* (University Park: Pennsylvania State University Press, 1977).

37. Editorial by Chen Duxiu in *Meizhou Pinglun*, December 22, 1918, reproduced in *Duxiu Wencun* [Surviving Writings of Chen Duxiu] (Hefei: Anhui Renmin Chubanshe, 1987), p. 388. Chen would cofound the Chinese Communist Party in 1921; on him see Lee Feigon, *Chen Duxiu, Founder of the Chinese Communist Party* (Princeton: Princeton University Press, 1983).

38. Cited in Xu, "The Age of Innocence," pp. 332–33.

39. See, for example, Koo to Lansing, November 25, 1918, in Record Group 03–12 (Archives of Chinese Embassy in Washington), box 8, folder 2, p. 477, at the Waijiaobu (Foreign Ministry) Archives, Academia Sinica, Taipei, Taiwan [Henceforth cited as Waijiaobu].

40. Ronald Wingate, *Wingate of the Sudan: The Life and Times of Sir Reginald Wingate, Maker of Anglo-Egyptian Sudan* (London: Murray, 1955), pp. 228, 232.

41. On the CPI's propaganda effort in Britain, see James D. Startt, "American Propaganda in Britain During World War I," *Prologue* 28, no. 1 (1996): 16–33; Peter Buitenhuis, "Selling the Great War," *The Canadian Review of American Studies* 7, no. 2 (1976): 139–50.

42. 'Abd al-Rahman Rafi'i, *Thawrat Sanat 1919: Tarikh Misr al-Qawmi min Sanat 1914 ila Sanat 1921* [The 1919 Revolution: The National History of Egypt, 1914–1921] (Cairo: Maktabat al-Nahda, 1955), p. 57; 'Abd al-Khaliq Lashin, *Sa'd Zaghlul wa-Dawruhu fi al-Siyasa al-Misriyya* [Sa'd Zaghlul and his Role in Egyptian Politics] (Beirut: Maktabat Madbuli, 1975), pp. 126–27.

43. Dae-Yeol Ku, *Korea Under Colonialism: The March First Movement and Anglo-Japanese Relations* (Seoul: Korea Branch of the Royal Asiatic Society, 1985), p. 45; Chong-sik Lee, *The Politics of Korean Nationalism* (Berkeley: University of California Press, 1963), p. 107.

44. Consulate general, Seoul, to State Department, January 10, 1919, cited in Frank R. Baldwin, "The March First Movement: Korean Challenge and Japanese Response" (Ph.D. diss., Columbia University, 1963), pp. 252–53.

45. Kenneth M. Wells, "Background to the March First Movement: Koreans in Japan," *Korean Studies* 13 (1989): 5–21, 12. See also Baldwin, "The March First Movement," p. 35, who writes that the New Korea Youth Association/Party was only formed, on an ad-hoc basis, in November; however, Lee, *Korean Nationalism*, p. 103, agrees with Wells that the organization had been founded that summer.

46. Baldwin, "The March First Movement," pp. 32–33.

47. Swaminath Natarajan, *A History of the Press in India* (Bombay: Asia Publishing House, 1962), p. 183.

48. Subramanya Aiyar to Woodrow Wilson, June 24, 1917, in the National Archives of India, New Delhi [NAI], Home Department/Political Branch, Deposit File, February 1918, File No. 36, entitled: "Action Taken in Regard to a Letter Sent by Sir Subramanya Aiyar to the President of the United States of America Invoking His Aid in Obtaining Home Rule for India," pp. 3–6. See also India Office Library, London [IOL], V/26/262/9 (Hunter Committee Report), Vol. VII, p. 3.

49. Address to a joint session of Congress, January 8, 1918, *PWW*, 45: 537–38; Diwakar Prasad Singh, *American Attitude towards the Indian Nationalist Movement* (New Delhi: Munshiram Manoharlal, 1974), pp. 216–17.

50. See, for example, "America Asks for War," *Amrita Bazar Patrika*, April 5, 1917.

51. "President Wilson's Speech and Needed Change in British Policy," *Mahratta*, October 6, 1918, pp. 473–74.

52. "The Lesson of the War," *Tribune* (Lahore), December 20, 1918, IOL, L/R/5/201, p. 3.

53. "India after the War," *Kesari* (Pune), n.d., IOL, L/R/5/200, p. 596.

54. See Roy's open letter to Wilson, written in late 1917, in M.N. Roy, *Selected Works of M.N. Roy*, vol. 1, Sibnarayan Ray, ed. (Delhi: Oxford University Press, 1987), pp. 67–83.

55. Li Dazhao, *Wei-er-xun yu pinghe* [Wilson and Peace], February 11, 1917, in Li Dazhao, *Li Dazhao wenji* [Writings of Li Dazhao] (Beijing: Renmin Chubanshe, 1984), 1: 271; and Li Dazhao, "*Bolshevism de shengli*" [The Victory of Bolshevism], *Xin Qingnian* [New Youth] 5, no. 5 (1918). Also Maurice J. Meisner, *Li Ta-chao and the Origins of Chinese Marxism* (Cambridge, Mass.: Harvard University Press, 1967), pp. 96–97.

56. Thirty-third INC session, Delhi, December 1918, Nehru Memorial Museum and Library, New Delhi, [NMML], All-India Congress Committee [AICC], File 1, Part II, p. 347.
57. Numerous such petitions are found in National Archive of the United Kingdom, Kew, England [NAUK], FO 608/211, fol. 126–36.
58. Memorandum, dated London, December 11, 1918, enc. in Tilak's letter to Khaparde, December 18, 1918, NAI, G.S. Khaparde Papers, File 1, pp. 1–2.
59. Tilak to D.W. Gokhale, dated London, January 23, 1919, NAI, Khaparde Papers, File 1, pp. 4–7.
60. Close to Tilak, January 14, 1919, quoted in T.V. Parvate, *Bal Gangadhar Tilak: A Narrative and Interpretative Review of his Life, Career, and Contemporary Events* (Ahmedabad: Navajivan, 1958), p. 463.
61. No date on petition, but the accompanying telegram is dated January 21, 1919. NAUK, FO 608/209, fol. 287.
62. January 21, 1919. NAUK, FO 608/209, fol. 287; Reinsch to Lansing, November 8, 1918, USNA, RG 256, 893.01/1. See also excerpts from the *Peking Leader*, November 3–5, 1919, enc. in RG 256, 893.00/5; and Foreign Minister of Canton Government to Lansing, January 23, 1919, RG 256, 893.00/18.
63. Wunsz King, *China at the Peace Conference in 1919* (New York: St. John's University Press, 1961), p. 3.
64. V.K. Wellington Koo and Cheng-ting T. Wang, *China and the League of Nations* (London: George Allen & Unwin, 1919).
65. A petition from Leon S. Farhj, an official at the Egyptian Ministry of Agriculture, December 11, 1918, and a petition from members of the Egyptian National Delegation, December 12, 1918, enc. in Gary to secretary of state, December 30, 1918, USNA, RG 256, 883.00/4 and FW 883.00/30.
66. For example, Zaghlul to Wilson, December 14, 1918, December 27, 1918, and January 3, 1919. Zaghlul sent Wilson quite a few letters and telegrams over the following months, and eight of those, including the ones quoted, are available most readily in George E. Noble, "The Voice of Egypt," *The Nation*, January 3, 1920, pp. 861–64.
67. See, for example, the list of signatories in a petition from residents of the Nile Delta town of Mansura, enc. in Gary to secretary of state, December 30, 1918, USNA, RG 256, 883.00/4.
68. Gary to Department of State, December 19, 1918, USNA, RG 256, 883.00/3.
69. New Korea Association to Lansing, December 2, 1918, USNA, RG 256, 895.00/1; Pamphlet entitled "Freedom and Peace with Korea under Japan?" March 1919, RG 256, 895.00/3; Korean National Independence Union to Robert Lansing, March 6, 1919, RG 256 895.00/4; Robert T. Oliver, *Syngman Rhee: The Man behind the Myth* (New York: Dodd, Mead, 1954), pp. 110–11, 113, 132.
70. Baldwin, "The March First Movement," pp. 35–36; Thomas F. Millard, *Democracy and the Eastern Question: The Problem of the Far East as Demonstrated by the Great War, and Its Relation to the United States of America* (London: G. Allen & Unwin, 1919), p. 40. Also see Lee, *Korean Nationalism*, pp. 103–04.

71. Lee, *Korean Nationalism*, p. 104; Baldwin, "The March First Movement," p. 246; Timothy Lee, "A Political Factor in the Rise of Protestantism in Korea: Protestantism and the March First Movement," *Church History: Studies in Christianity and Culture* 69 (2000): 116–42, 132.

72. Lee, *Korean Nationalism*, pp. 104–06. For more details on the February 8 movement in Tokyo, see Wells, "Koreans in Japan," pp. 11–17.

73. Oliver, *Syngman Rhee*, pp. 110–13, 132.

74. Ibid., p. 143; Rhee to Polk, June 19, 1919, USNA, RG 59, 895.01/4; Rhee to Wilson, June 27, 1919, RG 59, 895.01/8. On the position of the State Department see Grew to Hornbeck, March 28, 1919, RG 256, 895.00/8.

75. Timothy Lee, "Protestantism and the March First Movement," p. 132; Carter J. Eckert, Ki-Baik Lee, Young Ick Lew, Michael Robinson, and Edward W. Wagner, *Korea Old and New: A History* (Seoul: Ilchokak, 1991), p. 277; Lee, *Korean Nationalism*, pp. 106–07.

76. Cited in Baldwin, "The March First Movement," Appendix, pp. 224–27. A slightly different translation that does not significantly alter the meaning of the passage is offered in Han-Kyo Kim, "The Declaration of Independence, March 1, 1919: A New Translation," *Korean Studies* 13 (1989): 1–4.

77. Lee, *Korean Nationalism*, pp. 112–18.

78. Ibid., p. 122, citing the Japanese Gendarmerie Report.

79. Eckert, *Korea Old and New*, p. 279; Lee, *Korean Nationalism*, pp. 122–23.

80. Isma'il Sidqi Basha, *Mudhakkirati* [My Memoirs] (Cairo: Dar al-Hilal, 1950), pp. 46–49; Gary to the Secretary of State, March 10, 1919, USNA, RG 256, 883.00/37. See also Elie Kedourie, "Sa'd Zaghlul and the British," in Albert Hourani, ed., *Middle Eastern Affairs* 2 (Oxford: Oxford University Press, 1965), pp. 98–99.

81. Lashin, *Sa'd Zaghlul*, p. 128.

82. On the revolt of the peasants see Ellis Goldberg, "Peasants in Revolt: Egypt 1919," *International Journal of Middle East Studies* 24, no. 2 (1992): 261–80.

83. See PID reports in NAUK, FO 371/4373, pp. 35, 51. Also Gary to the secretary of state, March 10, 11, and 16, 1919, USNA, RG 256, 883.00/37, pp. 41 and 53.

84. Rafi'i, *Thawrat Sanat 1919*, p. 5. These events were reported in the United States, for example by *The Nation*, August 2, 1919, p. 135. See also Vatikiotis, *Modern Egypt*, pp. 266–67.

85. Tilak to D.W. Gokhale, London, February 6, 1919, NAI, Khaparde Papers, File 1, pp. 8–10.

86. Tilak to D.W. Gokhale, London, January 23, 1919, NAI, Khaparde Papers, File 1, pp. 4–7; unsigned memorandum entitled "How We Get On II," enc. in Tilak's letter from London March 20, 1919, NAI, Khaparde Papers, File 1, pp. 13–14.

87. Gandhi to Chelmsford, February 24, 1919 and March 11, 1919, NMML, Chelmsford Papers, roll 10.

88. Schmidt, "Democracy for China," p. 16; Chow Tse-tsung, *The May Fourth Movement: Intellectual Revolution in Modern China* (Cambridge, Mass.: Harvard University Press, 1960), pp. 92–93.

89. Zaghlul to Curzon, December 9, 1919, *British Documents on Foreign Affairs*, part II, series G, 1: 359–63; Kimm to Lansing, August 28, 1919, USNA, RG 59, 895.00/655;

90. Sun Yet-sen, *San Min Chu I: The Three Principles of the People*, trans. Frank W. Price (Shanghai: China Committee, Institute Pacific Relations, 1927), p. 84.

91. James Mayall, *Nationalism and International Society* (Cambridge: Cambridge University Press, 1990), pp. 44–45.

92. A.P. Thornton, *The Imperial Idea and Its Enemies: A Study in British Power*, 2nd ed. (London: Macmillan, 1985).

93. "After-Dinner Remarks," Paris, May 9, 1919, *PWW*, 58: 598.

CHAPTER 6

Alternative Visions of World Order in the Aftermath of World War I: Global Perspectives on Chinese Approaches

Dominic Sachsenmaier

World War I and Conceptions of World Order

> The Great War is not the manuscript for a new world history, but it is a transition that continues many elements from above and opens up new ones for the space below.[1]

With these words the Chinese scholar Liang Qichao (1873–1929) expresses a sentiment that was quite common during the years following the armistice of November 1918. In many parts of the world the Great War was understood as a watershed, a turning point that opened up possibilities for a new world order and new forms of internationalism. Many intellectuals in China, India, Europe, and other regions went even farther beyond Liang's assessment and predicted that the dusk of the war would be followed by the dawn of a new epoch. The disasters in Europe appeared to have shaken the foundations of the international structure enough to make profound adjustments palpable. The immediate aftermath of the war seemed to be the right time to promote great visions for the future and to critically reassess the recent past.

Understanding, contextualizing, and interpreting the Great War was believed to provide one of the keys that could open new doors toward a better future. Consequently, in such divergent societies as China, Germany, and Korea the war quickly acquired a highly symbolic power—its meaning was evoked, constructed, and instrumentalized by competing political camps, and it was done so in profoundly different ways.

There was a common belief that the fundaments of the international system had been eroded and that enormous opportunities for much of the non-Western world would emerge from the destruction in Europe. Even for cautious observers it appeared likely that the days of the previous Europe-centred global system were numbered and that many nations could be freed from Western domination. Many groups even assumed that the Great War had created a clean slate on which a uniform international system could be designed, finally replacing the complicated structure of regional, colonial, and national orders that had come to characterize the world. For most observers it seemed unthinkable that the world would again disintegrate into an uncoordinated system at a time when technological innovations such as the telegraph and the steamship had profoundly changed communication across vast distances, and when global economic patterns had started to emerge. A coherent world order also seemed likely since the colonial powers had long demonstrated the possibility of militaries with a worldwide reach.[2]

The wave of anticipations of a new world order also fostered the expectation that local political systems could be fundamentally reshaped. For example, in Germany, Italy, and other European societies, revolutionary movements sought to break with a traditional sociopolitical order, which in their view had proven to be detrimental in so many regards. In many colonies, such as India and Korea, and in states like China that were threatened by imperialism, the negotiations in Versailles were observed with great, Wilsonian hopes.[3] However, these were quickly shattered, since the American president's program had been primarily designed for Southeastern Europe and the Ottoman Empire, but not for the European colonies. Yet the wave of expectations created by the war had a lasting impact on political cultures in many societies outside Europe and the United States. Due to the allegedly open international situation and the new sense of urgency, the gap between rivalling political visions widened significantly in many societies during the years following the Great War.

Most of the competing efforts for national independence and cultural self-renewal were intrinsically connected with visions for the entire world. This only seemed to make sense since the great social, political, and cultural crises that had ravaged across many societies in Asia, Africa, and other continents had been closely connected with the expansion of the West and the formation of the prewar order. Thus, it was almost commonsensical to assume that national liberation or cultural emancipation could only be achieved by reordering the world at large. Consequently, within each country or region, multiple political and ideological forces worked on reshaping local polities in conjunction with restructuring the international community. Most political camps applied the same categories, the same interpretations of society and history to the levels of the global and the local. For example, socialist circles, which at the time started to grow significantly in many parts of the world, referred to the same Marxist concepts such as class struggle or modes of production when envisioning a postcapitalist international and domestic order.

After the Great War European civilization, or what was often closely associated with it, "modernity," continued to fascinate a large number of intellectuals and political activists in the non-Western world. In Europe, the intellectual climate after 1918 was largely characterized by doubts about the promises of Western civilization and modernity. Here the Great War aggravated a wave of cultural pessimism that two decades before had come to be labelled with terms such as *fin de siècle*, or "age of anxiety." By contrast, in the United States[4] and parts of East Asia, where the war in Europe had caused a short economic boom, optimism about the potentials of Western modernity prevailed—here much of society believed that although Europe had been weakened, some core facets of its civilization remained credible. Many thinkers in most parts of the non-Western world expected an end to colonialism but—quite different from today's situation—movements against Western dominance only rarely appeared in the form of cultural or religious countermovements. The war did not profoundly challenge the position of the West as the global source of cultural as well as political models. For example, most anticolonial or anti-imperialist movements in Africa, India, and other parts of the world continued to couch their agendas in Western terms such as nation building or class struggle. Around the time of World War I many self-strengthening programs were characterized by secularization efforts and at least some degree of antitraditionalism that was supposed to provide an answer to the sociocultural crises of the time. The March First Movement in Korea, Kemalism in Turkey, and the May Fourth Movements in China are examples of this trend. In these and other countries the war was followed by fierce political struggles between political visions and ideologies.

The great political tensions and social upheavals that many societies witnessed during the 1920s and 1930s were often among the consequences of World War I. If we include the rise of fascisms, the intensification of decolonization movements,[5] as well as the beginnings of socialism as existing alternatives in the picture, it may be not far-fetched to state that the war's implications for political cultures were arguably far greater than its immediate economic, military, and diplomatic consequences. The shockwaves of the Great War were less immediate and vehement than many had expected, and the lights did not truly go out for Europe after 1914.[6] Yet the Great War's consequences were profound, since the events in Europe triggered a cascade of tectonic movements in a substantial number of Western and non-Western societies. A global history of the Great War's impact on political movements as well as images of modernity and the West has yet to be written.[7] Already existing research provides us with a good understanding of the reactions within single world regions, but the transcultural connectedness of many political movements has not yet been sufficiently explored.[8]

This chapter will show how competing ideas about the future of China were inseparably connected with ideological visions of world order circulating on an international level. It will furthermore show that interpreting the meaning and implications of the Great War had become an important aspect of political theorizing and even social mobilization. Focusing on the immediate postwar period, the chapter will put a particular emphasis on intellectual movements that supported certain political ideologies as well as their sociocultural environment. It will mainly explore visions that emerged from politicized student movements and publications by prominent scholars. In all cases this chapter will sketch out some of the international dimensions that linked the rivaling political and intellectual camps in China with likeminded forces in the outside world.

The Chinese Context

Like many other societies China experienced a series of rapid and profound transformations during the decades leading up to World War I. In the eyes of many contemporary observers the changes that China underwent amounted to an unprecedented set of historical ruptures. Due to an unfavorable (but certainly entangled) combination of domestic turmoil and foreign encroachment that had erupted in events such as the Opium Wars and the Taiping Rebellion, the country had become politically destabilized during the nineteenth and early twentieth centuries. The Confucian state education system had been discontinued, which in conjunction with some other developments accelerated the demise of the scholar-official elite. In contrast to the last dynasty the new republic was now primarily led by men trained in modern sciences.[9] The rising importance of scientists within China's political sector is only one example for the wave of sociocultural changes that—to varying degrees—could be felt in all parts of Chinese society.[10] Thus, at a time when various Chinese governments sought to reshape China's outward connections into the diplomatic relationships of a sovereign country, the relationship between inner and outer, foreign and domestic, had become increasingly complex.[11]

Around the time of World War I political ideologies were hungrily absorbed, transformed, and adapted by Chinese intellectuals and political leaders. Political and intellectual elites were filled with a sense of urgency fuelled by the general perception that China's independence was doomed to further erode in a world that seemed to guarantee a dignified international status only to the most dynamic societies, particularly the fastest in changing. Sino-centric conceptions of world order could no longer be upheld, now that the former Middle Kingdom was seen as a developing country or even as—after the Ottoman Empire—another Sick Man of the East. Chinese nationalism developed, at least partly, out of a new global consciousness that seemed to place China on the lower rungs on the worldwide scale of power, influence, and development.[12] Consequently the educated sectors of Chinese society sought new sociopolitical models and apt ways of applying them to the specific situation in China. Around the turn of the twentieth century the number of Chinese translations of Western social theory had started to swell visibly.[13]

In the midst of this difficult domestic and international situation, almost all political, intellectual, and ideological camps in China resorted to discourses of national humiliation[14]—discourses that were based on new forms of political and cultural identities.[15] It seemed evident that if China would not be able to respond quickly and aptly to the challenges of the time, it would be further bullied by the international environment. The rise of Japan, which had defeated China in 1895, seemed to indicate that modernization was the only means to secure power and independence. Two decades later, the sense that China had to change in order to survive, that it had to advance in order to maintain some degree of autonomy, was common to most political and intellectual forces in the country. However, there was little consensus on which elements China should adopt from the outside and which aspects of its past it should keep and continue. It was not even clear what constituted the cores of "Chinese tradition," "modern culture," and "the West."

As in many colonial and semi-colonial structures, in China too the coastal cities and urban centers were the most immediately affected by the set of changes that in some cases have been labeled the "internationalization of China."[16] Here one could witness the transformations of urban life, mass politics, modern transportation, and the growing presence of international corporations almost on a daily basis.[17] Starting from the late nineteenth century significant changes in the urban public sphere were characterized by a growing internationally connected Chinese press.[18] Parallel to this process the first decades of the twentieth century saw the emergence of a intellectuals as a new milieu within China's social fabric. These people were highly educated and politically concerned, but in contrast to earlier Chinese scholar-officials they typically did not have a close connection with the political power center.[19] They did have, however, have access to international knowledge through translations of foreign works or by attending English-speaking institutions of higher learning. In addition, mass migration brought thousands of students mainly to Japan, but also to Europe and the United States.[20] Their exposure to internationally circulating ideas imbued a young generation of Chinese intellectuals with the confidence that their discussion rooms and seminars would be the laboratories from which the future of China would emerge. From their knowledge of the world and its systems of thought they staked their claim for playing a central role in shaping the future of China. Many intellectuals believed that their real or alleged cosmopolitanism represented the future toward which China needed to go.

Thus, the belief in the great potential of Western influences as catalysts for change was particularly popular among the younger generations of students.[21] At the same time, the disillusionment with the malfunctioning republic and the personal distance from political decision makers made many Chinese intellectuals increasingly receptive to radical ideas. Therefore, to the young pro-Westernization forces, nationalism did not necessarily mean defending their past heritage, but rather carried the potential to energize the nation by freeing the masses from both foreign and domestic oppression.[22] In their opinion China needed to adopt a new culture from Western examples that would prepare it for the modern world.[23] The concepts of "saving the country" (*jiuguo*) and "Enlightenment" (*qimeng*) became closely intertwined with each other. Many young intellectuals believed that China needed to unleash a great amount of creative social and cultural energy in order to keep the country afloat in the high tidal waves of international power politics. However, these basic commonalities were just an umbrella covering a wide spectrum of positions that associated themselves with the New Culture Movement.[24]

Like many other leading figures of the New Culture Movement, Chen Duxiu, one of the founders of the journal *New Youth* (*Xin Qingnian*) and later of the Chinese Communist Party,[25] regarded domestic traditions more than foreign encroachment as the root cause of China's maladies. However, it would be inappropriate to label the position of May Fourth leaders and others as unabashedly antitraditional. Most of the New Culture Movement's proponents had at least some of their intellectual roots in traditional Chinese scholarship, and did not tend to support iconoclasm and attacks on Chinese culture *in toto*.[26] For example, in an article entitled "What is the New Culture Movement," Chen Duxiu states that the new culture should complement and not replace Chinese tradition "with movements for new sciences, religions, virtues, as well as new forms of art, literature and music."[27] In the same article Chen asserts that relying on scientific evidence instead of hereditary teachings would help them overcome cultural isolationism and develop an open mindset capable of learning from the world. In his opinion the West was primarily denoted by a spirit of experimentalism, progress, and a daring desire to move ahead and leave the past behind. According to Chen Duxiu, Chinese culture would not be destroyed by scientism and progressivism, but rather gain the momentum and energy to break free from alleged societal shackles that had been locked for centuries. In fact most adherents of the Chinese student movement believed that only China's young intellectuals would be able to create a new culture and follow the footsteps of the European Enlightenment, from which a new nation could triumphantly emerge.[28]

The Great War—Reactions from the New Culture Movement

For student circles in Beijing and in other metropolitan areas the Great War became a defining moment: the events in Europe triggered the metamorphosis of parts of the New Culture Movement into the May Fourth Movement. In 1917 China had joined the war after long public debates and grave political tensions between Chinese leaders. Participating in an international war far from the home shores was indeed a historically unprecedented act for China,[29] and the expectations were high when China indeed emerged as part of the winning coalition. For example, on December 1, 1919 the prestigious newspaper *Morning Post* carried the headline "Congratulations: The Great Victory of the Entente Countries [leads to] World Peace."[30] The Chinese public followed the peace negotiations at Versailles and Wilson's programs with great anticipation and hopes. It was a common expectation that foreign concessions and other impingements on Chinese sovereignty would finally come to an end. The situation in China is just one example of the long waves of enthusiasm that the end of the war and the Wilsonian moment had generated.[31]

The May Fourth Movement, one of the intellectually most effervescent periods in modern Chinese history, gained its name from the student protests and strikes following the day when news of the humiliating conditions for China in the Versailles Peace Treaty reached the public. Hopes for full national sovereignty were shattered when it was announced that the German colonies in Shandong province had been secretly promised to Japan. Large parts of the Chinese urban public regarded this continuation of colonialism on Chinese soil as a severe blow to their country's national honor, particularly since China had supported the allies during the war and thus stood, at least nominally, in the ranks of the victorious nations. Student groups responded with protests that quickly found the support of other social groups and grew into nationwide demonstrations, strikes, and boycott movements.[32]

Before May 1919, the anticipation for a new, better world order had also run high among prominent Chinese intellectuals. For example, renowned scholars such as Hu Shi and the director of Beijing University, Cai Yuanpei, regarded the war's outcome as a triumph of democracy over militarism, authoritarianism, and imperialism. For them the slaughter at the Marne, Tannenberg, the Somme, and countless other battlefields was not senseless bloodshed but had a historical purpose for the entire world. In an article entitled "The European War and Philosophy," published in 1918, Cai portrayed the Great War as a battle of ideas. Germany, which according to Cai had adhered to the Nietzschean creed in the survival of the fittest, lost to the more altruistic philosophies of Russia and Western Europe. Whereas the Russian Revolution had tried to implement Tolstoy's principle of selfless love, the Entente countries had adopted the principle of mutual help. Cai concluded that the ultimate victory was to be in the hands of Western countries, since the Russian radicals disregarded the fact that Tolstoy's theory of selfless love had been developed for self-cultivation rather than as a political program for entire societies.[33] Similarly, Tao Lügong believed that the war had destroyed the "four old ideas" of secret diplomacy, militarism, dictatorship, and contempt for the rule of law. He predicted that future politics in Europe and the world at large would no longer adhere to any of these dated features of the old order, for an era of governance by ethical principles was in the offing.[34]

In many regards the end of the war and the surge of Wilsonian hopes led to an unprecedented support for liberal-democratic visions in China, particularly within circles of students and intellectuals.[35] Certainly Chinese liberalism was not a blunt copy of Western theories—even Chinese translations of Western authors such as John Stuart Mill and Adam Smith tended to focus more on social organisms or the invisible hand than on theories regarding the individuality of human actions and the pursuit of self-interest.[36]

The reception of internationally circulating ideas in China was always selective and cocreative. Nevertheless, prominent figures such as Hu Shi, who went to college in the United States and was a professor of philosophy at Beijing University, believed that it was possible to establish an American-inspired liberal democracy on Chinese soil, albeit in a modified form.[37] Hu's teacher at Columbia University, John Dewey, whose stay in China from 1919 to 1921 was a highly publicized event, cautioned that the special circumstances in China had to be taken into account when reflecting upon modernization and democratization efforts. Dewey and Hu commonly assumed that mass education would provide the fundaments for a flourishing liberal democracy.

Supporters of liberal-democratic models in China were driven by the belief that democracy, international law, and diplomacy would provide the best means for a peaceful transformation of the world. Their vision, which primarily focused on cooperation instead of conflict, needs to be seen in the context of the numerous intergovernmental and nongovernmental organizations flourishing during the 1920s, despite the initial setbacks suffered at the Versailles conference.[38] Even though some Chinese government circles actively pursued these pragmatist-liberal approaches,[39] the tide turned against moderate liberalism rather quickly after May 4, 1919. Certain prominent liberal philosophers continued to be influential thinkers, but an increasing number of students and other urban milieus started to favor more sudden and forceful approaches to China's transformation.[40] As in many other countries, the Wilsonian disillusionment strengthened the conviction that Western dominance could not be modified by working through the international institutions the West had created. In the eyes of many Chinese, more radical solutions were necessary for stabilizing China and reformulating international order. Faced with more radical opposition, moderate liberalism around leading figures such as Hu Shi was increasingly pushed toward more conservative positions.[41]

In the dozens, if not hundreds of journals affiliated with the New Culture Movement, the number of articles representing liberal-democratic worldviews declined significantly after May 1919. That is not to say that they disappeared entirely—a fair number of publications still continued to advocate the belief in an open world community of democratic nation states, and some writers even assumed that the Great War had brought the world closer to this ideal. For example, in an article published in late 1919, Wei Siluan, a member of the Young China Association,[42] refuted the notion that World War I had put a question mark on the eschatology of progress and sustained development. For him the atrocities in Europe did not reduce the modern European project to ashes. Arguing against cyclical theories of civilization that interpreted the Great War as the collapse of an overstretched cultural system, Wei Siluan suggested a model of spiral development. Admittedly Europe had been hurt, been thrown back, and some of its naïve optimism had been shattered; however, according to Wei the continent's physical destruction and economic crisis were outweighed by the spiritual benefits of the war. In his opinion the benefits and glimmers of hope that had emerged from the purgatory of the European battlefields, included the foundation of the League of Nations and the waves of democratization following the truce of 1918.[43] Along similar lines, Chen Qitian, another early member of the Young China Association and representative of its right wing, wrote five years later that the Great War had replaced "old nationalism" revolving around militarism, chauvinism, and imperialism, with "new nationalism," a form of collective identity characterized by cosmopolitanism, pacifism and humanitarianism.[44]

In the eyes of the majority of Chinese students and young intellectuals, however, the events of May 4, 1919 had shown that liberal-democratic rhetoric was only a veil for power politics. Many argued that, contrary to the high expectations of many Chinese, secret diplomacy, *realpolitik*, and other pillars of the prewar order had not disappeared from the world stage. A growing number of students now channeled their disillusionment with the new international system into renewed waves of attacks on Chinese customs and traditions. The outcome of the peace negotiations seemed to verify the assumption that only dynamic societies could grow strong enough to hold their own. Revolutionary changes in the international system thus had to be accompanied by revolutionary changes in non-Western societies. In the eyes of many young activists, Versailles seemed to have demonstrated to the world that international justice and dignity were luxuries only for the strong. According to the same activists, the very progressive spirit that appeared to form the basis of Western superiority and that Japan seemed to have copied so successfully, had to be injected into Chinese society and culture. The support for republican, democratic approaches that had grown among Chinese intellectuals after the Chinese Revolution in 1911, started to erode.

Together with the waning faith in the prospects of a liberal international community, Social Darwinism once again became influential among the educated parts of Chinese society. During the late nineteenth century, influential modernizers and reformers advocated evolutionary theories that were often only loosely related to notions of national competition. Some of the 1898 reformers such as Liang Qichao or Yan Fu had seen Social Darwinism as a tool to enhance the condition of the entire human species that also included the emancipation of women.[45] But around the time of the Chinese Revolution, when resentments against the Qing-dynasty were accompanied by anti-Manchu movements, racial concepts and identities started to become more influential in China.[46] The social groups that popularized racial and ethnic concepts in China were actually Chinese students returning from Western societies, where they had been exposed to racial theories and ethnic prejudices.[47]

With the enthusiasm surrounding the successful revolution of 1911 and Sun Yat-sen's advocacy of ethnically pluralistic forms of nationalism, the salience of Social Darwinism as an ingredient for political programs and ideologies had declined.[48] When Social Darwinism reemerged around the time of May Fourth, its parameters no longer appealed to the great reformers of 1898, but instead to the younger generations of intellectuals whose hopes for a new, open world order had proven to be mere illusions. Journals published in the aftermath of May Fourth contain a fairly large number of articles that perceive the events in Europe primarily from a Social Darwinian perspective. Some authors even went as far as to argue that the events between 1914 and 1918 were yet another indication of European superiority. Such individuals shared the opinion of writers such as Ernst Jünger, who asserted that only a supreme martial spirit in Europe could have led to such unprecedented warfare. In some eyes, the storms of steel between 1914 and 1918 had heightened national sentiments and revolutionary energies in the West that— when combined with materialism and industrialization—could provide societies with the necessary strength to survive in a merciless world.[49]

In many cases such interpretations of the war unabashedly referred to racism as a framework for placing the Great War into a historical and global context.[50] For example, an article written for the journal *New Youth* argued that Chinese culture was impeded by its own pacifist tendencies. Only a militaristic culture, aggressive spirit, and offensive mindset could prepare China for the great future conflicts between the white and the yellow races. For the author, both races that inhabited the Eastern and Western fringes of the Eurasian landmass were natural enemies and future conflicts were inevitable. He opined that different races could gain an advantage over each other by reaping the fruits of sciences, which were universal and laying on an open field of competition for different human groups. The article further states that those peoples who could not conquer nature through science were doomed to be conquered by others in the great Darwinian struggles looming over the horizon. Despite the war and through the war the West seemed to be still in an advantageous position.[51]

However, not all Social Darwinists interpreted the Great War as a bloody learning process that prepared Western powers better for the world orders to come. Some intellectuals, who shared the idea that the future would be characterized by a competition of civilizations or races, predicted that China would have a clear advantage over the West. For instance, an article published in November 1919 argued that China was in the unique position to learn from the West and combine the best elements of both cultures. By being able to pick and choose, to incorporate beneficial elements and reject potentially detrimental influences, China would be able to build a superior, in the author's words, "fitter" civilization. The West, the author predicted, would turn out to be unwilling and unable to learn from the East, mainly because of its own illusion of superiority, in addition to its language barriers.[52] Surrounded by mirrored cultural walls and too proud to learn, Europe would be unable to use other experiences as sources of inspiration. The article goes on to predict that this proud tower, into which Europe had retreated, would become a cultural prison and block Europe from learning, growing and changing. These examples show that Social Darwinism was not necessarily related to the notion of impermeable civilizational boundaries. Rather, cultural learning could be seen as a function of adaptation and thus make a human group more likely to proceed faster than its competitors. The different positions on the question of cultural learning reveal the great diversity that characterized Social Darwinism as an international school of thought.[53]

Social Darwinist theories remained influential after its surging prominence around the time of May Fourth, but the fastest growing political and intellectual milieu in China during the early 1920s were socialist and communist groupings.[54] Even Guomindang (Kuomintang) politicians had greeted the revolution of 1917 as a milestone on the way toward global justice, yet at that time, communist ideas were hardly known in China. But the October Revolution was far from an effective rallying call in China—only the great disillusionment with international standards and Western politics after Versailles turned an increasing number of Chinese intellectuals and activists toward the socialist camp. The Karakhan manifesto of 1919 that promised that the Soviet Union would relinquish all privileges and rights of Russia in China, was perceived as a marked contrast to the politics of the established international powers. In addition, the Leninist idea of the communist party's vanguard role tended to resonate with a sense of mission among many educated Chinese, a mission to mobilize the masses and awaken China.[55] Furthermore, the idea to partake in a global counterprogram to Western imperialism, to fight for an alternative vision that was rooted in the Enlightenment tradition, greatly attracted intellectuals who typically had been exposed to Western concepts since their early youth, and at best had rather tormented feelings toward Chinese political and cultural traditions. Lastly the internationally coordinated partification of the communist movement and the organizational as well as strategic support by the Comintern appealed to a generation of intellectuals whose faith in the ideal of open, democratic societies had been greatly shaken by the events following the end of World War I.

From its very beginning Chinese communism had been closely entangled with nationalist identities. The Leninist idea that proletarian nations needed to liberate themselves from imperialist-capitalist oppression was shifted further toward nationalist perspectives in Chinese communist circles. The positive benefits of communism for Chinese modernization and liberation were usually more in the foreground than the *telos* of a world revolution. It is thus not a great surprise that theories of the decline and fall of civilizations that had been an essential part of Social Darwinist and similar approaches, could also be found in early socialist or communist-inspired reactions to the Great War. Furthermore, Chinese thinkers often interpreted Lenin's vision of an imminent collapse of capitalism in ways that were close to theories of future competitions between different world regions.

Many early Chinese advocates of communist ideas believed that the Great War had revealed major disadvantaged of Europe, which had been hidden behind a façade of geopolitical dominance and cultural influence. For example, Li Dazhao, the head librarian of Beijing University who became one of the leading figures of the early Chinese Communist Party,[56] argued that the great powers of Western Europe had already reached their peak and were now in a stage of decline. By contrast—according to Li—countries such as Russia and China that had been rather slow in development were now filled with a surplus of energy that could catapult them to the top of the international system. He even assumed that in Russia a new civilization had emerged, which, founded upon the concepts of freedom and humanity, would offer many advantages to China and other underprivileged parts of the world.[57]

In a text entitled "The Victory of the People," Li Dazhao followed Lenin's interpretation of the war as a triumph of the common people and democracy over the capitalist class and despotism. Li Dazhao argued that now the social and political foundations for a new era of human existence, a higher and better stage of the human condition, had been laid.[58] This sparkling sense of optimism started to give way to visions of a more long-term struggle, but the Chinese Communist Party (CCP) remained committed to interpreting the war as an important transition point in human history. According to communist theory the war had brought an end to the unchallenged hegemony of imperialist and capitalist powers, particularly since now internationally coordinated countermovements of the oppressed classes and peoples had emerged. Expressed in Hegelian terms, European history had a purpose and hence the events after August 1914 also had to have a purpose.

Among those ideologies and political programs that had a great impact on China, none was as internationally coordinated as communism. As early as 1920, the Soviet Union dispatched two agents, Yang Mingzhu and Gregory Voitinsky, to China in order to prepare the founding of the CCP. A little later, prominent agents like Henk Sneevliet (alias Maring)[59] were supposed to help create a solid core of orthodox Marxists in the midst of the convoluted political situation exemplified by shifting alliances and overlapping ideologies. Initially the CCP ideology remained rather close to Moscow's doctrines, until Mao Zedong and others shifted the ideology's main emphasis away from the urban proletariat to the peasantry. The kind and degree of such intellectual and ideological coordination efforts may have been exceptional. But it should be considered that other systems of thought and ideologies that were prominent in China, also enjoyed international prominence and support structures.

Doubts about Modernity and Westernization Programs

For a considerable number of Chinese intellectuals the Great War was not another, admittedly atrocious, stage of human progression that despite all bloodshed, seemed to confirm the position of the West as the center of global transformations. A fair number of publications painted a picture of total economic decline and social instability in Europe,[60] and a group of thinkers referred to such reports when they argued that Western modernity was not only a promise, but also a threat.[61] Doubts about large-scale Westernization efforts that are often labeled as "conservative," reached back to the time before World War I and were as old as Chinese discourses of modernization. Against the rhetoric of revolutionary change, more cautious thinkers had long argued that transformations had to occur through moderate reforms and organic growth rather than quantum leaps.[62] The Great War strengthened such critical attitudes toward the notion that Europe was the world's only teaching civilization.

It would be wrong to assume that those groups, which sought to defend Chinese culture and tradition against iconoclastic national mobilization programs, were quite inimical to all internationally circulating discourses. Many theorists who voiced doubts about the project of Western modernity did not resort to blunt civilizational protectionism but rather promoted the goal of mutual cultural inspiration. At a closer look it even becomes apparent that traditionalist notions were connected with similar intellectual and political currents in the outside world.[63] On an international level no other non-Western public figure symbolized the notion of an Eastern remedy for the supposedly burned out, decaying European civilization as prominently as the Indian Nobel Prize Laureate Rabindranath Tagore.[64] The Indian poet maintained a great network of exchanges with supporters in North America, Europe, the Middle East, and other parts of the world. His connections with Chinese intellectuals eventually culminated in a visit to China in 1924, which however, was not well received in student circles.[65]

Some essential elements of traditionalist or culturalist thinking in China were thus being imported and adapted by internationally connected intellectuals. However, looking below the level of people who were actively engaged in international dialogues, it is certainly true that the bulk of Chinese people who shared certain reservations about the prospects of Westernization tended to have a Confucian educational background and little to no international exposure.[66] Their personal experiences may help explain why some thinkers were more sensitive to the cultural losses caused by modernization and internationalization than many young students of the New Culture Movement, who had been educated in the West or in "modern" Chinese schools. Older scholars and individuals who had been primarily trained in the Confucian education system experienced a combination of disadvantages that could be labelled as a "triple marginalization": in addition to the marginalization of China within the world and the marginalization of Confucian teaching within China, many had suffered from a personal marginalization within Chinese society—the great prestige and the main professional opportunities were at the hands of those who had some access to modern sciences and foreign languages.[67]

It is hardly surprising that the Great War became a major trope in the ranks of those who had long doubted the prospects of large-scale Westernization efforts. In many cases the events in Europe fortified such intellectual positions. For example, Yan Fu, who, like Liang Qichao had been known as a prominent advocate of Social Darwinism two decades before, experienced a major paradigm shift from the "Weberian" question of which elements of the West were missing in other cultures, to asking which elements in other cultures were missing in the West.[68] Referring to the Great War and Western Civilization, he noted that "three hundred years of evolutionary progress have come all down to nothing but four words: selfishness, slaughter, shamelessness and corruption."[69] Like many other thinkers Yan held that the today of the West could no longer symbolize the tomorrow of the rest since European civilization had collapsed morally, culturally, and politically. Now, he believed, the yesterday of East Asia could help the today of Europe. Such ideas circulated widely during the aftermath of the Great War.

Quite a substantial number of Chinese scholars had the chance to acquire a personal impression of Europe in the years following 1918. Some of them were visiting scholars at European universities, and others were accompanying diplomatic missions. Liang Qichao and the philosopher Zhang Junmai (otherwise know as Carsun Chang) were among the cultural delegates of the Chinese mission to Versailles. During their stay in Europe both traveled extensively through various countries and met intellectuals such as Romain Rolland, René Guénon and Thomas Mann. These public figures shared their doubts about the viability of the modern European path of continued industrial development, political revolutions, and social transformations. In Europe, critical voices arguing that modernity was little more than an empty, materialistic process were doubtlessly as old as modernity itself and had intensified during the last decades of the nineteenth century. Still, the experience of World War I further accentuated this tradition of voicing doubts about modernity and progress. For many thinkers, the events between 1914 and 1918 revealed the destructive potential of modernity, proving that the West's claim to civilizational superiority was specious.[70] Now an increasing number of poets and thinkers called for the salvation of Europe from its own culture, which they described as superficial, purely technological, rational, and dangerously naïve and brutal.

One of the most productive ensuing contacts between Chinese and European critics of "Western modernity" resulted from the exchanges between Zhang Junmai and Rudolf Eucken, a philosopher at the University of Jena and Nobel Prize Laureate in literature.[71] Eucken tirelessly averred that society needed to balance materialism and progressivism with self-cultivation and spiritual growth. Zhang Junmai was so impressed with Eucken's work that he decided to stay in Jena for several years to work with him on several common projects. He and Eucken even co-authored a book entitled *The Problem of Life in China and Europe* that was published in China and Germany.[72] The work presents China and Europe not as hermetically sealed civilizations but rather as organically grown cultural realms that had always been closely entangled with the world beyond. Zhang and Eucken then contrasted the allegedly communal traditions of Germany and China with the creed in the power of reason and individualism that, in their eyes, characterized the United States as well as a number of Western European societies. Stemming from these hypotheses, the book discusses the necessity to be "on guard against the Anglo-American notion that their way of life is the only possible, natural and superior one."[73]

After his return to China, Zhang Junmai continued to pursue his intellectual agenda. In later writings, such as the essay *My Political Impressions During my Stay in Europe From 1919 to 1921*,[74] Zhang warned of blindly copying European ideas and institutions. Arguing that Europe experienced a "kind of cultural crisis," he held that conscious choice and selection should be the guiding spirits for the modernization of China. For him China was now in the privileged position to have insight into the constructive and destructive potentials of European modernity. The Chinese now had the option to import only those elements that were compatible with their own situation and beneficial for the future. Zhang argued that such cultural eclecticism was possible, since the idea of coherent Eastern and Western cultures were nothing but gross generalizations. In this manner there was an alternative route for China between the options of wholesale Westernization on the one hand, and the complete denial of any European influence on the other. However, in contrast to intellectuals such as the aforementioned Wei Siluan, who believed that the war had actually strengthened European civilization, Zhang promoted the ideal of cultural learning not as an advantage of China in a cultural competition but as a necessary step toward global cross-fertilization. In Zhang's opinion the crisis-ridden nations of Europe and Chinese society could mutually benefit each other without completely losing their distinctive features and characteristics.

The idea that Europe needed to learn from China was now also advocated by the highly influential historian and public intellectual Liang Qichao. Decades before, he had been a staunch defender of Western learning but over the years had grown doubtful about radical modernization programs.[75] Liang was certainly one of the internationally most well connected Chinese intellectuals of his time, and in many regards he served as a transaction point between intellectual debates in China, Japan, and the West.[76] The war in Europe moved Liang further away from his previously rather teleological understandings of European civilization.[77] After returning home from a trip to Britain, France, Germany, and other countries from 1919 to 1920,[78] Liang Qichao published a monograph entitled *Impressions of My Travels in Europe*. The first part of this book, "Europe Before and After the Great War," is an account of Liang's stay in Europe and provides vivid accounts of the conditions in Europe.[79] For example it contains descriptions of pauperization in European cities, the growing gaps between the social classes as well as between urban and rural areas. The second part, "The Self-Awakening of the Chinese People," outlines the implications of the European crisis and the consequences of the new geopolitical constellation for Chinese society, culture, and politics.

In a similar way one can understand Liang's detailed accounts of the widespread pessimism among European intellectuals whom he described as "yelling about the end of the world and the decay of civilization."[80] He actually regarded Europe's overall dark cultural and intellectual climate as a more severe symptom of crisis than the material shortage from the destructions of war. For him, Europe was a continent that had awakened from a dream, that was devoid of any ideals or clear visions for the future, and that was desperately searching for new directions, commonly shared values and some sort of sociopolitical consensus. Before the war, Liang had praised Europe's endless resources of ambitious energies and cultural curiosity to discover the new and unknown as major advantages over China. During the 1920s, his accounts depicted Europe as intellectually as well as physically devastated—far more so than the Far East or any other civilization that had been shaken by European expansionism.

According to Liang Qichao, the dream of a man-made, scientific golden age had revealed itself as a nightmare, and the European project had turned into a pathological process. The specters that now haunted Europe were the growth of violent forces, the emergence of extreme contradictions, and the loss of any communal connectedness. According to Liang, Europe's revolutionary restlessness was now in the process of splitting up into a multitude of national and class-related protest movements. This in essence meant that the revolutionary energy that had driven Europe to the top was now in the process of turning against itself. If this process was not stopped and Europe would not change its historical trajectory, the Great War would be followed by additional, possibly even greater disasters and crises. In the same text Liang suggested that in the near future, national and socialist movements might merge and throw the continent into another lapse of severe domestic and international conflicts. He opined that it was mainly the method and the mentality of systematic scientific doubt that had robbed Europe of its spiritual stronghold: the consequences of scientific culture such as industrialization, urbanization, and social fragmentation had largely disintegrated the communal glue and cultural consensus that in the past had formed the bedrock of European societies.

His observations and theories prompted Liang Qichao to conclude that China could no longer learn from Europe but rather from Europe's fall. Like many Chinese intellectuals he believed that China's status as a "latecomer" and developing country now became an advantage, since, in Liang Qichao's own words, "knowing the disease is a good medicine."[81] According to him, communal values and traditional ties had the potential to enrich a culture focused on science and progress that could possibly prevent modernizing forces and energies from turning against themselves. For this reason, he admonished the Chinese youth movements to be patient and to carefully select between Chinese and Western elements when building the national culture of the future. He maintained that in the process of nation building "one should be neither bound by old Chinese thoughts nor by new Western thoughts." Any form of iconoclasm could be the wrong answer to the challenges of the time, since "what we consider to be new thoughts are criticized and regarded as outmoded in Europe itself." In the *Impressions of My Travels in Europe* Liang added that even if some ideas and concepts were completely new and propounded by the intellectual and political avant-garde of Europe, it would be a grave mistake to confuse "new" with "true."[82]

Still, just like Zhang Junmai and many other thinkers of his time, Liang Qichao did not simply prophesize the decline of the West. On the contrary, he predicted that European culture would critically reconsider its own civilizational premises and finally start approaching a more cautious, humble, and gentle form of modernity. Europe would learn to listen to the voices of less expansive and dynamic cultures such as China or India. For Liang, Europe had not only been dethroned as the world's great teacher, but was now placed in the role of a disoriented student who had to learn from other world regions that were culturally more intact and had more viable visions for the future. In other words, thinkers such as Liang Qichao or Zhang Junmai did not become cultural projectionists. Rather they remained committed to the ideal of cross-cultural exchanges but reversed the civilizational hierarchy that had been propagated since the nineteenth century. In their accounts, it was now the West that was primarily described through the cultural attributes it seemed to lack. Eastern cultures were now posited as alternative universalisms that could help stabilize a disintegrating West as well as an ever more fragile world. Efforts to maintain Chinese culture were intrinsically connected with a wider, global agenda.

Chinese Reactions to the Great War—A Transcultural Perspective

World War I was a global moment whose shockwaves could also be felt in those parts of the world that were only marginally affected by the military confrontation in Europe. The global economic and cultural consequences of the Great War have not been sufficiently explored by modern research yet, particularly from a transregional perspective. As the case of China indicates, the events in Europe could also have profound consequences for societies that did not play a central part in the four-year war effort—consequences that went far beyond new debates on world order. The shadows of doubt that the war cast on an imperialist world order and the ensuing Wilsonian hopes greatly energized the Chinese public. Whereas the Chinese Revolution of 1911 had mainly been the product of small elites, the protest movements in the wake of May Fourth forged an alliance between the new social milieu of young intellectuals and larger parts of society ranging from factory workers to clerks. Nationalist sentiments were further channeled into political movements that were not under government tutelage.[83]

However, Chinese reactions triggered by the war and Versailles were far from being similar to each other. Different intellectual and political

groupings fiercely disagreed about the implications of the war and the directions of future changes. The number of supporters of liberal democratic
ideals quickly thinned out after the disillusioning outcome of the Versailles
peace negotiations, and programs that sought to mobilize the nation by
radical means grew in strength. Coherence and collective power were increasingly seen as the true guarantors of dignity and independence for a country
in a violent, immoral, and unstable international system. Particularly for
younger Chinese intellectuals, the Great War and the Versailles negotiations
actually confirmed the necessity to push ahead with revolutionary changes.
However, the vision of these changes varied greatly among the polarized
right-wing and left-wing groups, both of which had emerged from the New
Culture Movement.

Contrary to the New Culture Movement, thinkers such as Zhang Junmai
and Liang Qichao, who had both grown more doubtful of the prospects of
Westernization, cautioned against naïve trust in the potentials of revolutionary transformations. Like many likeminded European thinkers they tended
to see a connection between the atrocities after the French Revolution and
the Great War, where—in their opinion—Europe had descended into an
abyss of mud, blood, and steel. Supporters of this camp came to understand
European civilization as a Faustian process that carried such a destabilizing
potential so as to lead the world into yet another series of disastrous collapses.
For these thinkers, the Great War was not a trumpet signal for another series
of revolutions but rather a clear warning that the global tide of transformations
needed to be critically reconsidered. In their eyes the project of modernity
could benefit from a revitalized Chinese past and from a reversed cultural
learning process that would no longer regard the West as the world's only
teaching civilization. This implied that China and other non-Western
cultures would now be in the position to universalize their cultures, and to
put an imprint on the value-systems and ideals that would underlie future
world orders.

An important feature of all political positions discussed in this chapter is
the global consciousness that characterized them. By the time of the May
Fourth Movement it was definitely impossible to conceive of China as its
own isolated universe, and to discuss the main directions for the future of
China, without paying due attention to the international situation at large.
Consequently, during the early 1920s all rivalling political as well as cultural
programs combined visions of world order with visions of domestic order.
The international constraints on the former Middle Kingdom made it clear
that the world needed to create an international environment allowing for a
repositioning and reconfiguration of China. For example, theories that
cautioned against blind faith in revolutionary change could only present

themselves as credible programs if they also developed visions for a world without imperialist rivalries. Likewise, early Chinese communists had to present their ideal of a proletarian revolution as part of a rising worldwide Hegelian tide in order not to be discarded as a group of blind idealists.

Most intellectual positions turned the humiliating new status of China as a developer into an asset.[84] The tool for shifting China's international position from a latecomer to a member of a group of frontrunners was usually a revision of the discourse of civilization. Followers of Social Darwinist, communist, and conservative ideologies could equally claim that China was an essential part of an alternative civilization that would rise up and replace at least parts of the allegedly burned out culture of Europe that in the past had attained a worldwide reach.[85] Across a wide range of political camps Chinese thinkers argued that their country had learned enough from the West to be internationally relevant, but that it was also untouched, unspoiled, and different enough to belong to the seeds of a better future be part of a true alternative. However, whether this alternative vision aimed at the globalization of Eastern ethics, a proletarian world revolution, or a Darwinian amalgamation of forces depended on one's individual viewpoint.

The increasing international entanglement and education of Chinese intellectuals was an important aspect of their rising global awareness. Most political groupings in China strengthened their exchange networks with likeminded forces in Europe and other parts of the world. The Chinese reception of internationally circulating ideologies and visions of world order was thus closely related to new worldwide sociocultural patterns and landscapes of knowledge. In the aftermath of World War I, political ideologies intensified their levels of international cooperation. The Soviet Union and the Communist International supplied likeminded groups around the world with financial support, agents, and ideological material. Furthermore, liberal forces were actively supported by government agencies, universities, associations, and other institutions in the United States and Western European countries. However, as a matter of fact, socialism, liberalism, and other global ideologies were not the only visions of political order being promoted by global networks of support. Quite to the contrary, even movements with a strictly anti-internationalist rhetoric that claimed to defend notions of "tradition" and "heritage" against global ideologies, were engaged in closely entangled transnational networks. This was true for traditionalist scholars, nationalist movements,[86] and also for the international fascist networks, which started to form a few years later.[87]

During the 1920s many advanced and developing societies were characterized by a tense political situation that was structured around the ideological triad of liberalism, socialism, and nationalism.[88] Needless to say, in all cases right-wing, left-wing, and liberal ideologies had overlapping agendas and mutually influenced each other. Furthermore, all international ideologies were altered and adapted to specific local contexts. Yet, it remains a remarkable matter of fact that during the 1920s, the rivaling political forces in such divergent countries as China and Germany, for instance, were divided into camps that in principle were quite comparable to each other.[89] Global moments and crises such as the Great War evoked a wide range of reactions around the world. Much of these different reaction patterns were embedded in political ideals and intellectual convictions that circulated in transnational networks of knowledge. The competing Chinese responses to World War I tended to be part of wider, transnational opinion networks.

Notes

1. Liang Qichao: "Ouyou Xinying lu jielu" [Condensed Record of Travel Impressions in Europe], in vol. 7 of *Yinbingshi heji* (Beijing: Zhonghua shuju, 1989), p. 2968.
2. For a more detailed description of this period and the emergence of levels of global consciousness see Michael Geyer and Charles Bright, "World History in a Global Age," *American Historical Review* 100, no. 4 (1995): 1034–60.
3. See the chapter by Erez Manela in this volume.
4. See, for example, David M. Kennedy, *Over There: The First World War and American Society* (Oxford: Oxford University Press, 1980). Needless to say, some American intellectuals shared European doubts about Western Civilization—for example Henry James in his novel *The Ivory Tower* (New York: Scribners, 1917).
5. For example Prasenjit Duara, "Introduction: The Decolonization of Asia and Africa in the Twentieth Century," in idem, ed., *Decolonization: Rewriting Histories* (New York: Routledge, 2004). Such a periodization is somewhat problematic since it does not account for the Latin American revolutions during the late eighteenth and nineteenth centuries.
6. After the famous quote by British foreign secretary Viscount Grey of Falloden during a blackout in July 1914 that was part of the war preparations: "The lights are going out all across Europe, and we shall not see them lit again in our lifetime."
7. A pioneering study, which focuses on doubts about Western modernity, is Michael Adas, "The Great War and the Decline of the Civilizing Mission," in L.J. Sears, ed., *Autonomous Histories, Particular Truths: Essays in Honor of John R.W. Small* (Madison: University of Wisconsin Monographs on Southeast Asia, 1993), pp. 101–21.
8. See, for example, about Africa: John Steele Gordon, "What We Lost in the Great War," *The Journal of African History* 44 (2003): 73–94; About Iran: Ali Mirsepassi, *Intellectual Discourse and the Politics of Modernization: Negotiating Modernity in Iran* (Cambridge, Mass.: Harvard University Press, 2000); about Europe: Belinda

Davis, "Experience, Identity, and Memory: the Legacy of World War One," *The Journal of Modern History* 75 (2003): 111–21.

9. See Hui Huang, "Overseas Chinese Studies and the Rise of Foreign Cultural Capital in Modern China," *International Sociology* 17, no. 1 (2002): 35–55.

10. Still a very valuable overview of China's economic and social transformations is Jürgen Osterhammel, *China und die Weltgesellschaft vom 18. Jahrhundert bis in die Gegenwart* (Munich: Beck, 1989).

11. Compare Wang Hui, *Xiandai zhongguo sixiang de xingqi* [The Rise of Modern Chinese Thought], vol.1 (Beijing: Sanlian Shudian, 2004), chapter 1.

12. For a discussion of the early 1900s see Rebecca E. Karl, "Creating Asia: China in the World at the Beginning of the Twentieth Century," *American Historical Review* 103, no. 4 (1998): 1096–118.

13. The rise of translations and the ensuing lexical changes in China are covered in Michael Lackner, Iwo Amelung, and Joachim Kurtz, eds., *New Terms for New Ideas: Western Knowledge & Lexical Change in Late Imperial China* (Leiden: Brill, 2001).

14. See Paul Cohen, "Remembering and Forgetting National Humiliation in Twentieth-Century China," *Twentieth-Century China* 27, no. 2 (2002): 1–39.

15. The concepts and categories for the new nation states such as ethnos, citizenship, or territorial sovereignty were taken from transnational discourses. For China see, for example, Prasenjit Duara, "Transnationalism in the Era of Nation States: China, 1900–1945," *Development and Change* 29, no. 4 (1998): 647–70.

16. For example, William Kirby, "The Internationalization of China," *China Quarterly* 150 (1997): 433–58.

17. See, for example, Leo Ou-fan Lee, "The Cultural Construction of Modernity in Urban Shanghai: Some Preliminary Explorations," in Wen-hsin Yeh, ed., *Becoming Chinese: Passages to Modernity and Beyond* (Berkeley: University of California Press, 2000), pp. 1–30.

18. See, for example, Bryna Goodman, guest ed., "Networks of News: Power, Language, and Transnational Dimensions of the Chinese Press, 1850–1949," *The China Review* 4, no. 1 (2004): 1–10.

19. For more details see Wen-hsin Yeh, *The Alienated Academy: Culture and Politics in Republican China, 1919–1937* (Cambridge, Mass.: Harvard University Press, 1990). See also Timothy B. Weston, *The Power of Position: Beijing University, Intellectuals, and Chinese Political Culture, 1898–1929* (Berkeley: University of California Press, 2004).

20. A statistical analysis is provided by Hui Huang, *The Chinese Construction of the West, 1862–1922: Discourses, Actors and the Cultural Field* (Ph.D. diss., University of North Carolina, 1996).

21. See, for example, Vera Schwarcz, *The Chinese Enlightenment: Intellectuals and the Legacy of the May Fourth Movement of 1919* (Berkeley: University of California Press, 1986).

22. John Fitzgerald, *Awakening China: Politics, Culture, and Class in the Nationalist Revolution* (Stanford: Stanford University Press, 1996).

23. See, for example, Weili Ye, *Seeking Modernity in China's Name: Chinese Students in the United States, 1920–1927* (Stanford: Stanford University Press, 2001).

24. Recent scholarship is becoming increasingly aware of the highly pluralistic character of the New Culture Movement. See, for example, the overview by Hung-Yok Ip, Tze-Ki Hon, and Chiu-Chun Lee, "The Plurality of Chinese Modernity: A Review of Recent Scholarship on the May Fourth Movement," *Modern China* 29, no. 4 (2003): 490–509.

25. Lee Feigon, *Chen Duxiu: Founder of the CCP* (Princeton: Princeton University Press, 1983).

26. A seminal study of the New Culture and May Fourth movements is still Chow Tse-tsung, *The May Fourth Movement: Intellectual Revolution in Modern China* (Cambridge, Mass.: Harvard University Press, 1960).

27. Chen Duxiu, "Xin Wenhua Yundong shi shenme?" *Xin Qingnian* 6, no. 1 (1920), p. 4.

28. See, for example, Gao Yuhan, "The Republic and the Self-Consciousness of Youth" [Gonghe quojia yu qingnian zhi zijue], *Xin Qingnian* 1, no. 1 (1915), pp. 1–8; Gao Yuhan, "Youth and the Future of the Nation" [Qingnian yu quojia zhi qiantu], *Xin Qingnian* 1, no. 5 (1916), pp. 1–7; Gao Yuhan, "The Enemies of Youth" [Qingnian zhi di], *Xin Qingnian* 1, no. 6 (1916), pp. 1–4.

29. See Xu Guoqi, *China and the Great War. China's Pursuit of a New National Identity and Internationalization* (Cambridge: Cambridge University Press, 2005). See also Klaus Mühlhahn, "China," in Gerhard Hirschfeld, Gerd Krumeich, and Irina Renz, eds., *Enzyklopädie Erster Weltkrieg* (Paderborn: Schöningh, 2002), pp. 412–16.

30. Chen Bao, "Gongzhu: xieyue guo da shengli shijie heping." *Morning Post*, December 1, 1919, "Congratulations: The Great Victory of the Entente Countries [leads to] World Peace."

31. A transcultural perspective of the hopes for independence in the aftermath of the Great War is provided by Erez Manela, *The Wilsonian Moment: Self-Determination and the International Origins of Anticolonial Nationalism* (Oxford: Oxford University Press, 2007).

32. See, for example, Elizabeth Perry, *Shanghai on Strike: The Politics of Chinese Labor* (Stanford: Stanford University Press, 1993).

33. Cai Yuanpei, "Ouzhan yu zhexue" [The European War and Philosophy], *Xin Qingnian* 5, no. 5 (1918): 491–96. A similar argument is provided by Tao Lügong, "Guanyu Ouzhan de yanshuo san pian—Ouzhan yihou de zhengzhi" [Three Lectures about the European War: Post-War European Politics] *Xin Qingnian* 5, no. 5 (1918): 470–72.

34. Tao Lügong, "Ouzhan yihou de zhengzhi " [Politics after the European War], *Xin Qingnian* 5, no. 5 (1918), pp. 439–41.

35. An account of Chinese liberalism is provided by Benjamin Tsai, *Enemies of the Revolution: Ideology and Practice in the Making of Chinese Liberalism, 1890–1927* (Ph.D. diss., University of Michigan, Ann Arbor, 2001).

36. "Generally on the topic of translations and cultural reformulations see Lydia He Liu, *Translingual Practice. Literature, National Culture, and Translated Modernity – China, 1900–1937* (Stanford: Stanford University Press, 1995). For the case of Yan Fu, (1853–1921) who translated many key works of Western social theory into Chinese, see Benjamin Schwartz, *In Search of Wealth and Power: Yan Fu and the West* (Cambridge, Mass.: Harvard University Press, 1964).

37. About Hu Shi see Jerome B. Grieder, *Hu Shi and the Chinese Renaissance: Liberalism in the Chinese Revolution, 1917–1937* (Cambridge, Mass.: Harvard University Press, 1970).

38. See Akira Iriye, *Cultural Internationalism and World Order* (Baltimore and London: Johns Hopkins University Press, 1997), chapter 2.

39. See, for example, S.H. Tan, "China's Pragmatist Experiment in Democracy: Hu Shih's Pragmatism and Dewey's Influence in China," *Metaphilosophy* 35, no. 1 (2004): 44–64.

40. Compare Wen-hsin Yeh, *The Alienated Academy*, chapter 7.

41. See, for example, Zhang Zhongdong, "Similarities and Differences between Hu Shi and Yin Haiguang during the Initial Stage of Anti-Communism," *Chinese Studies in History* 38, no. 1 (2004): 77–93.

42. After May Fourth, the Young China Association that was founded in 1918 and mainly recruited its members from students returned from overseas, started to split into right and left factions. The difference grew so big that the association fell apart in 1921. See Chow Tse-tsung, *The May Fourth Movement*, pp. 251–53.

43. Wei Siluan, "Renlei jinhua de geminghuang" [Aspects of Human Evolution], *Shaonian Zhongguo* 1, no. 1 (1919): 14–34.

44. Chen Qitian, "Xin guojiazhuyi yu zhongguo qiantu" [New Nationalism and China's Future], *Shaonian Zhongguo* 4, no. 9 (1924).

45. For more details see James Pusey, *China and Charles Darwin* (Cambridge, Mass.: Harvard University Press, 1983).

46. See, for example, Kauko Laitinen, *Chinese Nationalism in the Late Qing Dynasty: Zhang Binglin as an Anti-Manchu Propagandist* (London: Curzon Press, 1990).

47. Compare Weili Ye, *Seeking Modernity in China's Name*.

48. Ethnic and racial forms of nationalism were not really suitable as official state ideologies, since they would have inevitably put the political boundaries of China into question.

49. For example: Hua Lu, "Lessons and Warnings Derived from World War One," *Dongfang Zazhi* 21, no. 14 (1924): 17–22.

50. For the spread of racist theories in China see, for example, Kai-Wing Chow, "Imagining Boundaries of Blood: Zhang Binglin and the Invention of the Han 'Race' in Modern China," in Frank Dikotter, ed., *The Construction of Racial Identities in China and Japan: Historical and Contemporary Perspectives* (London: Hurst, 1997), pp. 34–52.

51. Liu Shuya, "Ouzhou zhanzheng yu qingnian zhi juewu" [World War One and the Awakening of Youth], *Xin Qingnian* 2, no. 2 (1919): 119–26.

52. Zong Zhikui, "Zhongguo Qingnian de fendou shenghuo yu chuangzao shenghuo " [Struggling Life and Creative Life of the Chinese Youth], *Shaonian Zhongguo* 1, no. 5 (1919), pp. 1–11.

53. See, for example, Mike Hawkins, *Social Darwinism in European and American Thought, 1860–1945* (Cambridge: Cambridge UP, 1997).

54. For a general account of the topic see, for example, Arif Dirlik, *The Origins of Chinese Communism* (Oxford: Oxford University Press, 1989).

55. Consequently the relationship between Communist intellectuals and workers was often somewhat contradictory in the China of the early 1920s. See Daniel Y. Kwan, *Marxist Intellectuals and the Chinese Labor Movement: A Study of Deng Zhongxia, 1894–1933* (Seattle: University of Washington Press, 1997).

56. For more details see Maurice M. Meisner, *Li Ta-chao and the Origins of Chinese Marxism* (Cambridge, Mass.: Harvard University Press, 1967). See also Michael Y.L. Luk, *The Origins of Chinese Bolshevism: An Ideology in the Making, 1920–1928* (Hong Kong: Oxford University Press, 1990).

57. Meisner, *Li Ta-chao and the Origins of Chinese Marxism*, pp. 64–65.

58. Li Dazhao, "The Victory of the People" [Shumin zhi shengli], *Xin Qingnian* 5, no. 5 (1918): 467–69. The article is part of a series entitled "Three Lectures on the European War."

59. See Anthony Saich, *The Origins of the First United Front in China: The Role of Sneevliet (Alias Maring)* (Leiden: Brill, 1991).

60. For example, Wang Guangqi, "Quan'ou geguo caizheng gaiguan" [A brief Summary of the Fiscal Situation in the Whole of Europe], *Shaonian Zhongguo* 4, no. 3 (May 1923): 1–7. In the following three issues of "Young China" Wang published a series of articles on the situation in Europe.

61. See Roland Felber, "Berichte von Chinesen über die Verhaltnisse in Berlin nach dem Ersten Weltkrieg," in Christoph Kaderas and Meng Hong, eds., *120 Jahre chinesische Studierende an deutschen Hochschulen* (Bonn: DAAD, 2000), pp. 128–38.

62. See Charlotte Furth, "Culture and Politics in Modern Chinese Conservatism," in idem, ed., *The Limits of Change: Essays on Conservative Alternatives in Republican China* (Cambridge, Mass.: Harvard University Press, 1976), pp. 22–56.

63. For example, see Michael Adas, "The Great War and the Decline of the Civilizing Mission," pp. 101–21.

64. About aspects of Tagore's intellectual agenda see Ashis Nandy, *The Illegitimacy of Nationalism: Rabindranath Tagore and the Politics of Self* (Oxford: Oxford University Press, 1994).

65. Tagore was even forced to cancel parts of his planned lecture series due to the wave of student protests. See Stephen N. Hay, *Asian Ideas of East and West: Tagore and His Critics in Japan, China, and India* (Cambridge, Mass.: Harvard University Press, 1970), pp. 148–49. See also Dominic Sachsenmaier, "Searching For Alternatives to Western Modernity. Cross-Cultural Approaches in the Aftermath of World War I," *Journal of Modern European History* 4, no. 2 (2006): 241–59.

66. Huang, *The Chinese Construction of the West*, pp. 179–83.

67. Compare Ying-shih Yu, "The Radicalization of China in the Twentieth Century," *Daedalus: China in Transformation* 122, no. 2 (1993): 125–50, who speaks of a "double marginalization" (excluding personal marginalization).

68. See Benjamin Schwarz, *In Search of Wealth and Power: Yen Fu and the West* (Cambridge, Mass.: Harvard University Press, 1964), pp. 229–36.

69. Quoted in Jonathan Spence, *The Search for Modern China* (London and New York: Norton, 1990), p. 302.

70. See Michael Adas, *Machines as the Measure of Men: Science, Technology, and Ideologies of Western Dominance* (Ithaca: Cornell University Press, 1989).

71. See Werner Meißner, *China zwischen nationalem "Sonderweg" und universaler Modernisierung: Zur Rezeption westlichen Denkens in China* (Munich: Beck, 1994). Eucken's works later became prominent in the early German Fascist movement.

72. Rudolf Eucken and Carsun Chang, *Das Lebensproblem in Europa und China* (Leipzig: Quelle and Meyer, 1922).

73. Ibid., p. 193.

74. Zhang Junmai, "1919 zhi 1921 nian lü Ouzhong zhi zhengzhi yinxiang ji wuren suode zhi jiaoxun" [My Political Impressions During My Stay in Europe from 1919 to 1921, and the Lessons that I Learned There], *Xinlu Banyuekan* 1, no. 5 (1928): 19-27.

75. For an intellectual biography see Tang Xiaobing, *Global Space and the Nationalist Discourse of Modernity: The Historical Thinking of Liang Qichao* (Stanford: Stanford University Press, 1996).

76. See Joshua A. Fogel, ed., *The Role of Japan in Liang Qichao's Introduction of Modern Western Civilization to China* (Berkeley: China Research Monograph Series 57, 2004).

77. Compare Tang Xiaobing, *Liang Qichao*, chapter 2.

78. For more details about Liang's travels in Europe see the classic account by Joseph R. Levenson, *Liang Ch'i-ch'ao and the Mind of Modern China* (Cambridge, Mass.: Harvard University Press, 1953).

79. Liang Qichao, *Ouyou Xinying lu jielu*, p. 2961.

80. Ibid., p. 2978.

81. Ibid., p. 2980.

82. Ibid., pp. 2980–81.

83. See Jürgen Osterhammel, *Shanghai, 30. Mai 1925. Die chinesische Revolution* (Munich: DTV, 1997), chapters 2 and 3.

84. About the global discourse of late development see Reinhard Bendix, "Strukturgeschichtliche Voraussetzungen der nationalen und kulturellen Identität in der Neuzeit," in Bernard Giesen, ed., *Nationale und kulturelle Identität: Studien zur Entwicklung des kollektiven Bewusstseins in der Neuzeit* (Frankfurt: Suhrkamp, 1991), pp. 39–55.

85. In that sense two different definitions of civilization, civilization as a potentially universal culture and civilization as a Spenglerian category for cultural distinctiveness,

were brought into the same theoretical frameworks. About the two main discourses of civilization during the early twentieth century see Prasenjit Duara, "Civilizations and Nations in a Globalizing World," in Dominic Sachsenmaier, Jens Riedel, and Shmuel Eisenstadt, eds., *Reflections on Multiple Modernities: European, Chinese, and Other Approaches* (Leiden: Brill, 2002), pp. 79–99.

86. A rich account of research approaches is provided by Craig Calhoun, "Nationalism, Modernism, and their Multiplicities," in Elizer Ben-Rafael and Yitzak Sternberg, eds., *Identity, Culture and Globalization* (Leiden: Brill, 2001): 445–70.

87. See, for example, Stein Ugelvik Larsen, ed., *Fascism outside Europe: The European Impulse against Domestic Conditions in the Diffusion of Global Fascism* (New York: Columbia University Press, 2001).

88. Compare Eric Hobsbawm, *The Age of Extremes: A History of the World, 1914–1991* (New York: Vintage, 1994).

89. See Dominic Sachsenmaier, "Politische Kulturen in China nach dem Ersten Weltkrieg—Gedanken zu einer globalhistorischen Perspektive," *Zeitschrift für Weltgeschichte* 4, no. 2 (2003): 55–68.

PART THREE

Movements Toward Alternative World Order

CHAPTER 7

Global Mobility and Nationalism: Chinese Migration and the Reterritorialization of Belonging, 1880–1910

Sebastian Conrad and Klaus Mühlhahn

Globalization is not only the catchword of the day. At the same time, it refers back to a longer history, and historians have in recent years begun to analyze its genealogy. The years between 1880 and 1914, in particular, have caught the attention of recent scholarship as a high time of global exchange and cross-border interaction.[1] The integration of the international economy, the political and imperial expansion of the West, and the increase in cultural exchanges across national borders contributed to a complex set of networks of global engagements. This did not go unnoticed by contemporaries who witnessed the process with enthusiasm, or apprehension. The integration of the world was indeed accompanied by the emergence of a form of global consciousness.[2]

The integration of the world, together with the global consciousness that corresponded with it, made possible, and produced, connections between processes that had until then developed largely within regional contexts. Social and political actors increasingly made reference to similar developments outside their own regions or states. Social phenomena and, above all, economic developments in seemingly distant societies were referred to as models and yardsticks; at the same time there emerged a growing awareness that what happened elsewhere no longer left one's own society unaffected. Even if the entanglement of the world did not encompass all societies and people in the same way, it had its effects on processes that for the main part had previously evolved in relative isolation. These effects could be homogenizing, but at the same time the growing interaction produced opposition and fragmentation—even if differences were increasingly expressed in similar ways.[3] Globalizing effects were palpable in realms ranging from knowledge and science to the arts, constitutional developments, and ideologies and worldviews. However, they could also be observed in a sphere would seemingly be at odds with the transnational promises of globalization: namely, nationalism.

In many regions, nationalism had a longer history that dated back, as in the case of Western Europe and Latin America, at least to the French Revolution and the Napoleonic wars. Also in other parts of the world, for example in Japan or China, early formations of nationalism emerged in the beginning of or during the nineteenth century. In many places, nationalism was the product of a complex set of social conditions and political discourses *within* a society and its regional contexts. However, these long-standing (and "internal") traditions of nationalism notwithstanding, the integration of the world at the end of the century worked as an additional and external factor that decisively influenced the trajectories of nationalism across the world. In many places (New Zealand, Australia, China, Persia, and Siam, among others) the nation-state was an invention of the late nineteenth century. Moreover, the emergence of a world order of nation-states went hand in hand with the spread of nationalism that now emerged virtually everywhere—for example, in Egypt, the Balkans, in India—as the privileged form of political discourse. Even in societies in which the nation-state looked back to a longer history, the discourse of nationalism was frequently influenced by the waves of globalization since the 1880s.[4]

This chapter argues that among the many dimensions of the increasing entanglement of the world, it was the process of mobility and migration that particularly affected the global discourse on what it meant to be a nation. The mobility of large numbers of people—not only of diplomats, tourists, and aristocrats on their Grand tour, but primarily of large groups of unskilled workers—was one of the defining characteristics of globalization in the late nineteenth century. Recent scholarship has shown that between 1840 and the 1930s, more than 150 million people left their countries of origin for elsewhere, often times to settle permanently. The 60 million Europeans that left the Old World in order to begin a life in the New World were complemented by large flows of people from India and Southern China to the areas in Southeast Asia and the Indian Ocean, and by large transborder migrations in

Northeast Asia.[5] However, these global movements were accompanied by the erection of global walls. The movement and circulation of people, in other words, proved to be a rather paradoxical process: a truly transnational phenomenon that at the same time reinforced national borders and mechanisms of exclusion.[6]

This reterritorialization of the world in the context of mobility and migration took different forms. Most tangibly, at the turn of the century, most states developed strategies to channel, control, and counter the steady human flow in and out of the country: by issuing passports, introducing ethnic quotas, reinforcing borders and immigration controls, by biometric technologies and limitations to citizenship. Before World War I, the character of national borders changed decisively, even if these changes were not visible on a map. What used to be largely symbolic lines were now turned into veritable impediments to free movement and mobility.[7] Second, the large flows of immigration contributed to the strengthening of notions of ethnic and racial limitations to national belonging. While the ethnic essentialization of nationality, too, often had a longer "internal" genealogy (as in the case of Antisemitism in Central Europe), the xenophobia elicited by mass migration since the late nineteenth century, frequently reinforced the ethnic connotations of nationality and citizenship. Finally, the global circulation of goods and people contributed to an awareness of the global and systemic context in which nation-states existed and asserted themselves.

In what follows, then, we will attempt to trace the effects of the globalization process, and in particular the increase in global mobility, as an additional and external factor that shaped—and synchronized—the discourse and practice of nationalism in very different locations. In making this point we will discuss one of the most significant examples of migration on a worldwide scale: Chinese migration that in fact can be seen as an epitome for the larger phenomenon of global flows of mobility so characteristic of the nineteenth century. It has been estimated that more than 19 million Chinese left their regions of origin to settle in Southeast Asia and the lands around the Indian Ocean and South Pacific. A central nodal point was the Straits Settlements, from which many traveled on to the Dutch Indies, Borneo, Burma, and places farther west. A second trajectory of Chinese mobility brought more than 30 million migrants to Manchuria and Siberia, a process that was facilitated by active homesteading policies by the Qing government and railroad construction since the 1890s.[8]

On a comparatively smaller scale, albeit of particular importance for the argument made here, were the contracts that migrants signed with European employers in the context of the so-called "coolie trade." It is important to note, as Wang Gungwu has argued extensively, that coolie migration in many cases followed patterns and models that had already structured earlier phases of transnational entanglement.[9] In particular, there had been a long history of migration of Chinese merchants, mainly to Southeast Asia. Mostly from prosperous and well-educated backgrounds, they went abroad and set up bases at ports, mines, and trading cities. They traveled back and forth frequently and despite long-term settlement in Southeast Asia, still considered their native places in China home.[10] While in some respects reproducing patterns of this earlier form of mobility, the large scale migration of Chinese labor was a novel phenomenon owing much to changes in the global economy. The emigration of workers to Brazil and Cuba began in the first half of the nineteenth century;[11] important steps on the path to Chinese mass migration were the gold rushes in California (1849) and Australia (1851) that triggered new forms of mobility on a global scale. The largely voluntary migration to the gold mines was not, however, part of what was formally to be called the coolie trade that only began with the recruitment of labor for the plantation economies and for the railway construction in the United States. The coolie trade implied a deep change in the features of emigration; the conditions of transport and the mechanisms of recruitment demonstrate the extent to which Chinese labor had already become a commodified good.[12] The large majority of emigrants moved to Singapore, which emerged as the largest coolie market in East Asia.[13] The global circulation of Chinese workers reached its peak in the last quarter of the nineteenth century.[14]

To many contemporary observers, the coolie trade had many commonalities with the earlier slave trade—like the brutal patterns of recruitment, frequent cases of kidnapping, inhuman conditions of transport, and the high mortality rate during plantation labor. In fact, both forms of social practice were at times hard to differentiate, in particular where—as in Cuba—Chinese and African slaves worked side by side on the same plantations.[15] The demand for Asian workers rose sharply after the slave trade had been limited and gradually abolished over the course of the century. The ensuing shortage of labor, particularly on the sugar plantations in the Caribbean, was increasingly met with workers from China, Java and India (and to a lesser extent from Japan, the Philippines, and Korea).[16] Adding to the effects of abolition, there was a second structural factor that influenced the dynamics of Chinese mobility, namely the changing power constellation in the epoch of high imperialism. In this time, most not-yet colonized regions of the world were appropriated by the colonizing powers, and western capital, settlers, and technology began to infiltrate the world in unprecedented ways. This process led to the expansion of the plantation complex—and, consequently, of the demand for mobile and flexible labor—even in regions that had not seen African slavery until then.[17]

The mobility of millions of Chinese workers was an essential and integral part of the global movement/displacement of workers that characterized the nineteenth century. The numerous Chinese Diaspora communities in Southeast Asia, Australia, the Americas, and Europe led to series of nationalistic reactions that contributed to a shift in the discourse and politics of nationalism in various places. At the same time, Chinese nationalism emerged as an answer to the problem of the dispersion of Chinese around the world. As we will attempt to show, the issue of Chinese mobility influenced a sense of nation in places as different as Australia, Thailand, Malaya, South Africa, Hawaii, the United States, Germany, and, last but not least, China itself.

What follows can be read as a contribution to a "spatial turn" in the historiography of nationalism. While most studies of nationalism privilege the temporal dimension by stressing continuities, national history, and the recourse to traditions (even if frequently "invented"), the spatial setting of nationalist practices is largely neglected. However, the constitution of the nation was not only a diachronic projection in time, but has also to be situated in its spatial contexts. This does not only refer to the obvious fact that the nation-state concept, in many countries, was an import.[18] Rather, it also means that the way the nation was defined, understood, and practiced owed more to the global context in which it was constituted than has hitherto been recognized.[19] The logic and dynamics of nationalism, as Rebecca Karl has argued for late Qing China, were not only shaped by diachronic "stages of development," but equally by a synchronic "staging of the world."[20] We will then proceed by discussing in turn, various regions that were all affected to a different degree by the immigration of Chinese workers in the nineteenth century. On the one hand, this approach allows us to take into account the specifics of different nationalisms, their peculiar prehistories, as well as the historical contexts in each region that we will discuss, and on the other, also to view the migration of Chinese workers as a truly global phenomenon simultaneously affecting different regions, albeit in different ways.

Chinese Coolies, German Nationalism, and the Yellow Peril

In 1894, a landlord by the name of Schmidt petitioned the Prussian government to allow for the "import of Chinese, a sober and diligent people with very modest needs."[21] Concomitantly, he wrote to the German legation in Peking and asked for "information on the question whether Chinese workers would be suitable for employment in Eastern Prussia, both in terms of the climate and the kind of agrarian work involved."[22] The intention was to replace the large numbers of agricultural workers in the Eastern provinces of Germany who had left for the industrial centers in the Rhein-Ruhr region or the United States—at a time when the labor-intensive cultivation of sugar beets demanded a larger rural work-force. Moreover, the idea to invite Chinese coolies to Prussia must be seen as a reaction to the influx of Polish workers across the near German-Russian borders, and to the perceived advantages of Chinese *vis-à-vis* Poles. "In contrast to the Poles," as one landowner put it, "the Chinese have a reputation of being solid and honest people."[23] But, while the landlords grew increasingly dependent upon Polish workers, nationalist public opinion viewed them as a threat to German national identity and cultural development in the Eastern provinces.[24]

The Prussian government inquired into the matter and ordered its consulates in the Chinese treaty ports to report on the political possibilities, the presumed economic benefits, and the cultural difficulties of such a project. The reactions of the German diplomats, however, were lukewarm, and the government decided to shelve the matter. Important factors in this decision were the vehement protests in the German press that did not subside until the plans were aborted. While the landowners were convinced that "our consumers, presumably, will not care who produced and supplied our products,"[25] public outcries indicated the opposite. Irrespective of transnational flows in the global economy, the comments in the press revealed a strong sense of culturally motivated protectionism. Social and economic issues, however, factored in as well, so that Socialist leader August Bebel foresaw a "storm of indignation to break out in the whole German working class" if the plans to import "unpretentious, diligent, modest Chinese workers who put up with anything" and would serve as instruments in the hands of the landowners materialized.[26]

At the outset, the plans to attract agricultural labor from China were thus implicated in the rhetoric of nationalism. The few advocates of the project saw the Chinese as a remedy against a growing Polish nationalism in the Prussian East. The majority of those publicly engaged in the issue, however, depicted the coolies themselves as the real threat to the German nation. The debate about Chinese workers was linked, on a popular level, to the discourse of the Yellow Peril. In Europe, this slogan gained currency in the 1890s as a transnational discourse, not precluding differences between European nations.[27] The fear of the "Mongolian race," as the Chinese were dubbed, was an expression of the dissemination of biological and racial categories that culminated, at the end of the nineteenth century, in the militaristic rhetoric of an imminent racial war. Apart from these racist overtones, the slogan had a number of different connotations, overlapping and sometimes contradicting each other. Economic interests were pivotal, both for those who feared Chinese competition with cheap industrial goods and for those who warned of Chinese wage dumping. The central dimension of the image of a Yellow Peril, however, was the demographic phantasm of Chinese mass mobility threatening to "flood" the "white" civilizations.[28] The rhetoric was also decidedly gendered, as the image of "blond and light-skinned girls who give themselves over to any guy who comes along" was at the heart of the paternalistic voices warning of Chinese promiscuity and of the dangers of a possible race mixing.[29]

Within the context of German nationalism, the trope of the Yellow Peril did not occupy a central position. However, it played a role in contributing to the racialization of German nationalism at the turn of the century. The power and influence it had were further enhanced by the fact that it was articulated with other discourses of exclusion like that of anti-Semitism. The frequent comparison of Chinese and Jews rested on the alleged economic capabilities of the Chinese that turned them into a "by far more dangerous people than the Jews." The possibility that these two marginalized groups might coalesce and unite the entrepreneurial capabilities of the Jews with the hard-working attitudes of the Chinese created further apprehension: "Between these two tribes the Germans would run the risk of being crushed entirely."[30] In the nationalist discourse of the German Empire, the anti-Chinese and anti-Jewish stereotypes thus frequently overlapped. In the 1890s, when anti-Semitism in Germany experienced a marked radicalization through biological and racial overtones, the trope of the Yellow Peril may very well have supplied a vocabulary through which this ethnicization of the nation could also be expressed. The anti-Semitic journal *Neue Deutsche Volkszeitung*, for example, saw "welcome parallels" between the "exclusion laws against the Chinese in North America and the need for a law banning the immigration of Jews" in Germany.[31] In the context of an influx of Jews from Russia and Galicia after 1890, in particular, the anti-Semitic press readily drew on anti-Chinese rhetoric and directed it against the Jews.[32]

The discourse of the Yellow Peril allowed German nationalists to link up local issues with larger global trends. In the absence of first-hand information and social experience with Chinese workers, the main arguments were formulated with direct reference to developments in Australia and the United States. The accounts of the xenophobic reactions and the subsequent measures of exclusion, mainly in California, were regularly employed as arguments against the recruitment of Chinese labor. "The three large colonial countries that have been in direct contact with the Chinese, namely North America, Australia, and South Africa, have had the worst possible experience and now are passionately opposed," as the *Deutsche Volkszeitung* phrased it in 1906, "to the yellow pest."[33] The fear of the Yellow Peril as a reaction to Chinese mobility can be read as the expression of a global consciousness and connected the trajectory of German nationalism to events as distant as San Francisco and New South Wales.

"White Australia" and the "Chinese Crisis"

Apart from the United States, the most frequent reference in German debates about the immigration of Chinese was to the case of Australia. A series of "letters from Australia" was published in the German press and warned of the perceived detrimental effects of an Asian influx on national character and solidarity. Due to its geographical setting and its long history of immigration, Australia, even until the present, has been particularly preoccupied with questions of race relations and with debates about its "Asian" or "Western" character. At the heart of this problematic, at least in the late nineteenth century, was the question of Chinese immigration. Since the 1880s, the "Chinese Question" emerged as the dominant issue of political, social, and cultural import. Around the turn of the century, it contributed to the definition of "White Australia" and indeed to the emergence of an Australian national identity.[34]

Chinese had migrated to Australia since the year 1848, when 120 farmers arrived to work in the wool production. After the transport of British convicts had ended in 1840, the lack of labor supply had led to attempts to meet this demand with Chinese coolies. However, the major influx was triggered by the gold rush in Australia in 1851, mainly in the Southeastern provinces of New South Wales and Victoria. Within a year, the number of immigrants had risen to 95,000, coming mainly from Great Britain, California (disappointed "Fortyniners") and China. In 1852, there were 2,666 Chinese in all Australia, their number rising steadily throughout the decade. In 1858, the Chinese population in Australia was at its height, at 38,742, equaling roughly 9 percent of the total population.

The presence of Chinese, in particular in the gold fields and mining towns, soon provoked unrest and spurts of violence, as in Lambing Flat in 1861, where more than 1000 Chinese were injured and some of them killed. The anti-Asian attitude of most local officials and representative bodies led to a number of limitations to Chinese immigration and to xenophobic regulations. For example, in 1874, the Amalgamated Miners' Association, prohibited its members from working in mines that employed Chinese workers.[35] However, it was not before the 1880s that the Chinese Question became an issue of general relevance and political implications. Typically, economic interests played a role, especially when union leaders claimed that employment of Chinese resulted in lower wages for white workers in mines and factories. In the course of continuing urbanization, massive economic growth and accompanying social change, the articulation of ethnic with class differences played an important part. But the calls for ethnic segregation were not motivated by economic considerations alone, instead mainly by political concerns and the ideal of ethnic homogeneity.[36]

For the fledgling Australian nationalism, anti-Chinese xenophobic racism served as a central ingredient in discourses of identity. In the century-long history of white settlement, it seemed difficult to find events that lend themselves as points of departure for the construction of a national founding myth. However, this is not to say, that notions of national belonging did not look back to a longer history. Russel Ward, in a now classic study, has gone so far as to argue that from the beginning of white settlement in 1788, there had emerged a form of solidarity among the convicts and immigrants from the lower strata. Ward argues that this "mateship" survived the social conflicts of industrialization and naturally fed into Australian nationalism at the end of the nineteenth century.[37] A more nuanced historical perspective that is not intent to contribute to this "Australian Legend," however, needs to take into account the history of interracial conflicts that pitted the settler communities against the native aborigines. The violent race relations extinguished large parts of the native population, often with the backing of the Colonial Office in London. At the same time, issues of ethnicity assumed center stage in debates about group loyalty and belonging.[38]

The relationship with Great Britain had been the central point of reference, both for a sense of (military) security, and for a feeling of cultural and political belonging. However, in the latter half of the century, the close ties to the British Empire were clearly on the wane. On the one hand, critics of the Empire, fearing involvement in British wars that would not be in Australia's interests called for the severing of ties, in sometimes anti-Semitic rhetoric. On the other hand, the call for an Australian federation was partly a reaction to limits set by the British government to Australian colonial ambitions as in the New Guinea crisis of 1883. The majority of Australians, however, saw the process by which Australia was moving out of Britain's political scope with growing apprehension. It was furthered by the unease with which the white majority viewed the peripheral situation of the continent, far away from Europe and the centers of the Empire and in the direct neighborhood of the "teeming millions" in Asia. Australia seemed in danger of becoming easy prey for aggressive imperialists in Asia. "The first war of the young Australian nation," as a delegate to the New South Wales Parliament warned, "will be with the Chinese."[39]

This double preoccupation, with a perceived lack of national substance and tradition, and with geopolitical marginality and danger, was the context within which the xenophobic reactions to Chinese workers were elevated, in public consciousness, to a question of national concern. Starting in 1881, the prime minister of New South Wales, Henry Parkes, initiated a politics of immigration control that was explicitly directed against Chinese workers. The Influx of Chinese Restriction Bill was not framed as an all-out prohibition of Chinese immigration, as this would not have found the consent of the British crown. However, by levying high tariffs as a condition for disembarking, the immigration control was, in social practice, almost total. It was intended, in the words of Parkes, "to terminate the landing of Chinese on these shores for ever."[40]

The heated public debate triggered by Parkes' vociferous calls for a White Australia culminated in the Chinese Crisis of the year 1888. The return of several hundred Asian workers who had visited their homelands and were now exempted from the immigration restrictions, prompted rumors of a Chinese design to establish diaspora communities that would later serve as a bridgehead for a Chinese invasion of Australia. In Sydney and Melbourne, large crowds took to the streets to protest against the imminent threat of a "Mongolian invasion,"[41] while Brisbane witnessed days of violent anti-Chinese riots. The protests united nationalists with the liberal bourgeoisie, but the most radical interventions came from the representatives of the working class movement who claimed to express the consensus of all-white Australians. The Chinese Crisis of 1888 triggered articulations and manifestations of national unity that in important ways prefigured the political and institutional unification of 1901.

The unification debate had been largely governed by political and economic considerations. Internally, the push for a federation came from the growing economic integration of the colonies and the advantages to be gained, especially for the manufacturing bourgeoisie, from a unified domestic market. The leading proponents of federation were keenly interested in the establishment of a unified internal market behind a high external tariff wall. Another crucial factor in the push for the federation was the perceived need to create a strong state apparatus to defend the interests of the ruling classes against the threat posed by the growing working class, particularly since the 1890s. However, more than these rationalities, anti-Chinese sentiments were instrumental in creating a hegemonic discourse of national purpose beyond individual and group interests.

As the leader of the Liberals in the new parliament, Alfred Deakin, made clear during the parliamentary debate, the White Australia policy signified more than just the exclusion of Asians from the new nation. It was to provide Australia's very foundation. "The unity of Australia is nothing," he declared, "if that does not imply a united race. Unity of race is an absolute to the unity of Australia. It is more actually in the last resort, than any other unity. After all, when the period of confused local politics and temporary political divisions was swept aside it was this real unity which made the Commonwealth possible."[42] Although the rhetoric of military threat was not as convincing as its proponents had anticipated, the warnings of the effects of a mixing of races and the imminent hybridization of Australia were particularly efficient as a rallying cry to enlist broad public support for a politics of "Australia for the Australians."

The perceived threat to the nation was thus articulated with convictions of a more general conflict between the white and yellow races. William Lane, the editor of the influential nationalist journal *The Boomerang*, gave these apprehensions vivid expression:

> It is more than a social or national movement that is upheaving itself around us, though those we have also; it is a true racial struggle that is going on today in Australia and Australia itself is the prize . . . Here we face the hordes of the East, as our kinsmen faced them in the dim distant centuries, and here we must beat them back if we would keep intact all that can make our lives worth living.[43]

Thus, the notion of race was at the core of a debate that essentially defined Australia *vis-à-vis* its external other.

Although the political goal of creating a unified and independent Australian federation had a longer prehistory and was driven by a variety of political and economic interests, the reactions to Chinese migration proved to be "the most important single component of Australian nationalism."[44] In the process of political unification, White Australia served as the founding consensus, and the racial overtones of the debate were the most important in cutting across class differences. At the same time, they helped to secure the necessary consent of the British Crown whose Secretary of State for the Colonies Chamberlain explicitly expressed his sympathy with "the determination of the white inhabitants of these colonies, who are in comparatively close proximity to millions and hundreds of millions of Asiatics, that there shall not be an influx of people alien in civilization, alien in religion, alien in customs."[45]

As a consequence of the exclusionist politics, the number of Chinese living in Australia gradually declined; in 1933, a mere 6404 Chinese (roughly 0.1 percent of the population) still lived on the continent. However, the dogma of White Australia remained a powerful force for some time to come, irrespective of quantities and statistics. In the early twentieth century, it was expanded to all nonwhites, including Pacific Islanders employed in the sugar industry in Queensland. Immigration controls were complemented by proactive politics to increase the birth rate of white Australians, and immigration quotas for Europeans were raised in order to contribute to an ethnically "pure" community. Long past the moment of its foundation, this image of a homogenous, white nation was repeatedly evoked in the context of Australian identity politics, most notably in the 1990s when the issue of Australia's place in Asia assumed center stage in public debates. The exclusionist and racial definition of the Australian nation, originally triggered by responses to Chinese mobility in the late nineteenth century, continued to inform the sense of nation on the continent.[46]

The Golden Door, Chinese Immigration, and Nativism in the United States

The most important precedent for the 1888 Influx of Chinese Restriction Act and the subsequent policies of exclusion, frequently alluded to in the Australian debates, was of course the 1882 Chinese Exclusion Act in the United States.[47] Chinese migration to North America is perhaps the best known part of the much bigger story of the Chinese Diaspora. While the Chinese came to America as early as 1785, it is above all, the pre-exclusion era (1848–1882) that witnessed massive Chinese immigration into the United States. During the gold rush, most Chinese workers went to mining areas. During the 1860–1880s, Chinese labor helped build the Western sections of the transcontinental railways. Chinese migrants also followed the transcontinental railways to central and eastern parts of America, even if their economic, political, and cultural center remained in the West. Until 1882, more than 317,000 Chinese entered the United States, the number of Chinese living permanently in the United States jumped from 25,000 in 1852 to more than 100,000 by 1880. Although the Exclusion Act did not completely halt Chinese immigration, the number of arrivals dwindled to insignificance immediately thereafter and never resumed the pre-exclusion levels, even after the partial repeal of exclusion in 1943.[48]

Local anti-Chinese sentiment had been evident since the Chinese first appeared in California, but public demonstrations of anti-Chinese feelings were limited until the economic depression of the 1870s left thousands unemployed.[49] Labor unions spearheaded the anti-Chinese movement in California that soon spread out to the East. It precipitated political pressure in Washington, forcing Congress to pass the first Chinese Exclusion Act in 1882. This banned the entry of Chinese laborers exempting only diplomats, tourists, merchants, teachers, and students. Chinese were also barred from being naturalized as American citizens.[50] Over the next decades the law was extended with ever stricter provisions. Exclusion reduced the influx, but many Chinese found a way around the laws. Some were smuggled in or jumped ship, and some entered claiming exempt status or citizen status. In order to determine the validity of such claims, immigration officials detained and interrogated Chinese applicants at entry ports. In San Francisco, the principal port of entry, a detention facility established on Angel Island processed thousands of arrivals between 1910–1940.[51]

The effects of the exclusion policy were multifaceted and complex. It affected the daily lives of Chinese in the United States and had repercussions on the labor market, city structures, and local business. In particular, the rise of nationalism in the United States as well as among overseas Chinese was intimately connected to the exclusion act. On the one hand, the discriminatory measures by state and federal governments prompted, as a reaction, the emergence of collective identities among Chinese groups that had hitherto been driven by factional strife and regional differences. The diaspora situation, often encouraged by nationalistic propaganda, furthered the notion of a common origin, a "mother country," across differences of ethnicity and language. Chinese language schools and a Chinese press further contributed to the emerging notion of Chineseness among emigrant communities. What was more, the American politics of exclusion facilitated transnational ties between Chinese communities; for example, in 1903 more than 100,000 Chinese living in the Philippines—at that time an American possession— joined in protests against the Exclusion laws.[52] Since the legal restrictions and discrimination in the United States were interpreted as the result of China's weakness on the global stage, the Chinese sense of nation was always tied to a notion of the geopolitical context within which the diaspora communities, China, and the United States were situated.[53]

However, the exclusion policy also had palpable effects on the way the nation was defined in the United States. Culminating in the Dillingham Report to the Congress on immigration issues in 1911, the xenophobic practices during the World War I, and the introduction of ethnic quotas in 1924, the anti-Chinese policies on local and national levels contributed to an American nationalism that was increasingly defined through the idea of common Caucasian ethnicity, rather than through civil rights and equal opportunities. Since the late nineteenth century, immigration law emerged as a dynamic site where ideas about race, immigration, citizenship, and nation were recast. Chinese exclusion, in particular, reflected, produced, and reproduced struggles over the makeup and character of the nation itself.

The debates about Chinese exclusion fed into a tradition of American nativism, a policy favoring the interests of established inhabitants over those of immigrants. Nativism was by no means a novel phenomenon. Although the United States has always portrayed itself as a sanctuary for the world's victims of oppression and poverty, nativism had a longer history that may be dated back to the Alien Acts in 1798 when Federalists in Congress attempted to suppress the newcomers' political activity. In the 1830s, nativists began focusing their attacks on Catholic immigrants. Nativism reached its political zenith in the mid-1850s with the meteoric rise of the "Know-Nothings," which in the long run failed to gain political influence.[54]

In the late nineteenth century, the antiradical impetus of nativist agitation was still highly influential, while the anti-Catholic thrust had largely disappeared.[55] But in the course of increased immigration—the so-called "new immigration," largely from Eastern and Southeastern Europe—the political apprehensions inextricably fused with xenophobic stereotypes.[56] As a result, calls for a politics of assimilation and Americanization increased—as did the demand for migration control.[57] The year 1882 is of particular importance here, since it not only saw the beginning of Chinese exclusion, but also the passing of the Immigration Act banning the immigration of paupers and convicts and thus ending the period of federal inaction toward immigration. As a result of powerful interactions between political institutions, ideological traditions, and organized social interests, the notions of race and class reinforced each other as categories of belonging and exclusion.[58]

The 1882 legislation established Chinese immigrants—defined by their race, class, and gender relations as the ultimate example of the dangerous, degraded alien—as the yardsticks by which in the following decades the desirability of other immigrant groups was measured. After 1882, calls to restrict or exclude other immigrant groups followed quickly, and these later campaigns were closely linked to the rhetoric and strategies of the anti-Chinese movement. In 1891, politician and historian Henry Cabot Lodge warned that the Slovak immigrants "are not a good acquisition for us to make, since they appear to have so many items in common with the Chinese."[59] One of the most significant consequences of Chinese exclusion was that it "provided a powerful framework to be used to racialize other threatening, excludable, and undesirable aliens."[60]

To be sure, ethnic solidarity was only one among many sources of American nationalism, alongside republicanism and civic voluntarism, patriotic cosmopolitanism, economic nationalism, and others. Moreover, it is important to recognize that the racialization of notions of belonging and citizenship did not begin with the influx of Chinese, but was also tied to a longer and intricate history of race relations within the United States. The relentless wars against native Americans and the discriminatory regulations concerning African Americans, in particular, had contributed to the emergence of a racially segregated society. However, articulating with this longer and internal history, the 1880s nevertheless stand out as an important watershed in the history of the ethnicization of American nationalism under the auspices of global mobility.[61] Analyzing this shift from internal marginalization to outward exclusion, Erika Lee has described "the Chinese exclusion laws as the main catalyst that transformed the United States into a gatekeeping nation."[62]

Migration, Ethnic Fragmentation and Nationalism in Colonial Malaysia

In what came to be perceived as the "West", a link between nationalism and Chinese migration emerged in several countries that included not only Australia and the United States, but also, for example, Hawaii and South Africa. Here the immigrating Chinese, in public discourse, were referred to not only as a social and economic threat, but also as the very incarnation, within the racial logic of the times, of ethnic difference. This is not to say that the identitarian effects of Chinese mobility were limited to societies that defined themselves as predominantly white. In fact, the race idiom became a language for similar fears and anxieties in places that had been under the influence of Chinese culture for centuries. This is particularly evident in the case of Southeast Asia. In this part of the world, conditions for the emergence of nationalism and nation building were markedly different than in Europe or North America. Traditionally, sultanates and kingdoms ruled over multiethnic societies, held together by common religious or cultural ties. In the nineteenth century, nation-states in Southeast Asia did not emerge on the basis of domestic developments, but rather resulted from colonial interventions and external efforts of state building. In the fragile and contested states created by colonial rulers, migration became a crucial factor that profoundly influenced the formation of nationalism.[63]

Chinese migration to Southeast Asia has a long, and unique, history that precedes Chinese migration to other regions in the world by at least two centuries.[64] Around 1900, Chinese living in Southeast Asia made up the biggest group among all Chinese living overseas by large margins. Then and still today, they comprise about 80 percent of all overseas Chinese. Several factors have historically facilitated this Chinese migration: The close diplomatic relations with the region that China long considered to be a peripheral part of the overarching Sinic world order; a considerable regional border-crossing migration in both directions that resulted in the formation of ethnic minorities in all of the neighboring countries along the Chinese border as well as in China proper; and, most importantly, important trade links between coastal cities in southern China and various regions in Southeast Asia that existed since the thirteenth century. It is important to point to the long-term factors behind this example of Chinese migration. When Chinese migration became a historical phenomenon in the nineteenth and twentieth centuries, it could operate on the basis of social and cultural patterns—such as ancestral home (*qiaoxiang*), native place, and homecoming—that were forged over a very long time.

Chinese migration since the sixteenth century flowed into practically all maritime areas of Southeast Asia. They eventually came to make up a majority of the population of Singapore and became significant minority populations in Indonesia, the Philippines, Thailand, Vietnam, and also the Malay Peninsula on which our discussion will focus.[65] By the turn of the eighteenth century, the Chinese had well established themselves in Malacca, many of them setting up shops in retail trade, and becoming what are called the "babas," or the Straits Chinese.[66] By the 1840s and 1850s, large numbers of Chinese entrepreneurs and workers became involved in gold and tin mining, a pursuit that had been the domain of the Sultans for centuries, but on a more limited scale.[67] Chinese tin mining and commercial activity, together accounting for over four fifths of total revenue, became important sources of funds for the colonial government so that "the main object of British policy towards the Chinese in the years after the Pangkor Engagement was to encourage tin mining and other commercial activities."[68]

With the British giving the Chinese *carte blanche* to pursue their economic ventures, the flow of Chinese immigrants looking to make their fortune in Malaya intensified. In order to meet the growing demand for labor, Chinese entrepreneurs primarily recruited people from southern China. After British intervention on the peninsula, mass recruitment proceeded on such a scale that within two decades the Chinese population had more than doubled in the Straits Settlements alone, increasing from 87,000 in 1871 to 183,000 in 1891.[69] In addition to Chinese coolies, the colonial authorities soon began to import contract workers from South India. The supply of labor from these places could be better controlled and easier regulated in accordance with the actual demands. Unlike in the case of the Chinese, the presence of Indians in Malaya was virtually nonexistent before British involvement in the region.[70] The first boom in demand for Indian coolies came after the establishment of sugar and coffee plantations. After the introduction of rubber to Malaya in 1905, the demand for Indian labor jumped to such high levels that the colonial government itself became directly involved in the recruitment process.[71] The system functioned so efficiently that in 1909, there were 21,963 assisted migrants per annum, and by 1913, the number had reached 91,236. The flow of Indian coolies continued unabated throughout the rubber boom and well into the 1920s.

The consequences of Chinese and Indian migration into Southeast Asia were far-reaching. The influx of Chinese and Indian immigrants around

1900 began to fundamentally change the composition of the population living on the Malay Peninsula. By the 1930s, Malays were outnumbered in their own country. Chinese and Indians together totaled 53.2 percent of the population of all of Malaya.[72] When the prospect of a Malay minority was becoming increasingly clear, British officials, speaking from their assumed role as trustees, reiterated their commitment to the special status of the Malays. In 1913, amidst concern that land was being consumed by Chinese and Indian landlords, the British introduced a new land alienation system. According to the Malay Reservation Enactment, certain reserved land that came to include areas as large as the entire state of Kelantan, could not be sold or transferred to non-Malays. In no state could the proportion of land reserved for Malays fall below 60 percent of total cultivable land. In 1933 the Aliens Ordinance was passed that finally set quotas on immigration to Malaya. British policies were to favor the Malays in terms of land, citizenship, education, language, and political opportunities in the civil service.

The definition of "Malay" in the Malay Reservation Enactment was the source of considerable indignation among the non-Malays. Under the definition, "Malay" was anyone who belonged to the Malay race, spoke Malay, and professed Islam, and as such included immigrants from the Dutch East Indies, while excluding Chinese and Indians who had lived on the peninsula for generations.[73] Problems with this definition were manifest in later debates about the status of non-Malay citizenship, as the British continued to regard all Chinese and Indians as temporary laborers, regardless of how long they had lived in Malaya.

While British policies effectively generated and perpetuated a social hierarchy that kept Malay elites in a position of power and Malay peasants committed to agriculture, Chinese migrant communities dominated local economies. The new majority of Chinese and Indian settlers were beginning to call the long-standing policy of "Malaya for the Malays" into question. The causes of Indian and Chinese nationalism were taken up by the overseas non-Malay communities. Tensions from newly awakened political awareness among Chinese, Malays, and Indians alike sparked the formation of several political parties that crossed the political spectrum but were often grouped along racial lines. The ramifications of the British colonial policy of encouraging Chinese commerce and recruiting Indian labor were to drastically alter the demography and politics of the Malay Peninsula.

Migration in this case precluded the emergence of a nationalism bridging over ethnic boundaries in a colonized space, and it also questioned the very possibility of creating an independent nation-state. It is on this basis that the various ethnic groups in the Federated Malay States strengthened their ties with their countries of origin, even if they had lived abroad for generations.

They increasingly connected with the rising nationalisms of their respective home countries.[74] In the case of Chinese communities, the Chinese government as well as local Chinese parties actively promoted and propagated a Chinese-ethnic nationalism that stressed the loyalty that overseas communities owed to the Chinese state, not to Malay.

To sum up, the history of Chinese migration into Malaysia demonstrates the complexity of the nexus between migration and nationalism. Prior to the colonial period and the influx of Chinese workers, nationalism simply did not exist. The influx of Chinese (and Indian) labor promoted by the British colonial administration in the long term obliterated the very possibility of an ethnically defined nation-state for native Malaysians, thus creating a fractured and heterogeneous society. The differential treatment of various groups by the colonial administration created deep divisions and sharpened a sense of ethnic particularity.[75] On the one hand, the colonial and postcolonial situation in an ethnically divided country such as the Federated Malay States generated, among the various groups, a sense of ethnic and national identity and gave way to nationalism narrowly confined within these groups. But on the other hand, Chinese and Indian migration tended to call into question the foundation of the independent Federation of Malaya in 1957 as a nation in its own right. The post-colonial multitude of nationalisms threatened rather then strengthened the prospectus of a common nationhood bridging over ethnic divisions.[76]

From Merchants and Coolies to "Overseas Chinese"

As we have shown, Chinese migration provoked nationalist reactions in many regions of the world and thereby accelerated the formation of nationalism in various places. At the same time, the departure of workers to foreign countries and above all discussions about their fate in their host countries was one of the factors that led to calls for a strengthening of nationalism in China. The global circulation of coolies, therefore, elicited nationalist responses not only in the countries in which Chinese immigration was perceived as an ethnic threat, but in China as well.

In the historiography of Chinese nationalism, the contribution of diaspora-Chinese is well known, but among them the large coolie migration does not play a central role. Instead, the focus is on the social elites and their involvement in the nationalist movement, both financially and ideologically.[77] In most accounts, the role of traders and merchants as suppliers of funds for the reformist groups and for the process of industrialization figures prominently.[78] Moreover, the large numbers of young activists that fled abroad in order to evade imprisonment were an important factor in the political history of nationalist revolution. Sun Yatsen has gone so far as to call the Chinese communities in Southeast Asia the "mother of the Chinese Revolution" of 1911.[79] While the diaspora elites occupy a firm place in the historiography of Chinese nationalism, the mass mobility of members of the underprivileged classes has been largely neglected. However, the global displacements of coolies, as we argue, was an equally important factor that worked toward the articulation of sentiments of Chinese nationality with broader, global currents.

In many ways the coolie phase within the history of Chinese migration was a transitional phenomenon. At the same time, it was much more than a centrifugal force that it has often been interpreted as. Many of the workers (Chinese: *Huagong*) not only send money back to their families at home along with letters and other items, they also eventually returned to China after their contract came to an end. Through their letters and upon their homecoming they brought with them stories of maltreatment and abuse by foreigners. Letters were often read in public in Chinese villages, schools, and market places.[80] As a consequence, the relationship between China and the overseas Chinese gradually changed, from indifference, if not open hostility, to engagement. The mistreatment and discrimination of Chinese in the so-called coolie trade became an issue that attracted widespread attention among intellectuals in China. Accusations of Western racism citing the fate of Chinese coolies indeed became a frequent topic in the writings and news-paper articles of early nationalist thinkers such as Zhi Gang, Zheng Guanying, Wang Zhichun, Xue Fucheng, Huang Zongxian, and others. The discrimination and inhumane treatment of Chinese workers by Western bosses was criticized in these texts as a violation of the principle of equality, regardless of race.[81] The coolie workers were now for the first time called compatriots (*tongbao*), as can be seen in an article in the *Beijing Guanhua Bao* (Beijing Mandarin Paper) of April 22, 1907: "The coolie workers (*Huagong*) from Shandong are our compatriots! Can we be quiet, when they are oppressed by foreigners? The Chinese people have the same talents as other races."[82]

The discursive incorporation of the migrant workers into the nation was thus directly linked to a global context. This sense of nation was articulated with the equally powerful global discourse of race and its exclusionary prac-tices. The growing awareness of the discrimination against Chinese coolies as well as the calls for racial equality reflected the emergence of a new political rhetoric and ideology that were clearly informed by the coolie phenomenon. It differed sharply from the terms traditionally used by the officials of the dynasty, who had stressed family ties and clan relationships that would bind together all Chinese people (*Huaren*) on the basis of a common Chinese culture. Within this new political discourse the Chinese people were being imagined as "race" (*minzu*) and as being entitled to the same rights as other races. The notion of race transcended earlier concepts of political solidarity and coherence within an empire composed loosely of clans and families and their loyalty to the emperor. Calls for racial equality were supposed to lead to the manifestation of a strong racial self-consciousness and the emergence of an organic society founded on racial nationalism. This in turn would enable China to effectively fight against colonialism, coolie trade, and slavery.[83] The discourse of racial nationalism emerged around 1900 in newspapers, study societies, and army clubs. The best known example is the treatise *Revolutionary Army* by a young officer by the name of Zou Yan. This popular nationalism was in many ways related to nationalist ideas as promoted by Liang Qichao and other well established intellectuals.[84]

The mobility of coolies was thus an important factor in the discourse of Chinese nationalism. But also among the migrant workers themselves, nationalism emerged as an ideology supplanting earlier forms of collective affinity. In the diaspora situation the notion of a shared Chineseness—across regional, linguistic, and cultural difference—was impressed upon the workers both by the hierarchies in the workplace and by nationalist propaganda. This fledgling sense of nation was reinforced through nationalist newspapers and Chinese language schools that frequently taught Mandarin instead of Southern Chinese dialects. While not all overseas workers turned nationalist, and some chose to affiliate with the host country, most coolies eventually came to perceive themselves as "Chinese," defined as a community resting on unalienable bonds of ethnicity, culture, and history.[85]

The migration of workers thus contributed to a nationalism "from below," but it also came to elicit attention among government officials. While the Chinese empire and its administration had long been negligent of, if not hostile to, the existence of overseas communities, this changed in the latter part of the nineteenth century. The existence of overseas Chinese was now generally recognized by the administration, as was the need to support them. A good example of the changing attitude of the government was the Imperial Delegation that China dispatched in 1873 to investigate into the working conditions of Chinese coolies in Cuba. Several years before the first consulates were established in the United States and Japan in 1878, this delegation is proof of a shift in foreign policy and the scope of international interventions. For the first time, a Chinese government assumed responsibility for workers who had left the sphere of Chinese "civilization" and had been treated as criminals only a few years ago.[86]

The concept of the Chinese nation began to change in the context of mobility and capitalism. This is apparent in the emergence of the concept of

Huaqiao, referring to all Chinese living overseas, across social and regional divides. The term came into use not until the end of the nineteenth century and quickly became associated with nationalism.[87] The *Huaqiao* concept was multi-layered and entailed claims on the political, legal, and discursive levels: On the political level the claim stands out that the *Huaqiao* owed allegiance to China and to the Qing throne, thereby negating British, Dutch, American, or German claims to the loyalty of Chinese subjects in their colonies.[88] On the legal level, the Chinese Empire or, after 1911, the Chinese Republic claimed to be entitled to provide protection for all overseas Chinese through its diplomatic representations. Finally, on the discursive level, the concept claimed that all Chinese wherever they lived were part of the Chinese nation and that all Chinese should pay their primary loyalty to China. This also meant to re-Sinicize those who had assimilated themselves to their host countries. In this discourse of *Huaqiao*, the Chineseness as found in culture, language, and ways of living and thinking was interpreted as a direct and strong link connecting overseas Chinese with China. It can be seen here, how the exterritorial concept of culture was now territorialized in the name of the nation.

There were, to be sure, many traditions and factors that contributed to a sense of nation in late Imperial China, and the large scale mobility of workers was only one among them. Thinking in national categories replaced earlier ideas of a cosmic and moral order guaranteed by the Imperial institutions in Beijing and legitimated by a common cultural identity. While the concept of Chinese "civilization" receded into the background, a new mental map of the world emerged in which China was but one out of many nation-states marked by clear cut borders and strong internal bonds.[89] In this process, opposition against the encroachments of Western imperialism played a crucial role; Kang Youwei's reform movement was but one expression within a complex and oftentimes contradicting set of nationalist discourses. An important source for nationalist inspiration was the Japanese experience that was witnessed first-hand by large numbers of Chinese reform-minded intellectuals.[90] There was also a political nationalism championed by cosmopolitan merchants and shop-keepers in Shanghai and other ports. Their nationalism was inclusive and invoked political rights for Chinese citizens *vis-à-vis* the state and foreign powers. Moreover, anti-Manchu sentiments against the Qing dynasty played a role as did a multiethnic, state-sponsored nationalism promoted later during the 1920s and 1930s by the Nationalist Party (Guomindang, GMD). The formation of different strands of Chinese nationalisms, in other words, drew on different resources and was negotiated in a situation of struggle and contestation.[91]

It is also important to note that in the context of migration, the sense of Chineseness was not only produced by demarcation or exclusion, but also

202 • Sebastian Conrad and Klaus Mühlhahn

through exchange and translation. Whether they were settlers or sojourners, Chinese overseas communities remained bi- or multicultural, even when they turned nationalist. They were able to access different languages and cultural systems, and to easily travel and mediate across borders. Most Chinese migrant communities lived in urban spaces that formed transit points for global networks of exchange and contact. These hubs were connected to each other in networks that transcended national boundaries. Sherman Cochran and David Strand have therefore concluded that "a greater China continued to emerge through migration, exile, and settlement beyond national borders, creating a complex, highly dispersed zone of contact."[92]

But it is no exaggeration to say that these ideas of a national community with ethnic and cultural borders as the basis for inalienable rights and duties were formed in a context in which the transnational mobility of Chinese workers played an important role.[93] The production of nationalism in China has to be seen against the backdrop of travel, transfer, and exchange, in which overseas Chinese figured prominently. When pondering the influence of coolie mobility, in particular, three aspects come to mind. On the one hand, nationalism in China had emerged as a theoretical or ideological concept championed largely by intellectuals and students. Yet, the transition from nationalist rhetoric to political practice proved to be more difficult and much slower than many intellectuals expected. In this context, the articulation of nationalist discourse with the issue of overseas migration and diaspora communities proved highly effective. The specific contribution of this interaction was a popularization of nationalist concepts that originally were ideas promoted by a small elite. Secondly, the reinforcement of the boundaries of the community through the notion of race was shaped in a context in which the politics of exclusion in places like California and Australia were explicitly directed against Chinese coolies. This not only influenced the mindset of overseas workers but was translated into political action in China as well. The anti-American boycott movement of 1905, for example, must be seen as a direct response to Washington's immigration restrictions and illustrates the global connections that were present in turn-of-the-century nationalist discourse.[94]

This brings us to the third level on which the circulation of labor was appropriated by nationalist discourses. The construction of China as a nation as well as the spread of nationalist ideas happened within a heightened recognition of the globe and its interdependence. The invention and promotion of racial nationalism was accompanied by an increasing awareness of being part of larger worldwide processes and developments. As Rebecca Karl pointed out in her study on Chinese nationalism, after China's defeat by Japan in 1895, and especially the failure of the reform movement three years later, there was a growing sense that China's predicament was not uniquely Chinese, nor was it solely the result of its relations with the Western powers.[95] Chen Duxiu is quoted by Karl as saying that "China is not the only country . . . being bullied . . . . Look at Poland, Egypt, the Jews, India, Burma, Vietnam . . . they all have been destroyed and turned into dependencies."[96] Indeed, the fate of overseas Chinese and of others such as colonized people that was seen as being similar to the treatment of black workers, Indian workers and so on, made the emerging Chinese public keenly aware that China's problem was shared by many emergent nations in a world of colonizers and colonized. Reports from overseas Chinese extolled the courageous struggles of these nations against much more powerful enemies and hailed them as apt models for China's own struggles. They had an immense impact on the nationalist discourse, so much so that by the early twentieth century more and more Chinese had come to accept the revolutionary praxis as the norm for building a new nation. The role of migration in the formation and rise of nationalism facilitated links connecting the Chinese plight to similar struggles around the world. Moreover, it demonstrates the global consciousness present in Chinese nationalism, as well as the intrinsic dialectics between integration into global structures and the discursive demarcation of boundaries.

Conclusion

We have argued that the mass mobility of people produced reactions that contributed to discourses of the nation on a global scale. The material process of mobility and migration was a reality that was increasingly difficult to neglect, but its various discursive effects were to prove as significant as its more tangible dimensions. A global consciousness emerged at the end of the nineteenth century that was closely linked to the experience of movements of people across state and cultural borders. It enabled political actors to articulate global structures with local/national settings and contributed to the "globalization" of phenomena that were both general and specific.

The discourse on mobility, in other words, influenced the trajectories of nationalism in highly diverse locations. This is not to deny the central role of complex sets of national traditions in the development of nationalism in Germany, Australia, the United States, Southeast Asia, and China. Many of the social actors and much of the political vocabulary and the cultural imaginaries of late nineteenth-century nationalism referred to continuities of nationalist sentiment. Apart from these long-standing traditions that had been fore-grounded by nationalist historiographies, however, the global interaction since roughly the 1880s, added an external factor to these internal histories. The synchronic articulation of national issues with larger trends and processes allowed social actors to link up with global contexts. These contexts did not create nationalism, but they influenced—and in some cases fundamentally shifted—the ways in which the nation was conceived and its mechanisms of inclusion and exclusion were practiced.

The effect of the increases in global mobility on discourses of nationalism can be observed, as has become evident in our discussion of Chinese migration, on at least three levels. One the one hand, many countries strengthened their immigration controls and devised ways to enforce control over the mobility of people, including passports, finger-prints, and other biometrical devices. The Chinese Exclusion Act in the United States is the best known example of a practice that most countries found increasingly difficult to ignore. Second, Chinese mobility contributed to the ethnicization of notions of national belonging, even if ethnic and racial criteria had a longer prehistory in most countries. The American Dillingham Report, the warnings of the Yellow Peril and the founding myth of a White Australia all were examples of this tendency. Finally, migration was an important factor working toward situating the nation in a systemic and global context, as the case of Chinese nationalism since the Sino-Japanese war clearly illustrates.

It appears, then, that global mobility, transnationalism, and nationalism were dynamically related to each other within a fluid global setting of migration and transfer. Mass migration influenced and defined a sense of nation for the host country and for the country of origin. The nationalizing effects were not at all homogenous. The political, economic, demographic, and cultural peculiarities of each context translated into very different constellations and nation-formation. However, in all cases, the sense of nation emerged at least partly in response to global currents. The existence of Chinese communities prompted questions concerning the cohesion and composition of the nation and fed into discourses of nationalism. In many countries, the trajectories of nationalism were significantly altered and acquired sharpness and profile in transnational contexts.

What is at issue here, then, is a revision of common assumptions concerning the history of nationalism. While an earlier trust in the long traditions and continuities of a national "essence" has long been deconstructed, most current theories of nationalism nevertheless privilege the temporal dimension of modern "imagined communities." While it is recognized that most national genealogies were indeed constructed in retrospect, the analytical focus remains on the connections of past, present, and future conceptualized strictly within national borders. However, our examples have shown that the particular form that nationalism and the representation of the nation-state took around the year 1900, were not mere invented traditions, but rather at least partly the effects of interactions and entanglements on a global scale.

The shifts and changes in the discourse of nationalism thus appear not only as effects of internal and diachronic modernization, as the familiar picture would suggest, but just as much of synchronous processes we retrospectively call globalization.

Notes

1. Anthony G. Hopkins, ed., *Globalization in World History* (New York: W.W. Norton, 2002); C.A. Bayly, *The Birth of the Modern World, 1780–1914: Global Connections and Comparisons* (Oxford: Blackwell, 2004); Jürgen Osterhammel and Niels P. Petersson, *Geschichte der Globalisierung: Dimensionen, Prozesse, Epochen* (München: Beck, 2003).
2. See T.N. Harper, "Empire, Diaspora and the Languages of Globalism, 1850–1914," in Hopkins, ed., *Globalization in World History* (London: Pimlico, 2002), pp. 141–66.
3. Bayly, *Birth*.
4. See ibid., pp. 199–243. See also Giovanni Arrighi, *The Long Twentieth Century: Money, Power, and the Origins of Our Times* (London: Verso, 1994), pp. 47–58.
5. Adam McKeown, "Global Migration, 1846–1940," *Journal of World History* 15, no. 2 (2004): 155–90.
6. Aristide R. Zolberg, "Global Movements, Global Walls: Responses to Migration, 1885–1925," in Wang Gungwu, ed., *Global History and Migrations* (Boulder: Westview Press, 1997), pp. 279–307.
7. See Simon A. Cole, *Suspect Identities: A History of Fingerprinting and Criminal Identification* (Cambridge, Mass.: Harvard University Press, 2001); Andreas Fahrmeir, Oliver Faron, and Patrick Weil, eds., *Migration Control in the North Atlantic World: The Evolution of State Practices in Europe and the United States from the French Revolution to the Inter-War Period* (New York: Berghahn Books, 2003); John Torpey, *The Invention of the Passport: Surveillance, Citizenship and the State* (Cambridge: Cambridge University Press, 2000); Jane Caplan and John Torpey, eds., *Documenting Individual Identity: The Development of State Practices in the Modern World* (Princeton: Princeton University Press, 2001); Radhika Singha, "Settle, Mobilize, Verify: Identification Practices in Colonial India," *Studies in History* 16, no. 2 (2000): 151–98.
8. McKeown, "Global Migration."
9. See Wang Gungwu, "Patterns of Chinese Migration in Historical Perspective," in Wang Gungwu, *China and the Chinese Overseas* (Singapore: Times Academic Press, 1991), pp. 3–22.
10. See Gungwu, "Patterns," and Dominic Sachsenmaier, "Die Identitäten der Überseechinesen in Südostasien im 20. Jahrhundert," in Hartmut Kaelble, Martin Kirsch, Alexander Schmidt-Gernig, eds., *Transnationale Öffentlichkeit und Identitäten im 20. Jahrhundert* (Frankfurt: Campus, 2002), pp. 211–35.
11. See Ching-Hwang Yen, *Coolies and Mandarins: China's Protection of Overseas Chinese during the Late Ch'ing Period (1851–1911)* (Singapore: Singapore University Press, 1985), pp. 46–47.

12. See Chen Sanjing, *Huagong yu Ouzhan* [The Chinese Labor Force in the First World War] (Taipei: Insitute of Modern History, Academia Sinica, 1986), pp. 25–60.
13. See Carl A. Trocki, *Opium and Empire: Chinese Society in Colonial Singapore, 1880–1910* (Ithaca: Cornell University Press, 1990).
14. See Yen, *Coolies and Mandarins*, pp. 335–47; Lynn Pan, *Sons of the Yellow Emperor: The Story of the Overseas Chinese* (London: Secker & Warburg, 1990).
15. See Pieter C. Emmer, ed., *Colonialism and Migration: Indentured Labor before and after Slavery* (Dordrecht: M. Nijhoff, 1986). Most recent scholarship, however, tends to stress the differences between indentured labor formally legitimized through contract and consent, and slave labor. See Stanley Engerman, "Contract Labor, Sugar, and Technology in the Nineteenth Century," *Journal of Economic History* 43 (1983): 635–59.
16. See Evelyn Hu-Dehart, "Chinese Coolie Labor in Cuba in the Nineteenth Century: Free Labor or Neo-Slavery," in *Slavery and Abolition* 14 (1993): 67–86.
17. David Northrup, *Indentured Labor in the Age of Imperialism, 1834–1922* (Cambridge: Cambridge University Press, 1995), pp. 17–20.
18. See the important discussion initiated by Partha Chatterjee, *Nationalist Thought and the Colonial World: A Derivative Discourse* (London: Zed Books for the United Nations University, 1986).
19. For a similar kind of argument, see Manu Goswami, *Producing India: From Colonial Economy to National Space* (Chicago: Chicago University Press, 2004).
20. Rebecca Karl, *Staging the World: Chinese Nationalism at the Turn of the Twentieth Century* (Durham: Duke University Press, 2002), p. 5.
21. See Federal Archives Berlin, R 8034 II, Nr. 5801, p. 52.
22. Secret Central Archives Berlin (GStA PK), I. HA, 87 B, No. 211, p. 155.
23. See Johannes Nichtweiß, *Die ausländischen Saisonarbeiter in der Landwirtschaft der östlichen und mittleren Gebiete des Deutschen Reiches. Ein Beitrag zur Geschichte der preußisch-deutschen Politik von 1890 bis 1914* (Berlin: Rütten & Loening, 1959); Ulrich Herbert, *Geschichte der Ausländerbeschäftigung in Deutschland 1880 bis 1980. Saisonarbeiter, Zwangsarbeiter, Gastarbeiter* (Berlin: J.H.W. Dietz, 1986).
24. Secret Central Archives Berlin (GStA PK), I. HA Rep 77, Tit. 922, No. 2.
25. *Illustrierte Landwirtschaftliche Zeitung*, January 6, 1897.
26. Stenographic Reports on the Proceedings of the German Reichstag, V. Session, February 8, 1898, pp. 892–903.
27. For different national variations, see the excellent study by Helmut Gollwitzer, *Die Gelbe Gefahr. Geschichte eines Schlagworts. Studien zum imperialistischen Denken* (Göttingen: Vandenhoeck & Ruprecht, 1962).
28. For the Yellow Peril, see Ute Mehnert, *Deutschland, Amerika und die "Gelbe Gefahr." Zur Karriere eines Schlagworts in der Großen Politik, 1905–1917* (Stuttgart: Steiner, 1995).
29. Stenographic Reports on the Proceedings of the German Reichstag, Session no. 200 on November 7, 1911, p. 7695. This discourse was particularly prevalent in the German colonies and concessions in China, from which it emanated.

In the colonies, the issue of how to handle mixed-marriages and their offspring touched on very real and urgent concerns. See Klaus Mühlhahn, *Herrschaft und Widerstand in der "Musterkolonie" Kiautschou: Interaktionen zwischen China und Deutschland, 1897–1914*, (München: Oldenbourg, 2000), pp. 188–99.

30. "Drohende Chinesen-Einwanderung" (June 14, 1889), in: GStA PK, I. HA Rep 77, Tit 922, No. 2.

31. Quoted from Kurt Wawrzinek, *Die Entstehung der deutschen Antisemitenparteien 1873–1890* (Berlin: E. Ebering, 1927), p. 44.

32. See Gollwitzer, *Die Gelbe Gefahr*, p. 174. For the fusion of anti-Slavism, anti-Semitism and the notion of the Yellow Peril in the ultranationalist thought of the German Empire see Uwe Puschner, *Die völkische Bewegung im wilhelminischen Kaiserreich. Sprache—Rasse—Religion* (Darmstadt: WBG, 2001), pp. 102–06.

33. Quoted from Federal Archives Berlin, R 8034 II, No. 4049.

34. For the following, see Charles A. Price, *The Great White Walls Are Built: Restrictive Immigration to North America and Australasia, 1838–1888* (Canberra: Australian Institute for International Affairs, in Conjunction with Australian National University Press, 1974).

35. See Andrew Markus, *Fear and Hatred: Purifying Australia and California 1850–1901* (Sydney: Hale & Iremonger, 1979), pp. 76–87.

36. For a comparative perspective, see Avner Offer, " 'Pacific Rim' Societies: Asian Labor and White Nationalism," in John Eddy and Deryck Schreuder, eds., *The Rise of Colonial Nationalism. Australia, New Zealand, Canada and South Africa First Assert Their Nationalities, 1880–1914* (Sydney: Allen & Unwin, 1988), pp. 227–47.

37. Russel B. Ward, *The Australian Legend* (Melbourne: Oxford University Press, 1958).

38. See Andrew Markus, *Australian Race Relations, 1778–1993* (St. Leonards, N.S.W.: Allen & Unwin, 1994); Charles D. Rowley, *The Destruction of Aboriginal Society* (Canberra: Australian National University Press, 1970).

39. Quoted in Jürgen Matthäus, *Nationsbildung in Australien von den Anfängen weißer Besiedlung bis zum Ersten Weltkrieg* (Frankfurt: P. Lang, 1993), p. 145. For a recent assessment of the place of Asia in Australian nationalism see David Walker, *Anxious Nation: Australia and the Rise of Asia 1850–1939* (St. Lucia: UQP Australian Studies, 1999).

40. Quoted in Matthäus, *Nationsbildung*, p. 145.

41. Quoted in D.M. Gibb, ed., *The Making of "White Australia"* (Melbourne: Victorian Historical Association, 1973), p. 77.

42. John A La Nauze, *Alfred Deakin: A Biography* (Melbourne: Melbourne University Press, 1965), pp. 280–81.

43. *The Boomerang*, August 4, 1888, p. 4.

44. Humphrey McQueen, *A New Britannia: An Argument concerning the Social Origins of Australian Radicalism and Nationalism* (Melbourne: Penguin Books, 1970), p. 41.

45. Quoted in Myra Willard, *History of the White Australia Policy to 1920* (Melbourne: Melbourne University Press, 1923), p. 112.

46. See Laksiri Jayasuriya, David Walker, Jan Gothard, eds., *Legacies of White Australia: Race, Culture and Nation* (Crawley: University of Western Australia Press, 2003).

47. For a comparison of nationalism in Australia and the United States, see Lyn Spillman, *Nation and Commemoration: Creating National Identities in the United States and Australia* (Cambridge: Cambridge University Press, 1997).

48. Him Mark Lai, "The United States," in Lynn Pan, ed., *The Encyclopedia of the Chinese Overseas* (London: Landmark Books, 1998), pp. 261–73; Michael H. Hunt, *The Making of a Special Relationship: The United States and China to 1914* (New York: Columbia University Press, 1983).

49. See Stuart C. Miller, *The Unwelcome Immigrant: The American Image of the Chinese, 1785–1882* (Berkeley: University of California Press, 1969).

50. Sucheng Chan, ed., *Entry Denied: Exclusion and the Chinese Community in America, 1882–1943* (Philadelphia: Temple University Press, 1991).

51. For the legal and administrative dimensions of exclusion politics see Lucy E. Salyer, *Laws Harsh as Tigers: Chinese Immigrants and the Shaping of Modern Immigration Law* (Chapel Hill: University of North Carolina Press, 1995). See also Aristide R. Zolberg, "The Great Wall Against China: Responses to the First Immigration Crisis, 1885–1925," in Jan Lucassen, Leo Lucassen, eds., *Migration, Migration History, History: Old Paradigms and New Perspectives* (Bern: Peter Lang, 1997), pp. 291–315.

52. Hunt, *Making of a Special Relationship*, p. 233.

53. Adam McKeown, "Conceptualizing Chinese Diasporas, 1842 to 1949," *Journal of Asian Studies* 58, no. 2 (1999): 306–37, here 326.

54. See the classic study by Ray A. Billington, *The Protestant Crusade, 1800–1860: A Study of the Origins of American Nativism* (New York: Rhinehart & Co., 1938). See also David H. Bennett, *The Party of Fear* (Chapel Hill: University of Carolina Press, 1988).

55. John Higham, *Strangers in the Land: Patterns of American Nativism, 1860–1925*, (New Brunswick, NJ: Rutgers University Press, 1955).

56. See Matthew Fry Jacobson, *Whiteness of a Different Color: European Immigrants and the Alchemy of Race* (Cambridge, Mass.: Harvard University Press, 1998).

57. Matthew Fry Jacobson, *Barbarian Virtues: The United States Encounters Foreign Peoples at Home and Abroad, 1876–1917* (New York: Hill & Wang, 2000); Gary Gerstle, *American Crucible: Race and Nation in the Twentieth Century* (Princeton: Princeton University Press, 2001).

58. David M. Reimers, *Unwelcome Strangers: American Identity and the Turn against Immigration* (New York: Columbia University Press, 1998); Erika Lee, "Enforcing the Borders: Chinese Exclusion along the U.S. Borders with Canada and Mexico, 1882–1924," *Journal of American History* 89 (2002): 54–86; Daniel J. Tichenor, *Dividing Lines: The Politics of Immigration Control in America* (Princeton: Princeton University Press, 2002).

59. Quoted from Jacobson, *Barbarian Virtues*, pp. 76–77.

60. Erika Lee, *At America's Gates: The Exclusion Era, 1882–1943* (Chapel Hill: University of North Carolina Press, 2003), p. 30. See also Nayan Shah,

Contagious Divides: Epidemics and Race in San Francisco's Chinatown (Berkeley: University of California Press, 2001).

61. Desmond King, *The Liberty of Strangers: Making the American Nation* (Oxford: Oxford University Press, 2005), chapter 4. For the 1920s, in particular, see Desmond King, *Making Americans: Immigration, Race, and the Origins of the Diverse Democracy* (Cambridge, Mass.: Harvard University Press, 2000).

62. Lee, *At America's Gates*, p. 9.

63. That colonial policies of segregation shaped an ethnic nationalism in Malaya, which prevailed in different ethnic communities, is also demonstrated by Charles Hirschman, "The Making of Race in Colonial Malaya: Political Economy and Racial Ideology," *Sociological Forum* 1, no. 2 (1986): 331–60.

64. For an general overview see Lynn Pan, "Migration," in Charles Hirschman, ed., *The Encyclopedia of the Chinese Overseas*, pp. 46–49. A discussion of current research on Chinese communities in East Asia is provided by Aihwa Ong, *Flexible Citizenship: The Cultural Logics of Transnationality* (Durham & London: Duke University Press, 1999).

65. See Pan, *Sons of the Yellow Emperor*; Wang Gungwu, *The Chinese Overseas: From Earthbound China to the Quest for Autonomy* (Cambridge, Mass.: Harvard University Press, 2000). See also Roderich Ptak, *China and the Asian Seas Trade, Travel, and Visions of the Other (1400–1750)* (Aldershot: Ashgate, 1998); and Roderich Ptak, *China's Seaborne Trade with South and Southeast Asia (1200–1750)* (Aldershot: Ashgate, 1999).

66. See here and in the following Victor Purcell, *The Chinese in Malaya* (London: Oxford University Press, 1948), pp. 16–19.

67. Donald R. Snodgrass, *Inequality and Economic Development in Malaysia* (Kuala Lumpur: Oxford University Press, 1980), p. 16.

68. John G. Butcher, *The British in Malaya 1880–1941: The Social History of a European Community in Colonial South-East Asia* (Kuala Lumpur: Oxford University Press, 1979), p. 9.

69. Snodgrass, *Inequality and Economic Development*, p. 24.

70. Ibid.

71. Michael Stenson, *Class, Race and Colonialism in West Malaysia: The Indian Case* (Vancouver: University of British Columbia Press, 1980), p. 18.

72. Abstract from 1931 Census, p. 90.

73. Leon Comber, *13 May 1969: A Historical Survey of Sino-Malay Relations* (Kuala Lumpur: Heinemann Asia, 1983).

74. Prasenjit Duara, "Nationalists among Transnationals: Overseas Chinese and the Idea of China, 1900–1911," in Aihwa Ong and Donald M. Nonini, eds., *Ungrounded Empires: The Cultural Politics of Modern Chinese Transnationalism* (London & New York: Routledge, 1997), pp. 39–60, here pp. 40–42; Yeu-Farn Wang, *The National Identity of the Southeast Asian Chinese* (Stockholm: Center for Pacific Asia Studies at Stockholm University, 1994).

75. See Sachsenmaier, "Die Identitäten der Überseechinesen," pp. 211–35.

76. Cheah Boon Keng, *Malaysia: The Making of a Nation* (Singapore: Institute of Southeast Asian Studies, 2002).

77. Anthony Reid, "Entrepreneurial Minorities, Nationalism, and the State," in Daniel Chirot and Anthony Reid, eds., *Essential Outsiders: Chinese and Jews in the Modern Transformation in Southeast Asia and Central Europe* (Seattle: University of Washington Press, 1997), pp. 33–74.

78. See, for example, Wang, *China and the Chinese Overseas*; Michael Godley, "The Treaty Port Connection," *Journal of Southeast Asian Studies* 12 (1981): 249–59; Michael Godley, *The Mandarin Capitalists from Nanyang: Overseas Chinese Enterprise in the Modernization of China, 1893–1911* (Cambridge: Cambridge University Press, 1981).

79. Quoted from Ching-Hwang Yen, *The Overseas Chinese and the 1911 Revolution, with Special Reference to Singapore and Malaya* (Kuala Lumpur: Oxford University Press, 1976), p. 263. See also L. Eve Armentrout Ma, *Revolutionaries, Monarchists and Chinatowns: Chinese Politics in the Americas and the 1911 Revolution* (Honolulu: University of Hawaii Press, 1990).

80. Charles W. Hayford, *To the People: James Yen and Village China* (New York: Columbia University Press, 1989).

81. See Wang Ermin, "Zhonguo jindai zhi ren quan xingjüe [The Recognition of Human Rights in Modern China]," *Xianggang Zhongwen Daxue Zhongguo wenhua yanjiusuo xuebao* 14 (1983): 67–82, here pp. 68–70.

82. See, for example, Kang Youwei's statements in Tang Zhijun, ed., *Kang Youwei zhenglunji* [The Political Writings of Kang Youwei] (Beijing: Zhonghua shuju,1981), pp. 201–10.

83. See Rebecca Karl, "Race, Ethnos, History in China at the Turn of the Twentieth Century," in Peter Osborne, Stella Sandford, eds., *Philosophies of Race and Ethnicity* (London: Continuum, 2002), pp. 97–113. For the concept of "race" in China see the not entirely convincing study by Frank Dikötter, *The Discourse of Race in Modern China: Historical and Contemporary Perspectives* (London: Hurst & Co., 1992). See also Frank Dikötter, ed., *The Construction of Racial Identities in China and Japan* (Honolulu: University of Hawaii Press, 1997).

84. See the excellent discussion by John Fitzgerald, *Awakening China: Politics, Culture, and Class in the Nationalist Revolution* (Stanford: Stanford University Press, 1996). The examples demonstrate that nationalism should awake the Chinese people and make them aware of discriminations, mistreatment of coolie labor, and other colonial cruelties.

85. Adam McKeown, *Chinese Migrant Networks and Cultural Change: Peru, Chicago, Hawaii, 1900–1936* (Chicago: University of Chicago Press, 2001), pp. 86–99.

86. See Robert L. Irick, *Ch'ing Policy toward the Coolie Trade, 1847–1878* (Taipei: Chinese Materials Center, 1982), pp. 273–388.

87. See Wang Gungwu, "South China Perspectives on Overseas Chinese," *The Australian Journal of Chinese Affairs* 13 (1985): 69–84.

88. Mühlhahn, *Herrschaft und Widerstand*, pp. 268–70.

89. See the classical study by Joseph Levenson, *Liang Ch'i-ch'ao and the Mind of Modern China* (Berkeley: University of California Press, 1953). For a critical assessment of his still influential thesis of a transition from culturalism to

nationalism see James Townsend, "Chinese Nationalism," in Jonathan Unger, ed., *Chinese Nationalism* (New York: M.E. Sharpe, 1996), pp. 1–30.

90. See Paula Harrell, *Sowing the Seeds of Change: Chinese Students, Japanese Teachers, 1895–1905* (Stanford: Stanford University Press, 1992); Ernest P. Young, *Chinese Leaders and Japanese Aid in the Early Republic*, in Akira Iriye, ed., *The Chinese and the Japanese: Essays in Political and Cultural Interactions* (Princeton: Princeton University Press, 1980), pp. 124–39; Douglas R. Reynolds, *China 1898–1912: The Xinzheng Revolution and Japan* (Cambridge, Mass.: Harvard University Press, 1993).

91. For different strands of Chinese nationalism, see Fitzgerald, *Awakening China*; Lowell Dittmer and Samuel S. Kim, eds., *China's Quest for National Identity* (Ithaca: Cornell University Press, 1993); Rebecca Karl, *Staging the World*; Prasenjit Duara, *Rescuing History from the Nation: Questioning Narratives of Modern China* (Chicago: University of Chicago Press, 1995), particularly pp. 17–50.

92. Sherman Cochran and David Strand, "Cities in Motion: An Introduction," Paper prepared for the conference on "Cities in Motion: Coast and Diaspora in Modern China" (University of California, Berkeley, November 15–17, 2002), p. 2. Cochran and Strand define "Zone of contact" as "a geographical term [that] connotes areas where separate national or cultural entities 'mingle' in defiance of a clearly drawn border and where 'foci of cultural contact in a zone of dispute' can stimulate 'cultural dissonance' as well as more open forms of conflict." See p. 2, note 1.

93. See Duara, "Nationalists Among Transnationals."

94. For the connection of the boycott movement and nationalism, see Shih-Shan Henry Tsai, "Reaction to Exclusion: The Boycott of 1905 and Chinese National Awakening," *The Historian* 39 (1976): 95–110; Delber McKee, *Chinese Exclusion versus the Open Door Policy, 1900–1906* (Detroit: Wayne State University Press, 1977); Wang Guanhua, *In Search of Justice: The 1905–1906 Chinese Anti-American Boycott* (Cambridge, Mass.: Harvard University Press, 2001); and Sin Kiong Wong, *China's Anti-American Boycott Movement in 1905: A Study in Urban Protest* (New York: Peter Lang, 2002).

95. Karl, *Staging the world*.

96. Ibid., 195.

CHAPTER 8

A Global Anti-Western Moment? The Russo-Japanese War, Decolonization, and Asian Modernity

Cemil Aydin

The Russo-Japanese War in 1905 was interpreted throughout the world as the first victory of an Asian nation belonging to the yellow race against a major white and Christian Western empire.[1] In fact, the world-historical significance of the Japanese victory over Russia was noted by a wide array of contemporary observers, writing in the immediate aftermath of the war.[2] This interpretation of the Japanese military victory transformed the character of reformist thought, perceptions of the Western Civilization and the critiques of international order in the major centers of the non-Western world, from Egypt, Iran, and Turkey to India, Vietnam, and China.[3] However, the celebration by Asian and African intellectuals of the Russo-Japanese War as a turning point in their critique of the Eurocentric world order was highly paradoxical. Japan fought the war with Russia over the control of Korea and Manchuria. It achieved its military victory partly due to the support it received from the Western superpower of the time, Great Britain, and partly due to the borrowing of huge sums of money from American banks. The Japanese elite was proud of the Anglo-Japanese Alliance, which symbolized the civilized status of their nation.[4]

More importantly, even the admirers of Japan among the anti-Western critics would concede that Japan's achievements were mainly due to its success in learning from the West. Yet, nationalist thinkers such as Egyptian leader Mustafa Kamil, who knew the alliance between Japan and Egypt's colonizer England very well, insisted that despite the vested interest of Britain in the Japanese victory, "a victory for Japan is a victory for the yellow race" against the British Empire.[5] Why then would so many Asian nationalists and other politicians as well as intellectuals, who were aware that the Japanese victory over Russia was strengthening the Pax Britannica in the Far East, still perceive it as a turning point in the history of decolonization from British and French imperial rule? Given these contradictory aspects of the worldwide interest in the Russo-Japanese War, how can we evaluate the significance of this event in global history?

This chapter suggests that the historical moment of the Russo-Japanese War can only be understood by examining the nature of the imperial world order that accompanied the globalization of Western modernity from the 1880s onward. This war became the key historical reference in resolving the tensions between the universalization of Eurocentric modernity through the agency of non-Western elites, and late nineteenth century race and civilization discourses that legitimized the European dominance. The very globalized nature of the debates on race, civilization, and progress that rendered the Japanese victory over Russia a turning point, both in the evolution of alternative anti-Western visions, especially Pan-Islamism and Pan-Asianism, and in the worldwide emulation of Western modernity in the form of constitutionalism and educational reforms. While examining the meaning of the Russo-Japanese War for the history of anti-Western critiques and conceptions of world order, this chapter will clarify not only the world-historical impact of the war as a global moment, but also the meaning of the boom of references to the Japanese modernization in Asian nationalist thought that had been characterized by the emulation of the Western model of modernity. Was the Japanese model ever seen as an alternative to Western modernity? What can we learn from the Asian responses to the Russo-Japanese War in rethinking the relationship between anti-Western critiques, visions of world order, and the imagination of a universal modernity?

The Russo-Japanese War as a Global Moment

The immediate political and cultural responses to the Japanese victory all over the world were a reflection of the scope and the synchronicity of the global intellectual sphere at that time. There was a surprising worldwide consensus on the larger historical and cultural meaning of the first modern war of the century. While most Asian and colored intellectuals, including African-Americans in the United States were welcoming Japan's military achievements as a moral contribution to their struggles, European observers predicted a potential threat from the rising Japanese power against their interests.[6] Newspapers in Iran, Turkey, and Egypt were filled with articles on Japan, discussing either the positive implications of Japanese military victories for the "awakening" of Asia, or the possible lessons other Asian societies could learn from the Japanese reforms.[7] It is important to note that there had been references to the Japanese model of reform since the mid-1890s in the writings of Turkish, Egyptian, and Chinese reformist and nationalists. Furthermore, especially after Japan's military victory against China in 1895, European newspapers and journals began to depict Japan as an exceptionally successful case of westernization and reform in the larger Asian continent that was failing in reforming itself. For example, Scottish engineer Henry Dyer's book on Japanese success, based on the author's long experience as a hired foreign expert in Japan, was published before the Russo-Japanese War.[8] Mostly relying on the European press coverage of Japan, nationalist thinkers of the Middle East, Southeast Asia, and East Asia also developed a keen interest in Japanese successes. Thus, the news of Japanese victory of Russia was not the first occasion when reformists and nationalists in different Asian countries, albeit in different intensity, wrote about Japanese achievements in modernization. Nevertheless, this victory led to a qualitative and quantitative change in the coverage of Japan in Asian papers, and in the production of nationalist discourses in Asia since observers increasingly referred to the Japanese model. These writings often included discussions of modernity, Western Civilization and international order.

The Russo-Japanese War propelled anticolonial nationalists to be more assertive and confident in invalidating several key discourses proclaiming the legitimacy of the Eurocentric world order. First of all, the scope of the responses to the war was great proof that the circulation of news and ideas had already created a global public sphere. The reading public consumed news about the Russo-Japanese War in a multitude of languages, due to the availability of accurate and fast reporting from the fronts through the telegraph network and international news agencies.[9] While the newspapers covered different battles of the war almost on a daily basis, the interpretations of the war and discussions about it were immediate among the reading public. Indian nationalist leader Jawaharlal Nehru noted in his autobiography how every morning he would impatiently check the English papers for recent news from the battles of the Russo-Japanese War, and how he felt sympathetic and proud of the Japanese victories.[10] Chinese nationalist leader Sun Yat-sen was amazed and pleased to receive congratulatory gestures and messages from Egyptians during his passage through the Suez Canal during the war. He witnessed how as a Chinese nationalist, he could establish bonds of solidarity with ordinary Egyptians, who would also think it appropriate to congratulate a Chinese passenger about the news of a Japanese victory.[11] Vietnamese nationalist Phan Bội Châu similarly emphasized the role of the Russo-Japanese war for his country's national awakening.[12] Burmese nationalist leader Ba Maw also noted, in his memoirs, the impact of the Japanese victory on his childhood psychology, (although he was too young to be considered a nationalist thinker in 1905).[13] The numerous articles and commentaries of Turkish, Arab, Persian, Indian, Vietnamese, and Chinese nationalists about the meaning of the Japanese victory popularized the shared interpretation of the war as proof of an Asian awakening and disproof of the Western claim to permanent racial and cultural superiority.

No local context could overlook the Russo-Japanese war in discourses on global relations among different races and civilizations. Even in the local contexts of Morocco, Burma, and the Philippines, where interest in the Japanese model of reform was not as immediate as it was in Iran, Egypt, the Ottoman Empire, or India, references to Japan increased over time in the decade following 1905.[14] Yet there were differences in the intensity of the writings on Japan in different local presses from Morocco to Vietnam and the Philippines in Asia, as some nationalist circles in Asia used the Japan metaphor more often than others. In this sense, responses to a global moment were conditioned by the local contexts, depending on press freedom, agenda of nationalist and colonial impulses, and domestic politics.

Furthermore, the similarities of the interpretation of the world historical significance of the war, by making reference to racial and cultural identities such as "yellow race," "white race," or "East and West," offer further proof of the existence of a shared global intellectual sphere. Nehru was not an exception when he eagerly discussed the positive implications of the Japanese victory for Indian nationalism. Alfred Zimmern, who later became one of the founders of the UNESCO, interrupted his Oxford University lectures on Greek history and spoke to his students about the "most important event which has happened, or is likely to happen, in our lifetime; the victory of a non-white people over a white people."[15]

One aspect of the various interpretations of the Russo-Japanese War was the fact that from Turkish and Indian nationalists to European intellectuals and African-American leaders, there was a surprising convergence in their ways of referring to the notions of race and civilization in interpreting the political meaning of this war. The globally shared but European originated terms, such as "East and West" and "yellow race and white race," became a transnational force, utilized in legitimizing and delegitimizing structures of international politics and competing visions of world order at the turn of the twentieth century. The global moment of the Russo-Japanese War influenced international history by challenging the established European discourse on racial hierarchies once and for all, thus delegitimizing the existing world order and encouraging alternative visions. For instance, when Abdullah Cevdet, the leading Ottoman Westernist and a believer in European ideas of race hierarchies, met Gustave Le Bon in 1905, he questioned Le Bon as to where European thinkers had erred in their placement of the Japanese at the hierarchy's bottom.[16] After 1905, no discussion of racism and innate civilizational hierarchies in world politics could avoid the example of Japan, which clearly challenged all that had been written by European social scientists and in European newspapers in the last quarter of the nineteenth century. The powerful interconnection among the trinity of the Eurocentric world order at the end of the nineteenth century, namely imperialism, modernity, and Orientalism/racism, forced anticolonial nationalists to redefine the relationship between civilization, race, and modern progress to claim their rightful position as equal members of the international system. The Russo-Japanese War clearly contradicted the racial arguments and the moral universe that justified the world order from 1882–1905, and thus it could be utilized to invalidate the prevailing notion of Western invincibility.[17]

Another reason for the global impact of the Russo-Japanese War derived from the fact that major nineteenth-century wars were taken as litmus tests for and validations of the ideals and moral values of the conflicting parties. By 1862, a leading reformist in the Ottoman State would refer to the Chinese defeat in the Opium Wars as proof of the necessity of change and the adoption of Western methods.[18] A successive series of European military victories in the process of worldwide colonization seemed to affirm the confident European perception of the global sphere as a hierarchy of races and civilizations. From the British show of superior military technology in suppressing the Egyptian nationalist movement at Tel al-Kabir in 1882 to the looting of the Chinese capital by a coalition of "civilized" nations in 1900, the high age of imperialism witnessed a series of military affirmations of Western hegemony.[19] Even when the legitimacy of global Western hegemony was contested by non-Western intellectuals, all knew that Western military power could not be as easily disputed. Therefore, Japan's military power gained great significance, as it showed that a non-Western nation could achieve military parity with a European empire after only three decades of successful reform.

The specific critiques of the West that pointed to the Russo-Japanese War were based on the realization that the idea of the superiority of the white race and Western Civilization had to be rejected in order to establish an alternative vision of post-imperial order. References to the rapid rise of Japan as the first Eastern nation to attain great power status inspired the imagining of a new world order in which Asia would be decolonized and become an equal partner with the West. Ottoman intellectual Ahmed Riza summarized this aspect of the war:

> How to explain the pretension of Europe, then, of wanting to civilize Asia, since, when a people of these regions endeavors to raise itself, [Europe] condemns it immediately as a "peril" of such and such color? . . . There are multiple well-merited lessons that the war permitted the Japanese to give to the "superior races". . . . One cannot doubt the preeminence of the social and political institutions of Japan, a so-called inferior race by most of those peoples upon whom the patent of superiority is conferred. The splendid victory of the Japanese has proved the Christian world arrogant; that it is not indispensable for a people to embrace Christianity in order to acquire morality, civilization, and an aptitude for progress. . . . Likewise events of the Far East have put forth evidence of the uselessness of interventions, frequent if pernicious, of Europe reforming a people. On the contrary, the more isolated and preserved from contact with European invaders and plunderers a people is, the better is the measure of [its] evolution toward a rational renovation.[20]

The Russo-Japanese War was especially important for the critique of European Orientalist discourses by the Asian nationalists and reformists. Due to the legal and political implications of the civilization discourse, Asian intellectuals were very sensitive about the politics surrounding the European colonial literature that had created and perpetuated an image of the Orient that, for the Asian intellectuals, bore no resemblance to the real East they knew or wanted to create.[21] Thus, they saw the European representation of the Orient as one of the greatest barriers to normal, healthy international relations based on mutual understanding and respect, because they presented the image of a society unfit for equality with the Occidental cultures. After the Japanese victory, Asian intellectuals became more confident in their campaign against the image of a decadent, inert East. Their concerns and critiques of Western viewpoints of Asia, and the invalidation of Western images with reference to Japan were embedded in the belief that the correction of misperceptions about Asians could in turn correct their problems in international affairs. In the conception of international law in the early twentieth century, each country could have full legal rights in the international society only if it was deemed civilized by the core European countries. The discourse that Orientals are incapable of being fully civilized was not only used by European newspapers and politicians to justify colonial adventures, but also became a scholarly opinion in mainstream texts on international law. For example, Iran, Siam, China, and Ethiopia were identified as not fully civilized states and thus not qualified to earn full legal equality in international law.[22]

Asian nationalists were also aware that the "correction" of the Western misperceptions of the Orient alone would not be sufficient to create a just international system, as they recognized power relations as equally important to the cultural vision of world order. Thus, Asian nationalists maintained a parallel conviction that only military power and industrial modernization could save the weak Asian nations from the powerful West. For example, leading Ottoman nationalists maintained that the Ottoman government should give up relying on diplomatic initiatives and appeals to international morality, and instead follow Japan's path of industrial and military self-strengthening. The Japanese achievement was proof that only a military victory, not just the knowledge of legal rights and civilized ideas, could secure equality and recognition in the chaotic and insecure international environment of the early twentieth century.[23] This ideal compelled many Asian nationalists to search for power alliances through Pan-Islamic and Pan-Asianist visions, against the perceived cooperation and unity of European powers in their policies toward Asian and African societies.

Geopolitical Impact: Ambivalent Appeal of Pan-Islamic and Pan-Asian Ideologies

The impact of the Russo-Japanese War on two major anti-Western visions of world order, namely Pan-Asianism and Pan-Islamism, was ambivalent in the sense that while the Japanese victory over Russia facilitated more assertive formulations of a new world order in Asia, there was no significant change in the existing world order. Both Pan-Asianism and Pan-Islamism emerged during the 1880s, and evolved into significant intellectual and political trends. The Russo-Japanese War strengthened the appeal of these two alternative visions of world order precisely because the war led to doubts about the long-term sustainability of the Eurocentric imperial world order in Asia.

European writers observed or predicted a general Asian awakening inspired by the Russo-Japanese War. The influential French journal *Revue du Monde Musulman*, published after 1906 under the auspices of the French Scientific Mission in Morocco, carried articles on the revival of Islam and Pan-Islamic currents in the post-Russo-Japanese War period.[24] Questions of Pan-Islamism, nationalist thought, and the revival of the East were major themes of this journal, which saw the dynamism and transnational networks in Asia as a confirmation of the triumph of modernity in those Westernizing world regions.[25] When the *Revue du Monde Musulman* carried an article on the impact of the Russo-Japanese War on the Muslim world in 1906, it predicted that the number of Muslim students going to Japan would increase.[26] However, before any students arrived in Tokyo, the leading Pan-Islamist activist and intellectual of this period, Abdurreşid Ibrahim, visited Tokyo and was hosted by Japan's Pan-Asianist groups for several months. In fact, the period after the Russo-Japanese War witnessed the first actual communication between Pan-Islamic and Pan-Asianists activists that led to long term intellectual and political cooperation.[27] The stories of the meetings between the representatives of the Pan-Islamic and Pan-Asianist movements in Tokyo and their attempts to foster global cooperation demonstrate the internationalist aspects and confinements of both of these movements. Abdurreşid Ibrahim and several prominent Japanese pan-Asianists, including Tôyama Mitsuru, Inukai Tsuyoshi, and Uchida Ryôhei, formed Ajia Gi Kai (Association for the Defense of Asia) in 1909 in order to institutionalize their contacts and hopes for futures cooperation. The new Asianist organization had ties with Konoe Atsumaro's Tôa Dôbunkai (East Asian Common Culture Society) as well as Kokuryûkai and Genyôsha, two major ultranationalist organizations advocating a more assertive role of Japan in Asia.[28]

There were several other Pan-Asianist organizations in Tokyo in the first decade of the twentieth century due to the large number of students, political activists, exiles, and merchants from China, India, the Philippines, Vietnam, and other Asian countries. Differing from the earlier organizations, Ajia Gi Kai specifically focused on improving the ties between the Muslim world and the Japanese Empire. Its objectives included the establishment of branches in China (meant for Chinese Muslims), India, Persia, Afghanistan, and Turkey to achieve the goal of "Asia for Asians." Ajia Gi Kai succeeded in registering nearly 40 members from different parts of the Muslim world, in addition to more than 100 Japanese.[29]

Abdurreşid Ibrahim's visit to Tokyo and the establishment of Ajia Gi Kai was an indication of a search for new power centers by a leading Pan-Islamic activist, and it was followed by a boom of Asianist publications in both Tokyo and Istanbul. Ajia Gi Kai published a journal in Japanese called *DaiTô* (The Great East) that included many articles on Islam and the Muslim world.[30] An Indian revolutionary and a Pan-Islamist himself, Muhammad Barakatullah started the publication of *Islamic Fraternity* in English, exemplifying the use of Tokyo as a center for Pan-Islamist and Asianist journals.[31] Muslims were not alone in their contacts with Japanese Pan-Asianists, who established contacts and networks among various nationalist groups from the Philippines, Vietnam, and China to India.[32] For awhile, Tokyo became an attractive destination for students, revolutionaries, intellectuals, and adventurers especially from East Asia. Barakatullah's collaborator Hasan Hatano Uhô, a Pan-Asianist convert to Islam, published other Islamic journals that contributed to the aura of a positive Japanese image in the Muslim world.[33] Hatano's book on Asian solidarity was later translated into Ottoman Turkish by Abdurreşid Ibrahim under the title *Asia in Danger* and published in Istanbul by a Pan-Islamist publication house, Sebilürreşad.[34] Meanwhile, in Istanbul, Ibrahim's own memoirs from his travels in Asia were published. His highly didactic discourse on lessons from Japan's achievements, and his Asianist perspective on world affairs shaped a highly pro-Japanese Muslim public opinion.[35] A Japanese Pan-Asianist and a Kokuryûkai member named Yamaoka Kôtarô accompanied Abdurreşid Ibrahim on the way back to the Muslim Middle East. He converted to Islam, visited Mecca, and gave lectures in Ottoman cities.[36] Finally and more importantly, the activities of this small group gradually shaped the imagination of Pan-Asianists and Pan-Islamists about an international solidarity that would go beyond the zones of the Islamic world or the Chinese cultural sphere.

Witnessing the larger Asian nationalist admiration for Japan, even from Islamic Asia with which Japanese Asianists were not very familiar, strengthened the arguments of those in Japan who advocated Japanese leadership of an awakening Asia. Thus, global responses to the Russo-Japanese War gave Pan-Asianists in Japan a new realist and confident voice. Although the ideal of Asian solidarity was not officially endorsed by the Japanese government, toward the end of the 1890s, even some of the high level Meiji bureaucrats began to consider Pan-Asianism as a potential counter to the aggressive policies of Western powers in East Asia. Prince Konoe Atsumaro's argument for solidarity with China exemplifies the appeal of Pan-Asianist ideas among the Japanese political and diplomatic elite. In an article published in *Taiyô* in 1898, Konoe predicted an inevitable racial struggle in East Asia between the white and yellow races, with both the Chinese and the Japanese siding together as the sworn enemies of the whites.[37] The early Asian Monroe Doctrine of Konoe Atsumaro was of a defensive nature, reflecting Japanese concerns about increased imperialist activity on a global scale and interventions in China, without making any grand claim of Japanese leadership in liberating Asia from colonialism. However, the Japanese victory over Russia in 1905 allowed the defensive concerns that constituted Konoe Atsumaro's Asian Monroe Doctrine to change into a confident assertion of Japan's regional hegemony and its overarching mission in the world, best seen in the intellectual career of Tokutomi Sôhô. As Japan came to be seen as the pioneer of Asian awakening and the model to illustrate the compatibility of Asian culture with universal modernity, a new vision of Japan's national mission emerged accordingly.[38]

Although the Asian Monroe Doctrine claimed to serve the Japanese national interest and appeared at a time when the idea of Japan's mission of leadership in Asia was beginning to penetrate public consciousness, it was still far from being a part of Japan's official foreign policy. Japanese policies toward Asia remained in harmony with the Anglo-Japanese Alliance, in spite of the support expressed by part of the Japanese elite for Asianist ideals or their sense of Asian identity. In some cases, differing visions of the role of Asianism in foreign policy led to conflicts among high-level bureaucrats. One well-known conversation in 1907 between Itô Hirobumi, then serving as Resident General in Korea, and Gotô Shinpei, President of the South Manchuria Railway Company, illustrates this division within the elite with regard to Asianism: In September of 1907, Gotô Shinpei (1857–1929) described his vision of Japan's World Policy to Itô Hirobumi. At the beginning of this policy report, Gotô expressed his belief that helping Chinese leaders to create *Tôyôjin no Tôyô* (Asia for Asians) represented the true aim of *Dai Ajia Shugi* (Great Asianism) and the best means of establishing a real peace in *Tôyô* (East Asia). Upon hearing this, Itô interrupted Gotô and asked him to stop and explain what he meant by the term Great Asianism. He cautioned Gotô of carelessness in expressing such ideas, pointing out that no benefit could come to Japan from the discourse of Great Asianism. Itô also warned that such references to Asianism would elicit misunderstanding in the eyes of Westerners, and would lead them to associate Japanese power and policies with their prejudiced concept of the Yellow Peril.[39]

From this conversation that took place in the context of efforts to define a long-term policy toward Russia, we can see that there were some top-level Japanese officials in the period following the Russo-Japanese War who sympathized with an Asianist orientation in foreign policy as Japanese national interest. They shared a belief in the cultural association with China and a feeling of pride that Japan alone had achieved a successful civilizational synthesis of East and West. They also perceived world events as constituting a racial conflict. Influential political figures such as Konoe Atsumaro, Inukai Tsuyoshi, Gotô Shinpei, Ôkuma Shigenobu, and Yamagata Aritomo all expressed Asianist ideals during their political careers.[40] In fact, Asian nationalists visiting Japan met with some of these leading Japanese statesmen.[41] However, on the whole, Japanese leaders cautioned that any kind of overt Asianist emphasis would threaten Japan's relationship with the Western powers and might provoke anti-Japanese views.[42] They made a deliberate effort to avoid appearing friendly to Japan's Asian nationalist admirers. Rather, they demonstrated Japan's pro-Western diplomacy by complying, in 1909, with a request from the French Embassy for the expulsion of a group of Vietnamese students who, inspired by Pan-Asianist ideals, had come to Japan to study the secrets of Japanese progress.[43] Similarly, it is highly instructive that, in 1910, Prime Minister Ôkuma Shigenobu wrote a preface to a translation of Lord Cromer's *Modern Egypt*, emphasizing that the British colonial experience in Egypt could serve as a model for Japan's management of Korea, at the same time that Egyptian nationalists were looking to Japan for inspiration in their national awakening.[44]

Similar to the experience of the relationship between the Japanese government and the Pan-Asianist movement, from 1905–1912, while Muslim intellectuals in the Ottoman State discussed the topic of Pan-Asianism, the Ottoman government continued a policy of cooperation with the Western powers without openly endorsing or supporting any Pan-Islamic movement. From the early 1880s to 1912, Pan-Islamism was an important topic among Muslim intellectual networks and the European writings on the rising nationalism and modernization movements in the Muslim world. But, during this period, it did not become an officially endorsed Ottoman policy, despite the fact that the Ottoman State and the institution of the Caliphate remained a central focus of Pan-Islamic imagination. Ottoman political leaders cautioned that any official indication of Pan-Islamic solidarity would lead to further suspicion of the Ottomans in the minds of the European powers. They insisted that the Ottoman State must focus on solving its own problems and give priority to its relations with the Europeans. After all, "while dreaming to save India from the British rule, the Ottoman State could lose Western Thrace just fifty miles away from its capital city."[45] When a leading Muslim modernist and Pan-Islamist from Russia, Ismail Bey Gaspıralı, (1851–1914), tried to establish the first major Pan-Islamic congress, he received no official blessing from the Ottoman government. As a venue for the Pan-Islamic congress, Gaspıralı had to choose British-controlled Cairo, because an Islamic congress could not meet in Istanbul as it would arouse Western powers' suspicion that the Ottoman government was officially mobilizing a reactionary anti-Western solidarity. Gaspıralı's project was partly inspired by his observations of the methods of the Pan-Slavic movement and his experience with the Muslim Congresses of Russia during 1905–1906.[46] Gaspıralı's appeal was for a cultural and social renewal, and for solving the common issues of Muslims in nonpolitical arenas, as he was careful to add that such a congress should not arouse the suspicion of the Great Powers. For example, in his petition to Abdulhamid II, the Ottoman Sultan, Gaspıralı assured him that the congress would not arouse any negative European public opinion.[47] Yet, he did not receive any response, despite the fact that Abdulhamid had a reputation for following Pan-Islamic policies.

The political situation of Pan-Asianist and Pan-Islamist trends in the aftermath of the Russo-Japanese War shows that both of these anti-Western transnational ideologies gained a new realist geopolitical currency, and in fact, they were being discussed as potential alternatives to the existing world order both by European-American and Asian intellectuals. However, neither the Japanese nor the Ottoman state openly endorsed Pan-Islamic and Pan-Asian programs in their foreign policy, although they may have benefited from the expectations, ideas and networks created by these two anti-Western visions.

Intellectual Impact: Japan as a Metaphor for Asian Modernities

The rise of Japan as the only nonwhite world power facilitated an increase of the Asian interest in the Japanese experience of modernization. In many circles, Japan began to serve as a metaphor for Asian modernity for the Ottomans, Egyptians, and Indians. The idea of a successful model of modernity in a non-European cultural zone was crucial for the nationalist claim to cultural authenticity, while at the same time embracing the universality of a Eurocentric model of progress and development. In this sense, Asian writings on the achievements of Japan's successful merger of traditional cultural elements with universal aspects of Western modernity were a form of affirmation that Ottomans, Egyptians, Iranians, or Indians could also modernize without any fear of loosing their national and cultural identity, and moreover, their authentic cultural and religious difference from Europe are never an obstacle for modernization.

Within that spirit, many reformers wanted to know what would be necessary to copy, for their own societies, in order to achieve what Japan had achieved in the three decades of reform after the Meiji Restoration.[48] The search for the secrets of Japan's progress was in harmony with the predominant appropriation of Social Darwinist notions of development and progress by Asian nationalists. Contrary to the deterministic interpretations of social Darwinism, and the writings of Herbert Spencer, reformists in Asia downplayed the determinism in favor of an optimistic and voluntaristic idea of reviving the nation or civilization.[49] For them, the actions and the willpower of the "young" nationalists of Asia were sufficient to overcome the seemingly scientific social and geographical determinants of Asian backwardness. Japan became the best example of a national willpower that could indeed close the developmental gap between Europe and Asia, a task previously deemed impossible according to the dominant social science theories or Darwinist and Spencerian notions of that time. This observation led to a search for the reasons, or "secrets," behind the "rise of Japan," and to reflections not only about the Meiji reform experience of the Japanese government, but also the character of the Japanese people. The Japanese model became an educational tool for almost all the conflicting ideological currents in the Ottoman State, Egypt and India, ranging from Social Darwinist secularists to Muslim and Hindu modernists, and from supporters of a strong monarchy to constitutionalists.

The secrets of Japanese progress were commonly attributed to Meiji state policies in compulsory public education, participatory politics and constitution, and to policies of industrial development. After describing the secrets of Japanese progress, one Egyptian paper expressed the hope that Japan would become Asia's teacher not only in the tangible skills of successful military technology, commerce, and agriculture, but also in the importance of education and patriotism.[50] Ottoman, Egyptian, and Indian writings on the secrets of Japanese progress reflected the dilemma on the issue of attributing Japanese success either to exceptional Japanese traits or to universally applicable policies that the Meiji leadership had executed. If the Japanese success was solely due to Japan's peculiar traditions and national culture, as several well-known European and Japanese interpretations argued, Japan could only be the exception that proved the rule of Asia's permanent backwardness. For example, Nitobe Inazô argued that the ethical training of Japanese individuals inherited from the martial tradition of the Samurai, *bushido*, explained Japan's extraordinary success in modernity. For Nitobe, to understand the principle and single driving force behind the success of Japan's transformation after the Meiji Restoration required more than a focus only on education or technological and industrial advances. "It is the spirit that quickeneth, without which the best of implements profiteth but little."[51] This meant that other Asian nations were still incapable of reaching the same high levels of progress and civilization. However, avoiding such a pessimistic conclusion, and in hopes of affirming an "awakening of Asia" through the symbol of Japan, other Asian commentators usually concluded that Japan's path to progress could be emulated by other Eastern nations, even if there remained certain peculiar aspects of Japanese culture that explained Japan's achievements.

We can see an example of the tension between a particularistic and a universalistic interpretation of Japan's achievement in the discussion arising from a conference on the Renaissance of Japan organized by the Committee of Union and Progress, the party of the 1908 Constitutional Revolution, in Istanbul in 1911. The audience included high ranking and influential figures such as the Ottoman Prince Abdülmecid Efendi and the Minister of Foreign Affairs, both of whom would naturally have been inclined to hear the secrets of Japanese success that could be taken as policy-oriented lessons for the Ottomans. The main speaker was the Austria-Hungarian advisor to the Ottoman Ministry of Justice, Comte Leon Ostrorog (1867–1932). Ostrorog explained the Japanese success not as a miracle, but as a consequence of the fundamental inclinations of the Japanese people, the most important of which was the recognition of the value of adopting the ways of a superior foreign civilization. In addition to underscoring Japan's historically "unique" ability to assimilate foreign cultures, Ostrorog's explanations represented major ideas of the exceptionality of Japan's modern successes that included, for example, references to *bushido* ethics. Ostrorog concluded that the Japanese had achieved constitutional reform, instituted military conscription and compulsory education, established universities, and reorganized the economy as a result of their exceptional national character.[52]

For Ottoman policymakers, the emphasis on Japan's uniqueness could be translated into an argument of fatalism and predeterminism. If it was Japanese culture that explained the country's success, it would have to be Ottoman-Muslim culture that prevented progress and halted reform efforts. This kind of culture-praise and culture-blame implied that it would be impossible for the Ottomans to repeat the great achievements of their Oriental brothers in Japan.[53] Thus, aware of these implications, contrary to Count Leon Ostrorog's emphasis on the role of peculiar Japanese characteristics, the conference organizer Salih Gourdji did not mention cultural factors in his introductory speech. Instead, he made comparisons between Japan and the Ottoman State, concluding that had the absolutist regime of Abdulhamid II not stopped the constitutional progress and put an end to political freedoms, the Ottomans could have enjoyed similar achievements. Thus, according to Gourdji, the Ottomans could also succeed if they took lessons from Japan's efforts at political participation and constitutional leadership.[54]

Despite the immense proliferation of writings on the Japanese model, Asian discourses on the Japanese achievements in modernization failed to offer any concrete alternative to Western modernity. Modernity was still seen as essentially one and universal, and Meiji Japan's achievement was to prove that this universal modernity was possible in the context of Japanese, Chinese, Indian, Turkish, Islamic, and Confucian cultures. Modernism was the dominant ideological trend in Asia, even among the seemingly anti-Western Pan-Asianists and Pan-Islamists. For example, there were no visible fundamentalist movements in the Islamic world during the 1882–1914 period, despite the critiques of European imperialism. As Asian nationalists observed differences among British, French, German, and American models of development and modernity, they could also imagine their own authentic version of modernity that nevertheless shared the essence of modern progress embodied in the West. Since nationalism required an assertion of cultural distinctiveness, there was no reason to copy another Asian nation's cultural attributes.

What Asian admirers learned from Japan was in fact a Japanese interpretation of Western modernity, and a validation of the earlier Asian interest in universalizing modernity. The experience of Asian students in Japan is a good example of this trend. For instance, for the more than ten thousand Chinese students who studied in Japan prior to World War I, studying in Japan was regarded primarily as a cheaper and more effective means to learn the Western-originated but still universal modernity from a nearby country that had already adopted it successfully. While Chinese intellectuals were in fact very much influenced by the Japanese interpretations of Western modernity through this student network, the fact remains that their ultimate goal was to learn what Japan had previously learned from the West, rather than any Japanese alternative to the West. Among Indian, Vietnamese, Turkish, and Arab students, those who chose to come to Japan must have done so more out of ideological inclinations than financial and geographical convenience.[55] Most people admired Japan's synthesis of Western modernity with its own cultural traditions. But they would also see Japanese modernity not as an alternative to the West, but rather as its most successful application.[56] Therefore, students who returned to their home countries from Japan did not find themselves in contradiction to those who came back from European countries, because Europe remained the ultimate model of modernity and reform.[57]

In sum, the Japanese model of modernization was valuable for Asian observers for three main reasons. First, it presented a shortcut to the Western level of civilization. According to the predominant views of modern world history, advanced Western nations had achieved their civilizational level over the course of several centuries. Non-Western intellectuals seeking to raise their own societies to an equal standard had to find some way to replicate the long years of Western development in a shorter period of time, especially given the widening power gap between the Western imperial powers and Asia. The success of the Japanese reforms since the Meiji Restoration was thus important as a demonstration of how progress could be achieved over just a few decades by cultivating patriotism, dedication to the nation, and social morality. If 30 years of rapid and selective state-led reforms had brought Japan to a level equal with the West, nationalists in Asia could also be optimistic about the future power and wealth of their own nations. The will to change, the energy to reform, and the availability of earlier models eliminated all the geographical, cultural, and historical constraints and conditions that European thinkers had identified as the causes of the rise of civilization in the West.

Second, the Japanese example showed that non-Western cultural and religious traditions did not necessarily have to be regarded as obstacles to modern progress. By the turn of the century, the nature of the relationship between traditional culture and universal modernity had already become an important question for the nationalist agenda. In the literature on Japan's modernization, the prevailing consensus held that Japan had successfully and intelligently selected the useful and essential aspects of Western civilization for adoption, without the need for appropriating "superficial and harmful" Western habits and denying its cultural heritage. In truth, the heritage that was preserved was more an invented image of traditional Japan than it was a reflection of the actual continuity of pre-Meiji Japanese culture.[58] However, this concept of a Japanese selectivity that could effectively synthesize Western and Eastern knowledge was very significant from the perspective of Asian nationalism, which had been preoccupied with the question of an East-West encounter and civilizational harmony since the 1880s.[59] For example, the Good Wife, Wise Mother ideology that Japan had adopted from European culture was regarded as a successful preservation of the Japanese tradition in a modernizing context, since women could actively serve the self-strengthening of the nation through Westernizing reforms without losing their traditional cultural role.[60] Throughout the Middle East, the imagery focusing on the progressive role of Japanese women in social life while preserving their traditional duties became a constant reference point among nationalists.[61] For intellectuals thinking within the paradigms of a synthesis between East and West, then, Japan presented a far better model than Germany or France, since it offered proof that native cultural traditions could indeed be compatible with modern civilization. For instance, the most prominent theorist of Turkish national identity, Ziya Gökalp, often referred to the Japanese historical experience in relation to his arguments that modern Turkey need not be afraid of losing its Muslim religion and national culture in the process of appropriating universal modernity.[62]

Third, the rise of Japan engendered optimism that it was not too late for Ottoman, Egyptian, and Indian reformers to bring their own societies to modernity and international equality. At the time of Japan's rise, Egypt and India were under colonial rule, while the Ottoman State, though politically independent, was still subject to unequal treaties and Western interventions into domestic affairs and had been dubbed the "sick man of Europe." A widespread mood of pessimism over the failure of the Ottoman reforms was combined with the newly popularized Darwinist ideologies of racial and civilizational hierarchies and led to the conviction that not only the Ottoman failures but the overall backwardness of Asian societies could be attributed to an inherent "incapability" of Easterners, as opposed to Westerners, to civilize themselves.[63] In this context, Japan's example of catching up with Western civilization in just three decades served as an inspiration to Ottoman reformers to rejuvenate radical reformism with renewed optimism.[64] Similarly, in colonized societies such as Egypt, Indonesia, and India, an emphasis on the racial and cultural similarity they shared with the Japanese under the banner of Eastern identity made it possible for the nationalist movements in those societies to find new legitimacy in their struggle against colonialism. After all, if "the Japanese could succeed, the Javanese could do it too," and thus they would not need the "civilizing mission" of the Dutch colonial rule.[65]

Conclusion

The Russo-Japanese War demonstrated that Western powers could no longer justify grabbing non-Western lands by pointing to the alleged superiority of the Western race and civilization. It was also a turning point in the history of both modernist ideologies and anti-Western critiques. From the Russo-Japanese War until World War I, the contradictions in the legitimacy structures of the international order, namely the civilizing mission ideology, became more obvious. Globally, the debates on the concept of racial hierarchies, and the ideas of Eastern and Western civilizations became more intensified and politicized. Three aspects of these debates are especially important for the historical trajectory of anti-Western critiques and alternative visions of world order. First, the Russo-Japanese War sealed the loss of legitimacy for the existing Eurocentric world order. Anticolonial nationalists and intellectuals all over Asia successfully utilized the Japanese victory to counter the earlier discourse of white race supremacy and the backwardness of the contemporary Oriental cultures. Second, Pan-Islamic and Pan-Asianist visions became part of the realist discourse of world politics. Nationalist movements all over Asia embraced the anti-Western internationalism of Pan-Asian and Pan-Islamic thought as a potential form of empowerment in their demands for autonomy and equality in the international system. Third, the Russo-Japanese War and the subsequent series of constitutional revolutions in Asia (Iran in 1906, Turkey in 1908, and China in 1911) established a self-consciousness of the era as the "awakening of the East," preceding the era of WWI described as the "decline of the West." Gradually, the meanings of "Asia" and "East" in relation to the West were redefined, in a reverse Orientalist strategy, to match the political realities of this period. The global moment of the Russo-Japanese War not only became a turning point in the history of decolonization of Asia, but also the precondition for the interpretation of World War I as the "decline of the West." In the long trajectory from the 1880s to the mid-1930s, recognizing the moment of 1905 would help us rethink the subjectivity of the non-Western world in the history of decolonization. Were there no "awakening East" associated with the 1905–1914 period, the "decline of the West" in World War I would be insufficient for describing the intellectual and political collapse of the Eurocentric world order during the interwar era.

Notes

1. Prasenjit Duara, ed., *Decolonization: Perspectives from Now and Then* (London: Routledge, 2004), pp. 2–3; Narangoa Li and Robert Cribbs, eds., *Imperial Japan and National Identities in Asia 1895–1945* (London: Routledge, 2003), pp. 2–3; Klaus Kreiser "Der japanische Sieg über Rußland (1905) und sein Echo unter den Muslimen" [The Japanese Victory over Russia (1905) and Its Echo in the Islamic World], *Die Welt des Islam* [The World of Islam] 21 (1984): 209–39.

2. For example, the German politician and diplomat Baron von Falkenegg wrote the following in his 1905 work: "Today there are indeed still thousands of Europeans supposedly versed in history who are extremely pleased with the victories of Japan over Russia. In fact they are ignorant of history and do not see that it was Europe and not Russia that was defeated in Manchuria." See Baron von Falkenegg, *Japan, die neue Weltmacht* [Japan, the Emerging World Power] (Berlin: Boll & Pickard, 1905). The image of Japan in England or America would differ according to the ideological perspective of the individual. While progressive anti-imperialist figures would welcome the rise of Japan as an obstacle to imperialism, the right wing figures would lament it as a dangerous Yellow Peril. For example, British socialist Henry Hyndman's journal *Justice* had many pro-Japanese articles. For a very sympathetic account of Japan's victory written by a Universalist minister, see Sidney L. Gulick, *The White Peril in the Far East: An Interpretation of the Significance of the Russo-Japanese War* (New York: Revell, 1905). For a very negative right-wing British account of Japan, see T.W.H. Crosland, *The Truth About Japan* (London: Richards, 1904).

3. For the most comprehensive work on Middle Eastern perceptions of Japan, see Renee Worringer, "Comparing Perceptions: Japan as Archetype for Ottoman Modernity, 1876–1918" (Ph.D. diss., University of Chicago, 2001). See also Anja Pistor-Hatam, "Progress and Civilization in Nineteenth-Century Japan: The Far Eastern State as a Model for Modernization," *Iranian Studies* 29, no. 1–2 (1996): 111–26; and Sugita Hideaki, "Japan and the Japanese as Depicted in Modern Arabic Literature," *Studies of Comparative Culture* 27 (1989): 21–40. For examples of primary sources of this literature, see Mustafa Kamil, *Al-Shams al-Mushriqah* (Cairo: Matbaat al-Liwa, 1904). For the reception of Mustafa Kamil's book on Japan in Southeast Asia, see Michael Laffan, "Watan and Negeri: Mustafa Kamil's 'Rising Sun' in the Malay World," *Indonesia Circle* 69 (1996): 157–75. For Malay interests in the Russo-Japanese War, see William R. Roff, *The Origins of Malay Nationalism* (*New Haven*: Yale University Press, 1967), pp. 91–100, 126–57.

4. Oka Yoshitake, "The First Anglo-Japanese Alliance in Japanese Public Opinion," in J.P. Lehmann, ed., *Themes and Theories in Japanese History* (London: Athlone Press, 1988), pp. 185–93.

5. Mustafa Kamil, "al-Harb al-Hadirah wa'l-Islam," *al-Liwa* (February 18, 1904): 1. For a discussion of Mustafa Kamil's ideas, see Renee Worringer, "Comparing Perceptions," pp. 350–56.

6. For the African American reactions to the Russo-Japanese War, see Marc Gallicchio, *Black Internationalism in Asia, 1895–1945: The African American*

Encounter with Japan & China (Chapel Hill: University of North Carolina Press, 2000), pp. 6–15.

7. Renee Worringer, " 'Sick Man of Europe' or 'Japan of the Near East'?: Constructing Ottoman Modernity in the Hamidian and Young Turk Eras," *International Journal of Middle Eastern Studies* 36, no. 2 (2004): 207–23; also Roxane Haag-Higuchi, "A Topos and Its Dissolution: Japan in Some 20th Century Iranian Texts," *Iranian Studies* 29, no. 1–2 (1996): 71–83.

8. Henry Dyer, *Dai Nippon, The Britain of the East: A Study in National Evolution* (London: Blackie & Son Limited, 1904).

9. For direct military reports from the fronts, see Ali Fuad Erden, *Musavver 1904–1905 Rus-Japon Seferi* (Istanbul: Kitaphane-yi Islam ve Askeri, 1905 or 1906). Japanese military power and history were well studied and written about by Ottoman military officer Pertev Bey, especially in his book Pertev Bey, *Rus-Japon Harbinden Alinan Maddi ve Manevi Dersler ve Japonlarin Esbabi Muzafferiyeti: Bir Milletin Tâli'I Kendi Kuvvetindedir!* [Material and Moral Lessons Taken from the Russo-Japanese War and the Reasons for Japan's Victory: A Nation's Good Fortune from its Own Power!] (Istanbul: Kanâ'at Kütüphanesi ve Matbaasi, 1911).

10. Jawaharlal Nehru, *An Autobiography* (Delhi: Oxford University Press, 1989), p. 16. See also Jawaharlal Nehru, *Toward Freedom* (Boston: Beacon Press, 1967), pp. 29–30.

11. Prasenjit Duara, "Transnationalism and the Predicament of Sovereignty: China, 1900–1945," *American Historical Review* 102, no. 4 (1997): 1030–52, 1038.

12. Phan Bội Châu, *Reflections from Captivity: Prison Notes*, trans. D. Marr (Athens, OH: Ohio University Press, 1978), pp. 23, 129.

13. Ba Maw, *Breakthrough in Burma: Memoirs of a Revolution, 1939–1946* (New Haven: Yale University Press, 1968), pp. 47–48.

14. For a comparison of the impact of the Russo-Japanese war in different national communities of intellectuals, see Gesa Westermann, "Japan's Victory in the Russo-Japanese War (1904–1905) from the Philippine, Vietnamese, and Burmese Perspectives" forthcoming in Rotem Kowner, ed., *Rethinking the Russo-Japanese War: Centennial Perspectives* (Dorset, UK: Global Oriental Publishers, 2006).

15. Hugh Tinker, *Race, Conflict and the International Order* (New York: St. Martin's Press, 1977), p. 39.

16. Şükrü Hanioğlu, *The Young Turks in Opposition* (New York: Oxford University Press, 1995), p. 210.

17. William Cleveland, *The Making of an Arab Nationalist: Ottomanism and Arabism in the Life and Thought of Sati' Al-Husri* (Princeton: Princeton University Press, 1971), pp. 37–38.

18. Münif Paşa, "Mukayese-i İlm ve Cehl," *Mecmua-i Fünün* 1 (1862): 28.

19. James Hevia, "Looting Beijing: 1860, 1900," in *Tokens of Exchange: The Problem of Translation in Global Circulations*, Lydia H. Liu, ed. (Durham: Duke University Press, 1999), pp. 192–213. During the suppression of the Boxer Rebellion, Japan joined the Western coalition, composed of soldiers from the United States, Austria-Hungary, Britain, France, Germany, Italy, and Russia.

20. Ahmed Riza, "La Leçon d'une Guerre," *Mechveret Supplement Français* 169 (1905): 1–2. The translation of this passage is taken from Renee Worringer, "Comparing Perceptions."

21. Şükrü Hanioğlu, *Preparation for a Revolution: The Young Turks, 1902–1908* (New York: Oxford University Press, 2001), p. 304.

22. Gerrit Gong quotes L. Oppenheim's *International Law: A Treatise* (London: Longmans, Green & Co., 1905) as an example, See Gerrit Gong, *The Standard of "Civilization" in International Society* (Oxford: Clarendon Press, 1984), p. 57.

23. Şükrü Hanioğlu, *Preparation for a Revolution*, pp. 304–05.

24. *Revue du Monde Musulman (RMM)*, first published in November 1906 (Paris: Mission Scientifique du Maroc, 1906–1926). The founding editor of *Revue du Monde Musulman*, Alfred Le Chatelier, was appointed Chair of Muslim Sociology at the College de France in 1903. See Susan Bayly, "Racial Readings of Empire: Britain, France, and Colonial Modernity in the Mediterranean and Asia," in Leila Fawaz and C.A. Bayly, eds., *Modernity and Culture from the Mediterranean to the Indian Ocean, 1890–1920* (New York: Columbia University Press, 2002), p. 296. See also Edmund Burke III, "The First Crisis of Orientalism," in Jean-Claude Vatin, Jacques Frémeaux, Laurence Michalak, and David Prochoska, eds., *Connaissances du Maghreb. Sciences Sociales et Colonisation* (Paris: CNRS, 1984), pp. 231–26.

25. For some of the articles on Pan-Islamism in the *Revue du Monde Musulman*, see L. Bouvat, "La Presse Anglaise et le Panislamisme," *RMM* 1, no. 3 (1907): 404–05; L. Bouvat, "Un Projet de parlement musulman international," *RMM* 7, no. 3 (1909): 321–22; A. Fevret, "Le Croissant contre la Croix," *RMM* 2, no. 7 (1907): 421–25; Ismael Hamet, "Le Congres Musulman Universal," *RMM* 4, no.1 (1908): 100–107; A. Le Chatelier, "Le Pan-Islamisme et le Progres," *RMM* 1, no. 4 (1907): 145–68.

26. F(ernard) Farjenel, "La Japon at L'Islam," *RMM* 1, no. 1 (1906): 101–14.

27. Selçuk Esenbel, "Japan's Global Claim to Asia and the World of Islam: Transnational Nationalism and World Power, 1900–1945," *The American Historical Review* 109, no. 4 (2004): 1140–70.

28. Tôa Dôbunkai was established in 1898 by Konoe Atsumaro with the purpose of studying China and developing cultural policies with an eye on a long-term alliance between Japan and China. Genyôsha was founded in 1881 by Hiraoka Kôtarô and Tôyama Mitsuru. Hiraoka (1851–1906) was a mine owner and former samurai who had taken part in the rebellion of Saigô Takamori. The aims that Genyôsha declared for itself were "to revere the Imperial Family," "to respect and honor the fatherland," and "to guard the rights of the people," yet they mostly focused on protecting and expanding Japanese interests in East Asia. During both the Sino-Japanese and the Russo-Japanese Wars, the society was involved in intelligence-gathering activities and covert operations. Kokuryûkai was formed by Uchida Ryôhei in 1901 as an offshoot of Genyôsha, with its purpose declared as the expulsion of Russia from the East Asian region up to the boundaries of the Amur River.

29. For information about its Japanese and Muslim members, see *Daitô* 4, no. 3 (1911): 64–65.
30. *Daitô* 3, no. 4 (1910): 2.
31. Mohammad Barakatullah, ed., *The Islamic Fraternity* (Tokyo: 1911–1912).
32. For an example of Kokuryûkai's increasing networking with Asian nationalists after the Russo-Japanese War, see Selcuk Esenbel, "Japanese Interest in the Ottoman Empire," in Bert Edstrom, ed., *The Japanese and Europe: Images and Perceptions* (Surrey: Curzon Press, 2000), pp. 112–20; El-Mostafa Rezrazi, "Pan-Asianism and the Japanese Islam: Hatano Uhô: From Espionage to Pan-Islamist Activity," *Annals of the Japan Association for Middle East Studies* 12 (1997): 89–112.
33. Hatano Uhô was an expert on Chinese Muslims and a graduate of Konoe Atsumaro's Tôa Dôbun Shoin in Shanghai.
34. Hatano Uhô, *Asya Tehlikede*, trans. Nakawa and (Abdurreşid) Ibrahim (Istanbul: Sebilürreşat, 1910).
35. Abdurreşid Ibrahim, *Alem-i Islam ve Japonya'da Intisari Islamiyet* (Istanbul: Ahmed Saki Bey Matbaasi, 1910 or 1911). For an assessment of the Japanese contacts of Abdurreşid Ibrahim and his pan-Asianism, see Selcuk Esenbel, Nadir Özbek, İsmail Türkoğlu, François Georgeon, and Ahmet Uçar "Ozel Dosya: Abdurresid Ibrahim 2," *Toplumsal Tarih* 4, no. 20 (1995): 6–23.
36. Sakamoto Tsutomu, "The First Japanese Hadji Yamaoka Kôtaro and Abdürreşid Ibrahim," in Selcuk Esenbel and Inaba Chiharu, eds., *The Rising Sun and the Turkish Crescent: New Perspectives on the History of Japanese-Turkish Relations* (Istanbul: Boğaziçi University Press, 2003), pp. 105–121; Nakamura Kôjirô, "Early Japanese Pilgrims to Mecca," *Report of the Society for Near Eastern Studies in Japan* [Nippon Orient Gakkai] 12 (1986): 47–57.
37. The name of the article was *Dôjinshu Dômei: Shina Mondai Kenkyû no Hitsuyô* [We Must Ally with Those of the Same Race, and We Must Study the China Problem]. See Marius Jansen, "Konoe Atsumaro," in Akira Iriye, ed., *The Chinese and the Japanese: Essays in Political and Cultural Interactions* (Princeton: Princeton University Press, 1980), p. 113.
38. In this context, Tokutomi Sohô (1863–1957) advocated a "Yellow Man's Burden," giving voice to an alternative to the idea of "The White Man's Burden" (Based on Rudyard Kipling's famous poem of 1899). Tokutomi Sohô, "Kôjin no omoni," *Kokumin Shimbun* (January 1906). See also Hirakawa Sukehiro, "Modernizing Japan in Comparative Perspective," *Comparative Studies of Culture* 26 (1987): 29.
39. Yamamura Shinichi, "Nihon Gaikô to Ajia Shugi no Kôsaku," in *Seiji Gaku Nenpô* (Tokyo, 1998), pp. 26–27. Taken from Tsurumi Yûsuke, *Gotô Shinpei*, 4 vols. (Tokyo: Keisô Shôbo, 1965–1967), pp. 960–61.
40. George Akita and Itô Takashi, "Yamagata Aritomo no 'jinshû kyôsô' ron" [Yamagata Aritomo's theory of racial conflict], in *Nihon Gaikô no kiki ninshiki* (Tokyo: Yamakawa Shuppansha, 1985), pp. 95–118.
41. For example, Abdurreşid Ibrahim, a Pan-Islamist who had connections to Russian, Ottoman and Egyptian Pan-Islamic circles was able to meet with

Ôkuma Shigenobu, Itô Hirobumi, and other leading statesmen of Japan, particularly due to the Japanese leaders' interest in meeting with a Muslim intellectual and Pan-Islamist activist. For the records of his conversation with Ôkuma Shigenobu in 1909, see Abdurreşid Ibrahim, *Alem-i Islam ve Japonya'da Intişari Islamiyet*, pp. 386–87. For Gotô Shinpei and Inukai Tsuyoshi's roles in helping an Indian revolutionary in Tokyo in 1917, see Tapan Mukherjee, *Taraknath Das: Life and Letters of a Revolutionary in Exile* (Calcutta: National Council of Education, Bengal, Jadavpur University, 1998), pp. 109–10. For the attention that Vietnamese nationalist Phan Boi Chau received from Inukai Tsuyoshi and Ôkuma Shigenobu, see David Marr, *Vietnamese Anti-Colonialism* (Berkeley: University of California Press, 1971), p. 113.

42. Yamamura Shinichi, "Nihon Gaikô to Ajia Shugi no Kôsaku," pp. 26–27.
43. David Marr, *Vietnamese Anti-Colonialism, 1885–1925* (Berkeley: University of California Press, 1971), pp. 146, 154–55.
44. Miura Tôru "Nihon no Chutô-Isuramu Kenkyû," *Gekkan Hyakka*, no. 365 (1993): 18–23. For Ôkuma Shigenobu's comments, see Evelyn Baring Cromer, *Saikin Ejiputo* [Modern Egypt] vol. 1 (Dainippon Bunmei Kyôkai, 1911), pp. 12–13.
45. For an example of how Ottoman intellectuals perceived Pan-Islamism as unrealistic around 1904 and 1905, see Yusuf Akçura, *Üç Tarzı Siyaset* (Ankara: Türk Tarih Kurumu Basımevi, 1987), pp. 39–40. In his work entitled *İttihad-i Islam* [Muslim Unity], Celal Nuri describes the objection of realist politicians of the Ottoman State in critique of the rising tide of Pan-Islamic ideas after the Balkan Wars. Those against the Ottoman leadership in the Muslim world saw the Ottoman State as an "old and sick grandfather (perhaps referring to the European notion of 'sick man of Europe'), in need of help himself," and believed that the Ottoman State was in no position to help the liberation of other Muslims. See Celal Nuri, *İttihad-i İslam: İslamin Mazisi, Hali, İstikbali* (Istanbul: Yeni Osmanli Matba'asi, 1913), pp. 10–11.
46. In his student years in Moscow (1865–1867), Ismail Gaspirali was socially adopted by a famous Pan-Slavist publisher and journalist, Mikhail Katkov, and witnessed the activities of the Moscow Slavic Benevolent Committee (which organized a Pan-Slavic Congress in 1867).
47. "İsmail Bey Gaspirali'nin 'Müslüman Kongresi' ile ilgili olarak Osmanli Padişahi II. Abdülhamid'e hitaben yazdiği mektubu," in Hakan Kirimli and Ismail Turkoglu, eds., *Ismail Bey Gaspıralı ve Dünya Müslümanları Kongresi*, Islamic Area Studies Project: Central Asian Research Series, vol. 4 (Tokyo: Tokyo University, 2002), p. 7.
48. "Japan at Turquie," *The Levant Herald Eastern Express* (May 15, 1912): 1, "This (Japanese) miracle, why would it not reproduce itself here? That which the Japanese did, could the Turks not do it too? . . . The response is not easy. It is necessary at first to realize the manner in which the Japanese have proceeded in their renovation. Thirsting for progress and comprehending well the impossibility of

getting there without specialists whose example they could heed, they placed some Europeans at the head of all their administrations."

49. For a discussion of the influnce of and responses to Social Darwinism and Herbert Spencer's ideas in different parts of Asia, see Prasenjit Duara, *Rescuing History from the Nation: Questioning Narratives of Modern China* (Chicago: University of Chicago Press, 1995), pp. 139–44; Şükrü Hanioğlu, *The Young Turks in Opposition*, pp. 200–12; Douglas Howland, "Society Reified: Herbert Spencer and Political Theory in Early Meiji Japan," *Comparative Studies in Society and History* 42, no. 1 (2000): 67–86; Hue-Tam Ho Tai, *Radicalism and the Origins of the Vietnamese Revolution* (Cambridge, Mass.: Harvard University Press, 1992), pp. 20–22.

50. "Luhmah buyna al-Sharqiyyin," *al-Liwa* (October 11, 1904): 1.

51. Nitobe Inazô, *Bushido: The Soul of Japan: An Exposition of Japanese Thought* (Tokyo: Kôdansha International, 1998), p. 188. Earliest version: Philadelphia: Leeds & Biddle, 1900.

52. Comte Leon Ostrorog, *Conference sur la Renaissance du Japon* (Istanbul: Ahmed Ihsan, 1911). This included Ostrorog's published proceedings as well as organizer M. Salih Gourdji's speech as a postscript between pp. 86 and 91. An Arabic translation of the book was produced by the former Ottoman Army officer and later Iraqi officer Taha al-Hashimi in 1925. See *Nahdat al-Yaban wa Ta'thir Ruh al-Ummah fi'l-Nahdah* [The Awakening of Japan and the Influence of the Nation's Spirit on the Awakening] (Baghdad: 1925). For comments on this lecture, see also Renee Worringer, "Comparing Perceptions," p. 267.

53. Şükrü Hanioğlu, *Preparation for a Revolution*, p. 304.

54. For Gourdji, in the three years since the Constitutional Revolution, there was not enough time to demonstrate comparable achievements by the constitutional Ottoman regime. See M. Salih Gourdji's postscript in Ostrorog, *Conference*, pp. 86–88.

55. On the Eastern Study Movement that sent students to Japan from Vietnam, see also Vuong Tri Nham, ed., *Phan Boi Chau and the Dong-DuMovement* (New Haven, Conn.: Yale Southeast Asia Studies, 1988).

56. For example, Ahmet Münir Ibrahim studied commerce at Waseda University, and sent articles to Sebilürreşat. Münir reportedly became a member of the Progressive Asian Student Society at Waseda, joining other students from China, Korea, India, Siam, and Japan. Ahmed Münir, "Hâricî Ticâret Vesile-i Sa'âdet-i Umûmidir," *Sebilürreşât* 12, no. 302 (1914): 290. Ahmet Münir, "Japonya Ticaret-i Bahriyesi," *Sebilürreşâta* 1, no. 8 (1912): 426–27. Münir also wrote a tribute to Emperor Meiji after his death: "Japonya Mikado'su Mutsuhito," *Sebilürreşât* 2, no. 9 (1912): 96–98. Another student, Hasan Fehmi, sent articles on the Japanese constitution and parliament emphasizing the key role played by the participatory political system for the empowerment of the Japanese nation. Hasan Fehmi, "Shuyûn: Japonya," *Sebilürreşad* 12, no. 295 (1914): 167.

57. For the derivative modernity concept, see Partha Chatterjee, *Nationalist Thought and the Colonial World: A Derivative Discourse* (Minneapolis: University of Minnesota Press, 1986).

58. Stephen Vlastos, ed., *Mirror of Modernity: Invented Traditions of Modern Japan* (Berkeley: University of California Press, 1998).

59. Albert Hourani, *Arabic Thought in the Liberal Age, 1798–1939* (Cambridge: Oxford University Press, 1962), p. 205.

60. Even as late as the Balkan Wars of 1911–1912, the example of Japanese women was invoked in order to ask for dedication and sacrifice from Ottoman Muslim women for the sake of the Ottoman State. See Zafer Toprak, *Milli Iktisat- Milli Burjuvazi* (Istanbul: Tarih Vakfi Yurt Yayinlari, 1995), p. 175. For the "Good Wife, Wise Mother" ideology, see Sharon Nolte and Sally Hastings, "Meiji State's Policy Toward Women," in Fail Lee Bernstein, ed., *Recreating Japanese Women, 1600–1945* (Berkeley and Los Angeles: University of California Press, 1991), pp. 151–74.

61. Egyptian modernist Qasim Amin's famous work *Tahrir al-Mar'ah*, written in 1899, spoke of Japanese women as an ideal example for Muslim women. Qasim Amin, *Tahrir al-Mar'ah* (Cairo: Dar al-Maarif, 1970). For the English translation, see Qasim Amin, *The Liberation of Women: A Document in the History of Egyptian Feminism*, trans. Samiha Sidhom Peterson (Cairo: American University in Cairo Press, 1992).

62. See Ziya Gökalp, "Medeniyetimiz" [Our Civilization], English translation in Niyazi Berkes, *Turkish Nationalism and Western Civilization: Selected Essays of Ziya Gökalp* (New York: George Allen & Unwin, 1959), p. 277. See also Uriel Heyd, *Foundations of Turkish Nationalism: The Life and Teachings of Ziya Gökalp* (London: Lucaz and Company Ltd., 1950).

63. I have discussed the shift in mood toward pessimism and radical ideologies of change in the last quarter of the twentieth century in my Master's thesis. See Cemil Aydin, "Mecmuai Fünün ve Mecmuai Ulum Dergilerinde Bilim ve Medeniyet Anlayişi" (Master's Thesis, Istanbul University, 1995).

64. Renee Worringer, "Comparing Perception," p. 222.

65. Indonesian nationalists metaphorically used the similarity between the words Japanese and Javanese to claim that the Javanese could one day become independent and advanced as well. *Islamic Fraternity* II-2, Tokyo (May 15, 1911).

CHAPTER 9

Bringing the "Black Atlantic" into Global History: The Project of Pan-Africanism

Andreas Eckert

Black Atlantic, Global History, and Pan-Africanism

Paul Gilroy's groundbreaking study on the "Black Atlantic" has revitalized scholarly interest in the connections between Africans, African-Americans and generally people of African descent on both sides of the Atlantic.[1] Gilroy argued that the Black Atlantic—the cultural web between diaspora Africans spread around Atlantic shores—has been crucial for modern sensibilities in the twentieth century.[2] In this context he makes the further point that "historians should take the Atlantic as a unit of analysis in their discussion of the modern world to produce an explicitly transnational perspective. . . ."[3] adding, "The history of the black Atlantic, continually criss-crossed by the movement of Black People—not only as commodities but engaged in various struggles toward emancipation, autonomy, and citizenship, is a means to reexamine the problems of nationality, location, identity, and historical memory."[4] Gilroy stresses the importance of the role of free travelers and of cultural exchanges among freed or free black populations in creating a shared Black Atlantic culture and shared black identities that transcend territorial boundaries.[5] He describes the African diaspora primarily in terms of what he calls "discontinuous" cultural exchange among diverse African diaspora populations. Drawing examples mainly from the English speaking black populations of England, the United States, and the Carribean, he argues that the shared cultural features of African diaspora groups "generally result far less from shared cultural memories of Africa than from these groups' mutually influential but culturally neutral responses to their exclusion from the benefits of the Enlightenment legacy of national citizenship and political equality in the West."[6]

In many ways the Black Atlantic seems to be an excellent subject for global historical approaches, although to date it hardly features in the realm of the historiography labelled "global." This has to do, among other things, with the fact that Gilroy's Black Atlantic is in some ways a narrow concept. He focuses mainly on cultural creativity and the intellectual links between the African diasporas in the United States and the United Kingdom, overlooking the southern part of the Atlantic, and the relations between Africa and Brazil, and conceding to intellectuals in Africa only a marginal position in his analysis. This chapter builds on Gilroy's analysis by systematically including the ideas and activities of Africans. In essence, it investigates the social and intellectual history of African, Caribbean, and African-American networks in the United States, Europe and Africa as part of the Black Atlantic between the 1880–1940s. The central focus will be on individuals and networks that could be linked to Pan-Africanist ideas.

In his concise definition, Kwame Anthony Appiah describes Pan-Africanism as "the political project calling for the unification of all Africans into a single African state to which those in the African diaspora could return. In its vaguer, more cultural forms, Pan-Africanism has pursued literary and artistic projects that bring together people in Africa and her diaspora."[7] Pan-Africanism was a very heterogeneous project initiated by intellectuals of African descent in North America and the Caribbean who thought of themselves as members of a single, "Negro" race. In this, Appiah adds, "they were merely following the mainstream of nineteenth-century thought in North America and Europe that developed an increasingly strong focus on the idea that human beings were divided into races, each of which had its own distinctive spiritual, physical, and cultural character."[8] In this way, they intentionally left out lighter-skinned North Africans, including the large majority who speak Arabic as their first language.

As Appiah rightly emphasizes, in the twentieth century, this way of thinking about African identity in racial terms has been challenged. In particular, the intellectuals born in Africa who took over the movement's leadership in the period after World War II developed a more geographical idea of African identity, although questions of race and culture continued to play an important role. However, the founders of the Organization of African Unity (OAU) such as Gamal Adbel Nasser of Egypt and Kwame Nkrumah of Ghana had a notion of Africa that was more straightforwardly continental. African unity for them was the unity of those who shared the African continent—though it continued to include, in some unspecified way, those whose ancestors had left the continent in the enforced exile of the slave trade. Nevertheless, the movement's intellectual roots lie firmly in the racial understanding of Africa in the thought of the African-American and Afro-Caribbean intellectuals who founded it. Because Pan-Africanism began as a movement in the New World, among the descendants of slave populations, and then spread back to Africa, it aimed to challenge antiblack racism on two fronts. On the one hand, it opposed racial domination in the diaspora; on the other, it challenged colonial domination that almost always was characterized by racism, in Africa itself. According to Appiah, "the stresses and strains that have sometimes divided the movement have largely occurred where these two rather different goals pulled it in different directions."[9] Especially during the twentieth century, Pan-Africanism was characterized by a continuous tension between concepts of "race," "culture," and "space"; often, as in the cases of Garveyism or Négritude (see below), it was a combination of all these concepts.

After the publication of some fundamental studies in the 1960s and early 1970s,[10] scholarly interest in Pan-Africanism remained low for a considerable period. This can partly be explained by the fact that, although prominent in the rhetoric of the new independent African nation states, Pan-Africanism did not play a significant role in political practice; the OAU, for instance, founded in 1963, soon became both inefficient and insignificant. Its replacement in 2001 by an apparently more dynamic African Union, pushed by none other than Libya's "leader of revolution" Muammar al Ghaddafi, may have stimulated some recent research on Pan-Africanism.[11] However, it was mainly the "discovery" of globalization by scholars that led to a renewed interest in diasporas, "transnational studies" and "global history." Consequently, there is a continuing and increasing interest in the history and significance of the African diaspora,[12] the global dispersal of peoples, and individuals of African descent, responsible for the emergence of Pan-African ideologies.

Pan-African history is principally connected with the dispersal of peoples of African origin brought about by the trans-Atlantic trade that took enslaved Africans to the Americas, at the beginning of the sixteenth century, and the subsequent emergence of global capitalism, European colonial rule, and imperialism. Numerous factors have pulled Africans into a global labor market for the last five centuries, from the slave plantations in the New World to the transitory black laborers who built railways and worked on other infrastructural projects in the Americas in the second half of the nineteenth century; to the African soldiers who fought (and died) in both world wars and to those Africans who worked in factories in France after 1945; to the current brain drain of African professionals and academics to the West.[13] A fresh look at African diasporas has led to a new assessment of the role of Africans in broad interregional and intercontinental networks. For instance, recent contributions to the debates concerning the Atlantic slave trade have attacked Eurocentric conceptions of Atlantic history and have emphasized that Africans made a major impact upon certain aspects of culture in the Western hemisphere.[14] The studies of Gilroy and others contributed to a fuller understanding of the roles, functions, and influences of Africans in relation to what we recognize as the modern world.[15] John Thornton emphasized the simple but easily overlooked fact that more Africans than Europeans reached the Americas until sometime early in the nineteenth century, and then powerfully stressed the role played by Africans in the construction of the Atlantic economy and the new colonial societies in the Americas.[16] According to Thornton, Africans (or at least African rulers) were creative participants, not passive and helpless victims, in these historical processes. "We must accept," Thornton writes, "that African participation in the slave trade was voluntary and under the control of African decision makers. This was not just at the surface level of daily exchange but even at deeper levels. Europeans possessed no means, either economic or military, to compel African leaders to sell slaves."[17] The critical role played by African agency in the operation of the Atlantic slave trade is partly accepted, partly still heavily disputed.[18] As regards the enslaved population in the diaspora, Thornton insists upon a high degree of continuity of traditions (such as language, music, dance, and religion) from Africa to the New World.[19] Others have demonstrated the continuous involvement of members of West African coastal communities in transoceanic networks. Parts of the area that Europeans called the Slave Coast (the coast of what is today Togo, Benin, and south-western Nigeria) were integrated into the Atlantic world not only by business links, but also by resultant cultural and social ties, on such a scale and intensity that the commercial and ruling elites might be considered to be participating in what may be reasonably termed an "Atlantic community."[20]

The twentieth century saw new and complex modes of migration from, to, and within Africa. While very few African-Americans or West Indians "returned" to Africa, many Africans went to Europe and the United States for business, education, and political purposes. In this context students especially played an important role in Pan-African networks.[21] African Americans and West Indians continued to play a considerable part in Pan-African ideologies and movements. Not only did their ideas and visions of the world travel more widely than in the preceding century, the protagonists themselves became much more mobile. The following pages represent an effort to follow their intellectual and social webs centred around the Atlantic, while focusing on both ideas and activities. This chapter, which attempts to establish a path through the many historical developments and historiographical debates linked to it, cannot be more than a survey of a confusing and complex phenomenon. However, it will be shown that Pan-Africanism is in many ways a topic par excellence for global and transnational history, as it implies processes transcending the nation-state as well as contacts and interaction over great distances.[22]

The Emergence of the Idea of Pan-Africanism in the Late Nineteenth Century

The idea of linking together the whole "Negro" race for political purposes was developed by a wide range of nineteenth-century, African-American intellectuals. It makes sense to speak of these nineteenth-century thinkers as Pan-Africanists, even though they did not use the term.[23] Appiah refers to the fact that like Pan-Slavism in Eastern Europe and the forms of romantic nationalism that created modern Germany and Italy, early Pan-Africanism reflected a philosophical tradition, derived from the German philosopher Johann Gottfried Herder. In Herder's opinion, peoples—or, as they were often called, nations—such as the Slavs, Germans, and Italians, were the central actors of world history. He suggested that their identities were expressed largely in language, in literature, and folk culture, and posited that such nations were naturally drawn together by the desire to live together in states, with shared language, culture, and traditions. In Herder's view the cultural oneness of a nation naturally led to political union.[24]

The first black intellectual to apply this theory in a systematic way to people of African descent was W.E.B. Du Bois in his lecture on "The Conservation of Races," published in 1897, in which he used the term Pan-Negroism.[25] Du Bois, who would become one of the most important African-American intellectuals and political activists as well as a crucial figure in the Pan-Africanist movement, was the first African-American who, in 1895, received a PhD from Harvard with a dissertation on "The Suppression of the African Slave Trade to the United States of America, 1683–1870."[26] He did some of his graduate work at the Friedrich Wilhelm University in Berlin, and was, therefore, thoroughly familiar with the intellectual traditions of modern European nationalism, as well as with the philosophical tradition that began with Herder. In "The Conservation of Races" Du Bois argued that "the history of the world is the history, not of individuals, but of groups, not of nations, but of races."[27] However, like so many other Western intellectuals of his day, he understood real nations to be divided along racial lines. He also argued that the differences among races were "spiritual, psychical, differences—undoubtedly based on the physical, but infinitely transcending them."[28] And, finally, he insisted that each race was "striving . . . in its own way, to develop for civilization its particular message"[29]—a statement which, as Appiah points out, was strongly reminiscent of Herder. The problem for the Pan-Negroism designed by Du Bois was how the "Negro people" were to deliver their message. Du Bois believed that African-Americans—according to him the "advance guard of the Negro people"[30]—were to play the leading role in this task. "He thought that they were especially well-suited for this task because some of them, like Du Bois himself, had been exposed to the best modern educations and the highest forms of knowledge."[31]

Though Du Bois's formulation had roots in the theories of European nationalism, he was also strongly influenced by a number of earlier African-American thinkers, who after the abolition of slave trade and slavery were convinced that a home was needed for blacks if they were to be free. Three black intellectuals of the nineteenth century, all of them occupied with the question of finding a territory for the "Negro race," can be seen as the fore-runners of Pan-Africanism.[32] Martin R. Delany (1812–1885) was a proponent of a common cause between all expatriated Africans, and of a return to Africa of those with skills to "raise" it to the new technological standards of the Europeans.[33] Alexander Crummell (1822–1898) was born in New York and was the first African-American to study at Cambridge University in England. He was an ordained Anglican clergyman and the first African-American intellectual to spend a significant amount of time in Liberia. In *The Future of Africa*, a collection of essays and lectures written while he was in Liberia and published in 1862, Crummell developed a vision of Africa as the "motherland of the Negro race." In "The English Language in Liberia," based on a lecture given on Liberian Independence Day in 1860, he argued that African-Americans who had been "exiled" in slavery to the New World had been given by divine providence "at least this one item of compensation, namely, the possession of the Anglo-Saxon tongue." Finally, Edward Blyden (1832–1912), who arguably was the most important early contributor to the ideologies of Pan-Africanism (and West African nationalism), and one of the first to articulate a notion of "African personality" and the uniqueness of the "African race." Blyden constantly traveled back and forth across the Atlantic. From Sierra Leone, he traveled to England and encouraged both the Church Missionary Society and the British government to expand their activities into Sierra Leone's hinterland. He believed that the expansion of "Christian Civilization" throughout the region could create the basis for the emergence of a large and influential West African state. In *Christianity, Islam and the Negro Race*, published in 1887, Blyden expressed the conviction that under-lies Du Bois's first explicit formulation of Pan-Africanism: "Among the conclusions to which study and research are conducting philosophers, none is clearer than this—that each of the races of mankind has a specific character and specific work."[34] Blyden argued that what he called Africa's current "state of barbarism" did not reflect any innate deficiency in the "Negro": "There is not a single mental or moral deficiency now existing among Africans . . . to which we cannot find a parallel in the past history of Europe."[35] Blyden's ideas became particularly influential amongst Western-educated West Africans. The Nigerian intelligentsia, for instance, adopted these ideas to defend themselves against European claims of superiority and European racism.[36] As Zachernuk shows in detail, the vague, unformed sense of being "Black Englishmen" was displaced by a sense of being black, and a part of the rising community of diaspora Africans. "The members of the educated community could become a genuine elite not by serving as agents of the Western penetration of the African darkness but by combining Western knowledge with their putative racial characteristics, acting in concert with other black elites of similar mind."[37] For West Africans, this identity could assume many forms—they could see themselves as Yoruba (a West African ethnic group that was particularly numerous among African slaves in Brazil), West Africans, Africans, or "Negroes"—but in what has been called the "cosmopolitan black ethos" of the period, all these identities were subsumed under their "common historical and racial identity with the Negroes of Black America."[38] Whatever Yoruba or West African qualities they held virtuous were virtues of the race affirmed against claims of European hegemony and superiority. Similarly, accomplishments by any black—West African or not—were taken as evidence of ability that pertained to all. The intelligentsia adopted this racial community for their own in diverse contexts, in the pursuit of what Blyden termed "race organisation and race consolidation."[39] The sense of shared identity lingered on through the interwar years, most powerfully among Nigerians abroad. For example, in 1934, Nnamdi Azikiwe would call from America, on "the Negro intellectual" in Africa, the West Indies, and the United States to kindle "a conception of race pride and race consciousness."[40] Accepting the premise of innate racial distinctions but proclaiming that African characteristics were not inferiorities, not only Blyden, but also members of the West African coastal elites sought to establish African standards of civilization by which European contributions might be judged valuable or not. The vision was that Africa would create a unique civilization on its own terms, learning from the West but not betraying its racial existence. The "inspiration of the race is in the race," Blyden argued.[41] Each race had its own particular genius and future, and "that only way must be found before there can be peace and harmony and progress."[42]

Pan-African Activities

Pan-Africanism as an intellectual movement began, then, in the works of Delany, Crummell, and Blyden, who all inspired Du Bois in systematizing Pan-African ideas around 1900. However, it should be emphasized that this African-American endeavour to define themselves rested in large part on a critique of Western Civilization rather than knowledge of Africa. Kwame Appiah sees Du Bois's views on race as a dialectical response to both European racism and a general African-American denial of racial difference:[43] countering racism meant abandoning notions of universal equality to assert pride in racial peculiarity. Marion Berghahn argues that Du Bois "looks for, and finds, in the African all those virtues which he had seen the West betray." More generally, the "New Negro had no intention of assimilating African ideas, languages, literature or music. What he had in mind was to define his own position vis-à-vis Africa."[44] There are hints that some of the West African intelligentsia faintly recognized these divergent perspectives. Later writers would recognize divergences more clearly, but for now they were less important than the need for mutual support. For instance, the Nigerian intelligentsia, prone themselves to the kind of dialectical response formulated by Du Bois, could hardly resist this propensity when it was reinforced by ideas from around the Atlantic. "In any case, as a minority in this discourse and without an overpowering presence within West Africa, they could not easily defy the trend. The Nigerian image of Africa developed for the 'African personality' showed its Atlantic affinities well into the interwar period."[45]

The emergence of Pan-Africanist ideas during the nineteenth century is linked to rather few individuals, who were characterized, among other things, by their ability to crisscross the Black Atlantic not only intellectually, but physically as well. Around 1900, the institutional history of Pan-Africanism began, and the key person in this context was Henry Sylvester Williams, a London barrister born in Trinidad.[46] He planned to bring together people of the African race in 1897, and in July 1900, after a preliminary conference in 1899, such a gathering took place in London. The actual word "Pan-Africanism" seems to have been coined at this meeting. It was still, however, a small event, bringing together only four African representatives—one each from Ethiopia, Sierra Leone, Liberia, and the Gold Coast colony—and a dozen representatives from North America (including Du Bois); eleven representatives came from the West Indies, five from London. The conference opened with the clearly stated aim of allowing black people to discuss the condition of the black race around the world. Its constitution aimed "to encourage a feeling of unity, to facilitate friendly intercourse among Africans in general; to promote and protect the interest of all subjects claiming African descent, wholly or in part, in British colonies and other places, especially in Africa, by circulating accurate information on all subjects, affecting their rights and privileges as subjects of the British Empire, and by direct appeals to the Imperial and local Governments."[47]

In the years prior to World War I there were little Pan-African activities at an international level.[48] Britain became something like a Pan-African center during this period, and mainly students from Africa and the West Indies were active in the Pan-African cause, while sometimes labeling themselves "Ethiopianists."[49] By 1904 there was an Ethiopian Association in Edinburgh, and in Liverpool, the same year, the Ethiopian Progressive Association (EPA) was founded "by West African and West Indian natives, students at the various colleges."[50] The Association seems to have had a short life, but it attempted to contact Du Bois in the United States and published at least one edition of a journal, *The Ethiopian Review*. The EPA aimed "to create a bond of union between a) all other members of the Ethiopian race at home and abroad, b) to further the interest and raise the social status of the Ethiopian race at home and abroad; and to try to strengthen the friendly relations of the said race and the other races of mankind."[51] Both individual West Africans and the organizations they formed were Pan-African in orientation. West Africans and those from the Caribbean often joined together to further their interests and made efforts to establish links with prominent African-Americans and their organisations. As the EPA expressed it, they were concerned with "matters of vital importance concerning Africa in particular and the Negro race in general." These concerns ranged from the 1906 Natal Uprising in South Africa, to discrimination in the West African Medical Service and the "pacification" campaigns in Nigeria. The students were also concerned to "raise the status of African people in general." For instance, they stressed the achievements of Edward Blyden and extolled the virtues of a glorious African past.[52]

J.E. Casely Hayford's (1866–1930) autobiographical novel *Ethiopia Unbound* was published in London in 1911 and provides some insight into the political concerns of Pan-African students at the time. Casely Hayford had been a law student in Cambridge and London and would become the founder of the National Congress of British West Africa, one of the first Pan-African organizations on the African continent. *Ethiopia Unbound*, one of the first African novels with a strong Pan-African theme, was dedicated to the "sons of Ethiopia the world wide over." In the novel West Africa is very much at the center of Casely Hayford's Pan-African world, a world that was based on the political traditions represented by Blyden. The hero of the novel, Kwamankra, praises Blyden's work as "universal, covering the whole race," designed "to reveal everywhere the African unto himself," "to lead him back into self respect" and to restore to him "his true place in creation on natural and national lines." In particular the novel is concerned with developing the "African nationality" and encouraging "race emancipation" and proudly claims that Africa was the "cradle of civilisation." It looks forward to the prospect of mobilizing those of African descent throughout the world in order to modernize African society while retaining its African features, as it argues Japan had done in the recent past. He also strongly favoured the creation of a university in West Africa that might become a center of excellence for students from the region and throughout the African diaspora.[53]

The next international Pan-African event was the First Pan-African Congress, convened by Du Bois in Paris, in February 1919. Du Bois was originally sent to France in 1918 by the National Association for the Advancement of Colored People (NAACP) to investigate the treatment of African-American soldiers in the U.S. army.[54] He had the support of the French Deputy from Senegal, Blaise Diagne, and the French President, Clemenceau. Fifty-seven delegates from Africa, the Caribbean, and the United States managed to attend the Congress.[55] Du Bois put forward a proposal for the creation of a new state in Africa based on Germany's former colonies. This would be supervised by the major powers, but would also take into account the views of "the civilised Negro world," a phrase that had mainly African-Americans in mind. Initially Du Bois proposed a permanent Pan-African secretariat based in Paris and hoped that the Congress would make the voice of the "children of Africa" heard at the postwar peace conference then in session in the French capitol. However, the Paris Pan-African Congress had little influence and its most significant resolutions demanded that the rights of Africans and those of African descent in the colonies and elsewhere should be protected by the League of Nations.[56] At this point, Du Bois proposed the idea that not only were blacks situated in a global network, but that their very presence and experience were crucial to how that network was constituted in the first place:

There are no races, in the sense of great, separate, pure breeds of men, differing in attainment, development, and capacity. There are great groups, now with common history, now with common interests, now with common ancestry; more and more common experience and present interest drive back the common blood and the world today consists, not of races, but of the imperial commercial group of master capitalists, international and predominantly white; the national middle classes of the several nations, white, yellow, and brown, with strong blood bonds, common languages, and common history; the international labouring class of all colors; the backward, oppressed groups of nature folk, predominantly yellow, brown, and black.[57]

One of the central themes here is that "common experience and present interest" undermine bonds based on blood alone. In the global economy of the twentieth century these "social races" represented broad hierarchical groupings in which class and colour were highly correlated. Thus capital and labor were now international-scale groupings with their respective linkages based on the commonality of a group's experience as exploiter and exploited; racially the former was white and the latter mixed. However, Du Bois was not suggesting that class had supplanted race. Indeed, class was "racialized" in this hierarchical scheme. "Capital ruled here, and the capitalists were white."[58]

In 1921 Du Bois and others organized a second Pan-African Congress that met in three sessions in London, Brussels, and Paris, this time with representatives from French and Portuguese colonies in Africa as well. They issued a final declaration that insisted on the "equality of the races," the diffusion of democracy, and the development of political institutions in the colonies. It also called for the "return" of Blacks to their own countries and once more urged the League of Nations to pay attention to both, race relations in the industrialized world and the condition of workers in the colonies. A third congress occurred in London in 1923 and continued, according to Du Bois, in Lisbon, though this appears to have been little more than an opportunity for him to talk to some people from the Portuguese colonies on his way from London to Liberia, where he was the official representative of the United States at the installation of the Liberian president.[59] The Pan-African Congress movement then effectively disappeared until the fifth congress in Manchester in 1945, during which the baton was handed from the diaspora community to the continent.[60] Du Bois's contribution now lay in the shadow of that of figures such as Kwame Nkrumah, who was to become Ghana's first prime minister. In Manchester, Du Bois was the only African-American present!

The Golden Age of Pan-Africanism: The Interwar Years

During the interwar years, in the heyday of the Pan-African-Congress movement, Pan-Africanism was shaped principally from three directions. First, it was considerably influenced by the growth of the Universal Negro Improvement Association (UNIA). Led by Marcus Garvey, a Jamaican immigrant to the United States, the UNIA became the largest black movement in the African diaspora and the most widespread black-led movement in world history. At its height in the early 1920s, the UNIA had an estimated two million members and sympathizers, and approximately one thousand chapters in 43 countries and territories. At the first UNIA international convention in 1920 that was attended by 2,000 delegates, the Declaration of the Rights of the Negro Peoples of the World was promulgated. It reiterated the earlier principles and condemned worldwide discrimination in all its forms and the inculcation of white superiority by the education system. It demanded "self-determination for all peoples" and espoused "the inherent right of the Negro to possess himself of Africa" and the "necessity of Negro nationalism, political power and control"; the "culmination of all the efforts of the UNIA must end in a Negro independent nation on the continent of Africa," to which all diaspora Africans could return. Garvey's surprising ignorance of the multiplicity of peoples and cultures in Africa resulted in his declaring himself provisional president of a future independent republic of Africa.[61] While the slogan of the movement was "Back to Africa," and Garvey did indeed plan a shipping line for the purpose, relatively few members of the organization actually left the New World for the Old. Nevertheless, Garvey's commitment to racial pride to the celebration of black historical achievement, and his concern to link the diaspora to the continent make him an important figure in the movement's history.[62]

Generally speaking, Garveyism had little (with some exceptions) following in Africa. One of the localities where Garveyism had a considerable impact on the African continent was South Africa, as reflected in eight official and numerous unofficial UNIA divisions. Within South Africa, Cape Town had the earliest and largest number of UNIA divisions of any locality in the 1920s and served as an important entrepot to distribute UNIA materials to other parts of the country. Furthermore, a small but disproportionately influential "American Negro" community in Cape Town became leading transmitters of Garveyism from the Americas into southern Africa.[63] The rise of Garveyism meant that many blacks in South Africa viewed African-Americans not just as models of a transnational black modernity that disproved white claims of inherent black inferiority, but as divinely-ordained liberators from South African white supremacy. Garveyites in South Africa, as elsewhere in the world, couched their political grievances and aspirations within a prophetic Christianity that featured a wide array of Judeo-Christian biblical texts, rituals, symbols, and metaphors to legitimate their claims for an independent Africa and for equal rights in the modern world. Finally, in addition to its obvious centrality in UNIA chapters, Garveyism, pervaded black South African politics generally, as it was an important unifying ideological influence for the UNIA, the African National Congress and the Industrial and Commercial Workers Union, the leading black South African organizations in the 1920s.[64]

The second important direction of Pan-Africanism was represented by cultural ideas emanating from the Caribbean and francophone West Africa in the 1920s and 1930s, and generally known as Négritude, which essentially argued that black people must regain their African culture. Never a formal organization, Négritude was a cultural project that emerged through intense discussions and intimate friendships among a diasporic peer group whose members shared similar colonial backgrounds and metropolitan challenges, as well as an interest in Africa.[65] Léopold Sédar Senghor, Aimé Césaire, and Léon-Gontran Damas, the main Négritude protagonists, were all products of colonial assimilation. Before leaving home to join the transnational group of colonial students and activists living in continental France in the 1930s, they were trained in overseas French schools to become members of the native elite in their home colonies. In the 1930s, Négritude was not a consciously organized movement. It consisted primarily of interminable discussions among students who shared ideas, explored Paris, and began to write poetry. They engaged contemporary currents of colonial thought, French culture, and black politics in order to fashion relationships to the colonial system in which they had been trained, to the French nation in which they now lived, and to the African societies to which they felt deeply connected. Over the course of their public lives, the three founders would each develop different conceptions of racial consciousness and cultural nationalism, but they agreed at its inception that Négritude was a rejection of assimilation, an identification with blackness, and a celebration of an African civilization that was conceptualized mainly as a distinctive culture.

Third, especially during the late 1920s and 1930s, Pan-Africanism was strongly influenced by the international communist movement and by socialist, anti-imperialist, and intenationalist perspectives, such as those developed by the International Trade Union Committee of Negro Workers. After World War I, the Soviet Union systematically supported liberation movements in the colonies in order to weaken the Western colonial powers. Since the mid-1920s, Germany, especially Berlin and Hamburg, became an important scene for the activities of "black revolutionaries."[66] According to the Trinidadian, George Padmore, a leading figure in the Pan-Africanist movement, who for many years was member of the Comintern head, Moscow did not want to bring attention to itself and carefully chose Germany as the center of anti-imperial activities:

> They assigned the responsibility of organizing the new anti-imperialist movement to the German Communists. . . . Shorn of her African and other colonies' defeat in the First World War, Germany was no longer a colonial power; and it was thought that an anti-imperialist call from Berlin would arouse less suspicion among colonial and dependent peoples than one coming from Western European capitals—London or Paris—possessing overseas empires.[67]

The so called "Negro Bureau," established in Hamburg in 1930, served as a center for the exchange of information. Directives from Moscow came there, and political operations were planned and directed. The rise of the Nazis to power in 1933 put an end to these activities.

In Moscow, the Comintern had established a school for students from African and Asian colonies. The curriculum was later described by Padmore as a three year program in "history, foreign languages, economics, political science, sociology, party and trade union organization, techniques of propaganda and agitation, public speaking and journalism . . . from a Marxist point of view."[68] However, to many African and Asian nationalists, the experience was a real disappointment. They complained bitterly about the poor food, bad accomodation, and low standard of English of the instructors. Jomo Kenyatta, later president of Kenya, was one of the spokesmen of the frustrated students. Because of his "petit bourgeois" criticisms, the Comintern considered him a poor prospect for either recruitment to the party or training as an agent.[69] During the 1930s, social unrest in many colonies and especially the international failure to act against the Italian fascist invasion of Ethiopia in 1935 served as new, strong political catalysts for black people both, within Africa and throughout the diaspora.[70]

These three very different trajectories of Pan-Africanism represented the rising mobility of colonized people and the emergence of politically active and well connected diaspora communities, a development that colonial powers regarded as a dangerous threat to their order of the world. The central vision behind the reflections and activities of Garvey, Senghor, Padmore, and others was to unify and integrate peoples of African descent all over the world and to challenge Western superiority. Thus Pan-Africanism played an important part in anti-imperial and anti-Western developments that led to the erosion of the global colonial order of the twentieth century. Similar to other non-European, anti-imperial, and pan-movements, Pan-Africanism combined a critique of Western politics and culture with a modernization project that—although conceptualized as an alternative modernity—included many elements of the dominant Western modernity.

Epilogue

While World War I helped stimulate political consciousness in both Africa and the political diaspora, World War II had a much more profound impact, especially on Africa, where Pan-African ideas had a strong appeal to some of the nationalist leaders, most notably Kwame Nkrumah.[71] Pan-Africanism in Africa was greatly stimulated by Nkrumah's career and by the end of formal British colonial rule in the Gold Coast in 1957. Nkrumah declared that "the independence of Ghana is meaningless unless it is linked up with the total liberation of the African continent." Independent Ghana became a beacon that drew many from the diaspora to Africa, but it also played an important role in building a new type of Pan-Africanism, centered on the African continent that, in 1963, culminated in the founding of the Organization of African Unity. However, the organization soon proved to be of little efficacy, and ideologies and problems of nation building soon superseded Pan-African visions and projects. Today, at the beginning of the twenty-first century, Pan-Africanism has little significance within Africa other than rhetoric. The main proponents of Pan-Africanism are within the black diaspora communities, mainly in the United States. Such ideas were strengthened by the Black Power movement of the 1960–1970s, with its strong political agenda and stress on cultural and artistic identification with Africa. While Pan-Africanism today may have lost much of its political influence, it could be said that for much of the twentieth century, the very complex Pan-Africanist networks, characterized by their diverse origins, contexts, aims, ideologies, and forms of organization, shaped the Black Atlantic and world history in significant ways. Moreover, the study of Pan-Africanism, with its focus on political history, broadens and substantiates the concept of Black Atlantic, while at the same time the project of Pan-Africanism represents both connections transcending national boundaries as well as the tensions and links between the local and the global.

Notes

1. Paul Gilroy, *The Black Atlantic: Modernity and Double Consciousness* (Cambridge, Mass.: Harvard University Press, 1993).
2. By now, the term Black Atlantic is widely used, mostly without further definition. Among the numerous publications (mostly in literary and cultural studies) using this term are Henry Louis Gates Jr. and William L. Andrews, eds., *Pioneers of the Black Atlantic: Five Slave Narratives from the Enlightenment* (Washington D.C.: Civitas, 1998); Joanne M. Braxton and Maria I. Diedrich, eds., *Monuments of the Black Atlantic: Slavery and Memory* (Muenster: LIT, 2004); Joanna Brooks, *"Face Zion forward": First Writers of the Black Atlantic, 1785–1798* (Boston: Northeastern University Press, 2002); John Cullen Gruesser, *Confluences: Postcolonialism, African-American Literary Studies, and the Black Atlantic* (Athens, GA: University of Georgia Press, 2005); Gesa Mackenthun, *Fictions of the Black Atlantic in American Foundational Literature* (London and New York: Routledge, 2004); J. Lorand Matory, *Black Atlantic Religion: Tradition, Transnationalism, and Matriarchy in the Afro-Brasilian Candomble* (Princeton: Princeton University Press, 2005); Allen J. Rice, *Radical Narratives of the Black Atlantic* (New York: Continuum, 2003); James Walvin, *Making the Black Atlantic: Britain and the African Diaspora* (New York and London: Cassell, 2000). The latter is part of a book series entitled "Black Atlantic." For a brief summary of the literature see

Andreas Eckert, "Atlantic History and the Black Atlantic," in Renate Pieper and Peer Schmidt, eds., *Latin America and the Atlantic World* (Cologne and Vienna: Böhlau, 2005), pp. 57–64.

3. Paul Gilroy, "Cultural Studies and Ethnic Absolutism," in Lawrence Grossberg, Cary Nelson, and Paula Treichler, eds., *Cultural Studies* (New York: Routledge, 1992), p. 192.

4 Gilroy, *Black Atlantic*, p. 103.

5. There is now some interesting research on these black Atlantic travelers, whose numerical significance is still disputed. The best-known case at least to Africanists is the history of Olaudah Equiano, who, as a slave of a naval captain, continually crisscrossed the Atlantic and later, as a free man, continued to travel between Europe, North America, and the Carribbean. See his controversial auto-biographical text, Olaudah Equiano, *The Life of Olaudah Equiano, or Gustavus Vasso the African* (Harlow: Longman, 1989) (orig. 1789). On Equiano see Vincent Carretta, *Equiano the African: Biography of a Self-Made Man* (Athens, GA: University of Georgia Press, 2005); James Walvin, *An African's Life: The Life and Times of Olaudah Equiano* (London: Cassell, 1998). On black sailors see W. Jeremy Bolster, *Black Jacks: African-American Seamen in the Age of Sail* (Cambridge, Mass.: Harvard University Press, 1997); and Peter Linebaugh and Marcus Rediker, *The Many-Headed Hydra: Sailors, Slaves, Commoners and the Hidden History of the Revolutionary Atlantic* (Boston: Beacon Press, 2000).

6. J. Lorand Matory, "The English Professors of Brazil: On the Diasporic Roots of the Yorùbá Nation," *Comparative Studies in Society and History* 41, no. 1 (1999): 73.

7. Kwame Anthony Appiah, "Pan-Africanism," in Kwame Anthony Appiah and Henry Louis Gates Jr., eds., *Africana: The Encyclopedia of the African and African-American Experience* (New York: Basic Civitas Books, 1999), p. 1485. For problems of definition see also Sidney J. Lemelle and Robin D.G. Kelley, "Imagining Home: Pan-Africanism Re-Visited," in Sidney J. Lemelle and Robin D.G. Kelley, eds., *Imagining Home: Class, Culture and Nationalism in the African Diaspora* (London and New York: Verso, 1994), pp. 1–16.

8. Appiah, "Pan-Africanism," p. 1485. There is now an abundant literature on this development. See, for example, George M. Frederickson, *Racism: A Short History* (Princeton: Princeton University Press, 2002).

9. See Appiah, "Pan-Africanism," p. 1485.

10. Most notably Immanuel Geiss, *The Pan-African Movement* (London: Methuen, 1974) (German orig. 1968); J. Ayodele Langley, *Pan-Africanism and Nationalism in West Africa 1900–1945: A Study in Ideology and Social Classes* (Oxford: Clarendon Press, 1973). Since then only one comprehensive scholarly study on Pan-Africanism has been published: P. Olisanwuche Esedebe, *Pan-Africanism: The Idea and Movement, 1776–1991* (Washington, D.C.: Howard University, 1994).

11. Hakim Adi and Marika Sherwood, "Preface," in Hakim Adi and Marika Sherwood, eds., *Pan-African History: Political Figures from Africa and the Diaspora since 1787* (London and New York: Routledge, 2003).

12. It is interesting to note that the first book to use the term "African diaspora" did not appear until 1976, in Martin Kilson and Robert Rotberg, eds., *The African*

Diaspora (Cambridge, Mass.: Harvard University Press, 1976). The actual use of the term represented a turning point in the field in that it signified an overt political consciousness that had been previously absent from much of the work in the field. Since then, numerous studies have appeared. See, among many others, Jana Braziel and Anita Mannur, eds., *Theorizing Diaspora* (Malden, Mass.: Blackwell, 2003); Robin Cohen, *Global Diaspora: An Introduction* (Seattle: University of Washington Press, 1997).

13. Emmanuel Akyeampong, "Africans in the Diaspora: The Diaspora and Africa," *African Affairs* 99 (2000): 186. Joseph Harris, "Introduction," in Joseph Harris, ed., *Global Dimensions of the African Diaspora*, 2nd ed. (Washington, D.C.: Howard University Press, 1993), pp. 3–10, distinguishes four phases of the African dispersion: "The primary stage is the original dispersion out of Africa; the secondary stage occurs with migrations from the initial settlement abroad to a second area abroad; the tertiary stage is movement to a third area abroad; and the circulatory stage involves movements among the several areas abroad and may include Africa." More recently, the frequency of migration processes and the easy availability of long-distance means of communication have added a strong dimension of "translocality" to many local communities in Africa. The rapidly expanding genre of local histories, written and published by nonacademic historians, attempts to make sense of these changes. See Axel Harneit-Sievers, ed., *A Place in the World: New Local Historiographies from Africa and South Asia* (Leiden: Brill, 2002).

14. For studies that focus on the North Atlantic to the virtual exclusion of the "Black Atlantic," see Bernard Bailyn, "The Idea of Atlantic History," *Itinerario* 20 (1996): 19–44; Bailyn, *Atlantic History. Concepts and Contours* (Cambridge, MA: Harvard University Press, 2005); David Hancock, *Citizens of the World: London Merchants and the Integration of the British Atlantic Community, 1735–1785* (Cambridge: Cambridge University Press, 1999); John J. McCusker and Kenneth Morgan, eds., *The Early Modern Atlantic Economy* (Cambridge: Cambridge University Press, 2000). For a more coherent view see Horst Pietschmann, ed., *Atlantic History: History of the Atlantic System, 1580 to 1830* (Göttingen: Vandenhoeck and Ruprecht, 2002).

15. While Gilroy's *Black Atlantic* is still regarded as the principal revisionist attack on the Eurocentric conception of Atlantic history, he very much approaches the issue from the perspective of the African (intellectual) diaspora; thus Africa figures in his treatment as an object of retrospective discovery, rather than as an active agent. For the development of a more "Africancentric" perspective see Robin Law and Paul Lovejoy, "The Changing Dimensions of African History: Reappropriating the Diaspora," in Simon McGrath, Charles Jedrej, Kenneth King, and Jack Thompson, eds., *Rethinking African History* (Edinburgh: Centre of African Studies, University of Edinburgh, 1997), pp. 181–200; Paul Lovejoy, "Identifying Enslaved Africans in the African Diaspora," in Paul Lovejoy, ed., *Identity in the Shadow of Slavery* (London: Continuum, 2000), pp. 1–29. For an uneven but ambitious set of overviews of where scholarship stood, often situating Gilroy and moving beyond him, see the special issue of the *African Studies Review* 43, no. 1

(2000) on "African Diaspora," especially Judith Byfield, "Rethinking the African Diaspora," pp. 1–9, as well as Tiffany Ruby Patterson and Robin D.G. Kelly, "Unfinished Migrations: Reflections on the African Diaspora in the Making of the Modern World," pp. 11–45. See also Christine Chivallon, "Beyond Gilroy's Black Atlantic: The Experience of the African Diaspora," *Diaspora* 11, no. 3 (2002): 359–82. See Hauke Dorsch, *Afrikanische Diaspora und Black Atlantic. Einführung in Geschichte und aktuelle Diskussion* (Münster: Lit, 2000), for a useful survey.

16. John Thornton, *Africa and Africans in the Making of the Atlantic World, 1400–1800*, 2nd ed. (Cambridge: Cambridge University Press, 1998).

17. Ibid., p. 125.

18. See, for example, Herbert Klein, *The Atlantic Slave Trade* (Cambridge: Cambridge University Press, 1999); David Eltis, *The Rise of African Slavery in the Americas* (Cambridge: Cambridge University Press, 2000). See also the articles in *William and Mary Quarterly*, 3rd ser. 58 (2001).

19. Thornton challenges in particular Sidney W. Mintz and Richard Price, *An Anthropological Approach to the Afro-American Past: A Caribbean Perspective* (Philadelphia: Institute for the Study of Human Issues, 1976), who emphasize the culturally deracinating effects of enslavement, transportation, and plantation life. For arguments along Thornton's lines see Law and Lovejoy, "Changing Dimensions," pp. 189–97; Michael A. Gomez, *Exchanging Our Country Marks: The Transformation of African Identities in the Colonial and Antebellum South* (Chapel Hill: University of North Carolina Press, 1998); Linda Heywood, ed., *Central Africans and Cultural Transformations in the American Diaspora* (Cambridge: Cambridge University Press, 2002). For interesting empirical evidence see Gwendolyn Midlo Hall, *Slavery and African Ethnicities in the Americas: Restoring the Links* (Chapel Hill: University of North Carolina Press, 2005).

20. Robin Law and Kristin Mann, "West Africa in the Atlantic Community: The Case of the Slave Coast." *William and Mary Quarterly* 46 (1999): 307–44; Kristin Mann and Edna Bay, eds., *Rethinking the African Diaspora: The Making of a Black Atlantic World in the Bight of Benin and Brazil* (London: F. Cass, 2001). The relationship between West Africa and Brazil is crucial here. See José C. Curto and Paul Lovejoy, eds., *Enslaving Connections: Changing Cultures of Africa and Brazil During the Era of Slavery* (Amherst: Humanity Books, 2004). For an intriguing example of some of the dynamics of reconnection between Africa and Africans in the diaspora during the nineteenth century see Matory, "English Professors."

21. Hakim Adi, *West Africans in Britain, 1900–1960: Nationalism, Pan-Africanism, and Communism* (London: Lawrence & Wishart, 1998); Philippe Dewitte, *Les Mouvements Nègres en France 1919–1939* (Paris: L'Harmattan, 1985); Andreas Eckert, "Universitäten und die Politik des Exils. Afrikanische Studenten und anti-koloniale Politik in Europa, 1900–1960," *Jahrbuch für Universitätsgeschichte* 7 (2004): 129–45.

22. These are central aspects of global history, at least according to Bruce Mazlish, "Comparing Global History to World History," *Journal for Interdisciplinary*

History 28 (1998): 385–95, and Bruce Mazlish, "An Introduction to Global History," in Bruce Mazlish and Ralph Buultjens, eds., *Conceptualizing Global History* (Boulder: Westview Press, 1993), pp. 1–24.

23. The following paragraphs are based on Appiah, "Pan-Africanism," p. 1485.
24. See Hans Kohn, *The Idea of Nationalism* (New York: Macmillan, 1967), especially pp. 431–32, which include relevant references to Herder's *On the New German Literature: Fragments of 1767*. Appiah, "Pan-Africanism," p. 1485.
25. W.E.B Du Bois, "The Conservation of Races," repr. in Eric J. Sundquist, ed., *The Oxford W.E.B. Du Bois Reader* (Oxford and New York: Oxford University Press, 1996), pp. 38–47.
26. The most comprehensive study on Du Bois is David Levering Lewis, *W.E.B. Du Bois: Biography of a Race, 1868–1919* (New York: H. Holt, 1993). See also David Levering Lewis, *W.E.B. Du Bois: The Fight for Equality and the American Century, 1919–1963* (New York: H. Holt, 2000).
27. Du Bois, "Conservation," p. 40.
28. Ibid., p. 41.
29. Ibid., p. 42.
30. Quoted in Appiah, "Pan-Africanism," p. 1485.
31. Ibid., p. 1485.
32. For the following sketches see ibid. and Adi and Sherwood, *Pan-African History*.
33. Cyril E. Griffith, *The African Dream: Martin Delany and the Emergence of Pan-African Thought* (University Park: Pennsylvania University Press, 1975).
34. Edward Wilmot Blyden, *Christianity, Islam and the Negro Race* (1887, repr. Edinburgh: University Press, 1967).
35. Ibid.
36. Philip S. Zachernuk, *Colonial Subjects: An African Intelligentsia and Atlantic Ideas* (Charlottesville: University Press of Virginia, 2000). For the general context see Richard Rathbone, "West Africa: Modernity and Modernization," in Jan-Georg Deutsch, Peter Probst and Heike Schmidt, eds., *African Modernities: Entangled Meanings in Current Debates* (Oxford: James Currey, 2002), pp. 18–30.
37. Zachernuk, *Colonial Subjects*, p. 67.
38. Michael J. Echeruo, *Victorian Lagos: Aspects of Nineteenth Century Lagos Life* (London: Macmillan, 1978), p. 109.
39. Blyden, *Christianity*, p. 140; Zachernuk, *Colonial Subjects*, pp. 67–68; Philip S. Zachernuk, "Critical Agents: Colonial Nigerian Intellectuals and their British Counterparts," in Chris Youé and Tim Stapleton, eds., *Agency and Action in Colonial Africa* (New York: Palgrave, 2001), pp. 156–71.
40. Nnamdi Azikiwe, *Liberia in World Politics* (1934, repr. Westport, Conn.: Negro Universities Press, 1970), p. 350. See also Zachernuk, *Colonial Subjects*, p. 69".
41. Blyden, *The African Problem and the Method of Its Solution* (1890), quoted by Zachernuk, *Colonial Subjects*, p. 70.
42. Edward Blyden, *African Life and Customs* (1908, repr. London: African Publication Society, 1969), p. 66. See also Zachernuk, *Colonial Subjects*, p. 70.
43. Kwame Anthony Appiah, *In My Father's House. Africa in the Philosophy of Culture* (New York: Oxford University Press, 1992), pp. 28–46.

44. Marion Berghahn, *Images of Africa in Black American Literature* (Chicago and London: University of Chicago Press, 1977), pp. 93 and 121; Zachernuk, *Colonial Subjects*, pp. 73–74.

45. Zachernuk, *Colonial Subjects*, p. 74; See also Langley, *Pan-Africanism*, pp. 34–40.

46. Owen Charles Mathurin, *Henry Sylvester Williams and the Origins of the Pan-African Movement* (Westport, Conn.: Greenwood Press, 1976). On the West Indian (intellectual) diaspora in Britain, of which Williams was a part, see now Bill Schwarz, ed., *West Indian intellectuals in Britain* (Manchester: Manchester University Press, 2003).

47. Quoted in Langley, *Pan-Africanism*, 27.

48. Geiss, *Pan-African Movement*.

49. Hakim Adi, "West African Students in Britain, 1900–60: The Politics of Exile," in David Killingray, ed., *Africans in Britain* (London: Frank Cass, 1994), pp. 107–28.

50. Adi, "West African Students in Britain," p. 11.

51. Quotes from ibid.

52. Quotes from ibid., pp. 11–12.

53. J.E. Casely Hayford, *Ethiopia Unbound: Studies in Race Relations* (1911, repr. London: Cass, 1969). See also Adi, "West African Students in Britain," Langley, *Pan-Africanism*; Robert W. July, *The Origins of Modern African Thought: Its Development in West Africa in the Nineteenth and Twentieth Centuries* (London: Faber, 1968), esp. pp. 433–37; Raymond Jenkins, "Gold Coasters Overseas, 1860–1919, with Specific Reference to Their Activities in Britain," *Immigrants and Minorities* 4 (1985): 5–52.

54. On the history of the NAACP see Manfred Berg, *The Ticket to Freedom. The NAACP and the Struggle for Black Political Integration* (Gainesville: University Press of Florida, 2005).

55. On this congress as well as the following ones see Geiss, *Pan-African Movement*; Lewis, *Du Bois*, vol. 2.

56. The Resolution is reprinted in W.E.B. Du Bois, *The World and Africa: An Inquiry into the Part Which Africa Has Played in World History* (New York: International Publishers, 1965), pp. 11–12.

57. Du Bois, "Of Work and Wealth," in Du Bois, *Darkwater: Voices from Within the Veil* (New York: Harcourt, Brace, 1920), p. 98.

58. See Thomas C. Holt, "Slavery and Freedom in the Atlantic World: Reflections on the Diasporan Framework," in Darlene Clark Hine and Jacqueline McLeod, eds., *Crossing Boundaries: Comparative History of Black People in Diaspora* (Bloomington: Indiana University Press, 1999), pp. 40–41.

59. Lewis, *Du Bois*, vol. 2.

60. Hakim Adi and Marika Sherwood, eds., *The 1945 Pan-African Congress Revisited* (London: New Beacon Books, 1995). On the continuing role of African-Americans in Pan-Africanist activities see Penny M. Von Eschen, *Race against Empire: Black Americans and Anticolonialism, 1937–1957* (Ithaca: Cornell University Press, 1997).

61. Quotes from Robert Hill, ed., *The Marcus Garvey and Universal Negro Improvement Association Papers*, vol. 1 (Berkeley: University of California Press, 1983).

62. Although no comprehensive biography exists, the literature on Marcus Garvey is extensive. See among others Tony Martin, *Race First: The Ideological and Organizational Struggles of Marcus Garvey and the Universal Negro Improvement Association* (Westport, Conn.: Greenwood Press, 1976); Rupert Lewis, *Marcus Garvey: Anti-Colonial Champion* (Trenton: Africa World Press, 1988); Judith Stein, *The World of Marcus Garvey: Race and Class in Modern Society* (Baton Rouge: Louisiana State University Press, 1986). See Lewis, *Du Bois*, vol. II, chapter 2, on the conflicts between Garvey and Du Bois.

63. For the following paragraphs see G. Pirio and Robert Hill, "Africa for the Africans: The Garvey Movement in South Africa, 1920–1940," in Shula Marks and Stanley Trapido, eds., *The Politics of Race, Class and Nationalism in Twentieth-Century South Africa* (London: Longman, 1987), pp. 209–53, and especially Robert T. Vinson, " 'Sea Kaffirs': 'American Negroes' and the Gospel of Garveyism in Early Twentieth Century South Africa," *Journal of African History* 47, no. 2 (2006), pp. 281–303.

64. Vinson, " 'Sea Kaffirs' ," pp. 281–82.

65. There is a vast literature on Negritude. The most recent publication is Gary Wilder, *The French Imperial Nation-State: Negritude and Colonial Humanism between the Two World Wars* (Chicago and London: Chicago University Press, 2005). For the following paragraph, see especially 151–57. See also Gary Wilder, "Practicing Citizenship in Imperial Paris," in Jean Comaroff and John L. Comaroff, eds., *Civil Society and the Political Imagination in Africa. Critical Perspectives* (Chicago and London: University of Chicago Press, 1999), pp. 44–71; Dominic Thomas, *Black France. Colonialism, Immigration, and Transnationalism* (Bloomington: Indiana University Press, 2007), especially chapter 2. An excellent biography of one of the main protagonists is Janet G. Vaillant, *Black, French, and African: A Life of Léopold Sédar Senghor* (Cambridge, Mass.: Harvard University Press, 1990).

66. For brief summaries of their activities see Peter Martin, "Schwarze Sowjets an Elbe und Spree?" in Peter Martin and Christine Alonzo, eds., *Zwischen Charleston und Stechschritt. Schwarze im Nationalsozialismus* (Hamburg: Dolling und Galitz, 2004), pp. 178–93; Geiss, *Pan-African Movement*, chapter 16.

67. George Padmore, *Pan-Africanism or Communism: The Coming Struggle for Africa* (London: D. Dobson, 1956), p. 323.

68. Ibid., p. 318.

69. See Bruce Berman, "Ethnography as Politics, Politics as Ethnography: Kenyatta, Malinowski, and the Making of 'Facing Mount Kenya,' " *Canadian Journal of African Studies* 30, no. 3 (1996): 323. See for the wider context Woodford McClellan, "African and Black Americans in the Comintern Schools, 1925–34," *International Journal of African Historical Studies* 26, no. 2 (1993): 371–90.

70. For the reaction of African students in Britain to the invasion in Ethiopia and the resulting activities see Adi, *West Africans*, pp. 67–70.

71. On Nkrumah see David Birmingham, *Kwame Nkrumah: Father of African Nationalism* (Athens: Ohio University Press, 1998).

Index